Introduction to Reliable Distributed Programming

Rachid Guerraoui · Luís Rodrigues

Introduction to

Reliable Distributed Programming

With 31 Figures

 Springer

Authors

Rachid Guerraoui

École Polytechnique Fédérale
de Lausanne (EPFL)
Faculté Informatique et Communications
Laboratoire Programmation Distribué (LPD)
Station 14
1015 Lausanne, Switzerland
Rachid.Guerraoui@epfl.ch

Luís Rodrigues

Universidade Lisboa
Faculdade de Ciências
Departamento de Informática
Bloco C6, Campo Grande
1749-016 Lisboa, Portugal
ler@di.fc.ul.pt

Library of Congress Control Number: 2006920522

ACM Computing Classification (1998): C.2, F.2, G.2

ISBN-10 3-540-28845-7 Springer Berlin Heidelberg New York
ISBN-13 978-3-540-28845-9 Springer Berlin Heidelberg New York

Springer is a part of Springer Science+Business Media

springer.com

© Springer-Verlag Berlin Heidelberg 2006
Printed in Germany

Typeset by the authors
Production: LE-TeX Jelonek, Schmidt & Vöckler GbR, Leipzig
Cover design: KünkelLopka Werbeagentur, Heidelberg

Printed on acid-free paper   45/3100/YL - 5 4 3 2 1 0

To May, Maria and Sarah.
To Hugo and Sara.

Preface

This book aims at offering an introductory description of distributed programming abstractions and of the algorithms that are used to implement them in different distributed environments. The reader is provided with an insight into important problems in distributed computing, knowledge about the main algorithmic techniques that can be used to solve these problems, and examples of how to apply these techniques when building distributed applications.

Content

In modern computing, a program usually executes on *several* processes: in this context, a process is an abstraction that may represent a computer, a processor within a computer, or simply a specific thread of execution within a processor. The fundamental problem in devising such distributed programs usually consists in having the processes *cooperate* on some *common* task. Of course, traditional centralized algorithmic issues, on each process individually, still need to be dealt with. The added difficulty here is in achieving a robust form of cooperation, despite failures or disconnections of some of the processes, inherent to most distributed environments.

Were no notion of cooperation required, a distributed program would simply consist of a set of detached centralized programs, each running on a specific process, and little benefit could be obtained from the availability of several machines in a distributed environment. It was the need for cooperation that revealed many of the fascinating problems addressed by this book, problems that need to be solved to make distributed computing a reality. The book, not only exposes the reader to these problems but also presents ways to solve them in different contexts.

Not surprisingly, distributed programming can be significantly simplified if the difficulty of robust cooperation is encapsulated within specific *abstractions*. By encapsulating all the tricky algorithmic issues, such distributed programming abstractions bridge the gap between network communication layers, usually frugal in terms of reliability guarantees, and distributed application layers, usually demanding in terms of reliability.

The book presents various distributed programming abstractions and describes algorithms that implement these abstractions. In a sense, we give the distributed application programmer a library of abstraction interface specifications, and give the distributed system builder a library of algorithms that implement the specifications.

A significant amount of the preparation time of this book was devoted to preparing the exercises and working out their solutions. We strongly encourage the reader to work out the exercises. We believe that no reasonable understanding can be achieved in a passive way. This is especially true in the field of distributed computing where a possible underlying anthropomorphism may provide easy but wrong intuitions. Many exercises are rather easy and can be discussed within an undergraduate teaching classroom. Some exercises are more difficult and need more time. These can typically be given as homeworks.

The book comes with a companion set of running examples implemented in the Java programming language, using the *Appia* protocol composition framework. These examples can be used by students to get a better understanding of many implementation details that are not covered in the high-level description of the algorithms given in the core of the chapters. Understanding such details usually makes a big difference when moving to a practical environment. Instructors can use the protocol layers as a basis for practical experimentations, by suggesting to students to perform optimizations of the protocols already given in the framework, to implement variations of these protocols for different system models, or to develop application prototypes that make use of the protocols.

Presentation

The book is written in a self-contained manner. This has been made possible because the field of distributed algorithms has reached a certain level of maturity where details, for instance, about the network and various kinds of failures, can be abstracted away when reasoning about the distributed algorithms. Elementary notions of algorithms, first order logics, programming languages, networking, and operating systems might be helpful, but we believe that most of our abstraction specifications and algorithms can be understood with minimal knowledge about these notions.

The book follows an incremental approach and was primarily built as a textbook for teaching at the undergraduate or basic graduate level. It introduces basic elements of distributed computing in an intuitive manner and builds sophisticated distributed programming abstractions on top of more primitive ones. Whenever we devise algorithms to implement a given abstraction, we consider a simple distributed system model first, and then we revisit the algorithms in more challenging models. In other words, we first devise algorithms by making strong simplifying assumptions on the distributed environment, and then we discuss how to weaken those assumptions.

We have tried to balance intuition and presentation simplicity, on the one hand, with rigor, on the other hand. Sometimes rigor was affected, and this might not have been always on purpose. The focus here is rather on abstraction specifications and algorithms, not on calculability and complexity. Indeed, there is no theorem in this book. Correctness arguments are given with the aim of better understanding the algorithms: they are not formal correctness proofs per se. In fact, we tried to avoid Greek letters and mathematical notations: references are given to papers and books with more formal treatments of some of the material presented here.

Organization

- In Chapter 1 we *motivate* the need for distributed programming abstractions by discussing various applications that typically make use of such abstractions. The chapter also presents the programming notations used in the book to describe specifications and algorithms.
- In Chapter 2 we present different kinds of *assumptions* that we will be making about the underlying distributed environment, i.e., we present different distributed system models. Basically, we describe the basic abstractions on which more sophisticated ones are built. These include process and communication link abstractions. This chapter might be considered as a reference throughout other chapters.

The rest of the chapters are each devoted to one family of related abstractions, and to various algorithms implementing them. We will go from primitive abstractions, and then use them to build more sophisticated ones.

- In Chapter 3 we introduce specific distributed programming abstractions: those related to the *reliable delivery* of messages that are *broadcast* to a group of processes. We cover here issues such as how to make sure that a message delivered by one process is delivered by all processes, despite the crash of the original sender process.
- In Chapter 4 we discuss *shared memory* abstractions which encapsulate simple forms of distributed storage objects with read-write semantics, e.g., files and register abstractions. We cover here issues like how to ensure that a value written (stored) within a set of processes is eventually read (retrieved) despite the crash of some of the processes.
- In Chapter 5 we address the *consensus* abstraction through which a set of processes can decide on a common value, based on values each process initially proposed, despite the crash of some of the processes.
- In Chapter 6 we consider variants of consensus such as atomic broadcast, terminating reliable broadcast, (non-blocking) atomic commitment, group membership, and view-synchronous communication.

The distributed algorithms we will study differ naturally according to the actual abstraction they aim at implementing, but also according to the assumptions on the underlying distributed environment (we will also say distributed system model), i.e., according to the initial abstractions they take for granted. Aspects such as the reliability of the links, the degree of synchrony of the system, and whether a deterministic or a randomized (probabilistic) solution is sought have a fundamental impact on how the algorithm is designed.

To give the reader an insight into how these parameters affect the algorithm design, the book includes several classes of algorithmic solutions to implement the same distributed programming abstractions for various distributed system models.

Covering all chapters, with their associated exercises, constitutes a full course in the field. Focusing on each chapter solely for the specifications of the abstractions and their underlying algorithms in their simplest form, i.e., for the simplest model of computation considered in the book (*fail-stop*), would constitute a shorter, more elementary course. Such a course could provide a nice companion to a more practice-oriented course possibly based on our protocol framework.

References

We have been exploring the world of distributed programming abstractions for more than a decade now. The material of this book was influenced by many researchers in the field of distributed computing. A special mention is due to Leslie Lamport and Nancy Lynch for having posed fascinating problems in distributed computing, and to the Cornell *school* of reliable distributed computing, including Ozalp Babaoglu, Ken Birman, Keith Marzullo, Robbert van Rennesse, Rick Schlicting, Fred Schneider, and Sam Toueg.

Many other researchers have directly or indirectly inspired the material of this book. We did our best to reference their work throughout the text. Most chapters end with a historical note. This intends to provide hints for further readings, to trace the history of the concepts presented in the chapters, as well as to give credits to those who invented and worked out the concepts. At the end of the book, we reference other books for further readings on other aspects of distributed computing.

Acknowledgments

We would like to express our deepest gratitude to our undergraduate and graduate students from Ecole Polytechnique Fédérale de Lausanne (EPFL) and the University of Lisboa (UL), for serving as reviewers of preliminary drafts of this book. Indeed, they had no choice and needed to prepare their exams anyway! But they were indulgent toward the bugs and typos that could be found in earlier versions of the book as well as associated slides, and they provided us with useful feedback.

Partha Dutta, Corine Hari, Michal Kapalka, Petr Kouznetsov, Ron Levy, Maxime Monod, Bastian Pochon, and Jesper Spring, graduate students from the School of Computer and Communication Sciences of EPFL, Filipe Araújo and Hugo Miranda, graduate students from the Distributed Algorithms and Network Protocol (DIALNP) group at the Departamento de Informática da Faculdade de Ciências da Universidade de Lisboa (UL), Leila Khalil and Robert Basmadjian, graduate students from the Lebanese University in Beirut, as well as Ali Ghodsi, graduate student from the Swedish Institute of Computer Science (SICS) in Stockholm, suggested many improvements to the algorithms presented in the book.

Several implementations for the "hands-on" part of the book were developed by, or with the help of, Alexandre Pinto, a key member of the *Appia* team, complemented with inputs from several DIALNP team members and students, including Nuno Carvalho, Maria João Monteiro, and Luís Sardinha.

Finally, we would like to thank all our colleagues who were kind enough to comment on earlier drafts of this book. These include Felix Gaertner, Benoit Garbinato and Maarten van Steen.

Rachid Guerraoui and Luís Rodrigues

Contents

1. Introduction

I know what you're thinking punk. You're thinking, did he fire six shots or only five? Well, to tell you the truth, I forgot myself in all this excitement. But being as this is a .44 Magnum, the most powerful handgun in the world and will blow your head clean off, you've got to ask yourself one question: do I feel lucky? Well do ya, punk?

(Dirty Harry)

This chapter first motivates the need for distributed programming abstractions. Special attention is given to abstractions that capture the problems that underlie robust forms of cooperation between multiple processes in a distributed system, usually called *agreement* abstractions. The chapter then advocates a modular strategy for the development of distributed programs by making use of those abstractions through specific Application Programming Interfaces (APIs).

A simple, concrete example API is also given to illustrate the notation and event-based invocation scheme used throughout the book to describe the algorithms that implement our abstractions. The notation and invocation schemes are very close to those we have used to implement our algorithms in the *Appia* protocol composition and execution framework.

1.1 Motivation

Distributed computing has to do with devising algorithms for a set of processes that seek to achieve some form of cooperation. Besides executing concurrently, some of the processes of a distributed system might stop operating, for instance, by crashing or being disconnected, while others might stay alive and keep operating. This very notion of *partial failures* is a characteristic of a distributed system. In fact, this notion can be useful if one really feels the need to differentiate a distributed system from a concurrent system. It is in order to quote Leslie Lamport here:

> "A distributed system is one in which the failure of a computer you
> did not even know existed can render your own computer unusable."

When a subset of the processes have failed, or become disconnected, the challenge is usually for the processes that are still operating, or connected to the majority of the processes, to synchronize their activities in a consistent way. In other words, the cooperation must be made robust to tolerate partial failures. This makes distributed computing a quite a hard, yet extremely stimulating, problem. As we will discuss in detail later in the book, due to several factors such as the asynchrony of the processes and the possibility of failures in the communication infrastructure, it may be impossible to accurately detect process failures, and, in particular, to distinguish a process failure from a network failure. This makes the problem of ensuring a consistent cooperation even more difficult. The challenge to researchers in distributed computing is precisely to devise algorithms that provide the processes that remain operating with enough consistent information so that they can cooperate correctly and solve common tasks.

In fact, many programs that we use today are distributed programs. Simple daily routines, such as reading e-mail or browsing the Web, involve some form of distributed computing. However, when using these applications, we are typically faced with the simplest form of distributed computing: *client-server* computing. In client-server computing, a centralized process, the *server*, provides a service to many remote *clients*. The clients and the server communicate by exchanging messages, usually following a request-reply form of interaction. For instance, in order to display a Web page to the user, a browser sends a request to the Web server and expects to obtain a response with the information to be displayed. The core difficulty of distributed computing, namely, achieving a consistent form of cooperation in the presence of partial failures, may pop up even by using this simple form of interaction. Going back to our browsing example, it is reasonable to expect that the user continues surfing the Web (by automatically being switched to other sites) if the site it is consulting fails, and even more reasonable that the server process keeps on providing information to the other client processes, even when some of them fail or get disconnected.

The problems above are already nontrivial to deal with when distributed computing is limited to the interaction between two parties, such as in the client-server case. However, there is more to distributed computing than handling client-server interactions. Quite often, not only two, but several processes need to cooperate and synchronize their actions to achieve a common goal. The existence of not only two, but multiple processes, does not make the task of distributed computation any simpler. Sometimes we talk about *multiparty* interactions in this general case. In fact, both patterns may coexist in a quite natural manner. Actually, a real distributed application would have parts following a client-server interaction pattern and other parts following a multiparty interaction pattern. This may even be a matter of perspective.

For instance, when a client contacts a server to obtain a service, it may not be aware that, in order to provide that service, the server itself may need to request the assistance of several other servers, with whom it needs to coordinate to satisfy the client's request. Sometimes, the expression peer-to-peer is used to emphasize the absence of a central server.

1.2 Distributed Programming Abstractions

Just like the act of smiling, the act of abstracting is restricted to very few natural species. By capturing properties that are common to a large and significant range of systems, abstractions help distinguish the fundamental from the accessory, and prevent system designers and engineers from reinventing, over and over, the same solutions for slight variants of the very same problems.

From The Basics. Reasoning about distributed systems should start by abstracting the underlying physical system: describing the relevant elements in an abstract way, identifying their intrinsic properties, and characterizing their interactions, lead us to define what is called a *system model*. In this book we will use mainly two abstractions to represent the underlying physical system: *processes* and *links*.

The processes of a distributed program abstract the active entities that perform computations. A process may represent a computer, a processor within a computer, or simply a specific thread of execution within a processor. To cooperate on some common task, the processes may typically need to exchange messages using some communication network. Links abstract the physical and logical network that supports communication among processes. It is possible to represent different realities of a distributed system by capturing different properties of processes and links, for instance, by describing the different ways these elements may fail.

Chapter 2 will provide a deeper discussion on the various distributed systems models that are used in this book.

To The Advanced. Given a system model, the next step is to understand how to build abstractions that capture recurring interaction patterns in distributed applications. In this book we are interested in abstractions that capture robust cooperation problems among groups of processes, as these are important and rather challenging. The cooperation among processes can sometimes be modeled as a distributed *agreement* problem. For instance, the processes may need to agree on whether a certain event did (or did not) take place, to agree on a common sequence of actions to be performed (from a number of initial alternatives), or to agree on the order by which a set of inputs need to be processed. It is desirable to establish more sophisticated forms of agreement from solutions to simpler agreement problems, in an incremental manner. Consider, for instance, the following situations:

- In order for processes to be able to exchange information, they must initially agree on who they are (say, using IP addresses) and on some common format for representing messages. They may also need to agree on some reliable way of exchanging messages (say, to provide TCP-like[1] semantics).
- After exchanging some messages, the processes may be faced with several alternative plans of action. They may then need to reach a *consensus* on a common plan, out of several alternatives, and each participating process may have initially its own plan, different from the plans of the other processes.
- In some cases, it may be acceptable for the cooperating processes to take a given step only if all other processes also agree that such a step should take place. If this condition is not met, all processes must agree that the step should *not* take place. This form of agreement is crucial in the processing of distributed transactions, where this problem is known as the *atomic commitment* problem.
- Processes may need not only to agree on which actions they should execute but to agree also on the order in which these actions need to be executed. This form of agreement is the basis of one of the most fundamental techniques to replicate computation in order to achieve fault tolerance, and it is called the *total order broadcast* problem.

This book is about mastering the difficulty underlying these problems, and devising *abstractions* that encapsulate such problems. In the following, we try to motivate the relevance of some of the abstractions covered in this book. We distinguish the case where the abstractions pop up from the natural distribution of the abstraction from the case where these abstractions come out as artifacts of an engineering choice for distribution.

1.2.1 Inherent Distribution

Applications which require sharing or dissemination of information among several participant processes are fertile for the emergence of distributed programming abstractions. Examples of such applications are information dissemination engines, multiuser cooperative systems, distributed shared spaces, cooperative editors, process control systems, and distributed databases.

Information Dissemination. In distributed applications with information dissemination requirements, processes may play one of the following roles: information producers, also called *publishers*, or information consumers, also called *subscribers*. The resulting interaction paradigm is often called *publish-subscribe*.

Publishers produce information in the form of notifications. Subscribers register their interest in receiving certain notifications. Different variants of

---

[1] Transmission Control Protocol, one of the main transport protocols used in the Internet (Postel 1981).

the publish-subscribe paradigm exist to match the information being produced with the subscribers' interests, including channel-based, subject-based, content-based, or type-based subscriptions. Independently of the subscription method, it is very likely that several subscribers are interested in the same notifications, which will then have to be multicast. In this case, we are typically interested in having subscribers of the same information receive the same set of messages. Otherwise the system will provide an unfair service, as some subscribers could have access to a lot more information than other subscribers.

Unless this reliability property is given for free by the underlying infrastructure (and this is usually not the case), the sender and the subscribers may need to coordinate to agree on which messages should be delivered. For instance, with the dissemination of an audio stream, processes are typically interested in receiving most of the information but are able to tolerate a bounded amount of message loss, especially if this allows the system to achieve a better throughput. The corresponding abstraction is typically called a *best-effort broadcast*.

The dissemination of some stock exchange information may require a more reliable form of broadcast, called *reliable broadcast*, as we would like all active processes to receive the same information. One might even require from a stock exchange infrastructure that information be disseminated in an ordered manner. In several publish-subscribe applications, producers and consumers interact indirectly, with the support of a group of intermediate cooperative brokers. In such cases, agreement abstractions may be useful for the cooperation among the brokers.

Process Control. Process control applications are those where several software processes have to control the execution of a physical activity. Basically, the (software) processes might be controlling the dynamic location of an aircraft or a train. They might also be controlling the temperature of a nuclear installation, or the automation of a car production system.

Typically, every process is connected to some sensor. The processes might, for instance, need to exchange the values output by their assigned sensors and output some common value, say, print a single location of the aircraft on the pilot control screen, despite the fact that, due to the inaccuracy or failure of their local sensors, they may have observed slightly different input values. This cooperation should be achieved despite some sensors (or associated control processes) having crashed or not observed anything. This type of cooperation can be simplified if all processes agree on the same set of inputs for the control algorithm, a requirement captured by the *consensus* abstraction.

Cooperative Work. Users located on different nodes of a network may cooperate in building a common software or document, or simply in setting up a distributed dialogue, say, for a virtual conference. A shared working space abstraction is very useful here to enable effective cooperation. Such distributed shared memory abstraction is typically accessed through *read* and *write* operations that the users exploit to store and exchange information. In its simplest form, a shared working space can be viewed as a virtual (distributed) register or a distributed file system. To maintain a consistent view of the shared space, the processes need to agree on the relative order among *write* and *read* operations on that shared board.

Distributed Databases. These constitute another class of applications where agreement abstractions can be helpful to ensure that all transaction managers obtain a consistent view of the running transactions and can make consistent decisions on the way these transactions are serialized.

Additionally, such abstractions can be used to coordinate the transaction managers when deciding about the outcome of the transactions. That is, the database servers on which a given distributed transaction has executed would need to coordinate their activities and decide on whether to commit or abort the transaction. They might decide to abort the transaction if any database server detected a violation of the database integrity, a concurrency control inconsistency, a disk error, or simply the crash of some other database server. As we pointed out, a distributed programming abstraction that is useful here is the *atomic commit* (or commitment) form of distributed cooperation.

1.2.2 Distribution as an Artifact

In general, even if the application is not inherently distributed and may not, at first glance, need sophisticated distributed programming abstractions. This need sometimes appears as an artifact of the engineering solution to satisfy some specific requirements such as *fault tolerance*, *load balancing*, or *fast sharing*.

We illustrate this idea through *state-machine replication*, which is a powerful way to achieve fault tolerance in distributed systems. Briefly, replication consists in making a centralized service highly available by executing several copies of it on several machines that are presumably supposed to fail independently. The service continuity is in a sense ensured despite the crash of a subset of the machines. No specific hardware is needed: fault tolerance through replication is software based. In fact, replication may also be used within an information system to improve the read access performance to data by placing it close to the processes where it is supposed to be queried.

For replication to be effective, the different copies must be maintained in a consistent state. If the state of the replicas diverge arbitrarily, it does not make sense to talk about replication. The illusion of *one* highly available service would fall apart and be replaced by that of several distributed services, each possibly failing independently. If replicas are deterministic, one of the simplest ways to guarantee full consistency is to ensure that all replicas receive the same set of requests in the same order. Typically, such guarantees are enforced by an abstraction called *total order broadcast*: the processes need to agree here on the sequence of messages they deliver. Algorithms that implement such a primitive are nontrivial, and providing the programmer with an abstraction that encapsulates these algorithms makes the design of replicated service easier. If replicas are nondeterministic, then ensuring their consistency requires different *ordering* abstractions, as we will see later in the book.

1.3 The End-to-End Argument

Distributed programming abstractions are useful but may sometimes be difficult or expensive to implement. In some cases, no simple algorithm is able to provide the desired abstraction and the algorithm that solves the problem can have a high complexity, e.g., in terms of the number of interprocess communication steps and messages. Therefore, depending on the system model, the network characteristics, and the required quality of service, the overhead of the abstraction can range from the negligible to the almost impairing.

Faced with performance constraints, the application designer may be driven to mix the relevant logic of the abstraction with the application logic, in an attempt to obtain an optimized integrated solution. The rationale for this would be that such a solution should perform better than a solution derived through a modular approach, where the abstraction is implemented as independent services that can be accessed through well-defined interfaces. The approach can be further supported by a superficial interpretation of the end-to-end argument: most complexity should be implemented at the higher levels of the communication stack. This argument could be applied to any form of (distributed) programming.

However, even if, in some cases, performance gains can be obtained by collapsing the application and the underlying layers, such an approach has many disadvantages. First, it is very error prone. Some of the algorithms that will be presented in this book have a considerable amount of difficulty and exhibit subtle dependencies among their internal elements. An apparently obvious "optimization" may break the algorithm correctness. It is in order to quote Knuth here:

"Premature optimization is the source of all evil."

Even if the designer reaches the amount of expertise required to master the difficult task of embedding these algorithms in the application, there are several other reasons to keep both implementations independent. The most important of these reasons is that there is usually no single solution for a given distributed computing problem. This is particularly true because of the variety of distributed system models. Instead, different solutions can usually be proposed and none of these solutions may strictly be superior to the others: each may have its own advantages and disadvantages, performing better under different network or load conditions, making different trade-offs between network traffic and message latency, and so on. Relying on a modular approach allows the most suitable implementation to be selected when the application is deployed, or even allows commuting at runtime among different implementations in response to changes in the operational envelope of the application.

Encapsulating tricky issues of distributed interactions within abstractions with well-defined interfaces significantly helps us reason about the correctness of the application, and port it from one system to the other. We strongly believe that, in many distributed applications, especially those that require many-to-many interaction, building preliminary prototypes of the distributed application using several abstraction layers can be very helpful.

Ultimately, one may indeed consider optimizing the performance of the final release of a distributed application and using some integrated prototype that implements several abstractions in one monolithic piece of code. However, full understanding of each of the enclosed abstractions in isolation is fundamental to ensure the correctness of the combined code.

1.4 Software Components

1.4.1 Composition Model

Notation. One of the biggest difficulties we had to face when thinking about describing distributed algorithms was to find out an adequate way to represent these algorithms. When representing a centralized algorithm, one could decide to use a programming language, either by choosing an existing popular one, or by inventing a new one with pedagogical purposes in mind.

Although there have indeed been several attempts to come up with distributed programming languages, these attempts have resulted in rather complicated notations that would not have been viable to describe general-purpose distributed algorithms in a pedagogical way. Trying to invent a distributed programming language was not an option. Had we the time to invent one successfully, at least one book would have been required to present the language itself.

Therefore, we have opted to use pseudo code to describe our algorithms. The pseudo code reflects a reactive computing model where components of the same process communicate by exchanging events: an algorithm is described as a set of event handlers. These react to incoming events and possibly trigger new events. In fact, the pseudo code is very close to the actual way we programmed the algorithms in our experimental framework. Basically, the algorithm description can be seen as actual code, from which we removed all implementation-related details that were more confusing than useful for understanding the algorithms. This approach hopefully simplifies the task of those who will be interested in building running prototypes from the descriptions found in this book.

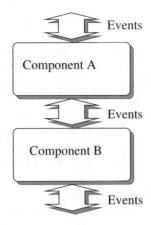

Fig. 1.1: Composition model

A Simple Example. Abstractions are typically represented through Application Programming Interfaces (API). We will informally discuss here a simple example API for a distributed programming abstraction.

To describe this API in particular, and our APIs in general, as well as the algorithms implementing these APIs, we shall consider, throughout the book, an *asynchronous event-based composition* model. Every process hosts a set of software modules, called *components* in our context. Each component is identified by a name, and characterized by a set of properties. The component provides an interface in the form of the events that the component accepts and produces in return. Distributed programming abstractions are typically made of a collection of components, at least one for every process, that are intended to satisfy some common properties.

Software Stacks. Components can be composed to build software stacks. At each process, a component represents a specific layer in the stack. The application layer is at the top of the stack whereas the networking layer is at the bottom. The layers of the distributed programming abstractions we will consider are typically in the middle. Components within the same stack communicate through the exchange of *events*, as illustrated in Figure 1.1. A given abstraction is typically materialized by a set of components, each running at a process.

According to this model, each component is constructed as a state-machine whose transitions are triggered by the reception of events. Events may carry information such as a data message, or a group membership information, in one or more *attributes*. Events are denoted by ⟨ *EventType* | *att1, att2, ...* ⟩.

Each event is processed through a dedicated handler by the process (i.e., by the corresponding component). The processing of an event may result in new events being created and triggering the same or different components. Every event triggered by a component of the same process is eventually processed, unless the process crashes. Events from the same component are processed in the order in which they were triggered. Note that this FIFO (*first-in-first-out*) order is only enforced on events exchanged among local components in a given stack. The messages among different processes may also need to be ordered according to some criteria, using mechanisms orthogonal to this one. We shall address this interprocess communication issue later in the book.

We assume that every process executes the code triggered by events in a mutually exclusive way. Basically, the same process does not handle two events concurrently. Once the handling of an event is terminated, the process keeps on checking if any other event is triggered. This periodic checking is assumed to be fair, and is achieved in an implicit way: it is not visible in the pseudo code we describe.

The code of each component looks like this:

---

upon event $\langle$ *Event1* $\mid$ att_1^1, att_1^2, ... $\rangle$ **do**
    something
    trigger $\langle$ *Event2* $\mid$ att_2^1,att_2^2, ... $\rangle$; *// send some event*

upon event $\langle$ *Event3* $\mid$ att_3^1, att_3^2, ... $\rangle$ **do**
    something else
    trigger $\langle$ *Event4* $\mid$ att_4^1, att_4^2, ... $\rangle$; *// send some other event*

This decoupled and asynchronous way of interacting among components matches very well the requirements of distributed applications: for instance, new processes may join or leave the distributed system at any moment and a process must be ready to handle both membership changes and reception of messages at any time. Hence, the order in which events will be observed cannot be defined *a priori*; this is precisely what we capture through our component model.

1.4.2 Programming Interface

A typical interface includes the following types of events:

- *Request* events are used by a component to request a service from another component: for instance, the application layer might trigger a *request* event at a component in charge of broadcasting a message to a set of processes in a group with some reliability guarantee, or proposing a value to be decided on by the group.
- *Confirmation* events are used by a component to confirm the completion of a request. Typically, the component in charge of implementing a broadcast

will confirm to the application layer that the message was indeed broadcast or that the value suggested has indeed been proposed to the group: the component uses here a *confirmation* event. Note that this is different from the actual delivery of the event to the application, as we discuss below.

- *Indication* events are used by a given component to *deliver* information to another component. Considering the broadcast example above, at every process that is a destination of the message, the component in charge of implementing the actual broadcast primitive will typically perform some processing to ensure the corresponding reliability guarantee, and then use an *indication* event to deliver the message to the application layer. Similarly, the decision on a value will be indicated with such an event.

A typical execution at a given layer consists of the following sequence of actions. We consider here the case of a broadcast kind of abstraction, e.g., the processes need to agree on whether or not to deliver a message broadcast by some process.

1. The execution is initiated by the reception of a *request* event from the layer above.
2. To ensure the properties of the broadcast abstraction, the layer will send one or more messages to its remote peers using the services of the layer below (using request events).
3. Messages sent by the peer layers are also *received* using the services of the underlying layer (through indication events).
4. When a message is received, it may have to be stored temporarily until the adequate reliability property is satisfied, before being *delivered* to the layer above (using an indication event).

This dataflow is illustrated in Figure 1.2. Events used to deliver information to the layer above are *indications*. In some cases, the layer may confirm that a service has been concluded using a specialized indication event, therefore called a *confirmation* event.

1.4.3 Modules

Not surprisingly, the modules described in this book perform some interaction with the correspondent modules on peer processes: after all, this is a book about distributed computing. It is, however, also possible to have modules that perform only local actions.

To illustrate the notion of modules, we use the example of a simple printing module. This module receives a print request, issues a print command, and then provides a confirmation of the print operation having been achieved. Module 1.1 describes its interface and Algorithm 1.1 is a straightforward implementation of it. The algorithm is to be executed by every process p_i.

Layer n+1

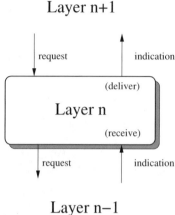

request   indication

(deliver)

Layer n

(receive)

request   indication

Layer n−1

Fig. 1.2: Layering

Module 1.1 Interface of a printing module

Module:

　　Name: Print.

Events:

　　Request: ⟨ *PrintRequest* | rqid, str ⟩: Requests a string to be printed. The token rqid is an identifier of the request.

　　Confirmation:⟨ *PrintConfirm* | rqid ⟩: Used to confirm that the printing request with identifier rqid succeeded.

Algorithm 1.1 Printing service

Implements:

　　Print.

upon event ⟨ *PrintRequest* | rqid, str ⟩ **do**

　　print str;

　　trigger ⟨ *PrintConfirm* | rqid ⟩;

To illustrate the way modules are composed, we use the printing module above to build a *bounded* printing service. The bounded printer only accepts a limited, predefined number of printing requests. The bounded printer also generates an indication when the threshold of allowed print requests is reached. The bounded printer uses the service of the (unbounded) printer introduced above and maintains a counter to keep track of the number of printing requests executed in the past. Module 1.2 provides the interface of the bounded printer and Algorithm 1.2 its implementation. The composition of the two modules is illustrated in Figure 1.3.

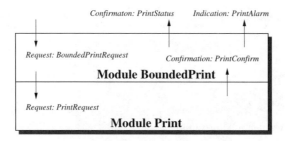

Fig. 1.3: A stack of printing modules

Module 1.2 Interface of a bounded printing module
___

Module:

    Name: BoundedPrint.

Events:

    Request: ⟨ *BoundedPrintRequest* | rqid, str ⟩: Request a string to be printed. The token rqid is an identifier of the request.

    Confirmation:⟨ *PrintStatus* | rqid, status ⟩: Used to return the outcome of the printing request: Ok or Nok.

    Indication:⟨ *PrintAlarm* ⟩: Used to indicate that the threshold was reached.

To make explicit the process of initializing the components, we assume that a special ⟨ *Init* ⟩ event is generated automatically by the runtime system when a component is created. This event is used to perform the initialization of the component. For instance, in the bounded printer example, this event is used to initialize the counter of executed printing requests.

1.4.4 Classes of Algorithms

As noted above, in order to provide a given service, a layer at a given process may need to execute one or more rounds of message exchange with the peer layers at remote processes. The behavior of each peer, characterized by the set of messages that it is capable of producing and accepting, the format of each of these messages, and the legal sequences of messages, is sometimes called a *protocol*. The purpose of the protocol is to ensure the execution of some *distributed algorithm*, the concurrent execution of different sequences of steps that ensure the provision of the desired service. This book covers several of these distributed algorithms.

To give the reader an insight into how design solutions and system-related parameters affect the algorithm design, this book includes five different classes of algorithmic solutions to implement our distributed programming abstractions, namely:

Algorithm 1.2 Bounded printer based on (unbounded) printing service

---

Implements:
    BoundedPrint.

Uses:
    Print.

upon event ⟨ *Init* ⟩ **do**
    bound := PredefinedThreshold;

upon event ⟨ *BoundedPrintRequest* | rqid, str ⟩ **do**
    if bound > 0 **then**
        bound := bound-1;
        trigger ⟨ *PrintRequest* | rqid, str ⟩;
        if bound = 0 **then trigger** ⟨ *PrintAlarm* ⟩;
    else
        trigger ⟨ *PrintStatus* | rqid, Nok ⟩;

upon event ⟨ *PrintConfirm* | rqid ⟩ **do**
    trigger ⟨ *PrintStatus* | rqid, Ok ⟩;

---

i. *fail-stop* algorithms, designed under the assumption that processes can fail by crashing but the crashes can be reliably detected by all the other processes;

ii. *fail-silent* algorithms, where process crashes can never be reliably detected;

iii. *fail-noisy* algorithms, where processes can fail by crashing and the crashes can be detected, but not always in an accurate manner (accuracy is only eventual);

iv. *fail-recovery* algorithms, where processes can crash and later recover and still participate in the algorithm; and

v. *randomized* algorithms, where processes use randomization to ensure the properties of the abstraction with some known probability.

These classes are not disjoint and it is important to notice that we do not give a solution from each class for every abstraction. First, there are cases where it is known that some abstraction cannot be implemented from an algorithm of a given class. For example, some of the coordination abstractions we consider in Chapter 7 do not have fail-noisy (and hence fail-silent) solutions and it is not clear how to devise meaningful randomized solutions to such abstractions. In other cases, such solutions may exist but devising them is still an active area of research.

Reasoning about distributed algorithms in general, and in particular about algorithms that implement distributed programming abstractions, first involves defining a clear model of the distributed system where these algorithms are supposed to operate. Put differently, we need to figure out what basic abstractions the processes assume in order to build more sophisticated ones. The basic abstractions we consider capture the allowable behavior of the processes and their communication links in the distributed system. Before delving into concrete algorithms to build sophisticated distributed programming abstractions, we thus need to understand such basic abstractions. This will be the topic of the next chapter.

1.5 Hands-On

Several of the algorithms that we will be presenting in the book have been implemented and made available as open source code. By using these implementations, the reader has the opportunity to run and experiment with the algorithms in a real setting, review the code, make changes and improvements to it and, eventually, take it as a basis to implement her own algorithms. Note that, when referring to the implementation of an algorithm, we will mainly use the word *protocol*. As noted before, the protocol describes not only the behavior of each participant but also the concrete format of the messages exchanged among participants.

The algorithms have been implemented in the Java programming language with the support of the *Appia* protocol composition and execution framework (Miranda, Pinto, and Rodrigues 2001). *Appia* is a tool that simplifies the development of communication protocols. To start with, *Appia* already implements a number of basic services that are required in several protocols, such as methods to add and extract headers from messages or launch timers: these are the sort of implementation details that may require the writing of a considerable number of lines of code when appropriate libraries are not available. Additionally, *Appia* simplifies the task of composing different protocol modules.

Central to the use of *Appia* is the notion of *protocol composition*. In its simpler form, a protocol composition is a stack of instances of the Layer class. For each different protocol module, a different specialization of the Layer class should be defined. In *Appia*, multiple instances of a given protocol composition may be created in run-time. Each instance is called a *channel*, as it is materialized as a stack of objects of the Session class. In *Appia*, modules communicate through the exchange of *events*. *Appia* defines the class Event, from which all events exchanged in the *Appia* framework must be derived. In order for a module to consume and produce events, a layer must explicitly declare the set of events *accepted, provided,* and *required*. When a layer requires an event, *Appia* checks if there is another layer in the composition that provides that event; if not, it generates an exception. This offers a simple way of detecting inconsistencies in the protocol composition.

At this point, it is probably useful to clarify the mapping between the abstract descriptions provided in the book and the corresponding concrete implementation in the *Appia* framework.

- While in the book we use pseudo code to describe the algorithms, in *Appia* the Java programming language is used to implement them.
- In the book we use the module concept to characterize the interface of a service. In the *Appia* implementation this interface is captured in the Layer class. The *Requests* accepted by the module are listed as *accepted* events. The *Indications* and *Confirmations* (if any) provided by the module are listed as *provided* events.
- Typically, there is a projection of the pseudo code that appears in an algorithm and the Java code of the corresponding Session class.

1.5.1 Print Module

Consider, for instance, the implementation of the Print module (Module 1.1). First, we define the events accepted and provided by this module. This is illustrated in Listing 1.1.

Listing 1.1. Events for the Print module

```
package appia.protocols.tutorialDA.print;

public class PrintRequestEvent extends Event {
    int rqid;
    String str;

    void setId(int rid);
    void setString(String s);
    int getId();
    String getString();
}
public class PrintConfirmEvent extends Event {
    int rqid;

    void setId(int rid);
    int getId();
}
```

Then, we implement the layer for this module. This is illustrated in Listing 1.2. As expected, the layer accepts the PrintRequestEvent and provides the PrintConfirmEvent. The PrintLayer is also responsible for creating objects of class PrintSession, whose purpose is described in the next paragraphs.

Listing 1.2. PrintLayer

```
package appia.protocols.tutorialDA.print;

public class PrintLayer extends Layer {

  public PrintLayer(){
    /* events that the protocol will create */
    evProvide = new Class[1];
    evProvide[0] = PrintConfirmEvent.class;

    /* events that the protocol requires to work. This is
     * a subset of the accepted events */
    evRequire = new Class[0];
```

```
    /* events that the protocol will accept */
    evAccept = new Class[2];
    evAccept[0] = PrintRequestEvent.class;
    evAccept[1] = ChannelInit.class;
  }

  public Session createSession() {
    return new PrintSession(this);
  }

}
```

Layers are used to describe the behavior of each module. The actual methods and the state required by the algorithm is maintained by Session objects. Thus, for every layer, the programmer needs to define the corresponding session. The main method of a session is the handle method, invoked by the *Appia* kernel whenever there is an event to be processed by the session. For the case of our Print module, the implementation of the PrintSession is given in Listing 1.3.

Listing 1.3. PrintSession

```
package appia.protocols.tutorialDA.print;

public class PrintSession extends Session {
    public PrintSession(Layer layer) {
        super(layer);
    }

    public void handle(Event event){
        if(event instanceof ChannelInit)
            handleChannelInit((ChannelInit)event);
        else if(event instanceof PrintRequestEvent){
            handlePrintRequest ((PrintRequestEvent)event);
        }
    }

    private void handleChannelInit(ChannelInit init) {
        try {
            init .go();
        } catch (AppiaEventException e) {
            e.printStackTrace();
        }
    }

    private void handlePrintRequest(PrintRequestEvent request) {
        try {
            PrintConfirmEvent ack = new PrintConfirmEvent ();

            doPrint (request.getString ());
            request.go();

            ack.setChannel(request.getChannel());
            ack.setDir(Direction. UP);
            ack.setSource(this);
            ack.setId (request.getId ());
            ack. init ();
            ack.go();
        } catch (AppiaEventException e) {
            e.printStackTrace();
```

```
        }
      }
  }
```

There are a couple of issues the reader should note in the previous code. First, as in most of our algorithms, every session should be ready to accept the ChannelInit event. This event is automatically generated and should be used to initialize the session state. Second, in *Appia*, the default behavior for a session is to always to move forward downward (or upward) in the stack the events it consumes. As it will become clear later in the book, it is often very convenient to have the same event processed by different sessions in sequence.

1.5.2 BoundedPrint Module

Having defined the events, the layer, and the session for the Print module, we can now perform a similar job for the BoundedPrint module (Module 1.2). As before, we start by providing the required events, as depicted in Listing 1.4. Note that we define the PrintAlarmEvent and the PrintStatusEvent.

We now use the opportunity to reinforce a very important feature of *Appia*. In *Appia*, the same event may be processed by several sessions in sequence. Therefore, *Appia* programmers avoid renaming events when they perform similar functions in different layers. In this case, instead of creating a new event BoundedPrintRequestEvent, that would have to be renamed PrintRequestEvent when propagated from the BoundedPrintLayer to the PrintLayer, we simply use the same event, PrintRequestEvent, in both layers. The order in which this event is processed (i.e, the fact that it is first processed by the BoundedPrintLayer and afterward by the PrintLayer) is defined by the composition of the stack, when the *Appia QoS* is declared.

Listing 1.4. Events for the BoundedPrint module

```
package appia.protocols.tutorialDA.print;

class PrintAlarmEvent extends Event {
}

class PrintStatusEvent extends Event {
    int      r_id ;
    Status   stat ;

    void setId (int rid );
    void setStatus (Status s);
    int getId ();
    int getStatus ();
}
```

We proceed to define the BoundedPrintLayer, as depicted in Listing 1.5. Since the BoundedPrint module uses the services of the basic Print module, it requires the PrintConfirmEvent produced by that module.

Listing 1.5. Bounded PrintLayer

```
package appia.protocols.tutorialDA.print;

public class BoundedPrintLayer extends Layer {

  public BoundedPrintLayer(){
    /* events that the protocol will create */
    evProvide = new Class[2];
    evProvide[0] = PrintStatusEvent.class;
    evProvide[1] = PrintAlarmEvent.class;

    /* events that the protocol require to work.
     * This is a subset of the accepted events */
    evRequire = new Class[1];
    evRequire[0] = PrintConfirmEvent.class;

    /* events that the protocol will accept */
    evAccept = new Class[3];
    evAccept[0] = PrintRequestEvent.class;
    evAccept[1] = PrintConfirmEvent.class;
    evAccept[2] = ChannelInit.class;
  }

  public Session createSession() {
    return new BoundedPrintSession(this);
  }

}
```

Subsequently, we can implement the session for the BoundedPrint module, depicted in Listing 1.6.

Listing 1.6. BoundedPrintSession

```
package appia.protocols.tutorialDA.print;

public class BoundedPrintSession extends Session {
    int bound;

    public BoundedPrintSession(Layer layer) {
        super(layer);
    }

    public void handle(Event event){
        if(event instanceof ChannelInit) {
            handleChannelInit((ChannelInit)event);
        }
        else if(event instanceof PrintRequestEvent) {
            handlePrintRequest ((PrintRequestEvent)event);
        }
        else if(event instanceof PrintConfirmEvent) {
            handlePrintConfirm ((PrintConfirmEvent)event);
        }
    }

    private void handleChannelInit(ChannelInit init) {
        try {
            bound = PredefinedThreshold;

            init .go ();
        } catch (AppiaEventException e) {
            e.printStackTrace();
        }
    }
```

```
private void handlePrintRequest(PrintRequestEvent request) {
    if (bound > 0){
        bound = bound -1;
        try {
            request.go ();
        } catch (AppiaEventException e) {
            e.printStackTrace();
        }
        if (bound == 0) {
            PrintAlarmEvent alarm = new PrintAlarmEvent ();
            alarm.setChannel (request.getChannel());
            alarm.setSource (this);
            alarm.setDir(Direction.UP);
            try {
                alarm.init ();
                alarm.go ();
            } catch (AppiaEventException e) {
                e.printStackTrace();
            }
        }
    }
    else {
        PrintStatusEvent status = new PrintStatusEvent ();
        status.setChannel (request.getChannel());
        status.setSource (this);
        status.setDir(Direction.UP);
        status.setId (request.getId ());
        status.setStatus (Status.NOK);
        try {
            status.init ();
            status.go ();
        } catch (AppiaEventException e) {
            e.printStackTrace();
        }
    }
}

private void handlePrintConfirm(PrintConfirmEvent conf) {
    PrintStatusEvent status = new PrintStatusEvent ();
    status.setChannel (request.getChannel());
    status.setSource (this);
    status.setDir(Direction.UP);
    status.setId (conf.getId ());
    status.setStatus (Status.OK);
    try {
        status.init ();
        status.go ();
    } catch (AppiaEventException e) {
        e.printStackTrace();
    }
}
}
```

1.5.3 Composing Modules

The two modules that we have described can now be easily composed using the *Appia* framework. The first step consists in creating a protocol composition by stacking the BoundedPrintLayer on top of the PrintLayer. Actually, in order to be able to experiment with these two layers, we further add on top

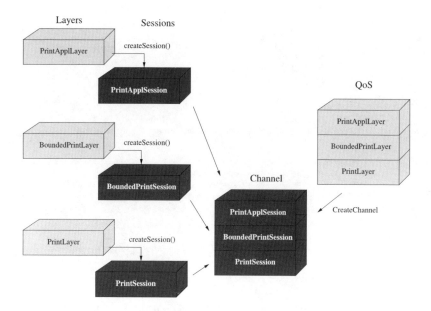

Fig. 1.4: Layers, Sessions, QoS and Channels

of the stack a simple application layer, named PrintApplicationLayer. This is a simple layer, that listens for strings on *standard input*, creates and sends a print request with those strings, and displays the confirmation and status events received.

A composition of layers in *Appia* is called a QoS (Quality of Service) and can simply be created by providing the desired array of layers, as shown in Listing 1.7. After defining a protocol composition, it is possible to create one or more communication *channels* that use that composition. Therefore, channels can be seen as instances of protocol compositions. Channels are made of *sessions*. When a channel is created from a composition, it is possible to automatically create a new session for every layer in the composition. The relation between Layers, Sessions, QoS, and Channels is illustrated in Figure 1.4. The code required to create a channel is depicted in Listing 1.7.

Listing 1.7. Creating a PrintChannel

```
package appia.protocols.tutorialDA.print;

public class Example {

    public static void main(String[] args) {
        /* Create layers and put them in a array */
        Layer [] qos =
            {new PrintLayer(),
             new BoundedPrintLayer(),
             new PrintApplicationLayer()};

        /* Create a QoS */
```

```
QoS myQoS = null;
try {
    myQoS = new QoS("Print_stack", qos);
} catch (AppiaInvalidQoSException ex) {
    System.err. println ("Invalid_QoS");
    System.err. println (ex.getMessage());
    System.exit(1);
}

/* Create a channel. Uses default event scheduler. */
Channel channel = myQoS.createUnboundChannel("Print_Channel");

try {
    channel.start ();
} catch(AppiaDuplicatedSessionsException ex) {
    System.err. println ("Error_in_start");
    System.exit(1);
}

/* All set. Appia main class will handle the rest */
System.out.println("Starting_Appia...");
Appia.run();
    }
}
```

The reader is now invited to install the *Appia* distribution provided as a companion of this book and try the implementations described above.

Try It To test the Print and BoundedPrint implementations, use the Example class, located in the demo.tutorialDA package.

To run a simple test, execute the following steps:

1. Open a shell/command prompt.
2. In the shell go to the directory where you have placed the supplied code.
3. Launch the test application:
   java demo/tutorialDA/Example
   Note: If the error NoClassDefError has appeared, confirm that you are at the root of the supplied code.

In the output displayed, each line starts with the name of the layer that is writing the output. The PrintApplication layer displays the identification of the next print request between parentheses. After you press the Enter key, that identification applies to the last typed text.

Now that the process is launched and running, you may try the following execution:

1. Type the text adieu (print request 1).
   • Note that Ok status was received for this text.
2. Type the text goodbye (print request 2).
   • Note that Ok status was received for this text.
3. Type the text adios (print request 3).
   • Note that Ok status was received for this text.
4. Type the text sayonara (print request 4).

- Note that `Ok` status was received for this text.
5. Type the text `adeus` (print request 5).
   - Note that an ALARM notification was received because the limit of the BoundedPrint layer, predefined value of 5, was reached.
   - Nevertheless an Ok status was received for this text.
6. Any further typed text will receive a `Not Ok` status.

2. Basic Abstractions

These are my principles. If you don't like them, I have others.

(Groucho Marx)

Applications that are deployed in practical distributed systems are usually composed of a myriad of different machines and communication infrastructures. Physical machines differ on the number of processors, type of processors, amount and speed of both volatile and persistent memory, and so on. Communication infrastructures differ on parameters such as latency, throughput, reliability, etc. On top of these machines and infrastructures, a huge variety of software components are sometimes encompassed by the same application: operating systems, file systems, middleware, communication protocols, each component with its own specific features.

One might consider implementing distributed services that are tailored to specific combinations of the elements listed above. Such implementations would depend on one type of machine, one form of communication, one distributed operating system, and so on. However, in this book, we are interested in studying abstractions and algorithms that are relevant for a wide range of distributed environments. In order to achieve this goal we need to capture the fundamental characteristics of various distributed systems in some basic abstractions, on top of which we can later define other more elaborate, and generic, distributed programming abstractions.

This chapter presents the basic abstractions we use to model a distributed system composed of computational entities (*processes*) communicating by exchanging messages.

Two kinds of abstractions will be of primary importance: those representing *processes* and those representing communication *links*. Not surprisingly, it does not seem to be possible to model the huge diversity of physical networks and operational conditions with a single process abstraction and a single link abstraction. Therefore, we will define different instances for each kind of basic abstraction. For instance, we will distinguish process abstractions according to the types of faults that they may exhibit.

Besides our process and link abstractions, we will introduce the *failure detector* abstraction as a convenient way to capture assumptions that might be reasonable to make on the timing behavior of processes and links. Later in the chapter we will identify relevant combinations of our three categories of abstractions. Such a combination is what we call a *distributed system model*.

This chapter also contains our first module descriptions, used to specify our basic abstractions, as well as our first algorithms, used to implement these abstractions. The specifications and the algorithms are rather simple and should help illustrate our notation, before proceeding in subsequent chapters to more sophisticated specifications and algorithms.

2.1 Distributed Computation

2.1.1 Processes and Messages

We abstract the units that are able to perform computations in a distributed system through the notion of *process*. We consider that the system is composed of N uniquely identified processes, denoted by $p_1, p_2, \ldots, p_N$. Sometimes we also denote the processes by p, q, r. The set of system processes is denoted by Π. Unless explicitly stated otherwise, it is assumed that this set is static (does not change) and processes do know of each other. Typically, we will assume that all processes of the system run the same local algorithm. The sum of these copies constitutes the actual distributed algorithm.

We do not assume any particular mapping of our abstract notion of process to the actual processors, processes, or threads of a specific computer machine or operating system. The processes communicate by exchanging messages and the messages are uniquely identified, say, by their original sender process using a sequence number or a local clock, together with the process identifier. Messages are exchanged by the processes through communication *links*. We will capture the properties of the links that connect the processes through specific link abstractions, which we will discuss later.

2.1.2 Automata and Steps

A *distributed algorithm* is viewed as a collection of distributed automata, one per process. The automaton at a process regulates the way the process executes its computation steps, i.e., how it reacts to a message. The *execution* of a distributed algorithm is represented by a sequence of steps executed by the processes. The elements of the sequences are the steps executed by the processes involved in the algorithm. A partial execution of the algorithm is represented by a finite sequence of steps; an infinite execution by an infinite sequence of steps.

Process

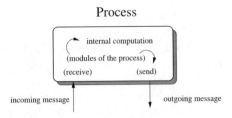

Fig. 2.1: Step of a process

It is convenient for presentation simplicity to assume the existence of a global clock, outside the control of the processes. This clock provides a global and linear notion of time that regulates the execution of the algorithms. The steps of the processes are executed according to ticks of the global clock: one step per clock tick. Even if two steps are executed at the same physical instant, we view them as if they were executed at two different times of our global clock. A *correct* process executes an infinite number of steps, i.e., every process has an infinite share of time units (we come back to this notion in the next section). In a sense, there is some entity, sometimes called a global scheduler, that schedules time units among processes, though the very notion of time is outside the control of the processes.

A process step consists in *receiving* (sometimes we will be saying *delivering*) a message from another process (global event), *executing* a local computation (local event), and *sending* a message to some process (global event) (Figure 2.1). The execution of the local computation and the sending of a message is determined by the process automaton, i.e., the algorithm. Local events that are generated are typically those exchanged between modules of the same process at different layers.

The fact that a process has no message to receive or send, but has some local computation to perform, is simply captured by assuming that messages might be *nil*, i.e., the process receives/sends the *nil* message. Of course, a process might not have any local computation to perform either, in which case it does simply not touch any of its local variables. In this case, the local computation is also *nil*.

It is important to notice that the interaction between local components of the very same process is viewed as a local computation and not as a communication. We will not be talking about messages exchanged between modules of the same process. The process is the unit of communication, just like it is the unit of failures, as we will discuss. In short, a *communication step* of the algorithm occurs when a process sends a message to another process, and the latter receives this message. The number of communication steps reflects the latency an implementation exhibits, since the network latency is typically a limiting factor of the performance of distributed algorithms.

An important parameter of the process abstraction is the restriction imposed on the speed at which local steps are performed and messages are exchanged. We will come back to this aspect when discussing timing assumptions later in this chapter.

Unless specified otherwise, we will consider *deterministic* algorithms. That is, for every step performed by any given process, the local computation executed by the process and the message sent by this process are uniquely determined by the message received by the process and its local state prior to executing the step.

In specific situations, we will also discuss *randomized* (or *probabilistic*) algorithms where processes make use of underlying *random* oracles to choose the local computation to be performed or the next message to be sent, from a set of possibilities.

2.1.3 Liveness and Safety

When we devise a distributed algorithm to implement a given distributed programming abstraction, we seek to satisfy the properties of the abstraction in all possible executions of the algorithm, i.e., in all possible sequences of steps executed by the processes according to the algorithm. The way these steps are scheduled is out of the control of the processes and depends on the global scheduler. The properties of the abstraction to be implemented need to be satisfied for a large set of possible interleaving of these steps. These properties usually fall into two classes: *safety* and *liveness*. Having in mind the distinction between these classes usually helps understand the two complementary faces of the abstraction and devise an adequate algorithm to implement it.

Basically, a **safety property** is a property of a distributed algorithm that can be violated at some time t and never be satisfied again after that time. Roughly speaking, safety properties state that the algorithm should not do anything wrong. To illustrate this, consider a property of perfect links (which we will discuss in more detail later in this chapter) that, roughly speaking, stipulates that no process should receive a message unless this message was indeed sent. In other words, communication links should not invent messages out of thin air. To state that this property is violated in some execution of an algorithm, we need to determine a time t at which some process receives a message that was never sent. This observation helps devise a correctness argument (by contradiction) for an algorithm presumably satisfying the property.

More precisely, a safety property is a property such that, whenever it is violated in some execution E of an algorithm, there is a partial execution E' of E such that the property will be violated in any extension of E'. In more sophisticated terms, we would say that safety properties are closed under execution prefixes.

Of course, safety properties are not enough. Sometimes, a good way of preventing bad things from happening consists in simply doing nothing. In many countries, some public administrations seem to understand this rule quite well and hence have an easy time ensuring safety.

Therefore, to define a useful abstraction, it is necessary to add some **liveness properties** to ensure that eventually something good happens. For instance, to define a meaningful notion of perfect links, we would require that if a correct process sends a message to a correct destination process, then the destination process should eventually deliver the message (besides the safety property which stipulates that messages should not be invented out of thin air and only delivered if priorly sent). To state that such a liveness property is violated in a given execution, we need to show that there is an infinite scheduling of the steps of the algorithm where the message is never delivered.

More precisely, a liveness property is a property of a distributed system execution such that, for any time t, there is some hope that the property can be satisfied at some time $t' \geq t$. It is a property for which, quoting Cicero, "While there is life there is hope."

The challenge is to guarantee both liveness and safety. (The difficulty is not in *talking*, or *not lying*, but in *telling the truth*.) Indeed, useful distributed services are supposed to provide both liveness and safety properties. In general, meeting an abstraction with only one kind of property is usually a sign of a flawed specification.

Consider, for instance, a traditional interprocess communication service such as TCP: it ensures that messages exchanged between two processes are neither lost or duplicated, and are received in the order in which they were sent. As we pointed out, requiring that messages are not lost is a liveness property. Requiring that the messages are not duplicated and received in the order in which they were sent, are safety property.

Although it is usually better, for modularity purposes, to separate the safety and liveness properties of an abstraction specification into disjoint classes, we will sometimes, and for the sake of conciseness, consider properties that are neither pure liveness nor pure safety properties, but rather a union of both.

2.2 Abstracting Processes

2.2.1 Process Failures

Unless it *fails*, a process is supposed to execute the algorithm assigned to it, through the set of components implementing the algorithm within that process. Our unit of failure is the process. When the process fails, all its components are assumed to fail as well, and at the same time.

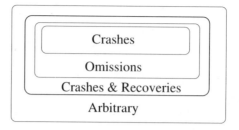

Fig. 2.2: Failure modes of a process

Process abstractions differ according to the nature of the failures that are considered. We discuss various forms of failures in the next section (Figure 2.2).

2.2.2 Arbitrary Faults and Omissions

A process is said to fail in an *arbitrary* manner if it deviates arbitrarily from the algorithm assigned to it. The *arbitrary fault* behavior is the most general one. In fact, it makes no assumptions on the behavior of faulty processes, which are allowed any kind of output and, therefore, can send any kind of message. These kinds of failures are sometimes called *Byzantine* (see the historical note at the end of this chapter) or *malicious* failures. Not surprisingly, arbitrary faults are the most expensive to tolerate, but this is the only acceptable option when an extremely high coverage is required or when there is the risk of some processes being controlled by malicious users that deliberately try to prevent correct system operation. An arbitrary fault needs not be intentional and malicious: it can simply be caused by a bug in the implementation, the programming language, or the compiler. This bug can thus cause the process to deviate from the algorithm it was supposed to execute.

A more restricted kind of fault to consider is the *omission* kind (Figure 2.2). An omission fault occurs when a process does not send (or receive) a message it is supposed to send (or receive), according to its algorithm. In general, omission faults are due to buffer overflows or network congestion. Omission faults result in lost messages. With an omission, the process deviates from the algorithm assigned to it by dropping some messages that should have been exchanged with other processes.

2.2.3 Crashes

An interesting particular case of omissions is when a process executes its algorithm correctly, including the exchange of messages with other processes, possibly until some time t, after which the process does not send any message to any other process. This is what happens if the process, for instance, crashes at time t and never recovers after that time. If, besides not sending any message after some time t, the process also stops executing any local computation after t, we talk about a *crash failure* (Figure 2.2), and a *crash-stop* process abstraction. The process is said to *crash* at time t. With this abstraction, a process is said to be *faulty* if it crashes. It is said to be *correct* if it does not ever crash and executes an infinite number of steps. We discuss two ramifications of the crash-stop abstraction.

It is usual to devise algorithms that implement a given distributed programming abstraction, say, some form of agreement, provided that a minimal number F of processes are correct, e.g., at least one, or a majority. This means that any number of processes can crash up to $F - 1$ times.

It is important to understand here that such an assumption does not mean that the hardware underlying these processes is supposed to operate correctly forever. In fact, the assumption means that, in every execution of the algorithm making use of that abstraction, it is very unlikely that more than a certain number F of processes crash, during the lifetime of that very execution. An engineer picking such an algorithm for a given application should be confident that the chosen elements underlying the software and hardware architecture make that assumption plausible. In general, it is also good practice, when devising algorithms that implement a given distributed abstraction under certain assumptions, to determine precisely which properties of the abstraction are preserved and which can be violated when a specific subset of the assumptions are not satisfied, e.g., when more than F processes crash.

Considering a crash-stop process abstraction boils down to assuming that a process executes its algorithm correctly, unless it crashes, in which case it does not recover. That is, once it crashes, the process does not ever perform any computation. Obviously, in practice, processes that crash can in general be restarted and hence do usually recover. In fact, it is usually desirable that they do.

It is also important to notice that, in practice, the crash-stop process abstraction does not preclude the possibility of recovery, nor does it mean that recovery should be prevented for a given algorithm (assuming a crash-stop process abstraction) to behave correctly. It simply means that the algorithm should not rely on some of the processes to recover in order to pursue its execution. These processes might not recover, or might recover only after a long period encompassing the crash detection and then the rebooting delay. In some sense, an algorithm that is not relying on crashed processes to recover would typically be faster than an algorithm relying on some of the processes to recover (we will discuss this issue in the next section). Nothing, however, prevents recovered processes from getting informed about the outcome of the computation and participating in subsequent instances of the distributed algorithm.

Unless explicitly stated otherwise, we will assume the crash-stop process abstraction throughout this book.

2.2.4 Recoveries

Sometimes, the assumption that certain processes never crash is simply not plausible for certain distributed environments. For instance, assuming that a majority of the processes do not crash, even only long enough for an algorithm execution to terminate, might simply be too strong.

An interesting alternative as a process abstraction to consider in this case is the *crash-recovery* one; we also talk about a *crash-recovery* kind of failure (Figure 2.2). In this case, we say that a process is faulty if either the process crashes and never recovers, or the process keeps infinitely often crashing and recovering. Otherwise, the process is said to be correct. Basically, such a process is eventually always (i.e., during the lifetime of the algorithm execution of interest) up and running. A process that crashes and recovers a finite number of times is correct in this model (i.e., according to this abstraction of a process).

According to the crash-recovery abstraction, a process can indeed crash: in such a case, the process stops sending messages, but might later recover. This can be viewed as an omission fault, with one exception, however: a process might suffer *amnesia* when it crashes and loses its internal state. This significantly complicates the design of algorithms because, upon recovery, the process might send new messages that contradict messages that the process might have sent prior to the crash. To cope with this issue, we sometimes assume that every process has, in addition to its regular volatile memory, a *stable storage* (also called a *log*), which can be accessed through *store* and *retrieve* primitives.

Upon recovery, we assume that a process is aware that it has crashed and recovered. In particular, a specific ⟨ Recovery ⟩ event is assumed to be automatically generated by the runtime environment in a similar manner to the ⟨ Init ⟩ event, executed each time a process starts executing some algorithm. The processing of the ⟨ Recovery ⟩ event should, for instance, retrieve the relevant state of the process from stable storage before the processing of other events is resumed. The process might, however, have lost all the remaining data that was preserved in volatile memory. This data should thus be properly reinitialized. The ⟨ Init ⟩ event is considered atomic with respect to recovery. More precisely, if a process crashes in the middle of its initialization procedure and recovers, say, without having processed the ⟨ Init ⟩ event properly, the process should invoke again the ⟨ Init ⟩ procedure before proceeding to the ⟨ Recovery ⟩ one.

In some sense, a crash-recovery kind of failure matches an omission fault if we consider that every process stores every update to any of its variables in stable storage. This is not very practical because access to stable storage is usually expensive (as there is a significant delay in accessing it). Therefore, a crucial issue in devising algorithms with the crash-recovery abstraction is to minimize the access to stable storage.

One way to alleviate the need for accessing any form of stable storage is to assume that some of the processes never crash (during the lifetime of an algorithm execution). This might look contradictory with the actual motivation for introducing the crash-recovery process abstraction in the first place. In fact, there is no contradiction, as we explain below. As discussed earlier, with crash-stop failures, some distributed-programming abstractions can be implemented only under the assumption that a certain number of processes never crash, say, a majority of the processes participating in the computation, e.g., four out of seven processes. This assumption might be considered unrealistic in certain environments. Instead, one might consider it more reasonable to assume that at least two processes do not crash during the execution of an algorithm. (The rest of the processes would indeed crash and recover.) As we will discuss later in the book, such an assumption makes it sometimes possible to devise algorithms assuming the crash-recovery process abstraction without any access to a stable storage. In fact, the processes that do not crash implement a virtual stable storage abstraction, and this is made possible without knowing in advance which of the processes will not crash in a given execution of the algorithm.

At first glance, one might believe that the crash-stop abstraction can also capture situations where processes crash and recover, by simply having the processes change their identities upon recovery. That is, a process that recovers after a crash, would behave, with respect to the other processes, as if it were a different process that was simply not performing any action. This could easily be done assuming a reinitialization procedure where, besides initializing its state as if it just started its execution, a process would also change its identity. Of course, this process should be updated with any information it might have missed from others, as if it did not receive that information yet. Unfortunately, this view is misleading, as we explain below. Again, consider an algorithm devised using the crash-stop process abstraction, and assuming that a majority of the processes never crash, say at least four out of a total of seven processes composing the system. Consider, furthermore, a scenario where four processes do indeed crash, and one process recovers. Pretending that the latter process is a different one (upon recovery) would mean that the system is actually composed of eight processes, five of which should not crash. The same reasoning can then be made for this larger number of processes. However, a fundamental assumption that we build upon is that the set of processes involved in any given computation is static, and the processes know of each other in advance.

A tricky issue with the crash-recovery process abstraction is the interface between software modules. Assume that some module of a process, involved in the implementation of some specific distributed abstraction, delivers some message or decision to the upper layer (say, the application layer), and subse-

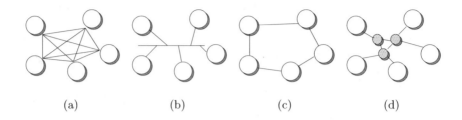

(a)   (b)   (c)   (d)

Fig. 2.3: The link abstraction and different instances

quently the process hosting the module crashes. Upon recovery, the module cannot determine if the upper layer (i.e., the application) has processed the message or decision before crashing or not. There are at least two ways to deal with this issue:

1. One way is to change the interface between modules. Instead of delivering a message (or a decision) to the upper layer (e.g., the application layer), the module may instead store the message (decision) in a stable storage that is exposed to the upper layer. It is then up to the upper layer to access the stable storage and exploit delivered information.
2. A different approach consists in having the module periodically deliver the message (or some decision) to the upper layer (e.g., the application layer) until the latter explicitly asks for the stopping of the delivery. That is, the distributed programming abstraction implemented by the module is in this case responsible for making sure the application will make use of the delivered information. Of course, the application layer needs in this case to check for duplicates.

2.3 Abstracting Communication

The *link* abstraction is used to represent the network components of the distributed system. Every pair of processes is connected by a bidirectional link, a topology that provides full connectivity among the processes. In practice, different topologies may be used to implement this abstraction, possibly using routing algorithms. Concrete examples of architectures that materialize the link abstraction, such as the ones illustrated in Figure 2.3, include the use of (a) a fully connected mesh, (b) a broadcast medium (such as an Ethernet), (c) a ring, or (d) a mesh of links interconnected by bridges and routers (such as the Internet). Many algorithms refine the abstract network view to make use of the properties of the underlying topology.

Messages exchanged between processes are uniquely identified and every message includes enough information for the recipient of a message to uniquely identify its sender. Furthermore, when exchanging messages in a request-reply manner among different processes, we usually assume that the processes have means to identify which reply message is a response to which request message. This can typically be achieved by having the processes generate (random) timestamps, based on sequence numbers or local clocks. This assumption alleviates the need for explicitly introducing these timestamps in the algorithm.

2.3.1 Link Failures

In a distributed system, it is possible for messages to be lost when transiting through the network. However, it is reasonable to assume that the probability for a message to reach its destination is nonzero because it is very unlikely that all messages exchanged among two processes are systematically lost unless there is a severe network failure (such as a network partition). A simple way to overcome the inherent unreliability of the network is to keep on retransmitting messages until they reach their destinations.

In the following, we will describe three different kinds of link abstractions. Some are stronger than others in the sense that they provide more reliability guarantees. All three are *point-to-point* link abstractions, i.e., they support the communication between pairs of processes. (In the next chapter, we will be defining broadcast communication abstractions.)

We will first describe the abstraction of *fair-loss* links, which captures the basic idea that messages might be lost but the probability for a message not to be lost is nonzero. Then we describe higher-level abstractions that could be implemented over *fair-loss* links using retransmission mechanisms to hide from the programmer part of the unreliability of the network. We will more precisely consider *stubborn* and *perfect* link abstractions, and show how they can be implemented on top of *fair-loss* links. As we pointed out earlier, unless explicitly stated otherwise, we will be assuming the crash-stop process abstraction.

We define the properties of each of our link abstractions using two kinds of primitives: *send* and *deliver*. The term *deliver* is preferred to the more general term *receive* to make clear that we are talking about a specific link abstraction to be implemented over the network. A message may typically be *received* at a given port of the network and stored within some buffer, and then some algorithm executed to make sure the properties of the required link abstraction are satisfied, before the message is actually *delivered*. When there is no ambiguity, we alternatively use the term *receive* to mean *deliver*. On the other hand, when implementing a communication abstraction A over a communication abstraction B, we will use sometimes the term *deliver* for A and *receive* for B to disambiguate.

A process invokes the *send* primitive of a link abstraction to request the sending of a message using that abstraction. When the process invokes that primitive, we say that the process sends the message. It might then be up to

---

Module 2.1 Interface and properties of fair-loss point-to-point links

Module:

    Name: FairLossPointToPointLinks (flp2p).

Events:

    Request: ⟨ *flp2pSend* | dest, m ⟩: Used to request the transmission of message m to process *dest*.

    Indication: ⟨ *flp2pDeliver* | src, m ⟩: Used to deliver message m sent by process *src*.

Properties:

    FLL1: *Fair-loss:* If a message m is sent infinitely often by process p_i to process p_j, and neither p_i nor p_j crash, then m is delivered an infinite number of times by p_j.

    FLL2: *Finite duplication:* If a message m is sent a finite number of times by process p_i to process p_j, then m cannot be delivered an infinite number of times by p_j.

    FLL3: *No creation:* If a message m is delivered by some process p_j, then m was previously sent to p_j by some process p_i.

---

the link abstraction to make some effort in transmitting the message to the target process, according to the actual specification of the abstraction. The *deliver* primitive is invoked by the algorithm implementing the abstraction on a destination process. When this primitive is invoked on a process p for a message m, we say that p delivers m.

2.3.2 Fair-Loss Links

The interface of the fair-loss link abstraction is described by Module 2.1, "FairLossPointToPointLinks (flp2p)." This consists of two events: a request event, used to send messages, and an indication event, used to deliver the messages. Fair-loss links are characterized by the properties FLL1–FLL3.

    Basically, the *fair-loss* property guarantees that a link does not systematically drop any given message. Therefore, if neither the sender process nor the recipient process crashes, and if a message keeps being retransmitted, the message is eventually delivered. The *finite duplication* property intuitively ensures that the network does not perform more retransmissions than that performed by the sending process. Finally, the *no creation* property ensures that no message is created or corrupted by the network.

2.3.3 Stubborn Links

We define the abstraction of *stubborn* links in Module 2.2, "StubbornPointTo-PointLink (sp2p)." This abstraction hides lower layer retransmission mecha-

---

Module 2.2 Interface and properties of stubborn point-to-point links

Module:

Name: StubbornPointToPointLink (sp2p).

Events:

Request: ⟨ sp2pSend | dest, m ⟩: Used to request the transmission of message m to process dest.

Indication:⟨ sp2pDeliver | src, m ⟩: Used to deliver message m sent by process src.

Properties:

SL1: *Stubborn delivery:* Let p_i be any process that sends a message m to a correct process p_j. If p_i does not crash, then p_j delivers m an infinite number of times.

SL2: *No creation:* If a message m is delivered by some process p_j, then m was previously sent to p_j by some process p_i.

---

nisms used by the sender process, when using actual fair-loss links, to make sure its messages are eventually delivered by the destination process.

Algorithm: Retransmit Forever. Algorithm 2.1, called "Retransmit Forever", describes a very simple implementation of a stubborn link over a fair-loss one. As the name implies, the algorithm simply keeps on retransmitting all messages sent. This overcomes possible omissions in the links. Note that we assume here the availability of a *timeout* service that can be invoked using the *startTimer* function and which triggers a *Timeout* event after a specified delay. This is a purely local mechanism, i.e., it can be implemented by a local counter and does not rely on any global synchronization mechanism.

We discuss, in the following, the correctness of the algorithm as well as some performance considerations.

Correctness. The *fair-loss* property of the underlying links guarantees that, if the target process is correct, it will indeed deliver, infinitely often, every message that was sent by every non-crashed process. This is because the algorithm makes sure the sender process will keep flp2pSending those messages infinitely often, unless that sender process itself crashes. The *no creation* property is simply preserved by the underlying links.

Performance. The algorithm is clearly not efficient and its purpose is primarily pedagogical. It is pretty clear that, within a practical application, it does not make much sense for a process to keep on, and at every step, restransmitting previously sent messages infinitely often. There are at least two complementary ways to prevent that effect and, hence, to make the algorithm more practical. First, it is very important to remember that the very notions of infinity and infinitely often are context dependent: they basically depend on the algorithm making use of stubborn links. After the algorithm making

---

Algorithm 2.1 Retransmit Forever

Implements:
    StubbornPointToPointLink (sp2p).

Uses:
    FairLossPointToPointLinks (flp2p).

upon event ⟨ *Init* ⟩ **do**
    sent := ∅;
    startTimer (TimeDelay);

upon event ⟨ *Timeout* ⟩ **do**
    forall $(dest, m) \in$ sent **do**
        trigger ⟨ *flp2pSend* | *dest, m* ⟩;
    startTimer (TimeDelay);

upon event ⟨ *sp2pSend* | dest, m ⟩ **do**
    trigger ⟨ *flp2pSend* | dest, m ⟩;
    sent := sent ∪ {(dest,m)};

upon event ⟨ *flp2pDeliver* | src, m ⟩ **do**
    trigger ⟨ *sp2pDeliver* | src, m ⟩;

---

use of those links has ended its execution, there is no need to keep on sending messages. Second, an acknowledgment mechanism can be added to notify a sender that it does not need to keep on sending a given set of messages any more. This mechanism can be performed whenever a target process has delivered (i.e., properly consumed) those messages, or has delivered messages that semantically subsume the previous ones, e.g., in stock exchange applications when new values might subsume old ones. Such a mechanism should however be viewed as an external algorithm, and cannot be integrated within our algorithm implementing stubborn links. Otherwise, the algorithm might not be implementing the stubborn link abstraction anymore, for the subsume notion is not part of the abstraction.

2.3.4 Perfect Links

With the stubborn link abstraction, it is up to the target process to check whether a given message has already been delivered or not. Adding mechanisms detecting and suppressing message duplicates, in addition to mechanisms for message retransmission, allows us to build an even higher level abstraction: the *perfect* link one, sometimes also called the *reliable link* abstraction. The perfect link abstraction specification is captured by the "PerfectPointToPointLink (pp2p)" module, Module 2.3. The interface of this module also consists of two events: a request event (to send messages) and an indication event (used to deliver messages). Perfect links are characterized by properties PL1–PL3.

Module 2.3 Interface and properties of perfect point-to-point links

Module:

> **Name:** PerfectPointToPointLink (pp2p).

Events:

> **Request:** ⟨ *pp2pSend* | *dest, m* ⟩: Used to request the transmission of message m to process *dest*.

> **Indication:**⟨ *pp2pDeliver* | *src, m* ⟩: Used to deliver message m sent by process *src*.

Properties:

> **PL1:** *Reliable delivery:* Let p_i be any process that sends a message m to a process p_j. If neither p_i nor p_j crashes, then p_j eventually delivers m.

> **PL2:** *No duplication:* No message is delivered by a process more than once.

> **PL3:** *No creation:* If a message m is delivered by some process p_j, then m was previously sent to p_j by some process p_i.

Algorithm 2.2 Eliminate Duplicates

Implements:
PerfectPointToPointLinks (pp2p).

Uses:
StubbornPointToPointLinks (sp2p).

upon event ⟨ *Init* ⟩ **do**
    delivered := ∅;

upon event ⟨ *pp2pSend* | dest, m ⟩ **do**
    trigger ⟨ *sp2pSend* | dest, m ⟩;

upon event ⟨ *sp2pDeliver* | src, m ⟩ **do**
    if ($m \notin$ delivered) **then**
        delivered := delivered ∪ { m };
        trigger ⟨ *pp2pDeliver* | src, m ⟩;

Algorithm: Eliminate Duplicates. Algorithm 2.2 ("Eliminate Duplicates") conveys a very simple implementation of a perfect link over a stubborn one. It simply keeps a record of all messages that have been delivered in the past; when a message is received, it is delivered only if it is not a duplicate. We discuss, in the following, the correctness of the algorithm as well as some performance considerations.

Correctness. Consider the *reliable delivery* property of perfect links. Let m be any message pp2pSent by some process p to some process q, and assume that none of these processes crash. According to the algorithm, process p sp2pSends m to q using the underlying stubborn link. Due to the *stubborn delivery* property of the underlying link, q eventually sp2pDelivers m, at least once, and hence pp2pDelivers m. The *no duplication* property follows from the test performed by the algorithm before delivering any message: whenever a message is sp2pDelivered and before pp2pDelivering that message. The *no creation* property simply follows from the *no creation* property of the underlying stubborn link.

Performance. Besides the performance considerations we discussed for our stubborn link implementation, i.e., Algorithm 2.1 ("Retransmit Forever"), and which clearly apply to the perfect link implementation of Algorithm 2.2 ("Eliminate Duplicates"), there is an additional concern related to maintaining the ever growing set of messages *delivered* at every process, given actual physical memory limitations.

At first glance, one might think of a simple way to circumvent this issue by having the target process acknowledge messages periodically and the sender process acknowledge having received such acknowledgments and promise not to send those messages any more. There is no guarantee, however, that such messages will not be still in transit and will later reach the target process. The latter might in this case deliver again, violating the *no creation* property. Additional mechanisms, e.g., timestamp-based, to recognize such old messages could, however, be used to circumvent this issue.

2.3.5 Logged Perfect Links

As we discuss below, the perfect link abstraction and the "Eliminate Duplicates" algorithm presented above are unsuitable for the crash-recovery process abstraction.

The problem with that algorithm for the crash-recovery process abstraction is easy to see. The algorithm uses a delivered variable to detect duplicates; but this variable is simply maintained in volatile memory. If a process crashes, the contents of this variable are lost. Upon recovery, the process will no longer remember which messages have already been delivered and might deliver the same message twice.

There is, however, a more subtle issue with the interface of the abstraction itself in the crash-recovery scenario. In this model, "delivering" a message by simply triggering an event does not provide any guarantee that the upper layer will properly handle the event. In fact, one layer can trigger an event and the process may crash immediately after, before the upper layer does anything useful with that event. One way to ensure that the upper layer eventually handles a "delivered" event is to redefine the very notion of "delivery." A suitable definition of "delivering" an event in the crash-recovery model consists of logging the event in a stable storage that is exposed to the upper layer.

Specification. The "LoggedPerfectPointToPointLink (log-pp2p)" module (Module 2.4) highlights the importance of this subtle interface issue. The

---

Module 2.4 Interface and properties of logged perfect point-to-point links

Module:

> **Name:** LoggedPerfectPointToPointLink (log-pp2p).

Events:

> **Request:** ⟨ *log-pp2pSend* | *dest, m* ⟩: Used to request the transmission of message m to process *dest*.

> **Indication:**⟨ *log-pp2pDeliver* | delivered ⟩: Used to notify the upper level of potential updates to the delivered log.

Properties:

> **LPL1:** *Reliable delivery:* Let p_i be any process that sends a message m to a process p_j. If p_i does not crash and p_j is correct, then p_j eventually delivers m.

> **LPL2:** *No duplication:* No message is delivered by a process more than once.

> **LPL3:** *No creation:* If a message m is delivered by some process p_j, then m was previously sent to p_j by some process p_i.

---

fundamental difference with the abstraction of perfect links presented in the previous section is in the manner messages are delivered. Instead of simply triggering an event to deliver a message, the logged perfect links abstraction relies on storing the message in a local log, which can later be read by the layer above. That layer is notified about changes in the log through specific events.

The act of delivering the message corresponds here to the act of logging the variable *delivered* with m in that variable. Hence, the properties of the abstraction are redefined in term of log operations.

Algorithm: Log Delivered. Algorithm 2.3 ("Log Delivered") conveys a very simple implementation of a logged perfect link over a stubborn one. As in the "Eliminate Duplicates" algorithm, it simply keeps a record of all messages that have been delivered in the past; however, here this record is kept in a stable storage that is exposed to the upper layer.

Correctness. The correctness argument is similar to that of the "Eliminate Duplicates" algorithm modulo the fact that delivering means here logging the message in stable storage.

Performance. In terms of messages, the performance of the "Log Delivered" algorithm is similar to that of the "Eliminate Duplicates." However, "Log Delivered" requires a log operation every time a new message is received.

2.3.6 On the Link Abstractions

Throughout this book, we will mainly assume perfect links (except in the crash-recovery case, as just discussed above). It may seem awkward to assume

---

Algorithm 2.3 Log Delivered

Implements:
    LoggedPerfectPointToPointLinks (log-pp2p).

Uses:
    StubbornPointToPointLinks (sp2p).

upon event ⟨ *Init* ⟩ **do**
    delivered := ∅;
    store (delivered);

upon event ⟨ *Recovery* ⟩ **do**
    retrieve (delivered);
    trigger ⟨ *log-pp2pDeliver* | delivered ⟩;

upon event ⟨ *log-pp2pSend* | dest, m ⟩ **do**
    trigger ⟨ *sp2pSend* | dest, m ⟩;

upon event ⟨ *sp2pDeliver* | src, m ⟩ **do**
    if (*m* ∉ delivered) **then**
        delivered := delivered ∪ { m };
        store (delivered);
        trigger ⟨ *log-pp2pDeliver* | delivered ⟩;

---

that links are perfect when it is known that real links may crash, lose, and duplicate messages. This assumption only captures the fact that these problems can be addressed by some lower level protocol. As long as the network remains connected, and processes do not commit an unbounded number of omission failures, link crashes may be masked by routing. The loss of messages can be masked through retransmission, as we have just explained through various algorithms. This functionality is often found in standard transport-level protocols such as TCP. These protocols are typically supported by the operating system and do not need to be reimplemented.

The details of how the perfect link abstraction is implemented is not relevant for the understanding of the fundamental principles of many distributed algorithms. On the other hand, when developing actual distributed applications, these details become relevant. For instance, it may happen that some distributed algorithm requires the use of sequence numbers and message retransmissions, even assuming perfect links. In this case, in order to avoid the redundant use of similar mechanisms at different layers, it may be more effective to rely just on weaker links, such as fair-loss or stubborn links. This is somehow what will happen when assuming the crash-recovery process abstraction.

Indeed, as we have seen, in the crash-recovery model, delivery is implemented by exposing a log maintained in stable storage. The upper layer is therefore required to keep its own record of which messages in the log it has already processed. Thus, the upper layer will generally have the ability to eliminate duplicates and can often operate using the weaker abstraction of stubborn links, avoiding the use of more expensive logged perfect links.

More generally, many networking issues should be considered when moving to concrete implementations. Among others:

- *Network topology awareness.* Many optimizations can be achieved if the network topology is exposed to the upper layers. For instance, communication in a local-area network exhibits a much lower latency than communication over wide-area links. Such facts should be taken into account by any practical algorithm.
- *Flow control.* In a practical system, the resources of a process are limited. This means that there is a limited number of messages a process is able to handle per unit of time. If a sender exceeds the receiver's capacity, messages may be lost. Practical systems must include feedback mechanisms to allow the senders to adjust their sending rate to the capacity of receivers.
- *Heterogeneity awareness.* In a real system, not all processes are equal. In fact, it may happen that some processes run on faster processors, have more memory, or can access more bandwidth than others. This heterogeneity may be exploited by an algorithm such that more demanding tasks are assigned to the most powerful processes first.

2.4 Timing Assumptions

An important aspect of the characterization of a distributed system is related to the behavior of its processes and links with respect to the passage of time. In short, determining whether we can make any assumption on time bounds on communication delays and (relative) process speeds is of primary importance when defining a model of a distributed system. We address some time-related issues in this section and then consider the *failure detector* abstraction as a meaningful way to abstract useful timing assumptions.

2.4.1 Asynchronous System

Assuming an *asynchronous* distributed system comes down to not making any timing assumption about processes and channels. This is precisely what we have been doing so far, when defining our process and link abstractions. That is, we did not assume that processes have access to any sort of physical clock, nor did we assume any bounds on processing or communication delays.

Even without access to physical clocks, it is still possible to measure the passage of time based on the transmission and delivery of messages, i.e., time is defined with respect to communication. Time measured this way is called *logical time*, and the resulting notion of a clock is called *logical clock*.

The following rules can be used to measure the passage of time in an asynchronous distributed system:

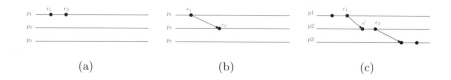

Fig. 2.4: The *happened-before* relation

- Each process p keeps an integer called *logical clock* l_p, initially 0.
- Any time an event occurs at process p, the logical clock l_p is incremented by one unit.
- When a process sends a message, it timestamps the message with the value of its logical clock at the moment the message is sent and tags the message with that timestamp. The timestamp of event e is denoted by $t(e)$.
- When a process p receives a message m with timestamp l_m, p increments its timestamp in the following way: $l_p = max(l_p, l_m) + 1$.

An interesting aspect of logical clocks is the fact that they capture cause-effect relations in systems where the processes can only interact through message exchanges. We say that an event e_1 may potentially have caused another event e_2, denoted as $e_1 \rightarrow e_2$, if the following relation, called the *happened-before* relation, applies:

- e_1 and e_2 occurred at the same process p and e_1 occurred before e_2 (Figure 2.4 (a)).
- e_1 corresponds to the transmission of a message m at a process p and e_2 to the reception of the same message at some other process q (Figure 2.4 (b)).
- there exists some event e' such that $e_1 \rightarrow e'$ and $e' \rightarrow e_2$ (Figure 2.4 (c)).

It can be shown that if the events are timestamped with logical clocks, then $e_1 \rightarrow e_2 \Rightarrow t(e_1) < t(e_2)$. Note that the opposite implication is not true.

As we discuss in the next chapters, even in the absence of any physical timing assumption, and using only a logical notion of time, we can implement some useful distributed programming abstractions. Many abstractions do, however, need some physical timing assumptions. In fact, even a very simple form of agreement, namely, *consensus*, is impossible to solve in an asynchronous system even if only one process fails, and it can only do so by crashing (see the historical note at the end of this chapter). In this problem, which we will address later in this book, the processes each start with an initial value, and have to agree on a common final value, from the initial values. The consequence of the consensus impossibilty is immediate for the impossibility of deriving algorithms for many agreement abstractions, including group membership or totally ordered group communication.

2.4.2 Synchronous System

While assuming an *asynchronous* system comes down to not making any physical timing assumption on processes and links, assuming a *synchronous* system comes down to assuming the following three properties:

1. *Synchronous computation.* There is a known upper bound on processing delays. That is, the time taken by any process to execute a step is always less than this bound. Remember that a step gathers the delivery of a message (possibly *nil*) sent by some other process, a local computation (possibly involving interaction among several layers of the same process), and the sending of a message to some other process.
2. *Synchronous communication.* There is a known upper bound on message transmission delays. That is, the time period between the instant at which a message is sent and the time at which the message is delivered by the destination process is smaller than this bound.
3. *Synchronous physical clocks.* Processes are equipped with a local physical clock. There is a known upper bound on the rate at which the local physical clock deviates from a global real-time clock. (Remember that we make here the assumption that such a global real-time clock exists in our universe, i.e., at least as a fictional device to simplify the reasoning about the processes, but it is not accessible to the processes.)

In a synchronous distributed system, several useful services can be provided. We enumerate some if them in the following:

- *Timed failure detection.* Every crash of a process may be detected within bounded time: whenever a process p crashes, all processes that did not crash detect the crash of p within a known bounded time. This can be achieved, for instance, using a heartbeat mechanism, where processes periodically exchange (heartbeat) messages and detect, within a limited time period, the crashes.
- *Measure of transit delays.* It is possible to get a good approximation of the delays of messages in the communication links and, from there, infer which nodes are more distant or connected by slower or overloaded links.
- *Coordination based on time.* One can implement a *lease* abstraction that provides the right to execute some action that is granted for a fixed amount of time, e.g., manipulating a specific file.
- *Worst-case performance.* By assuming a bound on the number of faults and on the load of the system, it is possible to derive *worst case response times* for any given algorithm. This allows a process to know when a message it has sent has been received by the destination process (provided that the latter is correct). This can be achieved even if we assume that processes commit omission failures without crashing, as long as we bound the number of these omission failures.

- *Synchronized clocks.* A synchronous system makes it possible to synchronize the clocks of the different processes in such a way that they are never
  apart by more than some known constant δ, known as the clock synchronization precision. Synchronized clocks allow processes to coordinate their
  actions and ultimately execute synchronized global steps. Using synchronized clocks makes it possible to timestamp events using the value of the
  local clock at the instant they occur. These timestamps can be used to order
  events in the system. If there was a system where all delays were constant,
  it would be possible to achieve perfectly synchronized clocks (i.e., where δ
  would be 0). Unfortunately, such a system cannot be built. In practice, δ
  is always greater than zero and events within δ cannot be ordered.

Not surprisingly, the major limitation of assuming a synchronous system is
the *coverage* of the system, i.e., the difficulty of building a system where
the timing assumptions hold with high probability. This typically requires
careful analysis of the network and processing load and the use of appropriate
processor and network scheduling algorithms. While this may be feasible
for some local area networks, it may not be so, or even desirable, in larger
scale systems such as the Internet. In this case, i.e., on the Internet, there
are periods where messages can take a very long time to arrive at their
destination. One should consider very large values to capture the processing
and communication bounds. This, however, would mean considering worst-
case values which are typically much higher than average values. These worst-
case values are usually so high that any application based on them would be
very inefficient.

2.4.3 Partial Synchrony

Generally, distributed systems appear to be synchronous. More precisely, for
most systems we know of, it is relatively easy to define physical time bounds
that are respected *most of the time.* There are however periods where the
timing assumptions do not hold, i.e., periods during which the system is asynchronous. These are periods where the network is, for instance, overloaded,
or some process has a shortage of memory that slows it down. Typically, the
buffer that a process might be using to store incoming and outgoing messages
may overflow, and messages may thus get lost, violating the time bound on
the delivery. The retransmission of the messages may help ensure the reliability of the channels but introduce unpredictable delays. In this sense, practical
systems are *partially synchronous.*

One way to capture partial synchrony is to assume that the timing assumptions only hold eventually (without stating when exactly). This boils
down to assuming that there is a time after which these assumptions hold
forever, but this time is not known. In a way, instead of assuming a synchronous system, we assume a system that is eventually synchronous. It is
important to notice that making such assumption does not in practice mean

that (1) there is a time after which the underlying system (including application, hardware, and networking components) is synchronous forever, nor does it mean that (2) the system needs to be initially asynchronous, and then only after some (long time) period becomes synchronous. The assumption simply captures the very fact that the system may not always be synchronous, and there is no bound on the period during which it is asynchronous. However, we expect that there are periods during which the system is synchronous, and some of these periods are long enough for an algorithm to terminate its execution.

2.5 Abstracting Time

2.5.1 Failure Detection

So far, we contrasted the simplicity with the inherent limitation of the asynchronous system assumption; the power with the limited coverage of the synchronous assumption; and we discussed the intermediate partially synchronous system assumption. Each of these assumptions makes sense for specific environments, and need to be considered as plausible when reasoning about general-purpose implementations of high-level distributed programming abstractions.

As far as the asynchronous system assumption is concerned, there are no timing assumption to be made and our process and link abstractions directly capture that case. These are, however, not sufficient for the synchronous and partially synchronous system assumptions. Instead of augmenting our process and link abstractions with timing capabilities to encompass the synchronous and partially synchronous system assumptions, we consider a separate and specific kind of abstraction to encapsulate those capabilities; namely, we consider *failure detectors*. As we will discuss in the next section, failure detectors provide information (not necessarily fully accurate) about which processes have crashed. We will, in particular, consider failure detectors that encapsulate timing assumptions of a synchronous system, as well as failure detectors that encapsulate timing assumptions of a partially synchronous system. Not surprisingly, the information provided by the first failure detectors about crashed processes will be more accurate than those provided by the others. Clearly, the stronger the timing assumptions we make on the distributed system (to implement the failure detector) the more accurate that information.

There are at least two advantages of the failure detector abstraction over an approach where we would directly make timing assumptions on processes and links. First, the failure detector abstraction alleviates the need for extending the process and link abstractions introduced earlier in this chapter with timing assumptions. As a consequence, the simplicity of those abstractions is preserved. Second, and as will see in the following, we can reason about the behavior of a failure detector using axiomatic properties with no explicit

---

Module 2.5 Interface and properties of the perfect failure detector

Module:

   Name: PerfectFailureDetector ($\mathcal{P}$).

Events:

   Indication: $\langle$ *crash* $\mid p_i$ $\rangle$: Used to notify that process p_i has crashed.

Properties:

   PFD1: *Strong completeness:* Eventually every process that crashes is permanently detected by every correct process.

   PFD2: *Strong accuracy:* If a process p is detected by any process, then p has crashed.

---

references about physical time. Such references are usually error prone. In practice, except for specific applications like process control, timing assumptions are indeed mainly used to detect process failures, i.e., to implement failure detectors.

2.5.2 Perfect Failure Detection

In synchronous systems, and assuming a process crash-stop abstraction, crashes can be accurately detected using *timeouts*. For instance, assume that a process sends a message to another process and awaits a response. If the recipient process does not crash, then the response is guaranteed to arrive within a time period equal to the worst case processing delay plus two times the worst case message transmission delay (ignoring the clock drifts). Using its own clock, a sender process can measure the worst case delay required to obtain a response and detect a crash in the absence of such a reply within the timeout period: the crash detection will usually trigger a corrective procedure. We encapsulate such a way of detecting failures in a synchronous system through the use of a *perfect failure detector* abstraction.

Specification. The perfect failure detector is denoted by $\mathcal{P}$, and it outputs, at every process, the set of processes that are detected to have crashed (we simply say *detected*). A perfect failure detector is characterized by the *accuracy* and *completeness* properties of Module 2.5. The act of detecting a crash coincides with the triggering of the event *crash*: once the crash of a process p is detected by some process q, the detection is permanent, i.e., q will not change its mind.

Algorithm: Exclude on Timeout. Algorithm 2.4, which we call "Exclude on Timeout", implements a perfect failure detector assuming a synchronous system. Communication links do not lose messages sent by a correct process to a correct process (perfect links), and the transmission period of every message is bounded by some known constant, in comparison to which the local processing time of a process, as well as the clock drifts, are negligible.

Algorithm 2.4 Exclude on Timeout

Implements:
    PerfectFailureDetector ($\mathcal{P}$).

Uses:
    PerfectPointToPointLinks (pp2p).

upon event ⟨ *Init* ⟩ **do**
    alive := Π;
    detected := $\emptyset$;
    startTimer (TimeDelay);

upon event ⟨ *Timeout* ⟩ **do**
    forall $p_i \in \Pi$ **do**
        if $(p_i \notin$ alive$) \wedge (p_i \notin$ detected$)$ **then**
            detected := detected $\cup \{ p_i \}$;
            trigger ⟨ *crash* | p_i ⟩;
        trigger ⟨ *pp2pSend* | p_i, [HEARTBEAT] ⟩;
    alive := $\emptyset$;
    startTimer (TimeDelay);

upon event ⟨ *pp2pDeliver* | src, [HEARTBEAT] ⟩ **do**
    alive := alive $\cup \{$ src $\}$;

The algorithm makes use of a specific timeout mechanism initialized with a timeout delay chosen to be large enough such that, within that period, every process has enough time to send a message to all, and each of these messages has enough time to be delivered at its destination (provided this destination process did not crash). Whenever the timeout period expires, the specific *Timeout* event is triggered. In order for the algorithm not to trigger an infinite number of failure detection events, ⟨ *crash* | p_i ⟩, for every faulty process p_i, once an event has been triggered for a given process p_i, we simply put that process in a specific variable *detected* and avoid triggering duplicate failure detection events for p_i.

Correctness. Consider the *strong completeness* property of a perfect failure detector. If a process p crashes, it stops sending heartbeat messages, and no process will deliver its messages: remember that perfect links ensure that no message is delivered unless it was sent. Every correct process will thus detect the crash of p.

Consider now the *strong accuracy* property of a perfect failure detector. The crash of a process p is detected by some other process q, only if q does not deliver a message from p before a timeout period. This can happen only if p has indeed crashed because the algorithm makes sure p must have otherwise sent a message, and the synchrony assumption implies that the message should have been delivered before the timeout period.

Performance. For presentation simplicity, we omitted a simple optimization which consists in not sending any heartbeat messages to processes that were detected to have crashed.

It is important to notice that the time to detect a failure depends on the timeout delay. A large timeout, say ten times the expected delay needed to send a message and deliver it to all processes, would reasonably cope with situations where the delay would be slightly extended. One would however detect, and hence react to, failures earlier with a shorter timeout. The risk here is that the probability to falsely detect a crash is higher. One way to cope with such a trade-off is to assume a imperfect failure detector, as we will discuss later.

2.5.3 Leader Election

Often, one may not need to detect which processes have failed, but rather need to elect a process that has *not* failed. This process may then act as the coordinator in some steps of a distributed algorithm. This process is in a sense *trusted* by the other processes and elected as their *leader*. The *leader election* abstraction we discuss here provides such support. It can also be viewed as a failure detector in the sense that its properties do not depend on the actual computation of the processes but rather on their failures. Indeed, as we will see here, the leader election abstraction can be implemented straightforwardly using a perfect failure detector.

More generally, the leader election abstraction consists in choosing one process to be selected as a unique representative of the group of processes in the system. For this abstraction to be useful in a distributed setting, a new leader should be elected if the current leader crashes. Such abstraction is particularly useful in a primary-backup replication scheme, for instance. Following this scheme, a set of replica processes coordinate their activities to provide the illusion of a unique fault-tolerant (highly available) service. Among the set of replica processes, one is chosen as the leader. This leader process, sometimes called the *primary*, treats the requests submitted by the client processes on behalf of the other replicas, called *backups*. Before a leader returns a reply to a given client, it updates its backups. If the leader crashes, one of the backups is elected as the new leader, i.e., the new primary.

Specification. We define the leader election abstraction more precisely through a specific indication, denoted by *leLeader* which, when triggered on a process p at some given time, means that the process is elected leader from that time on, until it crashes. The properties of the abstraction are given in Module 2.6.

The first property ensures the eventual presence of a correct leader. Clearly, it may be the case that, at some point in time, no process is leader. It may also be the case that no leader is running. The property ensures, however, that, unless there is no correct process, some correct process is eventually elected leader. The second property ensures the stability of the leader.

Module 2.6 Interface and properties of leader election

Module:

   Name: LeaderElection (le).

Events:

   Indication: $\langle$ *leLeader* $\mid p_i$ $\rangle$: Used to indicate that process p_i is the leader.

Properties:

   LE1: Either there is no correct process, or some correct process is eventually the leader.

   LE2: If a process is leader, then all previously elected leaders have crashed.

In other words, it ensures that the only reason to change the leader is if it
crashes. Indirectly, this property precludes the possibility for two processes
to be leader at the same time.

Algorithm: Monarchical Leader Election. Algorithm 2.5 implements
the leader election abstraction assuming a perfect failure detector. The algorithm assumes, furthermore, the existence of a ranking representing a total
order among processes agreed on a priori. This is encapsulated by some function O. This function would also typically be known by the user of the leader
election abstraction, e.g., the clients of a primary-backup replication scheme,
for optimization purposes as, in the absence of failures, requests would only
need to be sent to primaries.

   This function O associates, with every process, those that precede it in
the ranking. A process can become leader only if those that precede it have
crashed. Think of the function as representing the royal ordering in a monarchical system. The prince becomes leader if and only if the queen dies. If the
prince dies, maybe his little sister is the next on the list, and so on. Typically,
we would assume that $O(p_1) = \emptyset$, $O(p_2) = \{p_1\}$, $O(p_3) = \{p_1, p_2\}$, and so
forth. The order in this case is $p_1; p_2; p_3; ...; p_k; p_{k+1}$.

Correctness. Property *LE1* follows from the *completeness* property of the
failure detector whereas property *LE2* follows from the *accuracy* property of
the failure detector.

Performance. The process of becoming a leader is a local operation. The
time to react to a failure and become the new leader directly depends on the
latency of the failure detector.

2.5.4 Eventually Perfect Failure Detection

Just like we can encapsulate timing assumptions of a synchronous system
in a *perfect failure detector* abstraction, we can similarly encapsulate timing
assumptions of a partially synchronous system within an *eventually perfect
failure detector* abstraction.

Algorithm 2.5 Monarchical Leader Election

Implements:
　　LeaderElection (le).

Uses:
　　PerfectFailureDetector ($\mathcal{P}$).

upon event $\langle$ *Init* $\rangle$ **do**
　　suspected $:= \emptyset$;
　　leader $:= p_j : O(p_j) = \emptyset$;
　　trigger $\langle$ *leLeader* | leader $\rangle$;

upon event $\langle$ *crash* | p_i $\rangle$ **do**
　　suspected $:=$ suspected $\cup \{p_i\}$;

when exists p_i **such that** $O(p_i) \subseteq$ suspected **do**
　　leader $:= p_i$;
　　trigger $\langle$ *leLeader* | leader $\rangle$;

Specification. Basically, the eventually perfect failure detector abstraction guarantees that there is a time after which crashes can be accurately detected. This captures the intuition that, most of the time, timeout delays can be adjusted so they can lead to accurately detecting crashes. However, there are periods where the asynchrony of the underlying system prevents failure detection to be accurate and leads to false suspicions. In this case, we talk about failure *suspicion* instead of *detection*.

More precisely, to implement an eventually perfect failure detector abstraction, the idea is to also use a timeout, and to suspect processes that did not send heartbeat messages within a timeout delay. The original timeout might be considered quite short if the goal is to react quickly to failures. Obviously, a suspicion may be wrong in a partially synchronous system. A process p may suspect a process q, even if q has not crashed, simply because the timeout delay chosen by p to suspect the crash of q was too short. In this case, p's suspicion about q is false. When p receives a message from q, p revises its judgment and stops suspecting q. Process p also increases its timeout delay; this is because p does not know what the bound on communication delay will eventually be; it only knows there will be one. Clearly, if q now crashes, p will eventually suspect q and will never revise its judgment. If q does not crash, then there is a time after which p will stop suspecting q, i.e., the timeout delay used by p to suspect q will eventually be large enough because p keeps increasing it whenever it commits a false suspicion. This is because we assume that there is a time after which the system is synchronous.

An eventually perfect failure detector is denoted by $\Diamond\mathcal{P}$ ($\Diamond$ is used to denote "eventually" and $\mathcal{P}$ stands for "perfect"), and it can be described by the *accuracy* and *completeness* properties (EPFD1–2) of Module 2.7. A

Module 2.7 Interface and properties of the eventually perfect failure detector

Module:

    Name: EventuallyPerfectFailureDetector ($\Diamond\mathcal{P}$).

Events:

    Indication: $\langle$ *suspect* $\mid p_i$ $\rangle$: Used to notify that process p_i is suspected to have crashed.

    Indication: $\langle$ *restore* $\mid p_i$ $\rangle$: Used to notify that process p_i is not suspected anymore.

Properties:

    EPFD1: *Strong completeness:* Eventually, every process that crashes is permanently suspected by every correct process.

    EPFD2: *Eventual strong accuracy:* Eventually, no correct process is suspected by any correct process.

---

process p is said to be *suspected* by process q after q has triggered the event *suspect*(p_i) and until it triggers the event *restore*(p_i).

Algorithm: Increasing Timeout. Algorithm 2.6, which we have called "Increasing Timeout", implements an eventually perfect failure detector assuming a partially synchronous system. As for Algorithm 2.4 ("Exclude on Timeout"), we make use of a specific timeout mechanism initialized with a timeout delay. The main differences between Algorithm 2.6 and Algorithm 2.4 is that the first is prepared to suspect a process, and later receive a message from it (this means that the suspicion was not accurate); the timeout is in this case increased.

Correctness. The *strong completeness* property is satisfied as for Algorithm 2.4 ("Exclude on Timeout"). If a process crashes, it will stop sending messages, will be suspected by every correct process and no process will ever revise its judgment about that suspicion.

    Consider now the *eventual strong accuracy* property. Consider the time after which the system becomes synchronous, and the timeout delay becomes larger than message transmission delays (plus clock drifts and local processing periods). After this time, any message sent by a correct process to a correct process is delivered within the timeout delay. Hence, any correct process that was wrongly suspecting some correct process will revise its suspicion, and no correct process will ever be suspected by a correct process.

Performance. As for a perfect failure detector, the time to detect a failure depends on the timeout delay. The difference here is that the timeout can easily be adjusted to react quickly to failures. A wrong suspicion is somehow harmless as the very specification of the eventually perfect failure detector does not preclude false suspicions.

Algorithm 2.6 Increasing Timeout

Implements:
    EventuallyPerfectFailureDetector ($\Diamond\mathcal{P}$).

Uses:
    PerfectPointToPointLinks (pp2p).

upon event $\langle$ *Init* $\rangle$ **do**
    alive $:= \Pi$;
    suspected $:= \emptyset$;
    period $:=$ TimeDelay;
    startTimer (period);

upon event $\langle$ *Timeout* $\rangle$ **do**
    if (alive $\cap$ suspected) $\neq \emptyset$ **then**
        period $:=$ period $+ \Delta$;
    forall $p_i \in \Pi$ **do**
        if $(p_i \notin$ alive$) \wedge (p_i \notin$ suspected$)$ **then**
            suspected $:=$ suspected $\cup \{p_i\}$;
            trigger $\langle$ *suspect* $\mid p_i$ $\rangle$;
        else if $(p_i \in$ alive$) \wedge (p_i \in$ suspected$)$ **then**
            suspected $:=$ suspected $\setminus \{p_i\}$;
            trigger $\langle$ *restore* $\mid p_i$ $\rangle$;
        trigger $\langle$ *pp2pSend* $\mid p_i,$ [HEARTBEAT] $\rangle$;
    alive $:= \emptyset$;
    startTimer (period);

upon event $\langle$ *pp2pDeliver* $\mid$ src, [HEARTBEAT] $\rangle$ **do**
    alive $:=$ alive $\cup \{$src$\}$;

2.5.5 Eventual Leader Election

As we discussed earlier, instead of focusing on crashed processes, it may be better to look at correct ones. In particular, it is sometimes convenient to elect a correct process that will perform certain computations on behalf of the others. With a perfect failure detector, one could implement a perfect leader election abstraction with the properties of Module 2.6. This is impossible with an eventually perfect failure detector (see the exercises). Instead, what we can implement is a weaker leader election which ensures the unicity of the leader only *eventually*. As we will see later in the book, this abstraction is useful within consensus algorithms.

Specification. The *eventual leader detector* abstraction, with the properties (ELD1-2) stated in Module 2.8, and denoted by Ω, encapsulates a leader election algorithm which ensures that *eventually* the correct processes will elect the same correct process as their leader. Nothing precludes the possibility for leaders to change in an arbitrary manner and for an arbitrary period of time. Besides, many leaders might be elected during the same period of time without having crashed. Once a unique leader is determined, and does not

---

Module 2.8 Interface and properties of the eventual leader detector

Module:

   Name: EventualLeaderDetector (Ω).

Events:

   Indication: $\langle\ trust\ |\ p_i\ \rangle$: Used to notify that process p_i is trusted to be leader.

Properties:

   ELD1: *Eventual accuracy:* There is a time after which every correct process trusts some correct process.

   ELD2: *Eventual agreement:* There is a time after which no two correct processes trust different correct processes.

---

change again, we say that the leader has *stabilized*. Such a stabilization is guaranteed by the specification of Module 2.8.

Algorithm: Elect Lower Epoch. With a crash-stop process abstraction, Ω can be obtained directly from $\Diamond\mathcal{P}$. Indeed, it is enough to trust the process with the highest identifier among all processes that are not suspected by $\Diamond\mathcal{P}$. Eventually, and provided at least one process is correct, exactly one correct process will be trusted by all correct processes. Interestingly, the leader abstraction Ω can also be implemented with the process crash-recovery abstraction, also using timeouts and assuming the system to be partially synchronous.

Algorithm 2.7–2.8, called "Elect Lower Epoch", implements Ω in both crash-stop and crash-recovery models, assuming that at least one process is correct. Remember that this implies, with a process crash-recovery abstraction, that at least one process does not ever crash, or eventually recovers and never crashes again (in every execution of the algorithm).

In the algorithm, every process p_i keeps track of how many times it crashed and recovered, within an *epoch* integer variable. This variable, representing the *epoch number* of p_i, is retrieved, incremented, and then stored in stable storage whenever p_i recovers from a crash. The goal of the algorithm is to elect as a leader the active process with the lowest epoch, i.e., the one that has crashed and recovered less times.

Process p_i periodically sends to all processes a *heartbeat* message together with its current epoch number. Besides, every process p_i keeps a list of potential leader processes, within the variable *candidateset*. Initially, at every process p_i, *candidateset* is empty. Then, any process that does communicate with p_i is included in *candidateset*. A process p_j that communicates with p_i, after having recovered or being slow in communicating with p_i, is simply added again to *candidateset*, i.e., considered a potential leader for p_i.

Initially, the leader for all processes is the same, and is process p_1. After every timeout delay, p_i checks whether p_1 can still be the leader. This test

---

Algorithm 2.7 Elect Lower Epoch (initialization and recovery)

Implements:
    EventualLeaderDetector (Ω).

Uses:
    FairLossPointToPointLinks (flp2p).

upon event ⟨ *Init* ⟩ **do**
    leader := p_1;
    trigger ⟨ *trust* | leader ⟩;
    period := TimeDelay;
    epoch := 0;
    store(epoch);
    forall $p_i \in \Pi$ **do**
        trigger ⟨ *flp2pSend* | p_i, [HEARTBEAT, epoch] ⟩;
    candidateset := ∅;
    startTimer (period);

upon event ⟨ *Recovery* ⟩ **do**
    leader := p_1;
    trigger ⟨ *trust* | leader ⟩;
    period := TimeDelay;
    retrieve(epoch);
    epoch := epoch + 1;
    store(epoch);
    forall $p_i \in \Pi$ **do**
        trigger ⟨ *flp2pSend* | p_i, [HEARTBEAT, epoch] ⟩;
    candidateset := ∅;
    startTimer (period);

---

is performed through a function *select* that returns one process from a set of processes, or nothing if the set is empty. The function is the same at all processes and returns the same process (identifier) for the same given set (*candidateset*), in a deterministic manner and according to the following rule: among processes with the lowest epoch number, the process with the lowest identity is returned. This guarantees that, if a process p_j is elected leader, and p_j keeps on crashing and recovering forever, p_j will eventually be replaced by a correct process. By definition, the epoch number of a correct process will eventually stop increasing.

A process increases its timeout delay whenever it changes leader. This guarantees that, eventually, if leaders keep changing because the timeout delay is too short with respect to communication delays, the delay will keep increasing until it becomes large enough for the leader to stabilize when the system becomes synchronous.

Correctness. Consider the *eventual accuracy* property and assume by contradiction that there is a time after which a correct process p_i permanently trusts the same faulty process, say, p_j. There are two cases to consider (re-

---

Algorithm 2.8 Elect Lower Epoch (election)

---

upon event ⟨ *Timeout* ⟩ **do**
    newleader = *select*(candidateset);
    if (leader ≠ newleader) **then**
        period := period + Δ;
        leader := newleader;
        trigger ⟨ *trust* | leader ⟩;
    forall $p_i \in \Pi$ **do**
        trigger ⟨ *flp2pSend* | p_i, [HEARTBEAT, epoch] ⟩;
    candidateset := ∅;
    startTimer (period);

upon event ⟨ *flp2pDeliver* | src, [HEARTBEAT, epc] ⟩ **do**
    if exists $(s, e) \in$ candidateset **such that** (s=src) ∧ (e<epc) **then**
        candidateset := candidateset \ {(s, e)};
    candidateset := candidateset ∪ {(src, epc)};

---

member that we consider a crash-recovery process abstraction): (1) process p_j eventually crashes and never recovers again, or (2) process p_j keeps crashing and recovering forever.

Consider case (1). Since p_j crashes and does not ever recover again, p_j will send its *heartbeat* messages to p_i only a finite number of times. Due to the *no creation* and *finite duplication* properties of the underlying links (fair-loss), there is a time after which p_i stops delivering such messages from p_j. Eventually, p_j will be excluded from the set (*candidateset*) of potential leaders for p_i, and p_i will elect a new leader.

Consider now case (2). Since p_j keeps on crashing and recovering forever, its epoch number will keep on increasing forever. If p_k is a correct process, then there is a time after which its epoch number will be lower than that of p_j. After this time, either (2.1) p_i will stop delivering messages from p_j, and this can happen if p_j crashes and recovers so quickly that it does not have the time to send enough messages to p_i (remember that, with fair-loss links, a message is guaranteed to be delivered by its target only if it is sent infinitely often), or (2.2) p_i delivers messages from p_j but with higher epoch numbers than those of p_k.

In both cases, p_i will stop trusting p_j. Process p_i will eventually trust only correct processes.

Consider now the *eventual agreement* property. We need to explain why there is a time after which no two correct processes are trusted by two other correct processes. Consider the subset of correct processes in a given execution S. Consider, furthermore, the time after which (a) the system becomes synchronous, (b) the processes in S never crash again, (c) their epoch numbers stop increasing at every process, and (d) for every correct process p_i and every faulty process p_j, p_i stops delivering messages from p_j, or p_j's epoch number at p_i gets strictly larger than the largest epoch number of S's processes at p_i. Due to the assumptions of a partially synchronous system, the properties of the underlying fair-loss channels, and the algorithm, such time will eventually be reached. After it is reached, every correct process that is trusted by a correct process will be one of the processes in S. Due to the function *select*, all correct processes will trust the same process within this set.

2.6 Distributed System Models

A combination of (1) a process abstraction, (2) a link abstraction, and (possibly) (3) a failure detector abstraction defines a *distributed-system model*. In the following, we discuss several models that will be considered throughout this book to reason about distributed-programming abstractions and the algorithms used to implement them. We will also discuss some important properties of abstraction specifications and algorithms that will be useful reasoning tools for the following chapters.

2.6.1 Combining Abstractions

Clearly, we will not consider all possible combinations of basic abstractions. On the other hand, it is interesting to discuss more than one possible combination to get an insight into how certain assumptions affect algorithm's design. We have selected five specific combinations to define several different models studied in this book.

- **Fail-stop**. We consider the crash-stop process abstraction, where the processes execute the deterministic algorithms assigned to them, unless they possibly crash, in which case they do not recover. Links are considered to be perfect. Finally, we assume the existence of a perfect failure detector ($\mathcal{P}$) (Module 2.5). As the reader will have the opportunity to observe, when comparing algorithms in this model with algorithms in the four other models discussed below, making these assumptions (i.e., considering a fail-stop model) substantially simplifies the design of distributed algorithms.
- **Fail-silent**. We also consider here the crash-stop process abstraction together with perfect links. Nevertheless, we do not assume here any failure detection abstraction. That is, processes have no means to get any information about other processes having crashed.
- **Fail-noisy**. This case is somehow intermediate between the two previous models. We also consider here the crash-stop process abstraction together with perfect links. In addition, we assume here the existence of the eventually perfect failure detector ($\Diamond\mathcal{P}$) of Module 2.7 or the eventual leader detector (Ω) of Module 2.8.

- **Fail-recovery**. We consider here the crash-recovery process abstraction, according to which processes may crash and later recover and still participate in the algorithm. Algorithms devised with this basic abstraction in mind have to deal with the management of stable storage and with the difficulties of dealing with amnesia, i.e., the fact that a process may forget what it did prior to crashing. Links are assumed to be stubborn and we may rely on the eventual leader detector (Ω) of Module 2.8.

- **Randomized**. We will consider here a specific particularity in the process abstraction: algorithms may not be deterministic. That is, the processes may use a random oracle to choose among several steps to execute. Typically, the corresponding algorithms implement a given abstraction with some (hopefully high) probability. Randomization is sometimes the only way to solve certain problems or circumvent some inherent inefficiencies of deterministic algorithms.

It is important to note that some of the abstractions we study cannot be implemented in all models. For example, some the abstractions that we will consider in Chapter 6 do not have fail-silent solutions, and it is not clear how to devise meaningful randomized solutions to such abstractions. For other abstractions, such solutions may exist but devising them is still an active area of research. This is, for instance, the case for randomized solutions to the shared memory abstractions we consider in Chapter 4.

2.6.2 Measuring Performance

When we present an algorithm that implements a given abstraction, we analyze its cost mainly using two metrics: (1) the number of messages required to terminate an operation of the abstraction, and (2) the number of communication steps required to terminate such an operation. When evaluating the performance of distributed algorithms in a crash-recovery model, besides the number of communication steps and the number of messages, we also consider (3) the number of accesses to stable storage (also called logs).

In general, we count the messages, communication steps, and disk accesses in specific executions of the algorithm, specially executions when no failures occur. Such executions are more likely to happen in practice and are those for which the algorithms are optimized. It makes sense to plan for the worst, by providing means in the algorithms to tolerate failures, and hope for the best, by optimizing the algorithms for the case where failures do not occur. Algorithms that have their performance go proportionally down when the number of failures increases are sometimes called *gracefully degrading* algorithms.

Precise performance studies help select the most suitable algorithm for a given abstraction in a specific environment and conduct *real-time* analysis. Consider, for instance, an algorithm that implements the abstraction of perfect communication links and hence ensures that every message sent by a correct process to a correct process is eventually delivered by the latter.

It is important to note here what such a property states in terms of timing guarantees: for every execution of the algorithm, and every message sent in that execution, there is a time delay within which the message is eventually delivered. The time delay is, however, defined a posteriori. In practice one would require that messages be delivered within some time delay defined a priori, for every execution and possibly every message. To determine whether a given algorithm provides this guarantee in a given environment, a careful performance study needs to be conducted on the algorithm, taking into account various aspects of the environment, such as the operating system, the scheduler, and the network. Such studies are out of the scope of this book. We present algorithms that are applicable to a wide range of distributed systems, where bounded delays cannot be enforced, and where specific infrastructure-related properties, such as real-time demands, are not strictly required.

2.7 Hands-On

We now describe the implementation of some of the abstractions presented in this chapter. However, before proceeding, we need to introduce some additional components of the *Appia* framework.

2.7.1 Sendable Event

For the implementation of the protocols that we will be describing, we have defined a specialization of the basic *Appia* event, called SendableEvent. The interface of this event is presented in Listing 2.1.

Listing 2.1. SendableEvent interface

```
package appia.events;

public class SendableEvent extends Event implements Cloneable {
    public Object dest;
    public Object source;
    protected Message message;

    public SendableEvent();
    public SendableEvent(Channel channel, int dir, Session source);
    public SendableEvent(Message msg);
    public SendableEvent(Channel channel, int dir, Session source, Message msg);

    public Message getMessage();
    public void setMessage(Message message);
    public Event cloneEvent();
}
```

A SendableEvent owns three relevant attributes: a Message which contains the data to be sent on the network, the source which identifies the sending process, and the destination attribute which identifies the recipient processes.

Since our implementations are based on low-level protocols from the IP family, processes will be identified by a tuple (IP address, port). Therefore, both the source and the dest attributes should contain an object of type In-etWithPort (used by Java TCP and UDP interface).

2.7.2 Message and Extended Message

The Message component is provided by the *Appia* framework to simplify the task of adding and extracting protocol headers to/from the message payload. Chunks of data can be added to or extracted from the message using the auxiliary MsgBuffer data structure, depicted in Listing 2.2.

Listing 2.2. MsgBuffer interface

```
package appia.message;

public class MsgBuffer {
  public byte[] data;
  public int off;
  public int len;

  public MsgBuffer();
  public MsgBuffer(byte[] data, int off, int len);
}
```

The interface of the Message object is partially listed in Listing 2.3. Note the methods to push and popped MsgBuffers to/from a message, as well as methods to fragment and concatenate messages.

Listing 2.3. Message interface (partial)

```
package appia.message;

public class Message implements Cloneable {

  public Message();

  public int length();
  public void peek(MsgBuffer mbuf);
  public void pop(MsgBuffer mbuf);
  public void push(MsgBuffer mbuf);
  public void frag(Message m, int length);
  public void join(Message m);
  public Object clone() throws CloneNotSupportedException;
}
```

To ease the programming of distributed protocols in Java, the basic Message class was extended to allow arbitrary objects to be pushed and popped. The class that provides this extended functionality is the ExtendedMessage class, whose interface is depicted in Listing 2.4. This is the class that we will be using throughout this book.

Listing 2.4. ExtendedMessage interface (partial)

```
package appia.message;

public class ExtendedMessage extends Message {
```

```
public ExtendedMessage(); {

public void pushObject(Object obj);
public void pushLong(long l);
public void pushInt(int i);
/* ... */
public Object popObject();
public long popLong();
public int popInt();
/* ... */
public Object peekObject();
public long peekLong();
public int peekInt();
/* ... */
public Object clone() throws CloneNotSupportedException;
}
```

2.7.3 Fair-Loss Point-to-Point Links

The Fair-Loss Point-to-Point Links abstraction is implemented in *Appia* by the UdpSimple protocol. The UdpSimple protocol uses UDP sockets as unreliable communication channels. When a UdpSimple session receives a SendableEvent with the down direction (i.e., a transmission request) it extracts the message from the event and pushes it to the UDP socket. When a message is received from a UDP socket, a SendableEvent is created with the up direction.

2.7.4 Perfect Point-to-Point Links

The Perfect Point-to-Point Links abstraction is implemented in *Appia* by the TcpBasedPerfectP2P protocol. As its name implies, this implementation is based on the TCP protocol; more precisely, it uses TCP sockets as communication channels. When a TcpBasedPerfectP2P session receives a SendableEvent with the down direction (i.e., a transmission request) it extracts the message from the event and pushes it to the TCP socket. When a message is received from a TCP socket, a SendableEvent is created with the up direction.

A TcpBasedPerfectP2P session automatically establishes a TCP connection when requested to send a message to a given destination for the first time. Therefore, a single session implements multiple point-to-point links.

It should be noted that, in pure asynchronous systems, this implementation is just an approximation of the Perfect Point-to-Point Link abstraction. In fact, TCP includes acknowledgments and retransmission mechanisms (to recover from omissions in the network). However, if the other endpoint is unresponsive, TCP breaks the connection, assuming that the corresponding node has crashed. Therefore, TCP makes synchronous assumptions about the system and fails to deliver the messages when it erroneously "suspects" correct processes.

2.7.5 Perfect Failure Detector

In our case, the Perfect Failure Detector is implemented by the TcpBasedPFD, which is used only with the TcpBasedPerfectP2P protocol described above, built using TCP channels. When a TCP socket is closed, the protocol that implements TcpBasedPerfectP2P sends an event to the *Appia* channel. This event is accepted by the TcpBasedPFD protocol, which sends a Crash event to notify other layers. The implementation of this notification is shown in Listing 2.5. The protocols that use the TcpBasedPFD must declare that they will accept (and process) the Crash event generated by the TcpBasedPFD module. This is illustrated in the implementation of the reliable broadcast protocols, which are described in the next chapter.

To notify other layers of a closed socket, the TcpBasedPerfectP2P protocol must first create the corresponding TCP sockets. The way the TcpBasedPerfectP2P is implemented, these sockets are opened on demand, i.e., when there is the need to send/receive something from a remote peer. To ensure that these sockets are created, the TcpBasedPFD session sends a message to all other processes when it is started.

Note that the TcpBasedPFD abstraction assumes that all processes are started before it starts operating. Therefore, the user must start all processes before activating the perfect failure detector. Otherwise, the detector may detect as failed processes that have not yet been launched. Hence, in subsequent chapters, when using the perfect failure detector in conjunction with other protocols, the user will be requested to explicitly start the perfect failure detector. In most test applications, this is achieved by issuing the startpfd request on the command line. The implementation is illustrated in Listing 2.5.

Listing 2.5. Perfect failure detector implementation

```
package appia.protocols.tutorialDA.tcpBasedPFD;

public class TcpBasedPFDSession extends Session {
  private Channel channel;
  private ProcessSet processes;
  private boolean started;

  public TcpBasedPFDSession(Layer layer) {
    super(layer);
    started = false;
  }

  public void handle(Event event) {
    if (event instanceof TcpUndeliveredEvent)
      notifyCrash((TcpUndeliveredEvent) event);
    else if (event instanceof ChannelInit)
      handleChannelInit((ChannelInit) event);
    else if (event instanceof ProcessInitEvent)
      handleProcessInit((ProcessInitEvent) event);
    else if(event instanceof PFDStartEvent)
      handlePFDStart((PFDStartEvent) event);
  }

  private void handleChannelInit(ChannelInit init) {
```

```
    channel = init.getChannel();
    init.go();
  }

  private void handleProcessInit(ProcessInitEvent event) {
    processes = event.getProcessSet();
    event.go();
  }

  private void handlePFDStart(PFDStartEvent event) {
    started = true;
    event.go();
    CreateChannelsEvent createChannels =
      new CreateChannelsEvent(channel,Direction.DOWN,this);
    createChannels.go();
  }

  private void notifyCrash(TcpUndeliveredEvent event) {
    if(started){
      SampleProcess p = processes.getProcess((InetWithPort) event.who);
      if (p.isCorrect()) {
        p.setCorrect(false);
        Crash crash =
          new Crash(channel,Direction.UP,this,p.getProcessNumber());
        crash.go();
      }
    }
  }
}
```

2.8 Exercises

Exercise 2.1 *Explain under which assumptions the fail-recovery and the fail-silent models are similar (note that in both models any process can commit omission failures).*

Exercise 2.2 *Does the following statement satisfy the synchronous processing assumption:* on my server, no request ever takes more than one week to be processed?

Exercise 2.3 *Can we implement the perfect failure detector in a model where the processes could commit omission failures and where we cannot not bound the number of such failures? What if this number is bounded but unknown? What if processes that can commit omission failures commit a limited and known number of such failures and then crash?*

Exercise 2.4 *In a fail-stop model, can we determine a priori a time period such that, whenever a process crashes, all correct processes suspect this process to have crashed after this period?*

Exercise 2.5 *In a fail-stop model, which of the following properties are safety properties?*

1. *every process that crashes is eventually detected;*
2. *no process is detected before it crashes;*
3. *no two processes decide differently;*
4. *no two correct processes decide differently;*
5. *every correct process decides before t time units;*
6. *if some correct process decides, then every correct process decides.*

Exercise 2.6 *Consider any algorithm A that implements a distributed programming abstraction M using a failure detector D that is assumed to be eventually perfect. Can A violate the safety property of M if failure detector D is not eventually perfect, e.g., D permanently outputs the empty set?*

Exercise 2.7 *Specify a distributed programming abstraction M and an algorithm A implementing M using a failure detector D that is supposed to satisfy a set of properties, such that the liveness of M is violated if D does not satisfy its properties.*

Exercise 2.8 *Is there an algorithm that implements the leader election abstraction with the eventually perfect failure detector?*

2.9 Solutions

Solution 2.1 When processes crash, they lose the content of their volatile memory and they commit omissions. If we assume (1) that processes do have stable storage and store every update on their state within the stable storage, and (2) that they are not aware they have crashed and recovered, then the two models are similar. □

Solution 2.2 Yes. This is because the time it takes for the process (i.e. the server) to process a request is bounded and known: it is one week. □

Solution 2.3 It is impossible to implement a perfect failure detector if the number of omissions failures is unknown. Indeed, to guarantee the *strong completeness* property of the failure detector, a process p must detect the crash of another one, q, after some timeout delay. No matter how this delay is chosen, it can exceed the transmission delay times the number of omissions that q commits. This would lead to violating the *strong accuracy* property of the failure detector. If the number of possible omissions is known in a synchronous system, we can use it to calibrate the timeout delay of the processes to accurately detect failures. If the delay exceeds the maximum time during which a process can commit omission failures, without having actually crashed, it can safely detect the process as having crashed. □

Solution 2.4 No. The perfect failure detector only ensures that processes that crash are eventually detected: there is no bound on the time it takes for these crashes to be detected. This points out a fundamental difference between algorithms assuming a synchronous system and algorithms assuming a perfect failure detector (fail-stop model). In a precise sense, a synchronous model is strictly stronger. □

Solution 2.5

1. Eventually, every process that crashes is detected. This is a liveness property; we can never exhibit a time t in some execution and state that the property is violated. There is always the hope that eventually the failure detector detects the crashes.
2. No process is detected before it crashes. This is a safety property. If a process is detected at time t before it has crashed, then the property is violated at time t.
3. No two processes decide differently. This is also a safety property, because it can be violated at some time t and never be satisfied again.
4. No two correct processes decide differently. If we do not bound the number of processes that can crash, then the property turns out to be a liveness property. Indeed, even if we consider some time t at which two processes have decided differently, then there is always some hope that, eventually, some of the processes may crash and validate the property. This remains actually true even if we assume that at least one process is correct. Assume now that we bound the number of failures, say, by $F < N - 1$. The property is not any more a liveness property. Indeed, if we consider a partial execution and a time t at which $N - 2$ processes have crashed and the two remaining processes decide differently, then there is no way we can extend this execution and validate the property. But is the property a safety property? This would mean that in any execution where the property does not hold, there is a partial execution of it, such that no matter how we extend it, the property would still not hold. Again, this is not true. To see why, consider the execution where less than $F - 2$ processes have crashed and two correct processes decide differently. No matter what partial execution we consider, we can extend it by crashing one of the two processes that have decided differently and validate the property. To conclude, in the case where $F < N - 1$, the property is the union of both a liveness and a safety property.
5. Every correct process decides before t time units. This is a safety property: it can be violated at some l, where all correct processes have executed t of their own steps. If violated, at that time, there is no hope that it will be satisfied again.
6. If some correct process decides, then every correct process decides. This is a liveness property: there is always the hope that the property is satisfied. It is interesting to note that the property can actually be satisfied by

having the processes not do anything. Hence, the intuition that a safety property is one that is satisfied by doing nothing may be misleading.

□

Solution 2.6 No. Assume by contradiction that A violates the safety property of M if D does not satisfy its properties. Because of the very nature of a safety property, there is a time t and an execution R of the system such that the property is violated at t in R. Assume now that the properties of the eventually perfect failure detector hold after t in a run R' that is similar to R up to time t. A would violate the safety property of M in R', even if the failure detector is eventually perfect. □

Solution 2.7 An example of such abstraction is simply the eventually perfect failure detector. Note that such abstraction has no safety property. □

Solution 2.8 Recall that the leader election abstraction is defined with the following properties: (1) Either there is no correct process, or some correct process is eventually the leader; and (2) If a process is leader, then all previously elected leaders have crashed. It is impossible to implement such an abstraction with the eventually perfect failure detector, as we discuss below.

Consider an execution R_1 where no process fails; let p be the first process elected leader, and let t be the time at which p first declares itself leader. Consider an execution R_2, similar to R until time t, but where p crashes right after time t. Due to the first property of the leader election abstraction, another process is eventually elected. Denote that process by q, and let $t' > t$ be the time at which q first declares itself leader. With an eventually perfect failure detector, and until time t', there is no way to distinguish such execution from one, which we denote R_3, where p is actually correct (but whose messages got delayed until after t'). This execution R_3 violates the specification of the leader election abstraction (i.e., its second property). □

2.10 Historical Notes

- In 1978, the notions of causality and logical time were introduced in probably the most influential paper in the area of distributed computing by Leslie Lamport (1978).
- In 1982, agreement problems were considered in an arbitrary fault model, also called the malicious or the Byzantine model (Lamport, Shostak, and Pease 1982).
- In 1984, algorithms assuming that processes can only fail by crashing, and that every process has accurate information about which processes have

crashed (perfect failure detector) were called fail-stop algorithms (Schneider, Gries, and Schlichting 1984).

- In 1985, a fundamental result in distributed computing was established. It was proved that, even a very simple form of agreement, namely, consensus, is impossible to solve with a deterministic algorithm in an asynchronous system even if only one process fails, and it can only do so by crashing (Fischer, Lynch, and Paterson 1985).

- Also in 1985, the notions of safety and liveness were singled out. It was shown that any property of a distributed system execution can be viewed as a composition of a liveness and a safety property (Alpern and Schneider 1985).

- In 1988 (Dwork, Lynch, and Stockmeyer 1988), intermediate models between the synchronous and the asynchronous model, called partially synchronous models, were introduced.

- In 1989, the use of synchrony assumptions to build leasing mechanisms was explored (Gray and Cheriton 1989).

- In 1991, it was observed that, when solving various problems, in particular consensus, timing assumptions were mainly used to detect process crashes (Chandra and Toueg 1996; Chandra, Hadzilacos, and Toueg 1996). This observation led to the definition of an abstract notion of failure detector that encapsulates timing assumptions. For instance, the very fact that *consensus can be solved in partially synchronous systems* (Dwork, Lynch, and Stockmeyer 1988) is translated, in the failure detector terminology (Chandra, Hadzilacos, and Toueg 1996), into *consensus can be solved even with unreliable failure detectors* (e.g., eventually perfect failure detectors).

- The idea of stubborn communication channels was proposed in 1997 (Guerraoui, Oliveria, and Schiper 1997), as a pragmatic variant of perfect channels for the fail-recovery model, yet at a higher level than fair-loss links (Lynch 1996).

- In 2000, the notion of *unreliable failure detector* was precisely defined (Guerraoui 2000). Algorithms that rely on such failure detectors have been called *indulgent* algorithms (Guerraoui 2000; Dutta and Guerraoui 2002; Guerraoui and Raynal 2004).

- The notion of failure detector was also extended to the fail-recovery model (Aguilera, Chen, and Toueg 2000).

3. Reliable Broadcast

He said: "I could have been someone";
She replied: "So could anyone."
(The Pogues)

This chapter covers the specifications of *broadcast communication* abstractions. These are used to disseminate information among a set of processes and differ according to the reliability of the dissemination. For instance, *best-effort broadcast* guarantees that all correct processes deliver the same set of messages if the senders are correct. Stronger forms of reliable broadcast guarantee this property even if the senders crash while broadcasting their messages.

We will consider several related abstractions: *best-effort broadcast, (regular) reliable broadcast, uniform reliable broadcast, logged broadcast, stubborn broadcast, probabilistic broadcast, and causal broadcast.* For each of these abstractions, we will provide one or more algorithms implementing it, and these will cover the different models addressed in this book.

3.1 Motivation

3.1.1 Client-Server Computing

In traditional distributed applications, interactions are often established between two processes. Probably the most representative of this sort of interaction is the now classic *client-server* scheme. According to this model, a *server* process exports an interface to several *clients*. Clients use the interface by sending a request to the server and by later collecting a reply. Such interaction is supported by *point-to-point* communication protocols. It is extremely useful for the application if such a protocol is *reliable*. Reliability in this context usually means that, under some assumptions (which are, by the way, often not completely understood by most system designers), messages exchanged between the two processes are not lost or duplicated, and are delivered in the order in which they were sent. Typical implementations of this abstraction are reliable transport protocols such as TCP (Transmission Control Protocol (Postel 1981)). By using a reliable point-to-point communication protocol, the application is free from dealing explicitly with issues such as acknowledgments, timeouts, message retransmissions, flow control, and a number of other issues that are encapsulated by the protocol interface.

3.1.2 Multi-participant Systems

As distributed applications become bigger and more complex, interactions are no longer limited to bilateral relationships. There are many cases where more than two processes need to operate in a coordinated manner. Consider, for instance, a multiuser virtual environment where several users interact in a virtual space. These users may be located at different physical places, and they can either directly interact by exchanging multimedia information, or indirectly by modifying the environment.

It is convenient to rely here on *broadcast* abstractions. These allow a process to send a message within a *group* of processes, and make sure that the processes agree on the messages they deliver. A naive transposition of the reliability requirement from point-to-point protocols would require that no message sent to the group be lost or duplicated, i.e., the processes agree to deliver every message broadcast to them. However, the definition of agreement for a broadcast primitive is not a simple task. The existence of multiple senders and multiple recipients in a group introduces degrees of freedom that do not exist in point-to-point communication. Consider, for instance, the case where the sender of a message fails by crashing. It may happen that some recipients deliver the last message sent while others do not. This may lead to an inconsistent view of the system state by different group members.

Roughly speaking, broadcast abstractions provide reliability guarantees ranging from *best-effort*, which only ensures delivery among all correct processes if the sender does not fail, through *reliable*, which, in addition, ensures *all-or-nothing* delivery semantics, even if the sender fails, to *totally ordered*, which furthermore ensures that the delivery of messages follow the same global order, and *terminating*, which ensures that the processes either deliver a message or are eventually aware that they should never deliver the message. In this chapter, we will focus on best-effort and reliable broadcast abstractions. Totally ordered and terminating forms of broadcast will be considered in later chapters.

Module 3.1 Interface and properties of best-effort broadcast

Module:

    Name: BestEffortBroadcast (beb).

Events:

    Request: ⟨ *bebBroadcast* | m ⟩: Used to broadcast message m to all processes.

    Indication: ⟨ *bebDeliver* | src, m ⟩: Used to deliver message m broadcast by process *src*.

Properties:

    BEB1: *Best-effort validity:* For any two processes p_i and p_j. If p_i and p_j are correct, then every message broadcast by p_i is eventually delivered by p_j.

    BEB2: *No duplication:* No message is delivered more than once.

    BEB3: *No creation:* If a message m is delivered by some process p_j, then m was previously broadcast by some process p_i.

3.2 Best-Effort Broadcast

A broadcast abstraction enables a process to send a message, in a one-shot operation, to all processes in a system, including itself. We give here the specification and algorithm for a broadcast communication primitive with a weak form of reliability, called *best-effort broadcast*.

3.2.1 Specification

With best-effort broadcast, the burden of ensuring reliability is only on the sender. Therefore, the remaining processes do not have to be concerned with enforcing the reliability of received messages. On the other hand, no delivery guarantees are offered in case the sender fails. Best-effort broadcast is characterized by the properties BEB1-3 depicted in Module 3.1. BEB1 is a liveness property whereas BEB2 and BEB3 are safety properties. Note that broadcast messages are implicitly addressed to all processes. Remember also that messages are uniquely identified.

3.2.2 Fail-Silent Algorithm: Basic Broadcast

We provide here an algorithm (Algorithm 3.1) that implements best-effort broadcast using perfect links. This algorithm does not make any assumption on failure detection: it is a fail-silent algorithm. The idea is pretty simple. Broadcasting a message simply consists of sending the message on top of perfect links to every process in the system, as illustrated by Figure 3.1 (in the figure, white arrowheads represent request/indication events at the

---

Algorithm 3.1 Basic Broadcast

Implements:
     BestEffortBroadcast (beb).

Uses:
     PerfectPointToPointLinks (pp2p).

upon event ⟨ *bebBroadcast* | m ⟩ **do**
     forall $p_i \in \Pi$ **do**
          trigger ⟨ *pp2pSend* | p_i, m ⟩;

upon event ⟨ *pp2pDeliver* | p_i, m ⟩ **do**
     trigger ⟨ *bebDeliver* | p_i, m ⟩;

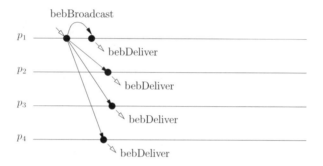

Fig. 3.1: Sample execution of basic broadcast

module interface and black arrowheads represent message exchanges). In the algorithm, called "Basic Broadcast", as long as the sender of a message does not crash, the properties of perfect links ensure that all correct processes eventually deliver the message.

Correctness. The properties of best-effort broadcast are trivially derived from the properties of the underlying perfect point-to-point links. *No duplication* and *no creation* are directly derived from PL2 and PL3. *Validity* is derived from PL1 and the fact that the sender sends the message to every other process in the system.

Performance. For every message that is broadcast, the algorithm requires a single communication step and exchanges N messages.

3.3 Regular Reliable Broadcast

Best-effort broadcast ensures the delivery of messages as long as the sender does not fail. If the sender fails, the processes might disagree on whether

---

Module 3.2 Interface and properties of regular reliable broadcast

Module:

    Name: (regular)ReliableBroadcast (rb).

Events:

    Request: ⟨ rbBroadcast | m ⟩: Used to broadcast message m.

    Indication: ⟨ rbDeliver | src, m ⟩: Used to deliver message m broadcast by process src.

Properties:

    RB1: *Validity:* If a correct process p_i broadcasts a message m, then p_i eventually delivers m.

    RB2: *No duplication:* No message is delivered more than once.

    RB3: *No creation:* If a message m is delivered by some process p_j, then m was previously broadcast by some process p_i.

    RB4: *Agreement:* If a message m is delivered by some correct process p_i, then m is eventually delivered by every correct process p_j.

---

or not to deliver the message. Actually, even if the process sends a message to all processes before crashing, the delivery is not ensured because perfect links do not enforce delivery when the sender fails. We now consider the case where agreement is ensured even if the sender fails. We do so by introducing a broadcast abstraction with a stronger form of reliability, called *(regular) reliable broadcast.*

3.3.1 Specification

Intuitively, the semantics of a reliable broadcast algorithm ensure that correct processes agree on the set of messages they deliver, even when the senders of these messages crash during the transmission. It should be noted that a sender may crash before being able to transmit the message, in which case no process will deliver it. The specification is given in Module 3.2. This extends the specification of Module 3.1 with a new liveness property: *agreement.* (The very fact that this is a liveness property might seem counterintuitive, as the property can be achieved by not having any process ever deliver any message. Strictly speaking, it is, however, a liveness property as it can always be ensured in extensions of finite executions. We will see other forms of *agreement* that are safety properties later in the book.)

3.3.2 Fail-Stop Algorithm: Lazy Reliable Broadcast

We now show how to implement regular reliable broadcast in a fail-stop model. In our algorithm, depicted in Algorithm 3.2, which we have called

"Lazy Reliable Broadcast", we make use of the best-effort abstraction described in the previous section as well as the perfect failure detector module introduced earlier.

To rbBroadcast a message, a process uses the best-effort broadcast primitive to disseminate the message to all. Note that this implementation adds some protocol headers to the messages exchanged. In particular, the implementation adds a message descriptor ("DATA") and the original source of the message to the message header. This is denoted by [DATA, s_m, m] in the algorithm. A process that gets the message (i.e., bebDelivers the message) delivers it immediately (i.e., rbDelivers it). If the sender does not crash, then the message will be rbDelivered by all correct processes. The problem is that the sender might crash. In this case, the process that delivers the message from some other process can detect that crash and relays the message to all. We note that this is a language abuse: in fact, the process relays a copy of the message (and not the message itself).

Our algorithm is said to be *lazy* in the sense that it retransmits a message only if the original sender has been detected to have crashed.

It is important to notice that, strictly speaking, two kinds of events can force a process to retransmit a message. (1) When the process detects the crash of the source, and (2) when the process bebDelivers a message and realizes that the source has already been detected to have crashed (i.e., the source is not anymore in the set *correct*). This might lead to duplicate retransmissions when a process bebDelivers a message from a source that fails, as we explain below. It is pretty clear that a process that detects the crash of a source needs to retransmit the messages already bebDelivered from that source. On the other hand, a process might bebDeliver a message from a source after it detected the crash of that source: it is thus necessary to check for the retransmission even when no new crash is detected.

Correctness. The *no creation* (resp. *validity*) property of our reliable broadcast algorithm follows from the *no creation* (resp. *validity*) property of the underlying best effort broadcast primitive. The *no duplication* property of reliable broadcast follows from our use of a variable *delivered* that keeps track of the messages that have been rbDelivered at every process. *Agreement* follows here from the *validity* property of the underlying best effort broadcast primitive, from the fact that every process relays every message it rbDelivers when it suspects the sender, and from the use of a perfect failure detector.

Performance. If the initial sender does not crash, to rbDeliver a message to all processes, the algorithm requires a single communication step and N messages. Otherwise, N^2 and, in the worst case (if the processes crash in sequence), N steps are required. .

3.3.3 Fail-Silent Algorithm: Eager Reliable Broadcast

In our "Lazy Reliable Broadcast" algorithm (Algorithm 3.2), if the *accuracy* property of the failure detector is not satisfied, then the processes might be

---

Algorithm 3.2 Lazy Reliable Broadcast

Implements:
 ReliableBroadcast (rb).

Uses:
 BestEffortBroadcast (beb).
 PerfectFailureDetector ($\mathcal{P}$).

upon event $\langle$ *Init* $\rangle$ **do**
 delivered := $\emptyset$;
 correct := Π;
 forall $p_i \in \Pi$ **do**
  from[p_i] := $\emptyset$;

upon event $\langle$ *rbBroadcast* | m $\rangle$ **do**
 trigger $\langle$ *bebBroadcast* | [DATA, self, m] $\rangle$;

upon event $\langle$ *bebDeliver* | p_i, [DATA, s_m, m] $\rangle$ **do**
 if ($m \notin$ delivered) **then**
  delivered := delivered $\cup$ \{m\}
  trigger $\langle$ *rbDeliver* | s_m, m $\rangle$;
  from[p_i] := from[p_i] $\cup$ \{(s_m, m)\}
  if ($p_i \notin$ *correct*) **then**
   trigger $\langle$ *bebBroadcast* | [DATA, s_m, m] $\rangle$;

upon event $\langle$ *crash* | p_i $\rangle$ **do**
 correct := correct \ \{p_i\}
 forall (s_m, m) $\in$ from[p_i] **do**
  trigger $\langle$ *bebBroadcast* | [DATA, s_m, m] $\rangle$;

---

relaying messages when it is not really necessary. This wastes resources but does not impact correctness. On the other hand, we rely on the *completeness* property of the failure detector to ensure the broadcast *agreement*. If the failure detector does not ensure *completeness*, then the processes might not be relaying messages that they should be relaying (e.g., messages broadcast by processes that crashed), and hence might violate *agreement*.

In fact, we can circumvent the need for a failure detector (i.e., the need for its *completeness* property) by adopting an *eager* scheme: every process that gets a message relays it immediately. That is, we consider the worst case, where the sender process might have crashed, and we relay every message. This relaying phase is exactly what guarantees the *agreement* property of reliable broadcast. The resulting algorithm (Algorithm 3.3) is called "Eager Reliable Broadcast."

The algorithm assumes a fail-silent model and does not use any failure detector: it uses only the best-effort broadcast primitive described in Section 3.2. In Figure 3.2a we illustrate how the algorithm ensures *agreement* even if the sender crashes: process p_1 crashes and its message is not bebDeliv-

---

Algorithm 3.3 Eager Reliable Broadcast

Implements:
    ReliableBroadcast (rb).

Uses:
    BestEffortBroadcast (beb).

upon event ⟨ *Init* ⟩ **do**
    delivered := ∅;

upon event ⟨ *rbBroadcast* | *m* ⟩ **do**
    delivered := delivered ∪ {*m*}
    trigger ⟨ *rbDeliver* | self, *m* ⟩;
    trigger ⟨ *bebBroadcast* | [DATA, self, *m*] ⟩;

upon event ⟨ *bebDeliver* | p_i, [DATA, s_m, *m*] ⟩ **do**
    if *m* ∉ delivered **do**
        delivered := delivered ∪ { m }
        trigger ⟨ *rbDeliver* | s_m, *m* ⟩;
        trigger ⟨ *bebBroadcast* | [DATA, s_m, *m*] ⟩;

---

ered by p_3 and p_4. However, since p_2 retransmits the message (bebBroadcasts it), the remaining processes also bebDeliver it and then rbDeliver it. In our "Lazy Reliable Broadcast" algorithm, p_2 will be relaying the message only after it has detected the crash of p_1.

Correctness. All properties, except *agreement*, are ensured as in the "Lazy Reliable Broadcast." The *agreement* property follows from the *validity* property of the underlying best-effort broadcast primitive and from the fact that every process immediately relays every message it rbDelivers.

Performance. In the best case, to rbDeliver a message to all processes, the algorithm requires a single communication step and N^2 messages. In the worst case (if processes crash in sequence), N steps and N^2 messages are required to terminate the algorithm.

3.4 Uniform Reliable Broadcast

With regular reliable broadcast, the semantics just require *correct* processes to deliver the same *set* of messages, regardless of what messages have been delivered by faulty processes. In particular, a process that rbBroadcasts a message might rbDeliver it and then crash, without any process having even bebDelivered that message. This scenario can also happen in both reliable broadcast algorithms we presented (eager and lazy). It is thus possible that no other process, including correct ones, ever rbDelivers that message. We now introduce a stronger definition of reliable broadcast, called *uniform* reliable

Module 3.3 Interface and properties of uniform reliable broadcast

Module:

    Name: UniformReliableBroadcast (urb).

Events:

    ⟨ *urbBroadcast* | *m* ⟩, ⟨ *urbDeliver* | *src, m* ⟩, with the same meaning and interface as in regular reliable broadcast.

Properties:

    RB1–RB3: Same as in regular reliable broadcast.

    URB4: *Uniform Agreement:* If a message m is delivered by some process p_i (whether correct or faulty), then m is also eventually delivered by every correct process p_j.

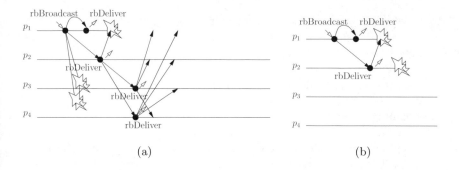

Fig. 3.2: Sample executions of reliable broadcast

broadcast. This definition is stronger in the sense that it guarantees that the set of messages delivered by *faulty* processes is always a *subset* of the messages delivered by correct processes.

3.4.1 Specification

Uniform reliable broadcast differs from reliable broadcast by the formulation of its *agreement* property. The specification is given in Module 3.3.

    Uniformity is typically important if processes might interact with the external world, e.g., print something on a screen, authorize the delivery of money through an ATM, or trigger a rocket. In this case, the fact that a process has delivered a message is important, even if the process has crashed afterward. This is because the process, before crashing, could have communicated with the external world after having delivered the message. The processes that did not crash should also be aware of that message having been delivered, and of the possible external action having been performed.

Figure 3.2b depicts an execution of a reliable broadcast algorithm that does not ensure uniformity. Both processes p_1 and p_2 rbDeliver the message as soon as they bebDeliver it, but crash before relaying the message to the remaining processes. Still, processes p_3 and p_4 are consistent among themselves (neither has rbDelivered the message).

3.4.2 Fail-Stop Algorithm: All-Ack Uniform Reliable Broadcast

Basically, our "Lazy Reliable Broadcast" and "Eager Reliable Broadcast" algorithms do not ensure *uniform agreement* because a process may rbDeliver a message and then crash. Even if this process has relayed its message to all processes (through a bebBroadcast primitive), the message might not reach any of the remaining processes. Note that even if we considered the same algorithms and replaced the best-effort broadcast abstraction with a reliable broadcast one, we would still not implement a uniform broadcast abstraction. This is because a process delivers a message before relaying it to all processes.

Algorithm 3.4, named "All-Ack Uniform Reliable Broadcast", implements the uniform version of reliable broadcast in the fail-stop model. Basically, in this algorithm, a process delivers a message only when it knows that the message has been *seen* (bebDelivered) by all correct processes. All processes relay the message once they have *seen* it. Each process keeps a record of which processes have already retransmitted a given message. When all correct processes have retransmitted the message, all correct processes are guaranteed to deliver the message, as illustrated in Figure 3.3.

Notice that the last *upon* statement of Algorithm 3.4 is different from the others we have considered so far in other algorithms: it is not triggered by an external event, i.e., originating from a different layer. Instead, it is triggered by an internal event originating from a predicate (*canDeliver*) becoming *true*.

Correctness. Integrity is directly derived from the properties of the underlying best-effort broadcast primitive. The *no creation* property is derived from that of the underlying best-effort broadcast. *No duplication* follows from the use of the *delivered* variable. As for *validity*, we rely on the *completeness* property of the failure detector and the *validity* property of the best-effort broadcast. *Uniform agreement* is ensured by having each process wait to urbDeliver a message until all correct processes have bebDelivered the message. We rely here on the *accuracy* property of the perfect failure detector.

Performance. In the best case, the algorithm requires two communication steps to urbDeliver a message to all processes. In the worst case, if the processes crash in sequence, $N + 1$ steps are required. The algorithm exchanges N^2 messages in each step. Therefore, uniform reliable broadcast requires one step more to deliver a message than its regular counterpart.

Algorithm 3.4 All-Ack Uniform Reliable Broadcast

Implements:
    UniformReliableBroadcast (urb).

Uses:
    BestEffortBroadcast (beb).
    PerfectFailureDetector ($\mathcal{P}$).

function canDeliver(m) **returns** boolean **is**
    return (correct $\subseteq$ ack$_m$);

upon event $\langle$ *Init* $\rangle$ **do**
    delivered := pending := $\emptyset$;
    correct := Π;
    forall m **do** ack$_m$:= $\emptyset$;

upon event $\langle$ *urbBroadcast* | m $\rangle$ **do**
    pending := pending $\cup$ {(self, m)};
    trigger $\langle$ *bebBroadcast* | [DATA, self, m] $\rangle$;

upon event $\langle$ *bebDeliver* | p_i, [DATA, s_m, m] $\rangle$ **do**
    ack$_m$:= ack$_m$ $\cup$ {p_i};
    if ((s_m, m) $\notin$ pending) **then**
        pending := pending $\cup$ {(s_m, m)};
        trigger $\langle$ *bebBroadcast* | [DATA, s_m, m] $\rangle$;

upon event $\langle$ *crash* | p_i $\rangle$ **do**
    correct := correct $\setminus$ {p_i};

upon exists (s_m, m) $\in$ pending **such that** canDeliver(m) $\wedge$ m $\notin$ delivered **do**
    delivered := delivered $\cup$ {m};
    trigger $\langle$ *urbDeliver* | s_m, m $\rangle$;

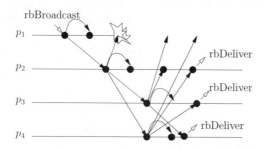

Fig. 3.3: Sample execution of all-ack uniform reliable broadcast

3.4.3 Fail-Silent Algorithm: Majority-Ack Uniform Reliable Broadcast

The "All-Ack Uniform Reliable Broadcast" algorithm of Section 3.4.2 (Algorithm 3.4) is not correct if the failure detector is not perfect. *Uniform*

Algorithm 3.5 Majority-Ack Uniform Reliable Broadcast

Implements:
    UniformReliableBroadcast (urb).

Extends:
    All-Ack Uniform Reliable Broadcast (Algorithm 3.4).

Uses:
    BestEffortBroadcast (beb).

function canDeliver(m) **returns** boolean **is**
    return $(|\text{ack}_m| > N/2)$;

// Except for the function above, and the non-use of the
// perfect failure detector, same as Algorithm 3.4.

---

agreement would be violated if *accuracy* is not satisfied and *validity* would be violated if *completeness* is not satisfied.

We now give a uniform reliable broadcast algorithm that does not rely on a perfect failure detector but assumes a majority of correct processes. We leave it as an exercise to show why the majority assumption is needed in a fail-silent model, without any failure detector. Algorithm 3.5, called "Majority-Ack Uniform Reliable Broadcast", is similar to the previous "All-Ack Uniform Reliable Broadcast" algorithm, except that processes do not wait until all correct processes have seen a message (bebDelivered the message), but only until a majority has seen the message. Hence, the algorithm is a simple extension of the original one (Algorithm 3.4), except that we modify the condition under which a message needs to be delivered.

Correctness. The *no creation* property follows from that of best-effort broadcast. The *no duplication* property follows from the use of the variable *delivered*.

To argue for the *uniform agreement* and *validity* properties, we first observe that if a correct process p_i bebDelivers any message m, then p_i urbDelivers m. Indeed, if p_i is correct, and given that p_i bebBroadcasts m (according to the algorithm), then every correct process bebDelivers and hence bebBroadcasts m. As we assume a correct majority, p_i bebDelivers m from a majority of the processes and urbDelivers it.

Consider now the *validity* property. If a correct process p_i urbBroadcasts a message m, then p_i bebBroadcasts m and hence p_i bebDelivers m: according to the observation above, p_i eventually urbDelivers m. Consider now *uniform agreement*, and let p_j be any process that urbDelivers m. To do so, p_j must have bebDelivered m from a majority of the processes. Due to the assumption of a correct majority, at least one correct process must have bebBroadcast m. Again, according to the observation above, all correct processes have beb-

Delivered m, which implies that all correct processes eventually urbDeliver m.

Performance. Similar to the "All-Ack Uniform Reliable Broadcast" algorithm.

3.5 Stubborn Broadcast

We now consider broadcast abstractions in a setting where processes can crash and recover, i.e., in the fail-recovery model. We first discuss the issue underlying fail-recovery when broadcasting messages and then give examples of specifications and underlying algorithms in this model.

3.5.1 Overview

It is first important to notice why the specifications we have considered for the fail-stop and fail-silent models are not adequate for the fail-recovery model. As we explain below, even the strongest of our specifications, uniform reliable broadcast, does not provide useful semantics in a setting where processes that crash can later recover and participate in the computation.

Consider a message m that is broadcast by some process p_i. Consider, furthermore, some other process p_j that crashes at some instant, recovers, and never crashes again. In the fail-recovery sense, process p_j is correct. With the semantics of uniform reliable broadcast however, it might happen that p_j delivers m, crashes without having processed m, and then recovers with no memory of m. Ideally, there should be some way for process p_j to find out about m upon recovery, and hence to be able to execute any associated action accordingly.

We start by presenting a generalization of the stubborn point-to-point communication idea to the broadcast situation. Correct processes are supposed to deliver all messages (broadcast by processes that did not crash) an infinite number of times, and hence eventually deliver such messages upon recovery. The corresponding specification is called *stubborn broadcast*.

3.5.2 Specification

The specification of stubborn broadcast we consider is given in Module 3.4, and we illustrate here the idea through the best-effort case. Stronger abstractions (regular and uniform) of stubborn broadcast could also be obtained accordingly. The key difference with the best-effort abstraction defined for the fail-no-recovery settings is in the stubborn (perpetual) delivery (even by recovered processes) of every message broadcast by a process that does not crash. As a direct consequence, the *no duplication* property is not ensured. The very fact that processes now have to deal with multiple deliveries is

---

Module 3.4 Interface and properties of stubborn best-effort broadcast

Module:

    Name: StubbornBestEffortBroadcast (sbeb).

Events:

    Request: ⟨ *sbebBroadcast* | m ⟩: Used to broadcast message m to all processes.

    Indication: ⟨ *sbebDeliver* | src, m ⟩: Used to deliver message m broadcast by process *src*.

Properties:

    SBEB1: *Best-effort validity:* If a process p_j is correct and another process p_i does not crash, then every message broadcast by p_i is delivered by p_j an infinite number of times.

    SBEB2: *No creation:* If a message m is delivered by some process p_j, then m was previously broadcast by some process p_i.

Algorithm 3.6 Basic Stubborn Broadcast

Implements:
    StubbornBestEffortBroadcast (sbeb).

Uses:
    StubbornPointToPointLink (sp2p).

upon event ⟨ *sbebBroadcast* | m ⟩ **do**
    forall $p_i \in \Pi$ **do**
        trigger ⟨ *sp2pSend* | p_i, m ⟩;

upon event ⟨ *sp2pDeliver* | src, m ⟩ **do**
        trigger ⟨ *sbebDeliver* | delivered ⟩;

---

the price to pay for saving expensive logging operations. Later on, we will also discuss an alternative abstraction (*logged broadcast*) where the issue of multiple deliveries is handled by logging messages.

3.5.3 Fail-Recovery Algorithm: Basic Stubborn Broadcast

Algorithm 3.6 implements stubborn best-effort broadcast using underlying stubborn communication links.

Correctness. The properties of stubborn broadcast are derived in the algorithm from the properties of stubborn links. In particular, *validity* is derived from the fact that the sender sends the message to every other process in the system.

Performance. The algorithm requires a single communication step for a process to deliver a message, and exchanges at least N messages. Of course, stubborn channels may retransmit the same message several times and, in practice, an optimization mechanism is needed to acknowledge the messages and stop the retransmission.

3.6 Logged Best-Effort Broadcast

We now consider an alternative broadcast abstraction for the fail-recovery model, which prevents multiple delivery of the same messages. In order to achieve this goal, we define the semantics of message delivery according to message logging, as we did for the logged perfect links abstraction in the previous chapter. Roughly speaking, a process is said to deliver a message when it logs the message, i.e., it stores it on stable storage. Hence, if it has delivered a message m, a process that crashes and recovers will still be able to retrieve m from stable storage and to execute any associated action accordingly.

3.6.1 Specification

The abstraction we consider here is called *logged broadcast* to emphasize the fact that the act of "delivering" corresponds to its "logging" in a local stable storage. Instead of simply triggering an event to deliver a message, logged broadcast relies on storing the message in a local log, which can later be read by the layer above. The layer is notified about changes in the log through specific events.

The specification is given in Module 3.5. The act of delivering the message corresponds here to the act of logging the variable *delivered* with m in that variable. Hence, *validity, no duplication,* and *no creation* properties are redefined in term of log operations. Note also that we consider here the best-effort case. As we discuss later, stronger abstractions (regular and uniform) can then be designed and implemented on top of this one.

3.6.2 Fail-Recovery Algorithm: Logged Basic Broadcast

Algorithm 3.7, called "Logged Basic Broadcast", implements logged best-effort broadcast. It has many similarities, in its structure, with Algorithm 3.1 ("Basic Broadcast"). The main differences are the following:

1. The "Logged Basic Broadcast" algorithm makes use of stubborn communication links between every pair of processes. Remember that these ensure that a message that is sent by a process that does not crash to a correct recipient is supposed to be delivered by its recipient an infinite number of times.

Module 3.5 Interface and properties of logged best-effort broadcast

Module:

    Name: LoggedBestEffortBroadcast (log-beb).

Events:

    Request: ⟨ *log-bebBroadcast* | m ⟩: Used to broadcast message m to all processes.

    Indication: ⟨ *log-bebDeliver* | delivered ⟩: Used to notify the upper level of potential updates to the delivered log.

Properties:

    LBEB1: *Best-effort validity:* If a process p_j is correct and another process p_i does not crash, then every message broadcast by p_i is eventually delivered by p_j.

    LBEB2: *No duplication:* No message is delivered more than once.

    LBEB3: *No creation:* If a message m is delivered by some process p_j, then m was previously broadcast by some process p_i.

---

2. The "Logged Basic Broadcast" algorithm maintains a log of all delivered messages. When a new message is received for the first time, it is appended to the log (delivered), and the upper layer is notified that the log has changed. If the process crashes and later recovers, the upper layer is also notified (as it may have missed a notification triggered just before the crash).

Correctness. The *no creation* property is derived from that of the underlying stubborn links, whereas *no duplication* is derived from the fact that the delivery log is checked before delivering new messages. The *validity* property follows from the fact that the sender sends the message to every other process in the system.

Performance. The algorithm requires a single communication step for a process to deliver a message, and exchanges at least N messages. Of course, stubborn channels may retransmit the same message several times and, in practice, an optimization mechanism is needed to acknowledge the messages and stop the retransmission. Additionally, the algorithm requires a log operation for each delivered message.

3.7 Logged Uniform Reliable Broadcast

In a manner similar to the crash-no-recovery case, it is possible to define both reliable and uniform variants of best-effort broadcast for the fail-recovery setting.

Algorithm 3.7 Logged Basic Broadcast

Implements:
    LoggedBestEffortBroadcast (log-beb).

Uses:
    StubbornPointToPointLink (sp2p).

upon event ⟨ *Init* ⟩ **do**
    delivered := ∅;
    store (delivered);

upon event ⟨ *Recovery* ⟩ **do**
    retrieve (delivered);
    trigger ⟨ *log-bebDeliver* | delivered ⟩;

upon event ⟨ *log-bebBroadcast* | m ⟩ **do**
    forall $p_i \in \Pi$ **do**
        trigger ⟨ *sp2pSend* | p_i, m ⟩;

upon event ⟨ *sp2pDeliver* | *src, m* ⟩ **do**
    if ((src, m) ∉ delivered) **then**
        delivered := delivered ∪ {(src, m)};
        store (delivered);
        trigger ⟨ *log-bebDeliver* | delivered ⟩;

Module 3.6 Interface and properties of logged uniform reliable broadcast

---

Module:

    Name: LoggedUniformReliableBroadcast (log-urb).

Events:

    ⟨ *log-urbBroadcast* | m ⟩, ⟨ *log-urbDeliver* | delivered ⟩ with the same
    meaning and interface as in logged best-effort broadcast.

Properties:

    LBEB1 (*Validity*), **LBEB2** (*No duplication*), and **LBEB3** (*No creation*),
    same as in logged best-effort broadcast.

    LURB1: *Uniform Agreement:* If a message m is delivered by some process,
    then m is eventually delivered by every correct process.

3.7.1 Specification

Module 3.6 defines a logged variant of the uniform reliable broadcast abstraction for the fail-recovery model. In this variant, if a process (either correct or not) delivers a message (i.e., logs the variable *delivered* with the message in it), all correct processes should eventually deliver that message. Not surprisingly, the interface is similar to that of logged best-effort broadcast.

3.7.2 Fail-Recovery Algorithm: Logged Majority-Ack URB

Algorithm 3.8, called "Logged Majority-Ack URB", implements logged uniform broadcast assuming a majority of the correct processes. The act of delivering (log-urbDeliver) a message m corresponds to logging the variable *delivered* with m in that variable. Besides *delivered*, the algorithm uses two other variables: *pending* and ack_m. Variable *pending* represents a set that gathers the messages that have been seen by a process but still need to be log-urbDelivered. This variable is logged. The ack_m set gathers, at each process p_i, the set of processes that p_i knows have seen m. The ack_m set is not logged: it can be reconstructed upon recovery. Messages are only appended to the *delivered* log when they have been retransmitted by a majority of the processes. This, together with the assumption of a correct majority, ensures that at least one correct process has logged the message, and this will ensure the retransmission to all correct processes.

Correctness. Consider the *agreement* property and assume some process p_i delivers (log-urbDelivers) a message m and does not crash. To do so, a majority of the processes must have retransmitted the message. As we assume a majority of the correct processes, at least one correct process must have logged the message (in *pending*). This process will ensure the eventual transmission (sp2pSend) of the message to all correct processes and all correct processes will hence acknowledge the message. Hence, every correct will deliver (log-urbDeliver) m. Consider the *validity* property and assume some process p_i broadcasts (log-urbBroadcasts) a message m and does not crash. Eventually, the message will be seen by all correct processes. As a majority is correct, a majority will retransmit the message: p_i will eventually log-urbDeliver m. The *no duplication* property is trivially ensured by the algorithm whereas the *no creation* property is ensured by the underlying channels.

Performance. Let m be any message that is broadcast (log-urbBroadcast) by some process p_i. A process delivers the message (log-urbDeliver) m after two communication steps and two causally related logging operations. (The logging of *pending* can be done in parallel).

3.8 Randomized Broadcast

This section considers randomized broadcast algorithms. These algorithms do not provide *deterministic* broadcast guarantees but, instead, only make probabilistic claims about such guarantees.

Of course, this approach can only be applied to applications that do not require full reliability. On the other hand, full reliability often induces a cost that is inacceptable in large-scale systems and, as we will see, it is often possible to build scalable randomized probabilistic algorithms while providing good reliability guarantees.

Algorithm 3.8 Logged Majority-Ack Uniform Reliable Broadcast

Implements:
　　LoggedUniformReliableBroadcast (log-urb).

Uses:
　　StubbornPointToPointLink (sp2p).

upon event ⟨ *Init* ⟩ **do**
　　forall m **do** $\text{ack}_m := \emptyset$;
　　pending := delivered := $\emptyset$;
　　store (pending, delivered);

upon event ⟨ *Recovery* ⟩ **do**
　　retrieve (pending, delivered);
　　trigger ⟨ *log-rbDeliver* | delivered ⟩;
　　forall $(s_m, m) \in$ pending **do**
　　　　forall $p_i \in \Pi$ **do trigger** ⟨ *sp2pSend* | p_i, [DATA, s_m, m] ⟩;

upon event ⟨ *log-urbBroadcast* | m ⟩ **do**
　　pending := pending $\cup \{(p_i, m)\}$;
　　store (pending);
　　$\text{ack}_m := \text{ack}_m \cup \{\text{self}\}$;
　　forall $p_i \in \Pi$ **do trigger** ⟨ *sp2pSend* | p_i, [DATA, p_i, m] ⟩;

upon event ⟨ *sp2pDeliver* | *src*, [DATA, s_m, m] ⟩ **do**
　　if $((s_m, m) \notin$ pending) **then**
　　　　pending := pending $\cup \{(s_m, m)\}$;
　　　　store (pending);
　　　　forall $p_i \in \Pi$ **do trigger** ⟨ *sp2pSend* | p_i, [DATA, s_m, m] ⟩;
　　if $(p_i \notin \text{ack}_m)$ **then**
　　　　$\text{ack}_m := \text{ack}_m \cup \{p_i\}$;
　　　　if $(|\text{ack}_m| > N/2) \wedge ((s_m, m) \notin$ delivered)**then**
　　　　　　delivered := delivered $\cup \{(s_m, m)\}$;
　　　　　　store (delivered);
　　　　　　trigger ⟨ *log-urbDeliver* | delivered ⟩;

3.8.1 The Scalability of Reliable Broadcast

As we have seen throughout this chapter, in order to ensure the reliability of broadcast in the presence of faulty processes (and/or links with omission failures), one needs to collect some form of *acknowledgment*. However, given limited bandwidth, memory, and processor resources, there will always be a limit to the number of acknowledgments that each process is able to collect and compute in due time. If the group of processes becomes very large (say, millions or even thousands of members in the group), a process collecting acknowledgments becomes overwhelmed by that task. This phenomenon is known as the *ack implosion* problem (see Figure 3.4a).

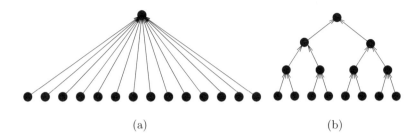

(a)   (b)

Fig. 3.4: Ack implosion and ack tree

There are several ways of mitigating the ack implosion problem. One way is to use some form of hierarchical scheme to collect acknowledgments, for instance, arranging the processes in a binary tree, as illustrated in Figure 3.4b. Hierarchies can reduce the load of each process but increase the latency in the task of collecting acknowledgments. Additionally, hierarchies need to be reconfigured when faults occur (which may not be a trivial task). Furthermore, even with this sort of hierarchies, the obligation to receive, directly or indirectly, an acknowledgment from every other process remains a fundamental scalability problem of reliable broadcast. In the next section we discuss how randomized approaches can circumvent this limitation.

3.8.2 Epidemic Dissemination

Nature gives us several examples of how a randomized approach can implement a fast and efficient broadcast primitive. Consider how epidemics are spread among a population. Initially, a single individual is infected; this individual in turn will infect some other individuals; after some period, the whole population is infected. Rumor spreading, or gossiping, is based exactly on the same sort of mechanism and has proved to be a very effective way to disseminate information.

A number of broadcast algorithms have been designed based on this principle and, not surprisingly, these are often called *epidemic, rumor mongering,* or *probabilistic broadcast* algorithms. Before giving more details on these algorithms, we first define the abstraction that they implement, which we call *probabilistic broadcast.* To illustrate how algorithms can implement the abstraction, we assume a model where processes can only fail by crashing.

3.8.3 Specification

Probabilistic broadcast is characterized by the properties PB1-3 depicted in Module 3.7. Note that only the *validity* property is probabilistic. The other properties are not.

Module 3.7 Interface and properties of probabilistic broadcast

Module:

    Name: ProbabilisticBroadcast (pb).

Events:

    Request: ⟨ *pbBroadcast* | m ⟩: Used to broadcast message m to all processes.

    Indication: ⟨ *pbDeliver* | src, m ⟩: Used to deliver message m broadcast by process *src*.

Properties:

    PB1: *Probabilistic validity:* There is a given probability such that for any two correct processes p_i and p_j, every message broadcast by p_i is eventually delivered by p_j with this probability.

    PB2: *No duplication:* No message is delivered more than once.

    PB3: *No creation:* If a message m is delivered by some process p_j, then m was previously broadcast by some process p_i.

As for previous communication abstractions we introduced in this chapter, we assume that messages are implicitly addressed to all processes in the system, i.e., the goal of the sender is to have its message delivered to all processes of a given group constituting what we call the system.

The reader may find similarities between the specification of probabilistic broadcast and the specification of best-effort broadcast presented in Section 3.2. In some sense, both are probabilistic approaches. However, in best-effort broadcast, the probability of delivery depends directly on the reliability of the processes: it is in this sense hidden under the probability of process failures. In probabilistic broadcast, it becomes explicit in the specification.

3.8.4 Randomized Algorithm: Eager Probabilistic Broadcast

Algorithm 3.9, called "Eager Probabilistic Broadcast", implements probabilistic broadcast. The sender selects k processes at random and sends them the message. In turn, each of these processes selects another k processes at random and forwards the message to those processes. Note that, in this algorithm, some or all of these processes may be exactly the processes already selected by the initial sender.

A step consisting of receiving a message and gossiping is called a *round*. The algorithm performs a maximum number of rounds r for each message.

The reader should observe here that k, also called the *fanout*, is a fundamental parameter of the algorithm. Its choice directly impacts the probability of reliable message delivery guaranteed by the algorithm. A higher value of k will not only increase the probability of having the entire population infected but will also decrease the number of rounds required to have the entire pop-

---

Algorithm 3.9 Eager Probabilistic Broadcast

Implements:
    ProbabilisticBroadcast (pb).

Uses:
    FairLossPointToPointLinks (flp2p).

upon event ⟨ *Init* ⟩ **do**
    delivered := ∅;

function pick-targets (ntargets) **returns** set of processes **is**
    targets := ∅;
    while (| targets | < ntargets) **do**
        candidate := random (Π);
        if (candidate ∉ targets) ∧ (candidate ≠ self) **then**
            targets := targets ∪ {candidate};
    return targets;

procedure gossip (msg) **is**
    forall t ∈ pick-targets (fanout) **do trigger** ⟨ *flp2pSend* | t, msg ⟩;

upon event ⟨ *pbBroadcast* | m ⟩ **do**
    gossip ([GOSSIP, self, m, maxrounds−1]);

upon event ⟨ *flp2pDeliver* | p_i, [GOSSIP, s_m, m, r] ⟩ **do**
    if (m ∉ delivered) **then**
        delivered := delivered ∪ {m}
        trigger ⟨ *pbDeliver* | s_m, m ⟩;
    if r > 0 **then** gossip ([GOSSIP, s_m, m, r − 1]);

---

ulation infected. Note also that the algorithm induces a significant amount of redundancy in the message exchanges: any given process may receive the same message more than once. The execution of the algorithm is illustrated in Figure 3.5 for a configuration with a fanout of 3.

The higher the fanout, the higher the load imposed on each process and the amount of redundant information exchanged in the network. Therefore, to select the appropriate k is of particular importance. The reader should also note that there are runs of the algorithm where a transmitted message may not be delivered to all correct processes. For instance, all the k processes that receive the message directly from the sender may select exactly the same k processes to forward the message to. In such a case, only these k processes will receive the message. This translates into the fact that the probability of reliable delivery is not 100%.

Correctness. The *no creation* and *no duplication* properties are immediate from the underlying channels we assume and the use of variable *delivery*. The probability of delivering a message to all correct processes depends on the size of the fanout and on the maximum number of rounds (maxrounds).

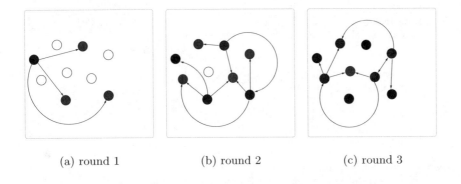

(a) round 1   (b) round 2   (c) round 3

Fig. 3.5: Epidemic (gossip) dissemination (fanout= 3)

Performance. The number of rounds needed for a message to be delivered by all correct processes also depends on the fanout. Roughly speaking, the higher the fanout, the higher is the number of messages exchanged at every round, and consequently the lower is the number of rounds needed for a message to reach all correct processes.

3.8.5 Randomized Algorithm: Lazy Probabilistic Broadcast

The "Eager Probabilistic Broadcast" algorithm we just described uses a gossip approach for the dissemination of messages. A major disadvantage of this approach is that it consumes a non negligible amount of resources with redundant transmissions. A way to overcome this limitation is to rely on a basic, possibly unreliable, but efficient broadcast primitive, when such a primitive is available. This primitive would be used to disseminate the messages first, and then the gossip approach would just be used as a backup to recover from message losses.

More precisely, we assume here the existence of a broadcast communication abstraction, defined by the primitives *unBroadcast* and *unDeliver*. We do not make specific assumptions on these, except that they could be used to exchange messages efficiently, without corrupting or adding messages to the system, and with nonzero probability of message delivery. The broadcast primitive could typically be implemented on top of fair-loss links. Of course, such a primitive might not always be available in settings that include a very large number of processes spread over the Internet.

Algorithm 3.10-3.11, called "Lazy Probabilistic Broadcast", assumes that each sender is transmitting a stream of numbered messages. Message omissions are detected based on gaps in the sequence numbers of received messages. Each message is disseminated using the unreliable broadcast primitive. For each message, some randomly selected receivers are chosen to store a copy

---

Algorithm 3.10 Lazy Probabilistic Broadcast (data dissemination)

Implements:
    ProbabilisticBroadcast (pb).

Uses:
    FairLossPointToPointLinks (flp2p);
    UnreliableBroadcast (un).

upon event ⟨ *Init* ⟩ **do**
    forall $p_i \in \Pi$ **do** delivered[p_i] := 0;
    lsn := 0; pending := stored := ∅;

procedure deliver-pending (s) **is**
    while exists [DATA, s, x, sn_x] ∈ pending **such that**
        sn_x = delivered[s]+1 **do**
            delivered[s] := delivered[s]+1;
            pending := pending \ {[DATA, s, x, sn_x]};
            trigger ⟨ *pbDeliver* | s, x ⟩;

procedure gossip (msg) **is**
    forall t ∈ pick-targets (fanout) **do**
    trigger ⟨ *flp2pSend* | t, msg ⟩;

upon event ⟨ *pbBroadcast* | m ⟩ **do**
    lsn := lsn+1; **trigger** ⟨ *unBroadcast* | [DATA, self, m, lsn] ⟩;

upon event ⟨ *unDeliver* | p_i, [DATA, s_m, m, sn_m] ⟩ **do**
    if (*random*() > store-threshold) **then**
        stored := stored ∪ { [DATA, s_m, m, sn_m] };
    if (sn_m = delivered[s_m]+1) **then**
        delivered[s_m] := delivered[s_m]+1;
        trigger ⟨ *pbDeliver* | s_m, m ⟩;
    else if (sn_m > delivered[s_m]+1) **then**
        pending := pending ∪ { [DATA, s_m, m, sn_m] };
        forall seqnb ∈ [delivered[s_m] + 1, sn_m − 1] **do**
            gossip ([REQUEST, self, s_m, seqnb, maxrounds−1]);
        startTimer (TimeDelay, p_i, sn_m);

---

of the message for future retransmission; they store the message for some maximum amount of time. The purpose of this approach is to distribute, among all processes, the load of storing messages for future retransmission.

Omissions can be detected using sequence numbers associated with messages. A process p detects that it has missed a message from a process q when p receives a message from q with a larger timestamp than what p was expecting from q. When a process detects an omission, it uses the gossip algorithm to disseminate a retransmission request. If the request is received by one of the processes that has stored a copy of the message, then this process retransmits the message. Note that, in this case, the gossip algorithm *does not* need to be configured to ensure that the retransmission request reaches

---

Algorithm 3.11 Lazy Probabilistic Broadcast (recovery)

---

upon event $\langle$ *flp2pDeliver* | p_j, [REQUEST, p_i, s_m, sn_m, r] $\rangle$ **do**
    if ([DATA, s_m, m, sn_m] $\in$ stored) **then**
        trigger $\langle$ *flp2pSend* | p_i, [DATA, s_m, m, sn_m] $\rangle$;
    else if ($r > 0$) **then** gossip ([REQUEST, p_i, s_m, sn_m, $r - 1$]);

upon event $\langle$ *flp2pDeliver* | p_j, [DATA, s_m, m, sn_m] $\rangle$ **do**
    if (sn_m = delivered[s_m]+1) **then**
        delivered[s_m] := delivered[s_m]+1;
        trigger $\langle$ *pbDeliver* | s_m, m $\rangle$;
        deliver-pending (s_m);
    else
        pending := pending $\cup$ { [DATA, s_m, m, sn_m] };

upon event $\langle$ *Timeout* | s, sn $\rangle$
    if sn = delivered[s]+1 **then** delivered[s] := delivered[s]+1;

---

all processes: it is enough that it reaches, with high probability, one of the processes that has stored a copy of the missing message. With small probability, recovery will fail. In this case, after some time, the message is simply marked as delivered, such that subsequent messages from the same sender can be delivered.

Correctness. The *no creation* and *no duplication* properties follow from the underlying channels and the use of timestamps. The probability of delivering a message to all correct processes depends here on the fanout (as in the "Eager Probabilistic Broadcast" algorithm) as well as on the reliability of the underlying disseminatination primitive.

Performance. Clearly, and assuming an underlying dissemination primitive that is efficient and reasonably reliable, the broadcasting of a message is much more effective than in the "Eager Probabilistic Broadcast" algorithm.

It is expected that, in most cases, the retransmission request message is much smaller that the original data message. Therefore, this algorithm is also much more resource effective than the "Eager Probabilistic Broadcast."

Practical algorithms based on this principle make a significant effort to optimize the number of processes that store copies of each broadcast message. Not surprisingly, the best results can be obtained if the physical network topology is taken into account: for instance, an omission in a link connecting a local area network (LAN) with the rest of the system affects all processes in that LAN. Thus, it is desirable to have a copy of the message in each LAN (to recover from local omissions) and a copy outside the LAN (to recover from the omission in the link to the LAN). Similarly, the retransmission procedure, instead of being completely random, may search first for a copy in the local LAN and only afterward at more distant processes.

3.9 Causal Broadcast

So far, we have not considered any ordering guarantee among messages delivered by different processes. In particular, when we consider a reliable broadcast abstraction, messages can be delivered in any order and the reliability guarantees are in a sense orthogonal to such an order.

In this section, we discuss the issue of ensuring message delivery according to *causal ordering*. This is a generalization of FIFO (*first-in first-out*) ordering, where messages from the same process should be delivered in the order in which they were broadcast.

3.9.1 Overview

Consider the case of a distributed message board that manages two types of information: proposals and comments on previous proposals. To make the interface user-friendly, comments are depicted attached to the proposal they are referring to.

In order to make it highly available, it is natural to implement the board application by replicating all the information to all participants. This can be achieved through the use of a reliable broadcast primitive to disseminate both proposals and comments. With a reliable broadcast, the following sequence would be possible: participant p_1 broadcasts a message m_1 containing a new proposal; participant p_2 delivers m_1 and disseminates a comment in message m_2; due to message delays, another participant p_3 delivers m_2 before m_1. In this case, the application at p_3 would be forced to keep m_2 and wait for m_1, in order not to present the comment before the proposal being commented. In fact, m_2 is causally after m_1 ($m_1 \rightarrow m_2$), and a causal order primitive would make sure that m_1 would have been delivered before m_2, relieving the application programmer from performing such a task.

3.9.2 Specifications

As the name indicates, a *causal order abstraction* ensures that messages are delivered respecting cause-effect relations. This is expressed by the *happened-before* relation described earlier in this book (Section 2.4.1). This relation, also called the *causal order* relation, when applied to the messages exchanged among processes, is captured by broadcast and delivery events. In this case, we say that a message m_1 may potentially have caused another message m_2 (or m_1 happened before m_2), denoted as $m_1 \rightarrow m_2$, if any of the following relations applies:

- m_1 and m_2 were broadcast by the same process p and m_1 was broadcast before m_2 (Figure 3.6a).
- m_1 was delivered by process p, m_2 was broadcast by process p, and m_2 was broadcast after the delivery of m_1 (Figure 3.6b).

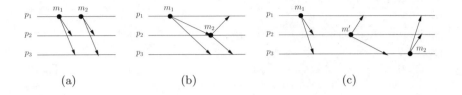

Fig. 3.6: Causal order of messages

Module 3.8 Causal order property

Module:

    Name: CausalOrder (co).

Events:

    Request: $\langle$ *coBroadcast* | m $\rangle$: Used to broadcast message m to Π.

    Indication: $\langle$ *coDeliver* | src, m $\rangle$: Used to deliver message m broadcast by process *src*.

Properties:

    CB: *Causal delivery:* No process p_i delivers a message m_2 unless p_i has already delivered every message m_1 such that $m_1 \rightarrow m_2$.

- there exists some message m' such that $m_1 \rightarrow m'$ and $m' \rightarrow m_2$ (Figure 3.6c).

Using the causal order relation, one can define a broadcast with the property CB in Module 3.8. The property states that messages are delivered by the broadcast abstraction according to the causal order relation. There must be no "holes" in the causal past, i.e., when a message is delivered, all preceding messages have already been delivered.

Clearly, a broadcast primitive that has only to ensure the *causal delivery* property might not be very useful: the property might be ensured by having no process ever deliver any message. However, the *causal delivery* property can be combined with both reliable broadcast and uniform reliable broadcast semantics. These combinations would have the interface and properties of Module 3.9 and Module 3.10, respectively.

To simplify, we call the first *causal order broadcast* and the second *uniform causal order broadcast* (we skip the term *reliable*). The reader might wonder at this point whether it would make sense to also consider a *causal best-effort broadcast* abstraction, combining the properties of best-effort broadcast with the *causal delivery* property. As we show through an exercise at the end of the chapter, this would inherently be also reliable.

Module 3.9 Properties of causal broadcast

Module:

   Name: ReliableCausalOrder (rco).

Events:

   ⟨ *rcoBroadcast* | m ⟩ and ⟨ *rcoDeliver* | src, m ⟩: with the same meaning
   and interface as the causal order interface.

Properties:

   RB1–RB4 from reliable broadcast and **CB** from causal order broadcast.

Module 3.10 Properties of uniform causal broadcast

Module:

   Name: UniformReliableCausalOrder (urco).

Events:

   ⟨ *urcoBroadcast* | m ⟩ and ⟨ *urcoDeliver* | src, m ⟩: with the same meaning
   and interface as the causal order interface.

Properties:

   URB1–URB4 from uniform reliable broadcast and **CB** from causal order
   broadcast.

3.9.3 Fail-Silent Algorithm: No-Waiting Causal Broadcast

Algorithm 3.12, called "No-Waiting Causal Broadcast", uses an underlying
reliable broadcast communication abstraction defined through rbBroadcast
and rbDeliver primitives. The same algorithm could be used to implement
a uniform causal broadcast abstraction, simply by replacing the underlying
reliable broadcast module by a uniform reliable broadcast module.

   The algorithm is said to be *no-waiting* in the following sense: whenever a
process rbDelivers a message m, it rcoDelivers m without waiting for other
messages to be rbDelivered. Each message m carries a control field called
$past_m$. The $past_m$ field of a message m includes all messages that causally
precede m. When a message m is rbDelivered, $past_m$ is first inspected: messages in $past_m$ that have not been rcoDelivered must be rcoDelivered before
m itself is also rcoDelivered. In order to record its own causal past, each
process p memorizes all the messages it has rcoBroadcast or rcoDelivered in
a local variable *past*. Note that *past* (and $past_m$) are ordered sets.

   As we pointed out, an important feature of Algorithm 3.12 is that the
rcoDelivery of a message is never delayed in order to enforce causal order. This
is illustrated in Figure 3.7. Consider, for instance, process p_4 that rbDelivers
message m_2. Since m_2 carries m_1 in its *past*, m_1 and m_2 are rcoDelivered in
order. Finally, when m_1 is rbDelivered from p_1, m_1 is discarded.

Correctness. All properties of reliable broadcast follow from the use of an
underlying reliable broadcast primitive and the no-waiting flavor of the algo-

---

Algorithm 3.12 No-Waiting Causal Broadcast

Implements:
    ReliableCausalOrder (rco).

Uses:
    ReliableBroadcast (rb).

upon event ⟨ *Init* ⟩ **do**
    delivered := ∅;
    past := ∅

upon event ⟨ *rcoBroadcast* | *m* ⟩ **do**
    trigger ⟨ *rbBroadcast* | [DATA, *past*, *m*] ⟩;
    past := past ∪ {(self,*m*)};

upon event ⟨ *rbDeliver* | p_i, [DATA, $past_m$, *m*] ⟩ **do**
    if (*m* ∉ delivered) **then**
        forall (s_n, n) ∈ $past_m$ **do** // in a deterministic order
            if (*n* ∉ delivered) **then**
                trigger ⟨ *rcoDeliver* | s_n, n ⟩;
                delivered := delivered ∪ {*n*}
                past := past ∪ {(s_n, n)};
        trigger ⟨ *rcoDeliver* | p_i, m ⟩;
        delivered := delivered ∪ {*m*};
        past := past ∪ {(p_i, m)};

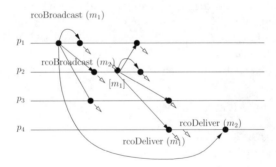

Fig. 3.7: Sample execution of causal broadcast with complete past

rithm. The causal order property is enforced by having every message carry its causal past and every process making sure that it rcoDelivers the causal past of a message before rcoDelivering the message.

Performance. The algorithm does not add additional communication steps or send extra messages with respect to the underlying reliable broadcast algorithm. However, the size of the messages grows linearly with time. In particular, the *past* field may become extremely large in long running executions, since it includes the complete causal past of the process.

In the next subsection, we present a simple scheme to reduce the size of *past*. We will later discuss an algorithm ("Waiting Causal Broadcast") that completely eliminates the need for exchanging past messages.

3.9.4 Fail-Stop Extension: Garbage Collecting the Causal Past

We now present a very simple optimization of the "No-Waiting Causal Broadcast" algorithm, depicted in Algorithm 3.13, to delete messages from the *past* variable. Algorithm 3.13 assumes a fail-stop model: it uses a perfect failure detector. The algorithm is a kind of distributed garbage collection scheme and it works as follows: when a process rbDelivers a message m, the process rbBroadcasts an *Ack* message to all other processes; when an *Ack* for message m has been rbDelivered from all correct processes, m is purged from *past*.

This distributed garbage collection scheme does not impact the correctness of our "No-Waiting Causal Broadcast" algorithm provided the *strong accuracy* property of the failure detector is indeed ensured. We purge a message only if this message has been rbDelivered by all correct processes.

If the *completeness* property of the failure detector is violated, then the only risk is to keep messages that could have been purged: correctness is not affected. In terms of performance, acknowledgment messages are indeed added (N^2 acknowledgment messages for each data message), but these can be grouped and performed in batch mode: they do not need to slow down the main path of rcoDelivering a message.

Even with this optimization, the *no-waiting* approach might be considered too expensive in terms of bandwidth. We present, in the following, an approach that tackles the problem at the expense of *waiting*.

3.9.5 Fail-Silent Algorithm: Waiting Causal Broadcast

Like Algorithm 3.12 ("No-Waiting Causal Broadcast"), Algorithm 3.14, called "Waiting Causal Broadcast", relies on an underlying reliable broadcast communication abstraction defined through rbBroadcast and rbDeliver primitives.

Instead of keeping a record of all past messages, however, the idea is to represent the past with a vector of *sequence numbers*. More precisely, *past* is now represented with an array of integers called a *vector clock*. The vector basically captures the causal precedence between messages. An auxiliary function *rank*, converts the process indentifier in an integer that can be used as an index in the vector (i.e., $rank(p_1)= 1$, ..., $rank(p_n)= n$).

Every process p maintains a vector clock that represents the number of messages that p has rcoDelivered from every other process, and the number of messages it has itself rcoBroadcast. This vector is then attached to every message m that p rcoBroadcasts. A process q that rbDelivers m compares

---

Algorithm 3.13 Garbage Collection of Past

Implements:
    ReliableCausalOrder (rco).

Extends:
    No-waiting Causal Broadcast (Algorithm 3.12).

Uses:
    ReliableBroadcast (rb);
    PerfectFailureDetector ($\mathcal{P}$).

upon event $\langle$ *Init* $\rangle$ **do**
    delivered := past := $\emptyset$;
    correct := Π;
    forall m **do** ack$_m$:= $\emptyset$;

upon event $\langle$ *crash* $\mid p_i$ $\rangle$ **do**
    correct := correct $\setminus \{p_i\}$;

upon exists $m \in$ delivered **such that** self $\notin$ ack$_m$ **do**
    ack$_m$:= ack$_m \cup \{$self$\}$;
    trigger $\langle$ *rbBroadcast* $\mid$ [ACK, m] $\rangle$;

upon event $\langle$ *rbDeliver* $\mid p_i$, [ACK, m] $\rangle$ **do**
    ack$_m$:= ack$_m \cup \{p_i\}$;
    if (correct $\subseteq$ ack$_m$) **then** past := past$\setminus\{(s_m, m)\}$;

---

this vector with its own vector to determine how many messages are missing (if any), and from which processes. Process q needs to rcoDeliver all these missing messages before it can rcoDeliver m.

As its name indicates ("Waiting Causal Broadcast"), and as we explain below, the algorithm forces (sometimes) processes to *wait* before rcoDelivering a message they had rbDelivered. This is the price to pay for limiting the size of the messages. Indeed, it is possible that a message may be prevented from being rcoDelivered immediately when it is rbDelivered, because some of the preceeding messages have not been rbDelivered yet. It is on the other hand possible that the rbDelivery of a single message triggers the rcoDelivery of several messages that were waiting to be rcoDelivered. For instance, in Figure 3.8, message m_2 is rbDelivered to p_4 before message m_1, but its rcoDelivery is delayed until m_1 is rbDelivered and rcoDelivered.

Correctness. The *no duplication* and *no creation* properties follow from those of the underlying reliable broadcast abstraction.

Consider a message m that is rcoDelivered by some correct process p. Due to the *agreement* property of the underlying reliable broadcast, every correct process eventually rbDelivers m. According to the algorithm, every correct process also eventually rbDelivers every message that causally precedes m. Hence, every correct process eventually rcoDelivers m. Consider now *validity*

Algorithm 3.14 Waiting Causal Broadcast

Implements:
    ReliableCausalOrder(rco).

Uses:
    ReliableBroadcast (rb).

upon event ⟨ *init* ⟩ **do**
    forall $p_i \in \Pi$ **do** VC[$rank(p_i)$] := 0;
    pending := $\emptyset$;

procedure deliver-pending **is**
    while exists $(s_x, [\text{DATA}, VC_x, x]) \in$ pending **such that**
        $\forall_{p_j}$:VC[$rank(p_j)$] $\geq$VC$_x$[$rank(p_j)$] **do**
            pending := pending $\setminus (s_x, [\text{DATA}, VC_x, x])$;
            trigger ⟨ *rcoDeliver* | s_x, x ⟩;
            VC[$rank(s_x)$] := VC[$rank(s_x)$]+1;

upon event ⟨ *rcoBroadcast* | m ⟩ **do**
    trigger ⟨ *rcoDeliver* | self, m ⟩;
    trigger ⟨ *rbBroadcast* | [DATA, VC, m] ⟩;
    VC[$rank$(self)] := VC[$rank$(self)] + 1;

upon event ⟨ *rbDeliver* | p_i, [DATA, VC_m, m] ⟩ **do**
    if $p_i \neq$ self **then**
        pending := pending $\cup$ $(p_i, [\text{DATA}, VC_m, m])$;
        deliver-pending;

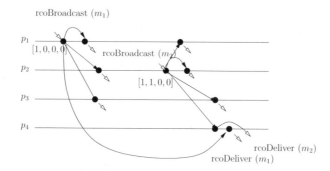

Fig. 3.8: Sample execution of waiting-causal broadcast

and a message m that is rcoBroadcast by some correct process p. According to the algorithm, p directly rcoDelivers m.

Consider now the *causal order* property. Due to the use of the vector clocks, if a message m_1 precedes m_2, no process rcoDelivers m_2 before rcoDelivering m_1.

Performance. The algorithm does not add any additional communication steps or messages to the underlying reliable broadcast algorithm. The size of the message header is linear with regard to the number of processes in the system.

Variant. We discuss through an exercise at the end of this chapter a uniform variant of the "Waiting Causal Broadcast" algorithm.

3.10 Hands-On

We now describe the implementation, in *Appia*, of several of the protocols introduced in this chapter.

3.10.1 Basic Broadcast

The communication stack used to illustrate the protocol is the following:

Application
Best-Effort Broadcast   **(implemented by Basic Broadcast)**
Perfect Point-to-Point Links   (implemented by TcpBasedPerfectP2P)

The implementation of this algorithm closely follows Algorithm 3.1 ("Basic Broadcast"). As shown in Listing 3.1, this protocol only handles three classes of events, namely, the ProcessInitEvent, used to initialize the set of processes that participate in the broadcast (this event is triggered by the application after reading the configuration file), the ChannelInit event, automatically triggered by the runtime when a new channel is created, and the SendableEvent. This last event is associated with transmission requests (if the event flows in the stack downward) or the reception of events from the layer below (if the event flows upward). Note that the code in these listing has been simplified. In particular, all exception handling code was deleted from the listings for clarity (but is included in the code distributed with the book).

The only method that requires some coding is the bebBroadcast() method, which is in charge of sending a series of point-to-point messages to all members of the group. This is performed by executing the following instructions for each member of the group: i) the event being sent is "cloned" (this effectively copies the data to be sent to a new event); ii) the source and destination address of the point-to-point message are set; iii) the event is forwarded to the layer below. There is a single exception to this procedure: if the destination process is the sender itself, the event is immediately delivered to the upper layer. The method to process messages received from the the layer below is very simple: it just forwards the message up.

Listing 3.1. Basic Broadcast implementation

```
package appia.protocols.tutorialDA.basicBroadcast;

public class BasicBroadcastSession extends Session {

    private ProcessSet processes;

    public BasicBroadcastSession(Layer layer) {
        super(layer);
    }


    public void handle(Event event){
        if(event instanceof ChannelInit)
            handleChannelInit((ChannelInit)event);
        else if(event instanceof ProcessInitEvent)
            handleProcessInitEvent((ProcessInitEvent) event);
        else if(event instanceof SendableEvent){
            if(event.getDir()==Direction.DOWN)
                // UPON event from the above protocol (or application)
                bebBroadcast((SendableEvent) event);
            else
                // UPON event from the bottom protocol (or perfect point2point links)
                pp2pDeliver((SendableEvent) event);
        }
    }

    private void handleProcessInitEvent(ProcessInitEvent event) {
        processes = event.getProcessSet();
        event.go();
    }

    private void handleChannelInit(ChannelInit init) {
        init.go();
    }

    private void bebBroadcast(SendableEvent event) {
        SampleProcess[] processArray = this.processes.getAllProcesses();
        SendableEvent sendingEvent = null;
        for(int i=0 ; i<processArray.length ; i++){
            // source and destination for data message
            sendingEvent = (SendableEvent) event.cloneEvent();
            sendingEvent.source = processes.getSelfProcess().getInetWithPort();
            sendingEvent.dest = processArray[i].getInetWithPort();
            // set the event fields
            sendingEvent.setSource(this); // the session that created the event
            if(i == processes.getSelfRank())
                sendingEvent.setDir(Direction.UP);
            sendingEvent.init();
            sendingEvent.go();
        }
    }

    private void pp2pDeliver(SendableEvent event) {
        event.go();
    }
}
```

Try It. The previous implementation may be experimented with using a simple test application, called SampleAppl. An optional parameter in the command line allows the user to select which protocol stack the application will use. The general format of the command line is the following:

```
java demo/tutorialDA/SampleAppl -f <cf> -n <rank> -qos <prot>
```

The `cf` parameter is the name of a text file with the information about the
set of processes, namely, the total number N of processes in the system and,
for each of these processes, its "rank" and "endpoint." The rank is a unique
logical identifier of each process (an integer from 0 to $N-1$). The "endpoint"
is just the host name or IP address and the port number of the process. This
information is used by low-level protocols (such as TCP or UDP) to establish the links among the processes. The configuration file has the following
format:

```
<number_of_processes>
<rank> <host_name> <port>
...
<rank> <host_name> <port>
```

For example, the following configuration file could be used to define a
group of three processes, all running on the local machine:

```
3
0 localhost 25000
1 localhost 25100
2 localhost 25200
```

The `rank` parameter identifies the rank of the process being launched
(and, implicitly, the address to be used by the process, taken from the configuration file).

As noted above, `prot` parameter specifies which abstraction is used by
the application. There are several possible values. To test our basic broadcast implementation, use the value "*beb*." After all processes are launched,
a message can be sent from one process to the other processes by typing a
`bcast <string>` in the command line and pressing the `Enter` key.

3.10.2 Lazy Reliable Broadcast

The communication stack used to illustrate the protocol is the following:

Application
Reliable Broadcast **(implemented by Lazy RB)**
Perfect Failure Detector (implemented by TcpBasedPFD)
Best-Effort Broadcast (implemented by Basic Broadcast)
Perfect Point-to-Point Links (implemented by TcpBasedPerfectP2P)

The implementation of this algorithm, shown in Listing 3.2, closely follows Algorithm 3.2 ("Lazy Reliable Broadcast"). The protocol accepts four events, namely, the ProcessInitEvent, used to initialize the set of processes that participate in the broadcast (this event is triggered by the application after reading the configuration file), the ChannelInit event, automatically triggered by the runtime when a new channel is created, the Crash event, triggered by the PFD when a node crashes, and the SendableEvent. This last event is associated with transmission requests (if the event flows in the stack downward) or the reception of events from the layer below (if the event flows upward). Note that the code in these listings has been simplified. In particular, all exception handling code was deleted from the listings for clarity (but is included in the code distributed with the book).

In order to detect duplicates, each message needs to be uniquely identified. In this implementation, the protocol uses the rank of the sender of the message and a sequence number. This information needs to be pushed into the message header when a message is sent, and then popped again when the message is received. Note that during the retransmission phase, it is possible for the same message, with the same identifier, to be broadcast by different processes.

In the protocol, broadcasting a message consists of pushing the message identifier and forwarding the request to the Best-Effort layer. Receiving the message consists of popping the message identifier, checking for duplicates, and logging and delivering the message when it is received for the first time. Upon a crash notification, all messages from the crashed node are broadcast again. Note that when a node receives a message for the first time, if the sender is already detected to have crashed, the message is immediately retransmitted.

Listing 3.2. Lazy Reliable Broadcast implementation

```
package appia.protocols.tutorialDA.lazyRB;

public class LazyRBSession extends Session {
    private ProcessSet processes;
    private int seqNumber;
    private LinkedList[] from;
    private LinkedList delivered;

    public LazyRBSession(Layer layer) {
        super(layer);
        seqNumber = 0;
    }

    public void handle(Event event){
        // (...)
    }

    private void handleChannelInit(ChannelInit init) {
        init.go();
        delivered = new LinkedList();
    }

    private void handleProcessInitEvent(ProcessInitEvent event) {
        processes = event.getProcessSet();
```

```
            event.go();
            from = new LinkedList[processes.getSize()];
            for (int i=0; i<from.length; i++)
                from[i] = new LinkedList();
      }

      private void rbBroadcast(SendableEvent event) {
            SampleProcess self = processes.getSelfProcess();
            MessageID msgID = new MessageID(self.getProcessNumber(),seqNumber);
            seqNumber++;
            ((ExtendedMessage)event.getMessage()).pushObject(msgID);
            bebBroadcast(event);
      }

      private void bebDeliver(SendableEvent event) {
            MessageID msgID = (MessageID) ((ExtendedMessage)event.getMessage()).peekObject();
            if ( ! delivered.contains(msgID) ){
                delivered.add(msgID);
                SendableEvent cloned = (SendableEvent) event.cloneEvent();
                ((ExtendedMessage)event.getMessage()).popObject();
                event.go();
                SampleProcess pi = processes.getProcess((InetWithPort) event.source);
                int piNumber = pi.getProcessNumber();
                from[piNumber].add(event);
                if ( ! pi.isCorrect() ){
                    SendableEvent retransmit = (SendableEvent) cloned.cloneEvent();
                    bebBroadcast(retransmit);
                }
            }
      }

      private void bebBroadcast(SendableEvent event) {
            event.setDir(Direction.DOWN);
            event.setSource(this);
            event.init ();
            event.go();
      }

      private void handleCrash(Crash crash) {
            int pi = crash.getCrashedProcess();
            System.out.println("Process "+pi+" failed.");
            processes.getProcess(pi).setCorrect(false);
            SendableEvent event = null;
            ListIterator it = from[pi].listIterator ();
            while(it.hasNext()){
                event = (SendableEvent) it.next();
                bebBroadcast(event);
            }
            from[pi].clear ();
      }
}
```

Try It. To test the implementation of the "Lazy Reliable Broadcast" protocol, we will use the same test application that we have used for the basic broadcast. Please refer to the corresponding "try it" section for details.

The `prot` parameter should be used in this case with value "*rb*." Note that the "Lazy Reliable Broadcast" algorithm uses the perfect failure detector module. As described in the previous chapter, this module needs to be activated. For this purpose, the test application also accepts the `startpfd` command; do not forget to initiate the PFD for every process by issuing the `startpfd` request on the command line before testing the protocol.

Hand-On Exercise 3.1 *This implementation of the Reliable Broadcast algorithm has a* delivered *set that is never garbage collected. Modify the implementation to remove messages that no longer need to be maintained in the* delivered *set.*

3.10.3 All-Ack Uniform Reliable Broadcast

The communication stack used to illustrate the protocol is the following:

Application
Uniform Reliable Broadcast **(implemented by All-Ack Uniform Reliable Broadcast)**
Perfect Failure Detector (implemented by TcpBasedPFD)
Best-Effort Broadcast (implemented by Basic Broadcast)
Perfect Point-to-Point Links (implemented by TcpBasedPerfectP2P)

The implementation of this protocol is shown in Listing 3.3. Note that the code in these listings has been simplified. In particular, all exception handling code was deleted from the listings for clarity (but is included in the code distributed with the book).

The protocol uses two variables, received and delivered to register which messages have already been received and delivered, respectively. These variables only store message identifiers. When a message is received for the first time, it is forwarded as specified in the algorithm. To keep track on who has already acknowledged (forwarded) a given message, a hash table is used. There is an entry in the hash table for each message. This entry keeps the data message itself (for future delivery) and a record of who has forwarded the message.

When a message has been forwarded by every correct process, it can be delivered. This is checked every time a new event is handled (as both the reception of messages and the crash of processes may trigger the delivery of pending messages).

Listing 3.3. All-Ack Uniform Reliable Broadcast implementation

---

```
package appia.protocols.tutorialDA.allAckURB;

public class AllAckURBSession extends Session {
  private ProcessSet processes;
  private int seqNumber;
  private LinkedList received, delivered;
  private Hashtable ack;
```

```
public AllAckURBSession(Layer layer) {
  super(layer);
}

public void handle(Event event) {
  // (...)
  urbTryDeliver();
}

private void urbTryDeliver() {
  Iterator  it = ack.values(). iterator ();
  MessageEntry entry=null;
  while( it.hasNext() ){
    entry = (MessageEntry) it.next();
    if(canDeliver(entry)){
      delivered.add(entry.messageID);
      urbDeliver(entry.event, entry.messageID.process);
    }
  }
}

private boolean canDeliver(MessageEntry entry) {
  int procSize = processes.getSize ();
  for(int i=0; i<procSize; i++)
    if(processes.getProcess(i). isCorrect() && (! entry.acks[i]) )
      return false;
  return ( (! delivered.contains(entry.messageID)) && received.contains(entry.messageID) );
}

private void handleChannelInit(ChannelInit init) {
  init .go();
  received = new LinkedList();
  delivered = new LinkedList();
  ack = new Hashtable();
}

private void handleProcessInitEvent(ProcessInitEvent event) {
  processes = event.getProcessSet();
  event.go();
}

private void urbBroadcast(SendableEvent event) {
  SampleProcess self = processes.getSelfProcess ();
  MessageID msgID = new MessageID(self.getProcessNumber(),seqNumber);
  seqNumber++;
  received.add(msgID);
  ((ExtendedMessage) event.getMessage()).pushObject(msgID);
  event.go ();
}

private void bebDeliver(SendableEvent event) {
  SendableEvent clone = (SendableEvent) event.cloneEvent();
  MessageID msgID = (MessageID) ((ExtendedMessage) clone.getMessage()).popObject();
  addAck(clone,msgID);
  if ( ! received.contains(msgID) ){
    received.add(msgID);
    bebBroadcast(event);
  }
}

private void bebBroadcast(SendableEvent event) {
  event.setDir(Direction.DOWN);
  event.setSource(this);
  event. init ();
  event.go();
```

```
  }

  private void urbDeliver(SendableEvent event, int sender) {
    event.setDir(Direction.UP);
    event.setSource(this);
    event.source = processes.getProcess(sender).getInetWithPort();
    event.init ();
    event.go ();
  }

  private void handleCrash(Crash crash) {
    int crashedProcess = crash.getCrashedProcess();
    System.out.println("Process_"+crashedProcess+"_failed.");
    processes.getProcess(crashedProcess).setCorrect(false);
  }

  private void addAck(SendableEvent event, MessageID msgID){
    int pi = processes.getProcess((InetWithPort)event.source).getProcessNumber();
    MessageEntry entry = (MessageEntry) ack.get(msgID);
    if(entry == null){
      entry = new MessageEntry(event, msgID, processes.getSize());
      ack.put(msgID,entry);
    }
    entry.acks[pi] = true;
  }
}
```

Try It. To test the implementation of the "All-Ack Uniform Reliable Broadcast" protocol, we will use the same test application that we have used for the basic broadcast. Please refer to the corresponding "try it" section for details.

The `prot` parameter that should be used in this case is "*urb.*" Note that the All-Ack Uniform Reliable Broadcast protocol uses the perfect failure detector module. As described in the previous chapter, this module needs to be activated. For this purpose, the test application also accepts the `startpfd` command; do not forget to initiate the PFD at every processes by issuing the `startpfd` request on the command line before testing the protocol.

Hand-On Exercise 3.2 *Modify the implementation to keep track just of the last message sent from each process in the received and delivered variables.*

Hand-On Exercise 3.3 *Change the protocol to exchange acknowledgments when the sender is correct, and only retransmit the payload of a message when the sender is detected to have crashed (just like in the Lazy Reliable Protocol).*

3.10.4 Majority-Ack URB

The communication stack used to illustrate the protocol is the following (note that a Perfect Failure Detector is no longer required):

Application
Uniform Reliable Broadcast   **(implemented by Majority-Ack URB)**
Best-Effort Broadcast   (implemented by Basic Broadcast)
Perfect Point-to-Point Links   (implemented by TcpBasedPerfectP2P)

The protocol works in the same way as the protocol presented in the prevous section, but without being aware of crashed processes. Besides that, the only difference from the previous implementation is the `canDeliver()` method, which is shown in Listing 3.4.

Listing 3.4. Indulgent Uniform Reliable Broadcast implementation

---

```
package appia.protocols.tutorialDA.majorityAckURB;

public class MajorityAckURBSession extends Session {

  private boolean canDeliver(MessageEntry entry) {
    int N = processes.getSize(), numAcks = 0;
    for(int i=0; i<N; i++)
      if(entry.acks[i])
        numAcks++;
    return (numAcks > (N/2)) && ( ! delivered.contains(entry.messageID) );
  }

    // Except for the method above, and for the handling of the crash event, same
    // as in the previous protocol
}
```

Try It. To test the implementation of the Majority-Ack uniform reliable broadcast protocol, we will use the same test application that we have used for the basic broadcast. Please refer to the corresponding "try it" section for details. The `prot` parameter that should be used in this case is *"iurb."*

Hand-On Exercise 3.4 *Note that if a process does not acknowledge a message, copies of that message may have to be stored for a long period (in fact, if a process crashes, copies need to be stored forever). Try to devise a scheme to ensure that no more than $N/2 + 1$ copies of each message are preserved in the system (that is, not all members should be required to keep a copy of every message).*

3.10.5 Probabilistic Reliable Broadcast

This protocol is based on probabilities and is used to broadcast messages in large groups. Instead of creating Perfect Point-to-Point Links, it use Unreliable Point-to-Point Links (UP2PL) to send messages just for a subset of the group. The communication stack used to illustrate the protocol is the following:

Application
Probabilistic Broadcast   **(implemented by Eager PB)**
Unreliable Point-to-Point Links   (implemented by TcpBasedPerfectP2P)

The protocol has two configurable parameters: i) *fanout* is the number of processes for which the message will be gossiped about; ii) *maxrounds*, is the maximum number of rounds that the message will be retransmitted.

The implementation of this protocol is shown on Listing 3.5. The gossip() method invokes the pickTargets() method to choose the processes to which the message is going to be sent and sends the message to those targets. The pickTargets() method chooses targets randomly from the set of processes. Each message carries its identification (as previous reliable broadcast protocols) and the remaining number of rounds (when the message is gossiped again, the number of rounds is decremented).

Listing 3.5. Probabilistic Broadcast implementation

```
package appia.protocols.tutorialDA.eagerPB;

public class EagerPBSession extends Session {

  private LinkedList delivered;
  private ProcessSet processes;
  private int fanout, maxRounds, seqNumber;

  public EagerPBSession(Layer layer) {
    super(layer);
    EagerPBLayer pbLayer = (EagerPBLayer) layer;
    fanout = pbLayer.getFanout();
    maxRounds = pbLayer.getMaxRounds();
    seqNumber = 0;
  }

  public void handle(Event event){
    // (...)
  }

  private void handleChannelInit(ChannelInit init) {
    init .go ();
    delivered = new LinkedList();
  }

  private void handleProcessInitEvent(ProcessInitEvent event) {
    processes = event.getProcessSet();
    fanout = Math.min (fanout, processes.getSize ());
    event.go ();
  }

  private void pbBroadcast(SendableEvent event) {
    MessageID msgID = new MessageID(processes.getSelfRank(),seqNumber);
    seqNumber++;
    gossip(event, msgID, maxRounds−1);
  }

  private void up2pDeliver(SendableEvent event) {
    SampleProcess pi = processes.getProcess((InetWithPort)event.source);
    int round = ((ExtendedMessage) event.getMessage()).popInt();
    MessageID msgID = (MessageID) ((ExtendedMessage) event.getMessage()).popObject();
```

```
    if ( ! delivered.contains(msgID) ){
      delivered.add(msgID);
      SendableEvent clone = null;
      clone = (SendableEvent) event.cloneEvent();
      pbDeliver(clone,msgID);
    }
    if(round > 0)
      gossip(event,msgID,round−1);
  }

  private void gossip(SendableEvent event, MessageID msgID, int round){
      int [] targets = pickTargets();
      for(int i=0; i<fanout; i++){
        SendableEvent clone = (SendableEvent) event.cloneEvent();
        ((ExtendedMessage) clone.getMessage()).pushObject(msgID);
        ((ExtendedMessage) clone.getMessage()).pushInt(round);
        up2pSend(clone,targets[i]);
      }
  }

  private int [] pickTargets() {
    Random random = new Random(System.currentTimeMillis());
    LinkedList targets = new LinkedList();
    Integer candidate = null;
    while(targets.size() < fanout){
      candidate = new Integer(random.nextInt(processes.getSize()));
      if ( (! targets.contains(candidate)) &&
                          (candidate.intValue() != processes.getSelfRank()) )
        targets.add(candidate);
    }
    int [] targetArray = new int[fanout];
    ListIterator it = targets.listIterator ();
    for(int i=0; (i<targetArray.length) && it.hasNext(); i++)
      targetArray[i] = ((Integer) it .next()).intValue();
    return targetArray;
  }

  private void up2pSend(SendableEvent event, int dest) {
    event.setDir(Direction.DOWN);
    event.setSource(this);
    event.dest = processes.getProcess(dest).getInetWithPort();
    event. init ();
    event.go();
  }

  private void pbDeliver(SendableEvent event, MessageID msgID) {
    event.setDir(Direction.UP);
    event.setSource(this);
    event.source = processes.getProcess(msgID.process).getInetWithPort();
    event. init ();
    event.go();
  }
}
```

Try It. To test the implementation of the probabilistic reliable broadcast protocol, we will use the same test application that we have used for the basic broadcast. Please refer to the corresponding "try it" section for details. The `prot` parameter that should be used in this case is *"pb <fanout> <maxrounds>"*, where the parameters are used to specify the fanout and the maximum number of message rounds.

Hands-On Exercises.

Hand-On Exercise 3.5 *The up2pDeliver() method performs two different functions: i) it delivers the message to the application (if it has not been delivered yet) and ii) it gossips about the message to other processes. Change the code such that a node gossips just when it receives a message for the first time. Discuss the impact of the changes.*

Hand-On Exercise 3.6 *Change the code to limit* i) *the number of messages each node can store, and* ii) *the maximum throughput (messages per unit of time) of each node.*

3.10.6 No-Waiting Causal Broadcast

The communication stack used to implement the protocol is the following:

Application
Reliable Causal Order **(implemented by No-Waiting CB)**
Delay
Reliable Broadcast (implemented by Lazy RB)
Perfect Failure Detector (implemented by TcpBasedPFD)
Best-Effort Broadcast (implemented by Basic Broadcast)
Perfect Point-to-Point Links (implemented by TcpBasedPerfectP2P)

The role of each of the layers is explained below.

SampleAppl: This layer implements the test application mentioned previously.

NoWaitingCO: This layer implements the causal order protocol. Each message, in the protocol, is uniquely identified by its source and a sequence number, as each process in the group has its own sequence number. The events that walk through the stack are not serializable, so we have chosen the relevant information of those events to send, as the past list. A message coming from the protocol is represented in Figure 3.9.

Delay: Test protocol used to delay the messages of one process/source when delivering them to one process/destination. This is used to check that messages are really delivered in the right order, even when delays are present. In short, this layer simulates network delays. Note that this layer does not belong to the protocol stack; it was developed just for testing.

LazyRB: Protocol that implements the reliable broadcast algorithm. The remaining layers are required by this protocol (see Chapter 3).

The protocol implementation is depicted in Listing 3.6.

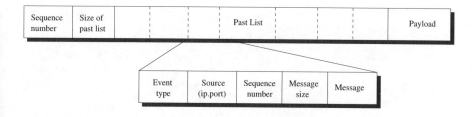

Sequence number	Size of past list			Past List				Payload

Event type	Source (ip.port)	Sequence number	Message size	Message

Fig. 3.9: Format of messages exchanged by CONoWaiting protocol

---

Listing 3.6. No-Waiting Reliable Causal Order Broadcast implementation

```
package appia.protocols.tutorialDA.noWaitingCO;

public class NoWaitingCOSession extends Session {
    Channel channel;
    ProcessSet processes = null;
    int seqNumber=0;
    LinkedList delivered; // Set of delivered messages.
    LinkedList myPast; // Set of messages processed by this element.

    public NoWaitingCOSession(Layer l) {
        super(l);
    }

    public void handle(Event e) {
        if (e instanceof ChannelInit)
            handleChannelInit((ChannelInit)e);
        else if (e instanceof ProcessInitEvent)
            handleProcessInit((ProcessInitEvent)e);
        else if (e instanceof SendableEvent){
            if (e.getDir()==Direction.DOWN)
                handleSendableEventDOWN((SendableEvent)e);
            else
                handleSendableEventUP((SendableEvent)e);
        }else{
            e.go();
        }
    }

    public void handleChannelInit (ChannelInit e){
        e.go();
        this.channel = e.getChannel();
        delivered=new LinkedList();
        myPast=new LinkedList();
    }

    public void handleProcessInit(ProcessInitEvent e) {
        processes = e.getProcessSet();
        e.go();
    }

    public void handleSendableEventDOWN (SendableEvent e){
        //cloning the event to be sent in oder to keep it in the mypast list ...
        SendableEvent e_aux=(SendableEvent)e.cloneEvent();
        ExtendedMessage om=(ExtendedMessage)e.getMessage();

        //inserting myPast list in the msg:
        for(int k=myPast.size();k>0;k--){
            ExtendedMessage om_k =
```

```
                (ExtendedMessage)((ListElement)myPast.get(k−1)).getSE().getMessage();
            om.push(om_k.toByteArray());
            om.pushInt(om_k.toByteArray().length);
            om.pushInt(((ListElement)myPast.get(k−1)).getSeq());
            InetWithPort.push((InetWithPort)((ListElement)myPast.get(k−1)).getSE().source,or
            om.pushString(((ListElement)myPast.get(k−1)).getSE().getClass().getName());
        }
        om.pushInt(myPast.size());
        om.pushInt(seqNumber);

        e.go();

        //add this message to the myPast list:
        e_aux.source = processes.getSelfProcess().getInetWithPort();
        ListElement le=new ListElement(e_aux,seqNumber);
        myPast.add(le);

        //increments the global seq number
        seqNumber++;
    }

    public void handleSendableEventUP (SendableEvent e){
        ExtendedMessage om=(ExtendedMessage)e.getMessage();
        int seq=om.popInt();

        //checks to see if this msg has been already delivered...
        if (! isDelivered((InetWithPort)e.source,seq)){

            //size of the past list of this msg
            int pastSize=om.popInt();
            for(int k=0;k<pastSize;k++){
                String className=om.popString();
                InetWithPort msgSource=InetWithPort.pop(om);
                int msgSeq=om.popInt();
                int msgSize=om.popInt();
                byte[] msg=(byte[])om.pop();

                // if this msg hasn't been already delivered,
                // we must deliver it prior to the one that just arrived!
                if (! isDelivered(msgSource,msgSeq)){
                    //composing and sending the msg!
                    SendableEvent se=(SendableEvent) Class.forName(className).newInstance(
                    se.setChannel(channel);
                    se.setDir(Direction.UP);
                    se.setSource(this);
                    ExtendedMessage aux_om = new ExtendedMessage();
                    aux_om.setByteArray(msg,0,msgSize);
                    se.setMessage(aux_om);
                    se.source=msgSource;

                    se.init ();
                    se.go();

                    //this msg has been delivered!
                    ListElement le=new ListElement(se,msgSeq);
                    delivered.add(le);
                    myPast.add(le);
                }
            }
        }

        //cloning the event just received to keep it in the mypast list
        SendableEvent e_aux=(SendableEvent)e.cloneEvent();

        e.setMessage(om);
        e.go();
```

```
                ListElement le=new ListElement(e_aux,seq);
                delivered.add(le);

                if (!e_aux.source.equals(processes.getSelfProcess().getInetWithPort()))
                    myPast.add(le);
            }
        }

        boolean isDelivered(InetWithPort source,int seq){
            for(int k=0;k<delivered.size();k++){
                InetWithPort iwp_aux =
                    (InetWithPort) ((ListElement)delivered.get(k)).getSE().source;
                int seq_aux=((ListElement)delivered.get(k)).getSeq();
                if ( iwp_aux.equals(source) && seq_aux==seq)
                    return true;
            }
            return false;
        }
    }
}

class ListElement{
    SendableEvent se;
    int seq;

    public ListElement(SendableEvent se, int seq){
        this.se=se;
        this.seq=seq;
    }

    SendableEvent getSE(){
        return se;
    }

    int getSeq(){
        return seq;
    }
}
```

Try It. To test the implementation of the no-waiting reliable causal order broadcast, we will use the same test application that we have used for the basic broadcast. Please refer to the corresponding "try it" section for details. The **prot** parameter that should be used in this case is "**conow**." Note that this protocol uses the perfect failure detector module. As described in the previous chapter, this module need to be activated. For this purpose, the test application also accepts the **startpfd** command; do not forget to initiate the PFD at every processes by issuing the **startpfd** request on the command line before testing the protocol.

To run some simple tests, execute the following steps:

1. Open three shells/command prompts.
2. In each shell go to the directory where you have placed the supplied code.
3. In each shell launch the test application, *SampleAppl*, giving a different *n* value (0, 1 or 2) and specifying the *qos* as **conow**.
   - In shell 0 execute:

           java demo/tutorialDA/SampleAppl \

```
-f demo/tutorialDA/procs \
-n 0 \
-qos conow
```

- In shell 1 execute:
  ```
  java demo/tutorialDA/SampleAppl \
      -f demo/tutorialDA/procs \
      -n 1 \
      -qos conow
  ```

- In shell 2 execute:
  ```
  java demo/tutorialDA/SampleAppl \
      -f demo/tutorialDA/procs \
      -n 2 \
      -qos conow
  ```

Note: If the error NoClassDefError has appeared, confirm that you are at the root of the supplied code.

Now that processes are launched and running, you may try the following two distinct executions:

1. Execution I:
   a) In shell 0, send a message **M1** (type **bcast M1** and press enter).
      - Note that all processes received **M1**.
   b) In shell 1, send a message **M2**.
      - Note that all processes received **M2**.
   c) Confirm that all processes have received **M1** and then **M2**, and note the continuous growth of the size of the messages sent.
2. Execution II: For this execution it is necessary to first modify file SampleAppl.java in package demo.tutorialDA. The sixth line of method get-COnoWChannel should be uncommented in order to insert a test layer that allows the injection of delays in messages sent between process 0 and process 2. After modifying the file, it is necessary to compile it.
   a) In shell 0, send a message **M1**.
      - Note that process 2 did not receive **M1**.
   b) In shell 1, send a message **M2**.
      - Note that all processes received **M2**.
   c) Confirm that all processes received **M1** and then **M2**. Process 2 received **M1** because it was appended to **M2**.

3.10.7 No-Waiting Causal Broadcast with Garbage Collection

The next protocol we present is an optimization of the previous one. It intends to circumvents its main disadvantage by deleting messages from the past list.

When the protocol delivers a message, it broadcasts an acknowledgment to all other processes; when an acknowledgment for the same message has been received from all correct processes, this message is removed from the past list.

The communication stack used to implement the protocol is the following:

SampleAppl
Reliable CO
(implemented by Garbage Collection Of Past)
Delay
Reliable Broadcast
(implemented by Lazy RB)
Perfect Failure Detector
(implemented by TcpBasedPFD)
Best-Effort Broadcast
(implemented by Basic Broadcast)
Perfect Point-to-Point Links
(implemented by TcpBasedPerfectP2P)

The protocol implementation is depicted in Listing 3.7.

Listing 3.7. No-Waiting Reliable Causal Order Broadcast with Garbage Collection implementation

```
package appia.protocols.tutorialDA.gcPastCO;

public class GCPastCOSession extends Session {
    Channel channel;
    int seqNumber=0;
    LinkedList delivered; // Set of delivered messages.
    LinkedList myPast; // Set of messages processed by this element.
    private ProcessSet correct; // Set of the correct processes.
    LinkedList acks; // Set of the msgs not yet acked by all correct processes.

    public GCPastCOSession(Layer l) {
        super(l);
    }

    public void handle(Event e) {
        if (e instanceof ChannelInit)
            handleChannelInit((ChannelInit)e);
        else if (e instanceof ProcessInitEvent)
            handleProcessInit((ProcessInitEvent)e);
        else if (e instanceof AckEvent)
            handleAck((AckEvent)e);
        else if (e instanceof SendableEvent){
            if (e.getDir()==Direction.DOWN)
                handleSendableEventDOWN((SendableEvent)e);
            else
                handleSendableEventUP((SendableEvent)e);
        }else if (e instanceof Crash)
            handleCrash((Crash)e);
        else{
            e.go();
        }
    }

    public void handleChannelInit (ChannelInit e){
```

```
   e.go();
   this.channel = e.getChannel();
   delivered=new LinkedList();
   myPast=new LinkedList();
   acks=new LinkedList();
}

public void handleProcessInit (ProcessInitEvent e){
   correct = e.getProcessSet();
   e.go();
}

public void handleSendableEventDOWN (SendableEvent e){
   // same as the handleSendableEventDOWN method of CONoWaitingSession
   // ...
}

public void handleSendableEventUP (SendableEvent e){
   ExtendedMessage om=(ExtendedMessage)e.getMessage();
   int seq=om.popInt();

   //checks to see if this msg has been already delivered...
   if (! isDelivered((InetWithPort)e.source,seq)){

      //size of the past list of this msg
      int pastSize=om.popInt();
      for(int k=0;k<pastSize;k++){
         String className=om.popString();
         InetWithPort msgSource=InetWithPort.pop(om);
         int msgSeq=om.popInt();
         int msgSize=om.popInt();
         byte[] msg=(byte[])om.pop();

         // if this msg hasn't been already delivered,
         // we must deliver it prior to the one that just arrived!
         if (! isDelivered(msgSource,msgSeq)){
            //composing and sending the msg!
            SendableEvent se =
               (SendableEvent) Class.forName(className).newInstance();
            se.setChannel(channel);
            se.setDir(Direction.UP);
            se.setSource(this);
            ExtendedMessage aux_om = new ExtendedMessage();
            aux_om.setByteArray(msg,0,msgSize);
            se.setMessage(aux_om);
            se.source=msgSource;

            se.init ();
            se.go();

            //this msg has been delivered!
            ListElement le=new ListElement(se,msgSeq);
            delivered.add(le);
            myPast.add(le);

            //let's send the ACK for this msg
            sendAck(le);
         }
      }

      //cloning the event just received to keep it in the mypast list
      SendableEvent e_aux=(SendableEvent)e.cloneEvent();

      e.setMessage(om);
      e.go();
```

```
                ListElement le=new ListElement(e_aux,seq);
                delivered.add(le);

                //this msg is already in the past list. It was added on the sending!!!!
                if(!e_aux.source.equals(correct.getSelfProcess().getInetWithPort()))
                    myPast.add(le);

                //let's send the ACK for this msg
                sendAck(le);
        }

}

private void sendAck(ListElement le){
    int index=−1;
    //search for it in the acks list:
    for(int i=0;i<acks.size(); i++){
        if(((AckElement)acks.get(i)).seq==le.seq &&
          ((AckElement)acks.get(i)).source.equals((InetWithPort)le.se.source)){
            index=i;
            i=acks.size();
        }
    }

    if(index==−1){
        //let's create it!
        AckElement ael=new AckElement(le.seq,(InetWithPort)le.se.source);
        acks.add(ael);
        index=acks.size()−1;
    }

    ((AckElement)acks.get(index)).regAck(correct.getSelfProcess().getInetWithPort());

    AckEvent ae=new AckEvent(channel, Direction.DOWN, this);
    ExtendedMessage om = new ExtendedMessage();
    InetWithPort.push((InetWithPort)le.se.source,om);
    om.pushInt(le.seq);
    ae.setMessage(om);
    ae.init();
    ae.go();
}

boolean isDelivered(InetWithPort source,int seq){
    // equal to the isDelivered method of CONoWaitingSession class
    // ...
}

public void handleAck(AckEvent e){
    //my ACK was already registered when the AckEvent was sent
    if(e.source.equals(correct.getSelfProcess().getInetWithPort()))
        return;

    ExtendedMessage om=(ExtendedMessage)e.getMessage();
    int seq=om.popInt();
    InetWithPort iwp=InetWithPort.pop(om);

    int index=−1;
    //search for it in the acks list:
    for(int i=0;i<acks.size(); i++){
        if(((AckElement)acks.get(i)).seq==seq &&
          ((AckElement)acks.get(i)).source.equals(iwp)){
            index=i;
            i=acks.size();
        }
    }
```

```
        if(index==−1){
            //let's create it!
            AckElement ael=new AckElement(seq,iwp);
            acks.add(ael);
            index=acks.size()−1;
        }

        ((AckElement)acks.get(index)).regAck((InetWithPort)e.source);

        // if all correct processes have already acked this msg
        if(getCorrectSize()==((AckElement)acks.get(index)).processes.size()) {
            // removes the entry for this msg from the myPast list
            for(int k=0;k<myPast.size();k++){
                if(((ListElement)myPast.get(k)).se.source.equals(iwp) &&
                   ((ListElement)myPast.get(k)).seq==seq){
                    myPast.remove(k);
                    k=myPast.size();
                }
            }
            // removes the entry for this msg from the acks list
            acks.remove(index);
        }
    }

    public void handleCrash(Crash e){
        correct.setCorrect(e.getCrashedProcess(),false);
        e.go();
    }

    private int getCorrectSize() {
        int i;
        int count=0;
        for (i=0 ; i < correct.getSize () ; i++)
            if ( correct.getProcess(i).isCorrect())
                count++;
        return count;
    }
}//end CONoWaitingSession

class ListElement{
    SendableEvent se;
    int seq;

    public ListElement(SendableEvent se, int seq){
        this.se=se;
        this.seq=seq;
    }

    SendableEvent getSE(){
        return se;
    }

    int getSeq(){
        return seq;
    }
}

class AckElement{
    int seq;
    InetWithPort source;
    LinkedList processes; // the set of processes that already acked this msg

    public AckElement(int seq, InetWithPort source){
        this.seq=seq;
        this.source=source;
        processes=new LinkedList();
```

```
        }
    void regAck(InetWithPort p){
        processes.add(p);
    }
}
```

Try It. To test the implementation of the no-waiting reliable causal order broadcast with the garbage collection protocol, we will use the same test application that we have used for the basic broadcast. Please refer to the corresponding "try it" section for details.

The `prot` parameter that should be used in this case is "*conowgc.*" Note that this protocol uses the perfect failure detector module. As described in the previous chapter, this module needs to be activated. For this purpose, the test application also accepts the `startpfd` command; do not forget to initiate the PFD at every processes by issuing the `startpfd` request on the command line before testing the protocol.

To run some simple tests, execute the following steps:

1. Open three shells/command prompts.
2. In each shell go to the directory where you have placed the supplied code.
3. In each shell launch the test application, *SampleAppl*, giving a different *n* value (0, 1 or 2) and specifying the *qos* as **conowgc**.

   - In shell 0 execute:
     ```
     java demo/tutorialDA/SampleAppl \
         -f demo/tutorialDA/procs \
         -n 0 \
         -qos conowgc
     ```

   - In shell 1 execute:
     ```
     java demo/tutorialDA/SampleAppl \
         -f demo/tutorialDA/procs \
         -n 1 \
         -qos conowgc
     ```

   - In shell 2 execute:
     ```
     java demo/tutorialDA/SampleAppl \
         -f demo/tutorialDA/procs \
         -n 2 \
         -qos conowgc
     ```

Note: If the error NoClassDefError has appeared, confirm that you are at the root of the supplied code.

Now that processes are launched and running, you may try the following three distinct executions:

1. Execution I and II: Since this protocol is very similar with the previous one, the two executions presented in the previous section can be applied to this protocol. Note that the line of code in *demo/tutorial-DA/SampleAppl.java* that has to be altered is now the seventh of the *getCOnoWGCChannel* method.

2. Execution III:(this execution is to be done with the delay layer in the protocol stack.)

   a) In shell 0, send a message **M1** (type **bcast M1** and press enter).
      - Note that process 2 did not receive **M1**.
   b) In shell 1, send a message **M2**.
      - Note the size of the message that was sent and note also that all processes received **M2**.
   c) In shell 2, send a message **M3**.
      - Note the smaller size of the message that was sent and note also that all processes received **M3**.
   d) Confirm that all processes received **M1**, **M2**, and **M3** in the correct order.

3.10.8 Waiting Causal Broadcast

The communication stack used to implement the protocol is the following:

SampleAppl
Reliable Casual Order   **(implemented by Waiting CO)**
Delay
Reliable Broadcast   (implemented by Lazy RB)
Perfect Failure Detector   (implemented by TcpBasedPFD)
Best-Effort Broadcast   (implemented by Basic Broadcast)
Perfect Point-to-Point Links   (implemented by TcpBasedPerfectP2P)

The protocol implementation is depicted in Listing 3.8.

Listing 3.8. Waiting Causal Broadcast implementation

```
package appia.protocols.tutorialDA.waitingCO;

public class WaitingCOSession extends Session{
    Channel channel;
    private ProcessSet correct; // Set of the correct processes.
    private LinkedList pendingMsg; // The list of the msg that are waiting to be delivered
    int [] vectorClock;

    public WaitingCOSession(Layer l){
        super(l);
    }
```

```
public void handle(Event e) {
    if (e instanceof ChannelInit)
        handleChannelInit((ChannelInit)e);
    else if (e instanceof ProcessInitEvent)
        handleProcessInit((ProcessInitEvent)e);
    else if (e instanceof SendableEvent){
        if (e.getDir()==Direction.DOWN)
            handleSendableEventDOWN((SendableEvent)e);
        else
            handleSendableEventUP((SendableEvent)e);
    }else{
        e.go();
    }
}

public void handleChannelInit (ChannelInit e){
    e.go();
    this.channel = e.getChannel();
    pendingMsg=new LinkedList();
}

public void handleProcessInit (ProcessInitEvent e){
    correct=e.getProcessSet();
    vectorClock=new int[correct.getSize()];
    Arrays.fill (vectorClock,0);
    e.go();
}

public void handleSendableEventDOWN (SendableEvent e){
    //i'm sending a msg therefore increments my position in the vector clock!
    vectorClock[correct.getSelfRank()]++;

    //add the vector clock to the msg from the appl
    ExtendedMessage om=(ExtendedMessage)e.getMessage();
    om.push(vectorClock);

    e.go();
}

public void handleSendableEventUP (SendableEvent e){
    //get the vector clock of this msg!
    ExtendedMessage om=(ExtendedMessage)e.getMessage();
    int [] vc_msg=(int[]) om.pop();

    if(canDeliver(correct.getRank((InetWithPort)e.source),vc_msg)){
        e.go();

        if (!e.source.equals(correct.getSelfProcess().getInetWithPort()))
            vectorClock[correct.getRank((InetWithPort)e.source)]++;

        checkPending();
    }else{
        om.push(vc_msg);
        pendingMsg.add(e);
    }
}

private boolean canDeliver(int rankSource,int[] vc_msg){
    boolean ret=false;
    if(vectorClock[rankSource] >= vc_msg[rankSource]-1)
        ret=true;

    for(int i=0;i < vectorClock.length;i++){
        if(i!=rankSource && vc_msg[i] > vectorClock[i])
            ret=false;
```

```
        }

        return ret;
    }

    private void checkPending(){
        // this  list  will  keep  the  information  about
        // which  messages  can  be  removed  from  the  pending  list!!!
        boolean[] toRemove=new boolean[pendingMsg.size()];
        Arrays. fill (toRemove,false);
        SendableEvent e_aux;

        //runs through the pending List to search for msgs that can already be delivered
        for(int  i=0;i<pendingMsg.size();i++){
            e_aux=(SendableEvent) pendingMsg.get(i);
            ExtendedMessage om=(ExtendedMessage)e_aux.getMessage();
            int [] vc_msg=(int[])om.pop();

            int sourceRank=correct.getRank((InetWithPort)e_aux.source);

            if(canDeliver(sourceRank,vc_msg)){
                e_aux.go();

                if (!e_aux.source.equals( correct . getSelfProcess (). getInetWithPort()))
                    vectorClock[correct . getRank((InetWithPort)e_aux.source)]++;

                toRemove[i]=true;
            }else{
                om.push(vc_msg);
            }
        }

        int countRemoved=0;
        //now, let's check the toRemove list to clean the pendingMsg list
        for(int  k=0;k<toRemove.length;k++){
            if(toRemove[k]){
                pendingMsg.remove(k−countRemoved);
                countRemoved++;
            }
        }
    }
}
```

Try It. To test the implementation of the no-waiting reliable causal order broadcast with garbage collection protocol, we will use the same test application that we have used for the basic broadcast. Please refer to the corresponding "try it" section for details.

The **prot** parameter that should be used in this case is "*cow*." Note that this protocol uses the perfect failure detector module. As described in the previous chapter, this module needs to be activated. For this purpose, the test application also accepts the **startpfd** command; do not forget to initiate the PFD at every process by issuing the **startpfd** request on the command line before testing the protocol.

To run some simple tests, follow the same steps as described in the two previous "try it" sections, except that the *qos* given must be **cow**. You may try the two following executions:

1. Execution I:

a) In shell 0, send a message **M1** (type **bcast M1** and press enter).
- Note that all processes received **M1**.

b) In shell 1, send a message **M2**.
- Note that all processes received **M2**.

c) Confirm that all processes received **M1** and then **M2**.

2. Execution II: For this execution it is necessary to first modify file *demo/-tutorialDA/SampleAppl.java*. The seventh line of the *getCOWChannel* method should be uncommented in order to insert a test layer that allows the injection of delays in messages sent between process 0 and process 2. After modifying the file, it is necessary to compile it.

a) In shell 0, send a message **M1**.
- Note that process 2 did not receive **M1**.

b) In shell 1, send a message **M2**.
- Note that process 2 also did not receive **M2**.

c) Wait for process 2 to receive the messages.
- Note that process 2 did not receive **M1**, immediately, due to the presence of the Delay layer; and it also did not receive **M2** immediately, because it had to wait for **M1** to be delivered, as **M1** preceded **M2**.

3.11 Exercises

Exercise 3.1 *Consider a process* p *that rbBroadcasts a message* m *in the "Lazy Reliable Broadcast" algorithm. Can* p *rbDeliver* m *before bebBroadcasting it.*

Exercise 3.2 *Modify the "Lazy Reliable Broadcast" algorithm to reduce the number of messages sent in case of failures.*

Exercise 3.3 *Some of the algorithms given in this chapter have the processes continuously fill their different message buffers without emptying them. Modify them to remove unnecessary messages from the following buffers:*

1. *from*[p_i] *in the "Lazy Reliable Broadcast" algorithm;*
2. delivered *in all reliable broadcast algorithms;*
3. pending *in the "All-Ack Uniform Reliable Broadcast" algorithm.*

Exercise 3.4 *What do we gain if we replace bebBroadcast with rbBroadcast in our "Majority-Ack Uniform Reliable Broadcast" algorithm?*

Exercise 3.5 *Consider our "All-Ack Uniform Reliable Broadcast" algorithm: what happens if each of the following properties of the failure detector is violated?*

1. *accuracy*
2. *completeness*

Exercise 3.6 *Our "All-Ack Uniform Reliable Broadcast" algorithm can be viewed as an extension of our "Eager Reliable Broadcast" algorithm. Would we gain anything by devising a uniform reliable broadcast algorithm that would be an extension of our "Lazy Reliable Broadcast" algorithm, i.e., can we have the processes not relay messages unless they suspect the sender?*

Exercise 3.7 *Can we devise a uniform reliable broadcast with an eventually perfect failure detector but without the assumption of a correct majority of the processes?*

Exercise 3.8 *Give the specification of a logged reliable broadcast abstraction (i.e., a weaker variant of Module 3.6) and an algorithm that implements it (i.e., a simpler variant of "Logged Majority-Ack URB").*

Exercise 3.9 *Our "Eager Probabilistic Broadcast" algorithm assumes that the connectivity is the same among every pair of processes. In practice, it may happen that some processes are at shorter distances and connected by more reliable links than others. For instance, the underlying network topology could be a set of local-area networks connected by long-haul links. Propose methods to exploit the topology in gossip algorithms.*

Exercise 3.10 *Compare our causal broadcast property with the following property: "if a process delivers messages m_1 and m_2, and $m_1 \to m_2$, then the process must deliver m_1 before m_2."*

Exercise 3.11 *Can we devise a best-effort broadcast algorithm that satisfies the* causal delivery *property without being a causal broadcast algorithm, i.e., without satisfying the* agreement *property of a reliable broadcast?*

Exercise 3.12 *Can we devise a broadcast algorithm that does not ensure the* causal delivery *property but only its nonuniform variant: no correct process p_i delivers a message m_2 unless p_i has already delivered every message m_1 such that $m_1 \to m_2$.*

Exercise 3.13 *Suggest a modification of the garbage collection scheme to collect messages sooner than in Algorithm 3.13.*

Exercise 3.14 *Give a variant of the "Waiting Causal Broadcast" algorithm that implements uniform causal broadcast.*

Algorithm 3.15 Simple optimization of Lazy Reliable Broadcast

---

upon event ⟨ *rbBroadcast* | *m* ⟩ **do**
    delivered := delivered ∪ {*m*}
    trigger ⟨ *rbDeliver* | self, *m* ⟩;
    trigger ⟨ *bebBroadcast* | [DATA, self, *m*] ⟩;

3.12 Solutions

Solution 3.1 The answer is yes. Every process anyway rbDelivers the messages as soon as it bebDelivers them. This does not add any guarantee with respect to rbDelivering the messages before bebBroadcasting them. The event that we would need to change in our "Lazy Reliable Broadcast" algorithm would simply be the rbBroadcast event, as depicted in Algorithm 3.15. □

Solution 3.2 In our "Lazy Reliable Broadcast" algorithm, if a process p rbBroadcasts a message and then crashes, N^2 messages are relayed by the remaining processes to retransmit the message of process p. This is because a process that bebDelivers the message of p does not know whether the other processes have bebDelivered this message or not. However, it would be sufficient in this case if only one process relays the message of p.

   In practice, one specific process, call it leader process p_l, might be more likely to bebDeliver messages: the links to and from this process would be fast and very reliable, the process would run on a reliable computer, etc. A process p_i would forward its messages to the leader p_l, which would coordinate the broadcast to every other process. If the leader is correct, every process will eventually bebDeliver and rbDeliver every message. Otherwise, we revert to the previous algorithm, and every process would be responsible of bebBroadcasting the messages that it bebDelivered. □

Solution 3.3 We discuss each of the three variables (message buffers) in the following.

- Consider variable $from[p_i]$ in the "Lazy Reliable Broadcast" algorithm: the array $from$ is used exclusively to store messages that are retransmitted in the case of a failure. Therefore they can be removed as soon as they have been retransmitted. If p_i is correct, they will eventually be bebDelivered. If p_i is faulty, it does not matter if the other processes do not bebDeliver them.
- Consider variable *delivered* in all reliable broadcast algorithms. Messages here cannot be removed. If a process crashes and its messages are retransmitted by two different processes, then a process might rbDeliver the same message twice if it empties the *deliver* buffer in the meantime. This would violate the *no duplication* property.

- Consider variable *pending* in the "All-Ack Uniform Reliable" broadcast algorithm: messages can actually be removed as soon as they have been urbDelivered.

□

Solution 3.4 Nothing, because the "Majority-Ack URB" algorithm does not assume and hence does not use the guarantees provided by the reliable broadcast algorithm.

Consider the following scenario, which illustrates the difference between using bebBroadcast and using rbBroadcast. A process p broadcasts a message and crashes. Consider the case where only one correct process q receives the message (bebBroadcast). With rbBroadcast, all correct processes would deliver the message. In the urbBroadcast algorithm, q adds the message in the *forward* buffer and then bebBroadcasts it. As q is correct, all correct processes will deliver it, and thus, we have at least the same guarantee as with rbBroadcast. □

Solution 3.5 Consider a system of three processes: p_1, p_2, and p_3. Assume, furthermore, that p_1 urbBroadcasts a message m. If *strong completeness* is not satisfied, then p_1 might never urbDeliver m if either of p_2 and p_3 crashes and p_1 never detects their crash or bebDelivers m from them: p_1 would wait indefinitely for them to relay m. In the case of both the regular and uniform reliable broadcast algorithms, the *validity property* can be violated. Assume now that *strong accuracy* is violated and p_1 falsely suspects p_2 and p_3 to have crashed. p_1 eventually urbDelivers m. Assume that p_1 crashes afterward. It might be the case that p_2 and p_3 never bebDelivered m and have no way of knowing about m and urbDeliver it: *uniform agreement* is violated. □

Solution 3.6 The advantage of the lazy scheme is that processes do not need to relay messages to ensure *agreement* if they do not suspect the sender to have crashed. In this failure-free scenario, only $N - 1$ messages are needed for all the processes to deliver a message. In the case of uniform reliable broadcast (without a majority), a process can only deliver a message when it knows that every correct process has seen that message. Hence, every process should somehow convey that fact, i.e., that it has seen the message. A lazy scheme would be of no benefit here. □

Solution 3.7 No. We explain why for the case of a system of four processes $\{p_1, p_2, p_3, p_4\}$ using what is called a *partitioning* argument. The fact that the correct majority assumption does not hold means that two out of the four processes may fail.

Consider an execution where process p_1 broadcasts a message m and assume that p_3 and p_4 crash in that execution without receiving any message

---

Module 3.11 Interface and properties of logged reliable broadcast

Module:

    Name: LoggedReliableBroadcast (log-rb).

Events:

    ⟨ *log-rbBroadcast* | *m* ⟩, ⟨ *log-rbDeliver* | delivered ⟩ with the same meaning
    and interface as in logged best-effort broadcast.

Properties:

    LURB1: *Validity:* If p_j is correct and p_i does not crash, then every message broadcast by p_i is eventually delivered by p_j.

    LURB2: *No duplication:* No message is delivered more than once.

    LURB3: *No creation:* If a message m is delivered by some process p_j, then m was previously broadcast by some process p_i.

    LURB4: *Agreement:* If a message m is delivered by some correct process, then m is eventually delivered by every correct process.

---

either from p_1 or from p_2. Due to the *validity* property of uniform reliable broadcast, there must be a time t at which p_1 urbDelivers message m.

Consider now an execution that is similar to this one except that p_1 and p_2 crash right after time t whereas p_3 and p_4 are correct: say, they have been falsely suspected, which is possible with an eventually perfect failure detector. In this execution, p_1 has urbDelivered a message m whereas p_3 and p_4 have no way of knowing about that message m and eventually urbDelivering it: *uniform agreement* is violated. □

Solution 3.8 Module 3.6 defines a logged variant of reliable broadcast. In this variant, if a correct process delivers a message (i.e., logs the variable *delivered* with the message in it), all correct processes should eventually deliver that message (i.e., log it in their variable *delivered*).

Algorithm 3.16 implements logged reliable broadcast using stubborn channels. To broadcast a message, a process first delivers it and then sends it to all other processes (using stubborn channels). When a message is received for the first time, it is delivered and sent to all processes. Upon recovery, a process retrieves the messages it has delivered and sends them to all other processes.

Consider the *agreement* property and assume some correct process p_i delivers a message m. If it does not crash, then p_i sends the message to all other processes and all correct processes will deliver the message based on the properties of the stubborn channels. If it crashes, there is a time after which p_i recovers, retrieves m and sends it to all processes. Again, all correct processes will deliver the message based on the properties of the stubborn channels. The *validity* property follows directly from the stubborn channels.

Algorithm 3.16 Reliable Broadcast with Log

Implements:
    LoggedReliableBroadcast (log-rb).

Uses:
    StubbornPointToPointLink (sp2p).

upon event ⟨ *Init* ⟩ **do**
    delivered := ∅;
    store (delivered);

upon event ⟨ *Recovery* ⟩ **do**
    retrieve (delivered);
    trigger ⟨ *log-rbDeliver* | delivered ⟩;
    forall $m \in$ delivered **do**
        forall $p_i \in \Pi$ **do**
            trigger ⟨ *sp2pSend* | p_i, m ⟩;

upon event ⟨ *log-rbBroadcast* | m ⟩ **do**
    delivered := delivered ∪ {m};
    store (delivered);
    trigger ⟨ *log-rbDeliver* | delivered ⟩;
    forall $p_i \in \Pi$ **do**
        trigger ⟨ *sp2pSend* | p_i, m ⟩;

upon event ⟨ *sp2pDeliver* | p_i, m ⟩ **do**
    if $m \notin$ delivered **then**
        delivered := delivered ∪ {m};
        store (delivered);
        trigger ⟨ *log-rbDeliver* | delivered ⟩;
        forall $p_i \in \Pi$ **do**
            trigger ⟨ *sp2pSend* | p_i, m ⟩;

The *no duplication* property is trivially ensured by the algorithm whereas the *no creation* property is ensured by the underlying channels.

Let m be any message that is broadcast by some process p_i. A process delivers the message m immediately and the other processes deliver it after one communication step. □

Solution 3.9 One approach consists in assigning weights to the links connecting processes. Weights reflect the reliability of the links. We could easily adapt our algorithm to avoid redundant transmission by gossiping through more reliable links with lower probability. An alternative approach consists in organizing the nodes in a hierarchy that reflects the network topology in order to reduce the traffic across domain boundaries. □

Solution 3.10 We need to compare the two following properties:

1. If a process delivers a message m_2, then it must have delivered every message m_1 such that $m_1 \rightarrow m_2$.
2. If a process delivers messages m_1 and m_2, and $m_1 \rightarrow m_2$, then the process must deliver m_1 before m_2.

Property 1 says that *any* message m_1 that causally precedes m_2 must only be delivered before m_2 if m_2 is delivered. Property 2 says that *any delivered* message m_1 that causally precedes m_2 must only be delivered before m_2 if m_2 is delivered.

Both properties are safety properties. In the first case, a process that delivers a message m without having delivered a message that causally precedes m violates the property and this is irremediable. In the second case, a process that delivers both messages without respecting the causal precedence might violate the property and this is also irremediable. The first property is, however, strictly stronger than the second. If the first is satisfied, then the second is. However, it can be the case that the second property is satisfied whereas the first is not: a process delivers a message m_2 without delivering a message m_1 that causally precedes m_1. $\square$

Solution 3.11 The answer is no. Assume by contradiction that some broadcast algorithm ensures causal order delivery and is not reliable but best-effort. We would define the abstraction implemented by such an algorithm with primitives coBroadcast and coDeliver. The only possibility for a broadcast to ensure the best-effort properties and not be reliable is to violate the *agreement* property: there must be some execution of the algorithm implementing the abstraction where some correct process p coDelivers a message m that some other process q does not ever coDeliver. Because the algorithm is best-effort, this can only happen if the original source of the message, say, r, is faulty.

Assume now that after coDelivering m, process p coBroadcasts a message m'. Given that p is correct and the broadcast is best-effort, all correct processes, including q, coDeliver m'. Given that m precedes m', q must have coDelivered m, a contradiction. Hence, any best-effort broadcast that satisfies the *causal delivery* property satisfies *agreement* and is thus also reliable. $\square$

Solution 3.12 Assume by contradiction that some algorithm does not ensure the *causal delivery* property but ensures its nonuniform variant. This means that the algorithm has some execution where some process p delivers some message m without delivering a message m' that causally precedes m. Given that we assume a model where processes do not self-destruct, p might very well be correct, in which case it violates even the nonuniform variant. $\square$

Solution 3.13 When removing a message m from the past, we can also remove all the messages that causally depend on this message—and then recursively those that causally precede these. This means that a message stored

---

Algorithm 3.17 Waiting Uniform Causal Broadcast

Implements:
    UniformCausalBroadcast (uco).

Uses:
    UniformReliableBroadcast (urb).

upon event ⟨ *init* ⟩ **do**
    forall $p_i \in \Pi$ **do** $VC[rank(p_i)] := 0$;
    pending $:= \emptyset$;
    ucoDel $:= 0$;

procedure deliver-pending() **is**
    while exists $(s_x, [\text{DATA}, VC_x, x]) \in$ pending **such that**
        $\forall_{p_j} : VC[rank(p_j)] \geq VC_x[rank(p_j)] \land$ ucoDel $\geq VC_x[rank(\text{self})]$ **do**
        pending $:=$ pending $\setminus (s_x, [\text{DATA}, VC_x, x])$;
        trigger ⟨ *ucoDeliver* | s_x, x ⟩;
        if $s_x \neq$ self **do**
            $VC[rank(s_x)] := VC[rank(s_x)]+1$;
        else
            ucoDel $:=$ ucoDel $+1$;

upon event ⟨ *ucoBroadcast* | m ⟩ **do**
    trigger ⟨ *urbBroadcast* | [DATA, VC, m] ⟩;
    $VC[rank(\text{self})] := VC[rank(\text{self})] + 1$;

upon event ⟨ *urbDeliver* | p_i, [DATA, VC_m, m] ⟩ **do**
    pending $:=$ pending $\cup (p_i, [\text{DATA}, VC_m, m])$;
    deliver-pending();

---

in the past must be stored with its own, distinct past. □

Solution 3.14 Notice first that the "Waiting Causal Broadcast" algorithm (Algorithm 3.14) does not implement uniform causal broadcast. A process rcoDelivers a message m before rbBroadcasting it. If p crashes, then no correct process might ever rcoDeliver m. Using an underlying uniform reliable broadcast does not make any difference, even if a process does not rcoDeliver a message until after it has urbBroadcast it.

We present below a variant of Algorithm 3.14 that relies on an underlying uniform reliable broadcast communication abstraction defined through primitives urbBroadcast and urbDeliver. The algorithm (Algorithm 3.17) implements a uniform causal broadcast abstraction defined through primitives ucoBroadcast and ucoDeliver. The function *rank* is the same as used in Algorithm 3.14.

When a process ucoBroadcasts a message m, it urbBroadcasts m but does not ucoDeliver it (unlike in Algorithm 3.14). In fact, no process ucoDelivers a message m before urbDelivering it. To preserve causality of messages that a process ucoDelivers from itself, we add a specific test (through variable *ucoDel*). □

3.13 Historical Notes

- The requirements for a reliable broadcast communication abstraction seem to have originated from the domain of aircraft control and the SIFT system in 1978 (Wensley 1978).
- The causal broadcast abstraction was discussed in 1987 (Birman and Joseph 1987a) following the notion of causality initially introduced in 1978 (Lamport 1978).
- Our "No-Waiting Causal Broadcast" algorithm was inspired by one of the earliest implementations of causal broadcast included in the ISIS toolkit (Birman and Joseph 1987b).
- Our waiting causal broadcast algorithm was based on the notion of vector clocks introduced in 1988 (Fidge 1988; Ladin, Liskov, Shrira, and Ghemawat 1990; Schwarz and Mattern 1992). To our knowledge, the most detailed description of the algorithm, including its correctness proof, was given in 1998 (Attiya and Welch 1998).
- Reliable and causal broadcast algorithms were presented in a very comprehensive way in 1994 (Hadzilacos and Toueg 1994).
- The problem of the uniformity of a broadcast was discussed in 1984 (Hadzilacos 1984) and then further explored in 1993 (Neiger and Toueg 1993).
- In this chapter, we presented algorithms that implement causal broadcast assuming that all messages are broadcast to all processes in the system. It is also possible to ensure causal delivery in the cases where individual messages may be sent to an arbitrary subset of group members, but the algorithms require a significantly larger amount of control information. These issues were addressed in 1991 (Raynal, Schiper, and Toueg 1991).
- The idea of applying epidemic dissemination to implementing probabilistically reliable broadcast algorithms have been explored since 1992 (Golding and Long 1992; Birman, Hayden, Ozkasap, Xiao, Budiu, and Minsky 1999; Eugster, Guerraoui, Handurukande, Kouznetsov, and Kermarrec 2003; Eugster, Guerraoui, and Kouznetsov 2004; Kouznetsov, Guerraoui, Handurukande, and Kermarrec 2001; Kermarrec, Massoulie, and Ganesh 2000; Xiao, Birman, and van Renesse 2002).
- A precise specification of a probabilistic broadcast algorithm was suggested in 2004 (Eugster, Guerraoui, and Kouznetsov 2004).
- The exploitation of topological features in probabilistic broadcast algorithms was proposed through a mechanism that assigns weights to link between processes in 1999 (Lin and Marzullo 1999). A similar idea, but using a hierarchy instead of weights, was proposed later to reduce the traffic across domain boundaries (Gupta, Kermarrec, and Ganesh 2002).

- The first probabilistic broadcast algorithm that did not depend on any global membership was given in 2003 (Eugster, Guerraoui, Handurukande, Kouznetsov, and Kermarrec 2003). The idea was refined since then (Voulgaris, Jelasity, and van Steen 2003; Jelasity, Guerraoui, Kermarrec, and van Steen 2004).
- The notion of message ages in probabilistic broadcast was introduced in 2001 (Kouznetsov, Guerraoui, Handurukande, and Kermarrec 2001) for purging messages and ensuring the scalability of process buffers. It was later refined to balance buffering among processes (Koldehofe 2003). The idea of flow control in probabilistic broadcast has been developed since 2002 (Rodrigues, Handurukande, Pereira, Guerraoui, and Kermarrec 2003; Garbinato, Pedone, and Schmidt 2004). Trade-offs between the fanout and the reliability of the dissemination were explored in 2000 (Kermarrec, Massoulie, and Ganesh 2000).

4. Shared Memory

I always tell the truth, even when I lie.
(Tony Montana – Scarface)

This chapter presents shared memory abstractions. These are distributed programming abstractions that encapsulate read-write forms of storage among processes. These abstractions are called *registers* because they resemble those provided by multiprocessor machines at the hardware level, though in many cases, including in this chapter, they are implemented over processes that communicate through message passing and do not share any hardware device. The register abstractions also resemble files in a distributed directory or shared working spaces in a distributed working environment. Therefore, understanding how to implement register abstractions helps us understand how to implement distributed file systems and shared workspaces.

We study here different variants of register abstractions. These differ according to the number of processes that are allowed to read and write on them, as well as on the semantics of their read operations in the face of concurrency and failures. We distinguish two kinds of semantics: *regular* and *atomic*. We will first consider the $(1, N)$ *regular* register abstraction. The notation $(1, N)$ means here that one specific process can write and any process can read. Then we will consider the $(1, N)$ *atomic* register and the (N, N) atomic register abstractions. We will consider these abstractions for three of the distributed system models identified in Chapter 2: the fail-stop, fail-silent, and fail-recovery models.

4.1 Introduction

4.1.1 Sharing Information in a Distributed System

In a multiprocessor machine, processes typically communicate through shared memory provided at the hardware level. The shared memory can be viewed as an array of shared registers. The act of building a register abstraction from a set of processes that communicate by message passing is sometimes called a *shared-memory emulation*. The programmer using this abstraction can develop shared memory algorithms without being aware that, behind the scenes, processes are actually communicating by exchanging messages, i.e., there is no physical shared memory. Such emulation is very appealing because programming with a shared memory is usually considered significantly easier than with message passing, precisely because the programmer can ignore the consistency problems introduced by the distribution of data.

As we pointed out, studying register specifications and algorithms is also useful when implementing distributed file systems as well as shared working spaces for collaborative work. For example, the abstraction of a distributed file that can be accessed through read and write operations is similar to the notion of a register. Not surprisingly, the algorithms that one needs to devise to build a distributed file system can be directly inspired by those used to implement register abstractions. Similarly, when building a shared workspace in collaborative editing environments, one ends up devising register-like distributed algorithms.

In the following, we will study two semantics of registers, namely, *regular* and *atomic*. When describing a register abstraction, we will distinguish the case where the register can be read and (or) written by exactly one process, and read and (or) written by all processes (i.e., any of the N processes in the system).

4.1.2 Register Overview

Assumptions. Registers store values that are accessed through two operations: *read* and *write*. The operations of a register are invoked by the processes of the system to exchange information through the register.

When a process invokes any of these operations and gets back a reply, we say that the process completes the operation. Each process accesses the registers in a sequential manner. That is, if a process invokes some operation (read or write on some register), the process does not invoke any further operation unless the previous one is complete.

To simplify, we also assume that every register (a) contains only positive integers and (b) is initialized to 0. In other words, we assume that some write operation was initially invoked on the register with 0 as a parameter and completed before any other operation was invoked. Also, for presentation simplicity, but still without loss of generality, we will also assume that (c) the values written in the register are uniquely identified, say, by using some unique timestamps provided by the processes (like we assumed in the previous chapters that messages that are sent or broadcast are uniquely identified.)

Some of the register abstractions and algorithms we will present make the assumption that specific processes can write and specific processes can read.

For example, the simplest case is a register with one writer and one reader, denoted by $(1,1)$: the writer is a specific process known in advance, and so is the reader. We will also consider registers with one writer and N readers (the writer is here a specific process and any process can be a reader). A register with X writers and Y readers is also called an (X, Y) register. When $X = Y = N$ (where N is the nu,mber of processes in the system) any process can be a writer and a reader at the same time.

Signature and Semantics. Basically, a read returns the value in the register and a write updates the value of the register. More precisely:

1. A read operation does not take any input parameter and has one ouput parameter. This output parameter presumably contains the current value of the register and constitutes the reply of the read invocation. A read does not modify the content of the register.
2. A write operation takes an input parameter and returns a simple confirmation that the operation has taken place. This confirmation constitutes the reply of the write invocation. The write operation aims at modifying the content of the register.

If a register is used (read and written) by a single process, and we assume there is no failure, we define the specification of a register through the following simple properties:

- **Liveness.** Every operation eventually completes.
- **Safety.** Every read returns the *last* value written.

In fact, even if a register is accessed by a set of processes one at a time (i.e., in a serial manner) and without crashing, we could still define the specification of the register using those simple properties. By serial access we mean that a process does not invoke an operation on a register if some other process has invoked an operation and has not received any reply. (Note that this notion is stronger than the notion of sequentiality introduced above.)

Failure Issues. If we assume that processes might fail, say, by crashing, we cannot require that any process that invokes an operation eventually completes that operation. Indeed, a process might crash right after invoking an operation and would not have the time to complete this operation (get the actual reply). We say that the operation has failed. (Remember that failures are unpredictable and this is precisely what makes distributed computing challenging.)

However, it makes sense to require that if a process p_i invokes some operation and does not subsequently crash, then p_i eventually gets back a reply to its invocation, i.e., completes its operation. That is, any process that invokes a read or write operation, and does not crash, should eventually return from that invocation. In this sense, its operation should not fail. This requirement makes the register *fault-tolerant*. It is also sometimes said to be *robust* or *wait-free*.

If we assume that processes access a register in a serial manner, we may, at first glance, still want to require from a read operation that it return the last value written. We need, however, to be careful here with failures in defining the very notion of *last*. To illustrate the underlying issue, consider the following situation.

- Assume that a process p_1 invokes a write on the register with value v_1 and completes its write. Later on, some other process p_2 invokes a write operation on the register with a new value v_2, and then p_2 crashes before the operation completes: before it crashes, p_2 does not get any confirmation that the operation has indeed taken place, i.e., the operation has failed. Now, if even later on process p_3 invokes a read operation on the register, what is the value supposed to be returned to p_3? Should it be v_1 or v_2?

In fact, we will consider both values to be valid replies. Intuitively, p_2 may or may not have the time to complete the write operation. In other words, when we require that a read returns the last value written, we consider the following two cases as possible:

1. The value returned has indeed been written by the last process that completed its write, even if some process invoked a write later but crashed. In this case, no future read should be returning the value of the failed write; everything happens as if the failed operation was never invoked.
2. The value returned was the input parameter of the last write operation that was invoked, even if by some process that crashed before the completion of the actual operation. Everything happens as if the operation that failed actually completed.

The difficulty underlying the problem of failure just discussed has actually to do with a failed write (i.e. of the crashed process p_2) being concurrent with a read (i.e., the one that comes from p_3 after the crash). This happens even if a process does not invoke an operation while some other process is waiting for a reply. This is a particular case of the more general case of concurrency, which we discuss now.

Concurrency Issues. In practice, executions are not serial (and clearly not sequential). What should we expect from a value returned by a read operation that is concurrent with some write operation? What is the meaning of the *last* write in this context? Similarly, if two write operations were invoked concurrently, what is the last value written? Can a subsequent read return one of the values, and then a read that comes even later return the other?

In this chapter, we will give the specifications of register abstractions (i.e., *regular* and *atomic*) that differ mainly in the way we address these questions, as well as algorithms that implement each of these specifications. Roughly speaking, a regular register ensures minimal guarantees in the face of concurrent and failed operations. An atomic register is stronger and provides strong properties even in the face of concurrency and failures. To make the specifications more precise, we first introduce some definitions that aim to capture the intuitions discussed above (remember that, by default, we assume that a process does nor recover after a crash; later in the chapter, we will consider the fail-recovery model).

4.1.3 Completeness and Precedence

We first define slightly more precisely the notions of *completeness* of an operation execution and *precedence* between operation executions, e.g., read or write executions. Note that when there is no possible ambiguity, we simply take *operations* to mean operation *executions*.

These notions are defined using the events that occur at the *boundary* of an operation at the process that invoked the operation: the *request invocation* (read or write invocation) and the *return confirmation* in the case of a write or the actual *reply value* in the case of a read invocation. Each of these events is assumed to occur at a single indivisible point in time. (Remember that we assume a fictional notion of global time, used to reason about specifications and algorithms. This global time is, however, not directly accessible to the processes.)

- We say that an operation is *complete* if *both* events at the boundaries of the operation have occured. This, in particular, means that the process which invoked the operation *op* did not crash before being informed that *op* is terminated, i.e., before the confirmation event occured in case of a write and a *reply value* in the case of a read invocation.
- A *failed* operation is one that was invoked (i.e., the request was issued), but the process which invoked it crashed before obtaining the corresponding confirmation.
- An operation *op* is said to *precede* an operation *op'* if the event corresponding to the confirmation of *op* precedes the event corresponding to the invocation of *op'*; It is important to note here that for an operation *op*, invoked by some process p_1, to *precede* an operation *op'* (invoked by a different process) p_2, *op* must be complete.
- If two operations are such that one precedes the other, then we say that the operations are *sequential*. Otherwise we say that they are *concurrent*.

Basically, the operation of a register can be viewed as a partial order of its read and write operations. If only one process invokes operations, then the order is total. When there is no concurrency and all operations are complete (serial execution), the order is also total.

- When a read operation r returns a value v, and that value v was the input parameter of some write operation w, we say that r (on v) has (was) *read from w*.
- A value v is said to be written when the write of v is complete.

In the following, we give specifications of various forms of registers and algorithms to implement them. The algorithms will implement arrays of registers as these will be useful in other algorithms. As a convention, the register under consideration will simply be denoted by *reg*.

4.2 $(1, N)$ Regular Register

We give here the specification and underlying algorithms of a $(1, N)$ *regular* register, i.e., one specific process, say, p_1 can invoke a write operation on the register, and any process can invoke a read operation on that register. The notion of regularity, which we explain below, is not considered for multiple writers. (There is no consensus in the distributed computing literature on how to generalize the notion of regularity to multiple writers).

4.2.1 Specification

The interface and properties of a $(1, N)$ regular register are given in Module 4.1. In short, a read that is not concurrent with any write returns the last value written. If there is a concurrent write, the read is allowed to return the last value written or the value concurrently being written. Note that if a process invokes a write and crashes (without recovering), the write is considered to be concurrent with any read that did not precede it. Hence, such a read can return the value that was supposed to be written by the failed write or the last value written before the failed write was invoked. Note also that, in any case, the value returned must be read from some write operation invoked on the register. That is, a value read must in any case be a value that some process has tried to write (even if the write was not complete): it cannot be invented out of thin air. This can be the initial value of the register, which we assume to have been written initially by the writer.

To illustrate the specification of a regular register, we depict in Figure 4.1 two executions. The first is not permitted by a regular register whereas the second is. In the first case, even when there is no concurrency, the read does not return the last value written.

4.2.2 Fail-Stop Algorithm: Read-One Write-All Regular Register

Algorithm 4.1 implements a $(1, N)$ regular register. The simplicity of this algorithm derives from the fact that it relies on a perfect failure detector (fail-stop model). The crash of a process is eventually detected by all correct processes (*strong completeness*), and no process is detected to have crashed until it has really crashed (*strong accuracy*).

The algorithm has each process store a copy of the *current* register value in a variable that is local to the process. In other words, the value of the register is replicated at all processes. The writer updates the value of all processes

---

Module 4.1 Interface and properties of a $(1, N)$ regular register

Module:

    Name: $(1, N)$RegularRegister (on-rreg).

Events:

    Request: ⟨ *on-rregRead | reg* ⟩: Used to invoke a read operation on register *reg*.

    Request: ⟨ *on-rregWrite | reg, v* ⟩: Used to invoke a write operation of value *v* on register *reg*.

    Confirmation: ⟨ *on-rregReadReturn | reg, v* ⟩: Used to return *v* as a response to the read invocation on register *reg* and indicates that the operation is complete.

    Confirmation: ⟨ *on-rregWriteReturn | reg* ⟩: Confirms that the write operation is complete.

Properties:

    RR1: *Termination:* If a correct process invokes an operation, then the process eventually receives the corresponding confirmation.

    RR2: *Validity:* A read returns the last value written, or the value concurrently written.

(a) non-regular   (b) regular

Fig. 4.1: Register execution

it does not detect to have crashed by broadcasting a WRITE message with the new value. All processes acknowledge the receipt of the new value with an ACK message. The write operation is considered complete when an acknowledgment has been received from every correct process. When the write of a new value is complete, all processes that did not crash have the new value. The reader simply returns the value it has stored locally. In other words, the reader *reads one value* and the writer *writes all values*. Hence the name of Algorithm 4.1: "Read-One Write-All."

    Besides a perfect failure detector, our algorithm makes use of two underlying communication abstractions: perfect point-to-point links as well as a best-effort broadcast.

    Notice that, as we pointed out, our "Read-One Write-All" algorithm (just like the many algorithms we will describe below) implements an array of registers. Indeed, we will be using multiple regular registers to build stronger abstractions later in this chapter and in the next chapter. Hence, our algo-

---

Algorithm 4.1 Read-One Write-All

Implements:
    $(1, N)$RegularRegister (on-rreg).

Uses:
    BestEffortBroadcast (beb);
    PerfectPointToPointLinks (pp2p);
    PerfectFailureDetector ($\mathcal{P}$).

upon event $\langle$ *Init* $\rangle$ **do**
    forall r **do**
        value[r] := 0;
        writeSet[r] := $\emptyset$;
    correct := Π;

upon event $\langle$ *crash* $|$ p_i $\rangle$ **do**
    correct := correct $\setminus \{p_i\}$;

upon event $\langle$ *on-rregRead* $|$ reg $\rangle$ **do**
    trigger $\langle$ *on-rregReadReturn* $|$ reg, value[reg] $\rangle$;

upon event $\langle$ *on-rregWrite* $|$ reg, val $\rangle$ **do**
    trigger $\langle$ *bebBroadcast* $|$ [WRITE, reg, val] $\rangle$;

upon event $\langle$ *bebDeliver* $|$ p_j, [WRITE, reg, val] $\rangle$ **do**
    value[reg] := val;
    trigger $\langle$ *pp2pSend* $|$ p_j, [ACK, reg] $\rangle$;

upon event $\langle$ *pp2pDeliver* $|$ p_j, [ACK, reg] $\rangle$ **do**
    writeSet[reg] := writeSet[reg] $\cup \{p_j\}$;

upon exists r **such that** correct $\subseteq$ writeSet[r] **do**
    writeSet[r] := $\emptyset$;
    trigger $\langle$ *on-rregWriteReturn* $|$ r $\rangle$;

---

rithm is designed to maintain the state of an array of registers. Similarly, all messages carry the identifier of the register which is the target of the operation being executed.

Correctness. The *termination* property is straightforward for any read invocation. A process simply reads its local value. For a write invocation, *termination* follows from the properties of the underlying communication abstractions (*reliable delivery* of perfect point-to-point communication and *validity* of best-effort broadcast) as well as the *completeness* property of the perfect failure detector (every crashed process is eventually detected by every correct process). Any process that crashes is detected and any process that does not crash sends back an acknowledgment which is eventually delivered by the writer.

Fig. 4.2: A non-regular register execution

Consider *validity*. Assume that there is no concurrency and all operations are complete. Consider a read invoked by some process p_i and assume, furthermore, that v is the last value written. Due to the *accuracy* property of the perfect failure detector, at the time when the read is invoked, all processes that did not crash have value v. These include p_i, which returns v, which is the last value written.

Assume now that the read is concurrent with some write of a value v and the value written prior to v was v' (this could be the initial value 0). Due to the properties of the communication abstractions (*no creation* properties), no message is altered and no value can be stored at a process unless the writer has invoked a write operation with this value as a parameter. Hence, at the time of the read, the value can either be v or v'.

Performance. Every write operation requires two communication steps corresponding to the WRITE and ACK exchange between the writer and all processes, and at most $2N$ messages. A read operation does not require any remote communication: it is purely local.

4.2.3 Fail-Silent Algorithm: Majority Voting Regular Register

It is easy to see that if the failure detector is not perfect, the "Read-One Write-All" algorithm (Algorithm 4.1) might not ensure the *validity* property of the register. We depict this possibility through the execution illustrated in Figure 4.2. Even without concurrency and without any failure, process p_2 returns a value that was not the last value written. This might happen if p_1, the process that has written that value, has falsely suspected p_2 to have crashed, and p_1 returned before making sure p_2 had locally stored the new value, 6.

In the following, we give a regular register algorithm in a fail-silent model. This algorithm does not rely on any failure detection scheme. Instead, the algorithm assumes a majority of the correct processes. We leave it as an exercise (end of this chapter) to show that this majority assumption is actually needed, even when an eventually perfect failure detector can be used.

The general principle of the algorithm requires for the writer and readers to use a set of *witness* processes that keep track of the most recent value of the register. The witnesses must be chosen in such a way that at least one witness participates in any pair of such operations, and does not crash in the meantime. Sets of witnesses must intuitively form *quorums*: their intersection should not be empty. This is ensured by the use of majorities, for which reason

---

Algorithm 4.2 Majority Voting (write)

Implements:
    $(1, N)$RegularRegister (on-rreg).
Uses:
    BestEffortBroadcast (beb);
    PerfectPointToPointLinks (pp2p).

upon event ⟨ *Init* ⟩ **do**
    forall r **do**
        $sn[r] := 0$;
        $v[r] := 0$;
        $acks[r] := 0$;
        $reqid[r] := 0$;
        $readSet[r] := \emptyset$;

upon event ⟨ *on-rregWrite* | r, val ⟩ **do**
    $sn[r] := sn[r] + 1$;
    $v[r] := val$;
    $acks[r] := 1$;
    trigger ⟨ *bebBroadcast* | [WRITE, r, $sn[r]$, val] ⟩;

upon event ⟨ *bebDeliver* | p_j, [WRITE, r, tstamp, val] ⟩ **do**
    if tstamp $> sn[r]$ **then**
        $v[r] := val$;
        $sn[r] := tstamp$;
        trigger ⟨ *pp2pSend* | p_j, [ACK, r, tstamp] ⟩;

upon event ⟨ *pp2pDeliver* | p_j, [ACK, r, ts] ⟩ **do**
    if ts$=sn[r]$ **then**
        $acks[r] := acks[r] + 1$;

upon exists r **such that** $acks[r] > N/2$ **do**
    trigger ⟨ *on-rregWriteReturn* | r ⟩;

Algorithm 4.2–4.3 is called a "Majority Voting" algorithm. The algorithm implements a $(1, N)$ regular register where one specific process is the writer, say, p_1, and any process can be the reader.

Similarly to our previous "Read-One Write-All" algorithm (Algorithm 4.1), our "Majority Voting" algorithm (Algorithm 4.2–4.3) also has each process store a copy of the *current* register value in a local variable. In addition, the "Majority Voting" algorithm relies on a timestamp (sometimes also called a sequence number) associated with each value stored locally at a process. This timestamp is defined by the writer p_1, and intuitively represents the version number of the value. It measures the number of times the write operation has been invoked.

For p_1 (the unique writer) to write a new value, it defines a new timestamp by incrementing the one it already had and associates it with the value to be written. Then p_1 broadcasts a WRITE message to all processes, and has

---

Algorithm 4.3 Majority Voting (read)

---

upon event ⟨ *on-rregRead* | r ⟩ **do**
    reqid[r] := reqid[r] +1;
    readSet[r] := ∅;
    trigger ⟨ *bebBroadcast* | [READ, r, reqid[r]] ⟩;

upon event ⟨ *bebDeliver* | p_j, [READ, r, id] ⟩ **do**
    trigger ⟨ *pp2pSend* | p_j,[READVALUE, r, id, sn[r], v[r]] ⟩;

upon event ⟨ *pp2pDeliver* | p_j, [READVALUE, r, id, tstamp, val] ⟩ **do**
    if id=reqid[r] **then**
        readSet[r] := readSet[r] ∪ {(tstamp, val)};

upon exists r **such that** (|readSet[r]| > N/2) **do**
    (v, ts) := highest(readSet[r]);
    v[r] := v;
    sn[r] := ts;
    trigger ⟨ *on-rregReadReturn* | r, v ⟩;

---

a majority adopt this value (i.e., store it locally) as well as its timestamp. Process p_1 considers the write to be complete (and hence returns the write confirmation) when p_1 has received an acknowledgment from a majority of the processes indicating that they have indeed adopted the new value and the corresponding timestamp. It is important at this point to note that a process p_i will adopt a value sent by the writer only if p_i has not already adopted a more recent value (with a larger timestamp). Process p_i might have adopted an old value if, for instance, p_1 has sent a value v_1, and then later a value v_2, and process p_i receives v_2 before v_1. This would mean that p_i was not in the majority that made it possible for p_1 to complete its writing of v_1 before proceeding to the writing of v_2.

To read a value, a reader process broadcasts a READ message to all other processes and selects the value with the largest timestamp from a majority. The processes in this majority act as witnesses of what was written before. This majority not need to be the same as the one used by the writter. Choosing the largest timestamp ensures that the last value is chosen, provided there is no concurrency. To simplify the presentation of our "Majority Voting" algorithm (Algorithm 4.2–4.3), the reader uses a function *highest* that returns the value with the largest timestamp from a set of pairs (value, timestamp) in the set of all pairs returned by a majority. Note that every request is tagged with a unique identifier, and that the corresponding replies carry this identifier. In the case of the writer, the tag is simply the timestamp associated with the value written. In the case of the reader, it is a specific sequence number solely used for identification purposes. In this way, the reader can figure out whether a given reply message matches a given request message (and is not an old reply). This is important here since the reader could, for instance, confuse two ACK messages: one for an old read invocation and one for a new one. This might lead to the violation the *validity* property of the register.

Clearly, and just like our "Read-One Write-All" algorithm, our "Majority Voting" algorithm implements an array of registers. The algorithm is designed to maintain the state of an array of registers. It keeps an array of all relevant state variables, indexed by the identifier of each register. Similarly, all messages carry the identifier of the register which is the target of the operation being executed.

Correctness. The *termination* property follows from the properties of the underlying communication abstractions and the assumption that of a majority of the correct processes exists in the system.

Consider now *validity*. Consider first the case of a read that is not concurrent with any write. Assume, furthermore, that a read is invoked by some process p_i and the last value written by the writer p_1, say, v, has timestamp sn_1 at p_1. This means that, at the time when the read is invoked, a majority of the processes have timestamp sn_1, and there is no larger timestamp in the system. This is because the writer uses increasing timestamps.

Before returning from the read operation, p_i consults a majority of the processes and hence gets at least one value with timestamp sn_1. This is because majorities always intersect (i.e., they form quorums). Process p_i hence returns value v with timestamp sn_1, which is indeed the last value written. Consider now the case where the read is concurrent with some write of value v and timestamp sn_1, and the previous write was for value v' and timestamp $sn_1 - 1$. If any process returns sn_1 to p_i, then p_i will return v, which is a valid reply. Otherwise, at least one process will return $sn_1 - 1$ and p_i will return v', which is also a valid reply.

Performance. Every write operation requires one communication roundtrip between the writer and a majority of the processes, and every read requires one communication roundtrip between the reader and a majority of the processes. In both operations, at most $2N$ messages are exchanged.

4.3 $(1, N)$ Atomic Register

We give here the specification and underlying algorithms of a $(1, N)$ atomic register. The generalization to multiple writers will be discussed in the next section.

4.3.1 Specification

With a regular register specification, nothing prevents a process from reading a value v and then v', even if the writer process has written v' and then v, as long as the writes and the reads are concurrent. Furthermore, consider a

(a) non-atomic   (b) atomic

Fig. 4.3: Register executions

register on which only one write operation is invoked by the writer p_1, say, with some value v, and p_1 crashes before returning from the operation and does not recover, i.e., the operation is not complete. A subsequent reader might read v whereas another, coming even later, might not, i.e., it might return the initial value of the register. An atomic register is a regular register that prevents such behavior.

The interface and properties of a $(1, N)$ atomic register are given in Module 4.2. A $(1, N)$ atomic register is a regular register that, in addition to the properties of a regular register (Module 4.1) ensures a specific *ordering* property which, roughly speaking, prevents an old value from being read once a new value has been read.

Typically, with a $(1, N)$ atomic register, a reader process cannot read a value v', after some value v was read (possibly by some other process), if v' was written before v. In addition, consider a register on which one write operation was invoked and the writer that invoked this operation, say, with some value v, crashed before returning from the operation, i.e., the operation is not complete. Once a subsequent reader reads v, no subsequent reader can read the initial value of the register.

The execution depicted in Figure 4.3b is that of an atomic register whereas the execution depicted in Figure 4.3a is not. In the execution of Figure 4.3a, the *ordering* property of an atomic register should prevent the read of process p_2 from returning 6 and then 5, given that 5 was written before 6.

It is important to note that none of our previous algorithms implements a $(1, N)$ atomic register. We illustrate this through the execution depicted in Figure 4.4 as a counterexample for our "Read-One Write-All" regular register algorithm (Algorithm 4.1), and the execution depicted in Figure 4.5 as a counterexample for our "Majority Voting" regular register algorithm (Algorithm 4.2–4.3).

- The scenario of Figure 4.4 can occur with Algorithm 4.1 if during the second write operation of p_1, the new value 6 is received and read by p_2 before it is received by p_3. Before receiving the new value, p_3 will continue to read the previous value 5 even if its read operation occurs after the read by p_2.

Module 4.2 Interface and properties of a $(1, N)$ atomic register

Module:

Name: $(1, N)$AtomicRegister (on-areg).

Events:

Request: ⟨ *on-aregRead | reg* ⟩: Used to invoke a read operation on register *reg*.

Request: ⟨ *on-aregWrite | reg, v* ⟩: Used to invoke a write operation of value v on register *reg*.

Confirmation: ⟨ *on-aregReadReturn | reg, v* ⟩: Used to return v as a response to the read invocation on register *reg* and indicates that the operation is complete.

Confirmation: ⟨ *on-aregWriteReturn | reg* ⟩: Confirms that the write operation has taken place at register *reg* and is complete.

Properties:

AR1: *Termination:* If a correct process invokes an operation, the process eventually receives the corresponding confirmation (same as RR1).

AR2: *Validity:* A read returns the last value written, or the value concurrently written (same as RR2).

AR3: *Ordering:* If a read returns v_2 after a read that precedes it has returned v_1, then v_1 cannot be written after v_2.

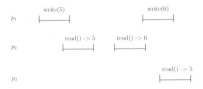

Fig. 4.4: Violation of atomicity in the "Read-One Write-All" regular register algorithm

- The scenario of Figure 4.5 can occur with Algorithm 4.2-4.3 if p_2 has accessed p_1 and p_4 in its second *read* while p_3 has accessed p_4 and p_5 while p_1 is performing is second write (after p_2 has been updated but before the update of p_3, p_4 and p_5). Clearly, this can also occur for Algorithm 4.1.

In the following, we give algorithms that implement the $(1, N)$ atomic register abstraction. We first describe how to automatically transform any (fail-stop or fail-silent) $(1, N)$ regular algorithm into a $(1, N)$ atomic register algorithm. Such a transformation is modular and helps understand the fundamental difference between atomic and regular registers. It does not however lead to efficient algorithms. We will later describe how to extend our regular register algorithms in an ad hoc way and obtain efficient $(1, N)$ atomic register algorithms.

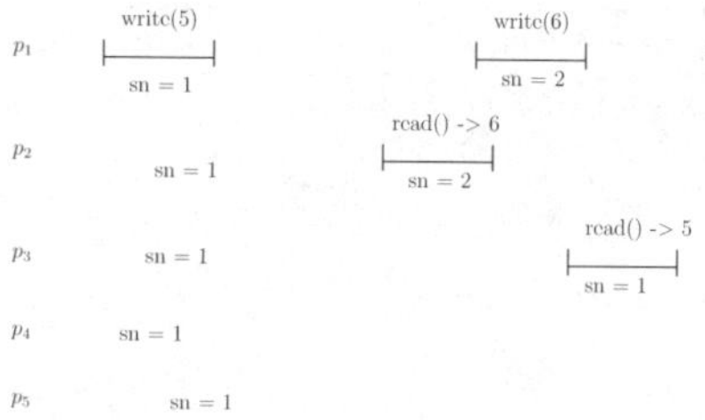

Fig. 4.5: Violation of atomicity in the "Majority Voting" regular register algorithm

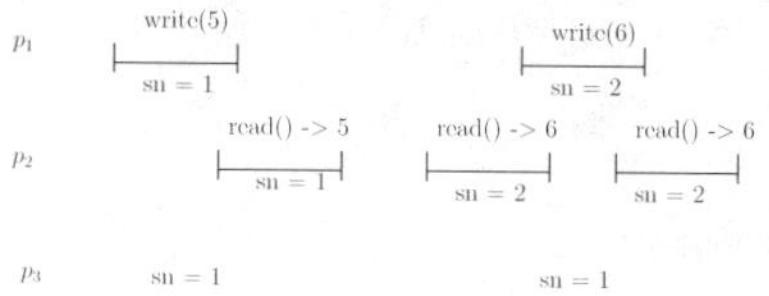

Fig. 4.6: A $(1, N)$ atomic register execution

4.3.2 Transformation: From $(1, N)$ Regular to $(1, N)$ Atomic

For pedagogical reasons, we divide the problem of transforming any $(1, N)$ regular register into a $(1, N)$ atomic register algorithm in two parts. We first explain how to transform any $(1, N)$ regular register algorithm into a $(1, 1)$ atomic register algorithm and then how to transform any $(1, 1)$ atomic register algorithm into a $(1, N)$ atomic register algorithm. It is important to note that these transformations do not use any other means of communication between processes than the underlying registers.

From $(1, N)$ Regular to $(1, 1)$ Atomic. The first transformation is given in Algorithm 4.4 and its underlying idea is simple. To build a $(1, 1)$ atomic register with p_1 as a writer and p_2 as a reader, we make use of one $(1, N)$ regular register of which the writer is also p_1 and the reader is also p_2. Furthermore, the writer p_1 maintains a timestamp that it increments and associates with every new value to be written. The reader also maintains a timestamp, together with a variable to locally store the latest value read from the register. Intuitively, the goal of storing this value is to make sure that an old value is not returned after a new one has been returned.

In Algorithm 4.4 there is a one-to-one mapping between the atomic registers maintained by the algorithm (as before, the algorithm maintains an array of such registers) and the underlying regular registers. That is, once an operation is invoked on an atomic register of index n, the same index is used to select the corresponding regular register.

Algorithm 4.4 From $(1, N)$ Regular to $(1, 1)$ Atomic Registers

---

Implements:
    $(1, 1)$AtomicRegister (oo-areg).

Uses:
    $(1, N)$RegularRegister(on-rreg).

upon event ⟨ *Init* ⟩ **do**
    forall r **do**
        ts$[r] := 0$;
        sn$[r] := 0$;
        v$[r] := 0$;

upon event ⟨ *oo-aregWrite* | r, val ⟩ **do**
    ts$[r] :=$ ts$[r] + 1$;
    trigger ⟨ *on-rregWrite* | r, (ts$[r]$,val) ⟩;

upon event ⟨ *on-rregWriteReturn* | r ⟩ **do**
    trigger ⟨ *oo-aregWriteReturn* | r ⟩;

upon event ⟨ *oo-aregRead* | r ⟩ **do**
    trigger ⟨ *on-rregRead* | r ⟩;

upon event ⟨ *on-rregReadRet* | r, (tstamp,val) ⟩ **do**
    if tstamp $>$ sn$[r]$ **then**
        sn$[r] :=$ tstamp; v$[r] :=$ val;
    trigger ⟨ *oo-aregReadReturn* | r, v$[r]$ ⟩;

We now explain the steps underlying each (read or write) operation of a single atomic register. To make the explanation clear, we refer to the atomic register as *atomicReg* and to the underlying regular register as *regularReg*.

- To write a value v in the atomic register *atomicReg*, the writer p_1 increments its timestamp and writes it, together with v in the underlying regular register *regularReg*.
- To read a value in the atomic register *atomicReg*, the reader p_2 reads the value in the underlying regular register *regularReg* as well as the associated timestamp. If the timestamp read is larger than the one previously locally stored by the reader p_2, then p_2 writes the new timestamp, together with the corresponding new value just read, and returns the latest. Otherwise, the reader simply returns the value it had already locally stored.

Correctness. The *termination* property of the atomic register follows from the one of the underlying regular register.

Consider *validity*. Assume first a read that is not concurrent with any write, and the last value written by p_1, say, v, is associated with timestamp sn_1. The timestamp stored by p_2 is either sn_1, if p_2 has already read v in some previous read, or a strictly lower value. In both cases, due to the *validity* property of the regular register, a read by p_2 will return v. Consider now the case where the read is concurrent with some write of value v and timestamp sn_1, and the previous write was for value v' and timestamp $sn_1 - 1$. The timestamp stored by p_2 cannot be strictly larger than sn_1. Hence, due to the *validity* property of the underlying regular register, p_2 will return either v or v'; both are valid replies.

Consider now *ordering*. Assume p_1 writes value v and then v'. Assume p_2 returns v' for some read and consider any subsequent read of p_2. The timestamp stored locally at p_2 is either the one associated with v' or a larger one. According to the transformation algorithm, there is no way p_2 can return v.

Performance. Interestingly, writing in the atomic register requires only a local computation (incrementing a timestamp) in addition to writing in the regular register. Similarly, reading from the atomic register requires only a local computation (performing a test and possibly some affectations) in addition to reading from the regular register. This observation means that no messages need to be added to an algorithm that implements a $(1, 1)$ regular register in order to implement an $(1, N)$ atomic register.

From (1, 1) Atomic to (1, N) Atomic. We describe here an algorithm that implements the abstraction of a $(1, N)$ atomic register out of $(1, 1)$ atomic registers. To get an intuition of the transformation, think of a teacher, i.e., the writer, who needs to communicate some information to a set of students, i.e., the readers, through the abstraction of a traditional blackboard. In some sense, a board is typically a $(1, N)$ register, as long as only the teacher writes on it. It is, furthermore, atomic as it is made of a single physical entity.

Assume, however, that the teacher cannot physically gather all students within the same classroom, and hence cannot use one physical board for all. Instead, this global board needs to be emulated using one or several electronic boards (e-boards) that could also be written by one person but could only be read by one person, say, every student can have one or several of such boards at home that only he or she can read.

It makes sense to have the teacher write each new piece of information on at least one e-board per student. This is intuitively necessary for the students to eventually read the information provided by the teacher, i.e., to ensure the *validity* property of the register. This is, however, not enough if we want to guarantee the *ordering* property of an atomic register. Indeed, assume that the teacher writes two consecutive pieces of information, X and then Y. It might happen that a student reads Y and then, later on, some other student reads X, say, because the information flow from the teacher to the first student is faster than the flow to the second student. This case of *ordering* violation is similar to the situation of Figure 4.4.

One way to cope with this issue is for every student, before terminating the reading of some information, to transmit this information to all other students, through other e-boards. That is, every student would use, besides the e-board devoted to the teacher to provide new information, another one for the student to write new information on. Whenever a student reads some information from the teacher, he or she first writes this information on the e-boards of all other students before returning the information. Old and new information are distinguished using timestamps.

The transformation we give in Algorithm 4.5–4.6 implements an array of $(1, N)$ atomic registers. The one considered in the algorithm is denoted by r. The writer in r is p_1, and the building of r makes use of a number of $(1, 1)$ atomic registers.

These $(1, 1)$ registers are used in the following way:

1. A series of N $(1, 1)$ atomic registers, with identities stored in variables $writer[r, 1]$, $writer[r, 2]$, ..., $writer[r, N]$. These registers are used to communicate between the writer, i.e., p_1, and each of the N readers. In all these registers, the writer is p_1. The reader of register $writer[r, k]$ is p_k.
2. A series of N^2 $(1, 1)$ atomic registers, with identities stored in variables $readers[r, 1, 1]$, ..., $readers[r, i, j]$, ..., $readers[r, N, N]$. These registers are used to communicate between the readers. The register with identifier $readers[r, i, j]$ is used to inform reader p_i about the last value read by reader p_j.

Algorithm 4.5–4.6 also relies on a timestamp ts that indicates the version of the current value of the register. For presentation simplicity, we also make use here of a function *highest* that returns the pair (timestamp, value) with the largest timestamp in a set of such pairs.

Correctness. Due to the *termination* property of the underlying $(1, 1)$ atomic registers and the fact that the transformation algorithm contains no loop or wait statement, every operation eventually returns.

Similarly, due the *validity* property of the underlying $(1, 1)$ atomic registers, and the fact that the value with the largest timestamp is chosen to be returned, we also derive the *validity* of the $(1, N)$ atomic register.

Consider now the *ordering* property. Consider a write w_1 of a value v_1 with timestamp s_1 that precedes a write w_2 with value v_2 and timestamp s_2 ($s_1 < s_2$) (in register r). Assume that some read operation returns v_2: According to the algorithm, for any j in $[1, N]$, p_i has written (s_2, v_2) in $readers[r, i, j]$. Due to the *ordering* property of the underlying $(1, 1)$ registers, every subsequent read will return a value with a timestamp at least as large as s_2, i.e., there is no way to return v_1.

Performance. Every write operation into the $(1, N)$ register requires N writes into $(1, 1)$ registers. Every read from the $(1, N)$ register requires one read from N $(1, 1)$ registers and one write into N $(1, 1)$ registers.

We give, in the following, two ad hoc $(1, N)$ atomic register algorithms. The first one is a fail-stop and the second is a fail-silent algorithm. These are adaptations of the "Read-One Write-All" and "Majority Voting" $(1, N)$

Algorithm 4.5 From $(1, 1)$ Atomic to $(1, N)$ Atomic Registers (write)

Implements:
    $(1, N)$AtomicRegister (on-areg).

Uses:
    $(1, 1)$AtomicRegister (oo-areg).

upon event $\langle$ *Init* $\rangle$ **do**
    $i := rank$ (self); // rank of the process (integer in range $1 \ldots N$)
    forall r **do**
        $\text{ts}[r] := 0$;
        $\text{acks}[r] := 0$;
        $\text{readval}[r] := 0$;
        $\text{readSet}[r] := \emptyset$;
        $\text{reading}[r] := \text{true}$;
        for $j = 1$ **to** N **do** // assign namespace of $(1, 1)$ atomic registers
            $\text{writer}[r, j] := (r - 1)(N^2 + N) + j$;
            for $k = 1$ **to** N **do**
                $\text{readers}[r, j, k] := (N^2 + N)(r - 1) + jN + k$;

upon event $\langle$ *on-aregWrite* $\mid$ r, v $\rangle$ **do**
    $\text{ts}[r] := \text{ts}[r] + 1$;
    $\text{reading}[r] := \text{false}$;
    for $j = 1$ **to** N **do**
        trigger $\langle$ *oo-aregWrite* $\mid$ writer[r,j], (ts[r], v) $\rangle$;

upon event $\langle$ *oo-aregWriteReturn* $\mid$ writer$[r, j]$ $\rangle$ **do**
    $\text{acks}[r] := \text{acks}[r] + 1$;

upon exists r **such that** $(\text{acks}[r] = N) \wedge \neg \text{reading}[r]$ **do**
    $\text{acks}[r] := 0$;
    $\text{reading}[r] := \text{true}$;
    trigger $\langle$ *on-aregWriteReturn* $\mid$ r $\rangle$;

---

regular register algorithms, respectively. Both algorithms require fewer messages than we would obtain through the automatic transformations described above.

4.3.3 Fail-Stop Algorithm: Read-Impose Write-All $(1, N)$ Atomic Register

If the goal is to implement a register with one writer and multiple readers, i.e., $(1, N)$, the "Read-One Write-All" regular register algorithm (Algorithm 4.1) clearly does not work: the scenario depicted in Figure 4.4 illustrates this case.

To cope with this case, we define an extension to the "Read-One Write-All" regular register algorithm (Algorithm 4.1) that circumvents the problem by having the reader also *impose*, on all other processes, the value it is about to return. In other words, the read operation acts also as a write. The resulting

---

Algorithm 4.6 From $(1, 1)$ Atomic to $(1, N)$ Atomic Registers (read)

---

upon event $\langle$ *on-aregRead* | r $\rangle$ **do**
    readSet[r] := ∅;
    for $j = 1$ **to** N **do**
        trigger $\langle$ *oo-aregRead* | readers[r, i, j] $\rangle$;

upon event $\langle$ *oo-aregReadReturn* | readers[r, i, j], (tstamp, v) $\rangle$ **do**
    readSet[r] := readSet[r] ∪ {(tstamp, v)};

upon exists r **such that** |readSet[r]| = N) **do**
    trigger $\langle$ *oo-aregRead* | writer[r, i] $\rangle$;

upon event $\langle$ *oo-aregReadReturn* | writer[r, i], (tstamp, v) $\rangle$ **do**
    (maxts, readval[r]) := *highest* (readSet[r] ∪ {(tstamp, v)});
    for $j = 1$ **to** N **do**
        trigger $\langle$ *oo-aregWrite* | readers[r, j, i], (maxts, readval[r]) $\rangle$;

upon event $\langle$ *oo-aregWriteReturn* | readers[r, j, i] $\rangle$ **do**
    acks[r] := acks[r] + 1;

upon exists r **such that** acks[r] = N ∧ reading[r] **do**
    acks[r] := 0;
    trigger $\langle$ *on-aregReadReturn* | r, readval[r] $\rangle$;

---

algorithm (Algorithm 4.7–4.8) is named "Read-Impose Write-All". The writer uses a timestamp to date the values it is writing: it is this timestamp that ensures the *ordering* property of every execution. A process that is asked to store a value that is older than the one it has does not modify its value. We will discuss the need for this test, as well as the need for the timestamp, through an exercise (at the end of this chapter).

Correctness. Termination and *validity* are ensured as in our "Read-One Write-All" algorithm (Algorithm 4.1). Consider now *ordering*. Assume p_1 writes a value v and then v', which is associated with some timestamp sn. Assume, furthermore, that some reader p_i reads v' and, later on, some other process p_j invokes another read operation. At the time where p_i completes its read, all processes that did not crash have a timestamp that is at least as large as sn. According to the "Read-One Impose-All" algorithm, there is no way p_j will later on change its value with v, as this has a smaller timestamp because it was written by p_1 before v'.

Performance. Every write or read operation requires two communication steps, corresponding to the roundtrip communication between the writer or the reader and all processes. At most $2N$ messages are needed in both cases.

Algorithm 4.7 Read-Impose Write-All (part I)

Implements:
   $(1, N)$AtomicRegister (on-areg).

Uses:
   BestEffortBroadcast (beb);
   PerfectPointToPointLinks (pp2p);
   PerfectFailureDetector ($\mathcal{P}$).

upon event ⟨ *Init* ⟩ **do**
   correct := Π;
   forall r **do**
      v[r] := 0;
      sn[r] := 0;
      readval[r] := 0;
      rqid[r] := 0;
      reading[r] := false;
      writeSet[r] := $\emptyset$;

upon event ⟨ *crash* | p_i ⟩ **do**
   correct := correct \ $\{p_i\}$;

upon event ⟨ *on-aregRead* | r ⟩ **do**
   rqid[r] := rqid[r] + 1;
   reading[r] := true;
   readval[r] := v[r];
   trigger ⟨ *bebBroadcast* | [WRITE, r, reqid[r], sn[r], v[r]] ⟩;

upon event ⟨ *on-aregWrite* | r, val ⟩ **do**
   rqid[r] := rqid[r] + 1;
   trigger ⟨ *bebBroadcast* | [WRITE, r, reqid[r], sn[r] + 1, val] ⟩;

4.3.4 Fail-Silent Algorithm: Read-Impose Write-Majority $(1, N)$ Atomic Register

In the following, we consider a fail-silent model. We describe an adaptation of our "Majority Voting" $(1, N)$ regular register algorithm (Algorithm 4.2–4.3) to implement a $(1, N)$ atomic register.

This adaptation, called "Read-Impose Write-Majority", is depicted in Algorithm 4.9–4.10. The implementation of the write operation is similar to that of the "Majority Voting" algorithm (Algorithm 4.2–4.3): the writer simply makes sure a majority adopts its value. The implementation of the read operation is however, different. A reader selects the value with the largest timestamp frm a majority, as in the "Majority Voting" algorithm, but now also imposes this value and makes sure a majority adopts it before completing the read operation: this is the key to ensuring the *ordering* property of an atomic register.

Algorithm 4.8 Read-Impose Write-All (part II)

---

upon event ⟨ *bebDeliver* | p_j,[WRITE, r, id, tstamp, val] ⟩ **do**
    if tstamp > sn[r] **then**
        v[r] := val;
        sn[r] := tstamp;
    trigger ⟨ *pp2pSend* | p_j, [ACK, r, id] ⟩;

upon event ⟨ *pp2pDeliver* | p_j, [ACK, r, id] ⟩ **do**
    if id = reqid[r] **then**
        writeSet[r] := writeSet[r] ∪ {p_j};

upon exists r **such that** correct ⊆ writeSet[r] **do**
    writeSet[r] := ∅;
    if (reading[r] = true) **then**
        reading[r] := false;
        trigger ⟨ *on-aregReadReturn* | r, readval[r] ⟩;
    else
        trigger ⟨ *on-aregWriteReturn* | r ⟩;

It is important to notice that the "Majority Voting" algorithm can be seen as a particular case of the "Read-Impose Write-Majority" algorithm in the following sense: given that there is only one reader in the "Majority Voting" algorithm, the reader simply adopts the value read (i.e., imposes it on itself) and makes sure to include itself in the majority.

Correctness. *Termination* and *validity* are ensured as in Algorithm 4.2–4.3 ("Majority Voting"). Consider now the *ordering* property. Assume that a read invocation r_1, by process p_i, returns a value v_1 from a write invocation w_1, by process p_1 (the only writer); a read invocation r_2, by process p_j, returns a different value v_2 from a write invocation w_1, also by process p_1; and r_1 precedes r_2. Assume by contradiction that w_2 precedes w_1. According to the algorithm, the sequence number that p_1 associated with v_1, ts_k, is strictly larger than the one p_1 associated with v_2, $ts_{k'}$. Given that r_1 precedes r_2, when r_2 was invoked, a majority has a timestamp that is at least $ts_{k'}$. Hence p_j cannot return v_2, because v_2 has a strictly smaller sequence number than v_1. A contradiction.

Performance. Every write operation requires two communication steps corresponding to one roundtrip exchange between p_1 and a majority of the processes. $2N$ messages are exchanged. Every read requires four communication steps corresponding to two roundtrip exchanges between the reader and a majority of the processes. $4N$ messages are exchanged.

Algorithm 4.9 Read-Impose Write-Majority (part I)

Implements:
    $(1, N)$AtomicRegister (on-areg).

Uses:
    BestEffortBroadcast (beb); PerfectPointToPointLinks (pp2p).

upon event ⟨ *Init* ⟩ **do**
    forall r **do**
        sn[r] := 0;
        v[r] := 0;
        acks[r] := 0;
        reqid[r] := 0;
        readval [r] := 0;
        reading[r] := false;
        readSet[r] := ∅;

upon event ⟨ *on-aregWrite* | r, val ⟩ **do**
    reqid[r] := reqid[r] + 1;
    sn[r] := sn[r] + 1;
    v[r] := val;
    acks[r] := 1;
    trigger ⟨ *bebBroadcast* | [WRITE, r, reqid, sn[r], val] ⟩;

upon event ⟨ *bebDeliver* | p_j, [WRITE, r, id, t, val] ⟩ **do**
    if t > sn[r] **then**
        sn[r]:= t; v[r] := val;
    trigger ⟨ *pp2pSend* | p_j, [ACK, r, id] ⟩;

upon event ⟨ *pp2pDeliver* | p_j, [ACK, r, id] ⟩ **do**
    if reqid[r] = id **then**
        acks[r] := acks[r] + 1;

4.4 (N, N) Atomic Register

4.4.1 Multiple Writers

So far, we have focused on registers with a single writer. That is, our specifications of regular and atomic registers do not provide any guarantees when multiple processes write in a register. It is natural to ask what should be ensured in the case of multiple writers.

One difficulty underlying this question has to do with defining the *validity* property in the case of multiple writers. Indeed, this property requires that a read that is not concurrent with any write should return the *last* value written. But if two processes have written different values concurrently, say, v and v', before some other process invokes a read operation, then what should this read return? Assuming we make it possible for the reader to return either v or v', do we allow a concurrent reader, or even a reader that comes later, to

---

Algorithm 4.10 Read-Impose Write-Majority (part II)

---

upon exists r **such that** acks[r] $> N/2$ **do**
    if reading[r] = true **then**
        reading[r] := false;
        trigger ⟨ *on-aregReadReturn* | r, readval[r] ⟩;
    else
        trigger ⟨ *on-aregWriteReturn* | r ⟩;

upon event ⟨ *on-aregRead* | r ⟩ **do**
    reqid[r] := reqid[r] + 1;
    readSet[r] := ∅;
    trigger ⟨ *bebBroadcast* | [READ, r, reqid[r]] ⟩;

upon event ⟨ *bebDeliver* | p_j, [READ, r, id] ⟩ **do**
    trigger ⟨ *pp2pSend* | p_j, [READVALUE, r, id, sn[r], v[r]] ⟩;

upon event ⟨ *pp2pDeliver* | p_j, [READVALUE, r, id, ts, val] ⟩ **do**
    if reqid[r] = id **then**
        readSet[r] := readSet[r] ∪ { (ts, val) };

upon exists r **such that** |readSet[r]| $> N/2$ **do**
    (tstamp,readval[r]) := *highest*(readSet[r]);
    acks[r] := 0;
    reading[r] := true;
    trigger ⟨ *bebBroadcast* | [WRITE, r, reqid[r], tstamp, readval[r]] ⟩;

---

return the other value? What about a failed write? If a process writes a value v and crashes before completing the write, does a reader need to return v or can it return an older value?

In the following, we address these questions and generalize the specification of atomic registers to multiple writers.

4.4.2 Specification

In short, an (N, N) atomic register ensures that failed writes appear either as if they were never invoked or if they were complete, i.e., as if they were invoked and terminated. (Clearly, failed read operations do always appear as if they were never invoked.) In addition, even in the face of concurrency, the values returned by reads could have been returned by a serial execution (called a *linearization* of the actual execution), where any operation takes place at some instant between its invocation and reply instants. The execution is in this sense *linearizable*, i.e., there is a way to *linearize* it.

A (N, N) atomic register is a generalization of a $(1, N)$ atomic register in the following sense: every execution of a $(1, N)$ atomic register is an execution of an (N, N) atomic register. The interface and properties of an (N, N) atomic register are given in Module 4.3.

Module 4.3 Interface and properties of an (N, N) atomic register

Module:

   Name: (N, N)AtomicRegister (nn-areg).

Events:

   Same as for a regular register (just replace "on-" by "nn-" on the interface).

Properties:

   NAR1: *Termination:* Same as RR1.

   NAR2: *Atomicity:* Every failed operation appears to be complete or does not appear to have been invoked at all, and every complete operation appears to have been executed at some instant between its invocation and the corresponding confirmation event.

To study the implementation of (N, N) atomic registers, we adopt the same modular approach as for the $(1, N)$ case. We first describe a general transformation that implements an (N, N) atomic register using $(1, N)$ atomic registers. This transformation does not rely on any other way of exchanging information among the processes, besides the underlying $(1, N)$ atomic registers. This helps understand the fundamental difference between both abstractions. We will also study ad hoc and efficient (N, N) atomic register algorithms in various models.

4.4.3 Transformation: From $(1, N)$ Atomic to (N, N) Atomic Registers

To get an intuition of this transformation, think of emulating a general (atomic) blackboard to be used by a set of teachers to provide information to a set of students. Teachers would like to be able to write and read information on a single common board. However, what is available are simply boards where only one teacher can write information. If every teacher uses his or her own board to write information, then it will not be clear for a student which information to select and still ensure the atomicity of the common board, i.e., the illusion of one physical common board that all teachers share. The difficulty is actually for any given student to select the latest information written. Indeed, if some teacher A writes X and then some other teacher B later writes Y, then a student that comes afterward should read Y. But how can the student know that Y is indeed the latest information, given that what is available are simply individual boards, one for each teacher?

This can in fact be ensured by having the teachers coordinate their writing to create a causal precedence among the information they write. Teacher B that writes Y could actually read the board of teacher A and, when finding X, associate with Y some global timestamp that denotes the very fact that Y is indeed more recent than X. This is the key to the transformation algorithm we present below.

The transformation algorithm (Algorithm 4.11), implements an array of (N, N) atomic registers. Each register, denoted by r, uses N $(1, N)$ atomic registers, whose identities are stored in variables $writer[r, 1], \ldots, writer[r, N]$. Every register $writer[r, i]$ contains a value and an associated timestamp. Basically, to write a value v in r, process p_j reads all $(1, N)$ registers and selects the largest timestamp, which it increments and associates with the value v to be written. Then p_j writes in $writer[r, j]$ the value with the associated timestamp.

To read a value from r, process p_j reads all registers from $writer[r, 1]$ to $writer[r, N]$, and returns the value with the largest timestamp. To distinguish values that are associated with the same timestamp, p_j uses the identity of the processes that have originally written those values and order them accordingly, i.e., p_j uses the indices of the registers from which it has read these timestamps. We define in this way a total order among the timestamps associated with the values, and we abstract away this order within a function *highest-ts* that returns the timestamp with the highest order. We also make use of a similar function, called *highest-val*, but with a different signature, that returns the value with the largest timestamp, from a set of triplets (timestamp, value, process identity).

Correctness. The *termination* property of the (N, N) register follows from that of the $(1, N)$ register, whereas *atomicity* follows from the total order used to write values: this order respects the real-time order of the operations.

Performance. Every write operation into the (N, N) atomic register requires N reads from each of the $(1, N)$ registers and one write into a $(1, N)$ register. Every read from the (N, N) register requires N reads from each of the $(1, N)$ registers.

1. Assume we apply the transformation of Algorithm 4.11 to the "Read-One Impose-All" fail-stop algorithm (Algorithm 4.7–4.8) in order to obtain an (N, N) atomic register algorithm. Every read in the (N, N) register would involve N (parallel) communication roundtrips between the reader and all other processes. Furthermore, every write operation in the (N, N) register would involve N (parallel) communication roundtrips between the writer and all other processes (to determine the largest timestamp), and then another communication roundtrip between the writer and all other processes (to perform the actual writing).

2. Similarly, assume we apply the transformation of Algorithm 4.11 to "Read-Majority Impose-Majority" algorithm (Algorithm 4.9–4.10) in order to obtain a (N, N) atomic register algorithm. Every read in the (N, N) register would involve N communication roundtrips between the reader and a majority of the processes (to determine the latest value), and then N other communication roundtrips between the reader and a majority of the processes (to impose that value). Furthermore, every write operation in the (N, N) register would involve N parallel communication roundtrips between the writer and a majority (to determine the

---

Algorithm 4.11 From (1, N) Atomic to (N, N) Atomic Registers

Implements:
  (N, N)AtomicRegister (nn-areg).

Uses:
  (1, N)AtomicRegisters(o-areg).

upon event ⟨ *Init* ⟩ **do**
  i := *rank* (self); // rank of the process (integer in range 1 ... N)
  forall r **do**
    writeval[r] := 0;
    writing[r] := false;
    readSet[r] := ∅;
    for j = 1 **to** N **do** // assign namespace of (1, N) atomic registers
      writer[r, j] := (r − 1)N + j;

upon event ⟨ *nn-aregWrite* | r, v ⟩ **do**
  writeval[r] := v;
  writing[r] := true;
  readSet[r] := ∅;
  for j = 1 **to** N **do**
    trigger ⟨ *on-aregRead* | writer[r,j] ⟩;

upon event ⟨ *nn-aregRead* | r ⟩ **do**
  readSet[r] := ∅;
  for j = 1 **to** N **do**
    trigger ⟨ *on-aregRead* | writer[r,j] ⟩;

upon event ⟨ *on-aregReadReturn* | writer[r,j], (tstamp,val) ⟩ **do**
  readSet[r] := readSet[r] ∪ { (tstamp, val) };

upon exists r **such that** |readSet[r]| = N **do**
  (t, v) := *highest* (readSet[r]);
  if writing[r] **then**
    writing[r] := false;
    trigger ⟨ *on-aregWrite* | writer[r,i], (t+1, writeval[r]) ⟩;
  else
    trigger ⟨ *nn-aregReadReturn* | r, v ⟩;
upon event ⟨ *on-aregWriteReturn* | writer[r,i] ⟩ **do**
  trigger ⟨ *nn-aregWriteReturn* | r ⟩;

---

largest timestamp) and then another communication roundtrip between the writer and a majority (to perform the actual writing).

We present, in the following, ad hoc algorithms that are more efficient than the algorithms we obtain through the automatic transformations. We describe first a fail-stop algorithm and then a fail-silent algorithm.

4.4.4 Fail-Stop Algorithm: Read-Impose Write-Consult (N, N) Atomic Register

We describe below an adaptation of our $(1, N)$ "Read-Impose Write-All" algorithm (Algorithm 4.7–4.8) to deal with multiple writers. To get an idea of the issue introduced by multiple writers, it is important to first figure out why the "Read-One Impose-All" algorithm cannot afford multiple writers. Consider indeed the case of two processes trying to write in a register implemented using the "Read-Impose Write-All" algorithm: say, processes p_1 and p_2. Different values would be associated with the same timestamp. To address this issue, the idea is to use the identity of the processes in the comparison, i.e., use the lexicographical order. (The idea of making use of process identities in the comparisons was also key in our transformation from $(1, N)$ to (N, N) atomic.) The resulting algorithm, called "Read-Impose Write-Consult" (Algorithm 4.12–4.13), is an extension of "Read-Impose Write-All" algorithm (Algorithm 4.7–4.8) that implements a (N, N) atomic register.

Correctness. The *termination* property of the register follows from the *completeness* property of the failure detector and the underlying channels. The *atomicity* property follows from the *accuracy* property of the failure detector.

Performance. Every read in the (N, N) register requires four communication steps: 4N messages are exchanged. Every write requires two communication steps: 2N messages are exchanged.

4.4.5 Fail-Silent Algorithm: Read-Impose Write-Consult-Majority (N, N) Atomic Register

We describe here how to obtain an algorithm that implements an (N, N) atomic register in a fail-silent model as an extension of our "Read-Impose Write-Majority" algorithm, i.e., Algorithm 4.9–4.10, that implements a $(1, N)$ atomic register. Let us first discuss the issue of multiple writers in Algorithm 4.9–4.10. Consider the case where a process p_1 makes a long sequence of write operations. Further, assume that some other process p_2 is never included in the majority required to complete those operations. When process p_2 tries to write using its local timestamp, its write operation will fail because its timestamp will be considered smaller than the current value by those processes involved in the majority required to terminate p_1's write operations. Intuitively, the problem is that now the timestamps are generated independently by each processes, something that did not happen with a single writer. What we actually expect from the timestamps is that (a) they be totally ordered, and (b) they reflect the precedence relation between operations. They should not be generated independently by multiple writers, but should in our example reflect the fact that the writing of Y precedes the writing of Z. In the case of multiple writers, we have to deal with the problem of how to determine a timestamp in a distributed fashion. The idea

---

Algorithm 4.12 Read-Impose Write-Consult (part I)

Implements:
    (N, N)AtomicRegister (nn-areg).

Uses:
    BestEffortBroadcast (beb);
    PerfectPointToPointLinks (pp2p);
    PerfectFailureDetector ($\mathcal{P}$).

upon event ⟨ *Init* ⟩ **do**
    correct := Π;
    i := *rank* (self);
    forall *r* **do**
        writeSet[r] := ∅;
        reading[r] := false;
        reqid[r] := 0;
        readval[r] := 0;
        v[r] := 0;
        ts[r] := 0;
        mrank[r] := 0;

upon event ⟨ *crash* | p_i ⟩ **do**
    correct := correct \ {p_i};

upon event ⟨ *nn-aRegRead* | r ⟩ **do**
    reqid[r] := reqid[r]+1;
    reading[r] := true;
    writeSet[r] := ∅;
    readval[r] := v[r];
    trigger ⟨ *bebBroadcast* | [WRITE, r, reqid[r], (ts[r], mrank[r]), v[r]] ⟩;

upon event ⟨ *nn-aRegWrite* | r, val ⟩ **do**
    reqid[r] := reqid[r]+1;
    writeSet[r] := ∅;
    trigger ⟨ *bebBroadcast* | [WRITE, r, reqid[r], (ts[r] + 1, i), val] ⟩;

---

is to have every writer consult first other writers to collect their timestamps, and then to determine its timestamp by choosing the largest, i.e., we add one communication roundtrip between the writer and all processes (that did not crash). (The idea of consulting other writers is also key to our transformation above from $(1, N)$ to (N, N) atomic.)

We describe in Algorithm 4.14–4.15 the events that need to be modified or added to Algorithm 4.9–4.10 ("Read-Impose Write-Majority") in order to deal with multiple writers. More precisely, the read procedure of our (N, N) atomic register algorithm ("Read-Impose Write-Consult-Majority") is similar to that of Algorithm 4.9–4.10. The write procedure is different in that the writer first determines a timestamp to associate with the new value to be written by reading a majority of the processes. It is also important to notice

---

Algorithm 4.13 Read-Impose Write-Consult (part II)

---

upon event ⟨ *bebDeliver* | p_j,[WRITE, r, id, (t,j), val] ⟩ **do**
    if (t,j) > (ts[r], mrank[r]) **then**
        v[r] := val;
        ts[r] := t;
        mrank[r] := j;
    trigger ⟨ *pp2pSend* | p_j, [ACK, r, id] ⟩;

upon event ⟨ *pp2pDeliver* | p_j, [ACK, r, id] ⟩ **do**
    if id = reqid[r] **then**
        writeSet[r] := writeSet[r] ∪ {p_j};

upon exists r **such that** correct ⊆ writeSet[r] **do**
    writeSet[r] := ∅;
    if (reading[r] = true) **then**
        reading[r] := false;
        trigger ⟨ *nn-aregReadReturn* | r, readval[r] ⟩;
    else
        trigger ⟨ *nn-aregWriteReturn* | r ⟩;

---

that the processes distinguish values with the same timestamps using process identifiers. We assume that every value written is tagged with the identity of the originator process. A value v is considered more recent than a value v' if v has a strictly larger timestamp, or v and v' have the same timestamp and v was written by p_i whereas v' was written by p_j such that $i > j$. As in previous algorithms, we use a function *highest-ts* that returns the timestamp with the largest order and a similar function, called *highest-val*, that returns the value with the largest timestamp.

Correctness. The *termination* property of the register follows from the correct majority assumption and the underlying channels. The *atomicity* property follows from the quorum property of the majority.

Performance. Every read or write in the (N, N) register requires four communication steps corresponding to two roundtrip exchanges between the reader or the writer and a majority of the processes. In each case, at most $4N$ messages are exchanged.

4.5 $(1, N)$ Logged Regular Register

So far, we considered register specifications and implementations under the assumption that processes that crash do not recover. In other words, processes that crash, even if they recover, are excluded from the computation: they can neither read nor write in a register. Furthermore, they cannot help other processes reading or writing by storing and witnessing values. We revisit here this assumption and take into account processes that recover after crashing.

Algorithm 4.14 Read-Impose Write-Consult-Majority (part I)

Implements:
    (N, N)AtomicRegister (nn-areg).

Uses:
    BestEffortBroadcast (beb);
    PerfectPointToPointLinks (pp2p).

upon event $\langle$ *Init* $\rangle$ **do**
    i := *rank* (self);
    forall *r* **do**
        writeSet[r] := $\emptyset$;
        readSet[r] := $\emptyset$;
        reading[r] := false;
        reqid[r] := 0;
        v[r] := 0;
        ts[r] := 0;
        mrank[r] := 0;

upon event $\langle$ *nn-aregRead* | r $\rangle$ **do**
    reqid[r] := reqid[r] + 1;
    reading[r] := true;
    readSet[r] := $\emptyset$;
    writeSet[r] := $\emptyset$;
    trigger $\langle$ *bebBroadcast* | [READ, r, reqid[r]] $\rangle$;

upon event $\langle$ *nn-aregWrite* | r, val $\rangle$ **do**
    reqid[r] := reqid[r] + 1;
    writeval[r] := val;
    readSet[r] := $\emptyset$;
    writeSet[r] := $\emptyset$;
    trigger $\langle$ *bebBroadcast* | [READ, r, reqid[r]] $\rangle$;

upon event $\langle$ *bebDeliver* | p_j, [READ, r, id] $\rangle$ **do**
    trigger $\langle$ *pp2pSend* | p_j, [READVALUE, r, id, (ts[r], mrank[r]), v[r]] $\rangle$;

upon event $\langle$ *pp2pDeliver* | p_j, [READVALUE, r, id, (t,rk), val] $\rangle$ **do**
    if id = reqid[r] **then**
        readSet[r] := readSet[r] $\cup$ {$((t, rk), val)$};

That is, we give register specifications and algorithms that implement these specifications in the fail-recovery model.

4.5.1 Precedence in the Fail-Recovery Model

To define register semantics in a fail-recovery model, we first revisit the notion of precedence introduced earlier, assuming, by default, fail-no-recovery models.

Algorithm 4.15 Read-Impose Write-Consult-Majority (part II)

---

upon exists r **such that** $|readSet[r]| > N/2$ **do**
    ((t,rk), v) := *highest* (readSet[r]);
    readval[r] := v;
    if reading[r] **then**
        trigger ⟨ *bebBroadcast* | [WRITE, r, reqid[r], (t,rk), readval[r]] ⟩;
    else
        trigger ⟨ *bebBroadcast* | [WRITE, r, reqid[r], (t+1,i), writeval[r]] ⟩;

upon event ⟨ *bebDeliver* | p_j,[WRITE, r, id, (t,j), val] ⟩ **do**
    if (t,j) > (ts[r], mrank[r]) **then**
        v[r] := val;
        ts[r] := t;
        mrank[r] := j;
    trigger ⟨ *pp2pSend* | p_j, [ACK, r, id] ⟩;

upon event ⟨ *pp2pDeliver* | p_j, [ACK, r, id] ⟩ **do**
    if id = reqid[r] **then**
        writeSet[r] := writeSet[r] ∪ {p_j};

upon exists r **such that** $|writeSet[r]| > N/2$ **do**
    if (reading[r] = true) **then**
        reading[r] := false;
        trigger ⟨ *nn-aregReadReturn* | r, readval[r] ⟩;
    else
        trigger ⟨ *nn-aregWriteReturn* | r ⟩;

- We say that an operation *op1* (e.g., read or write) *precedes* an operation *op2* (e.g., read or write) if any of the following two conditions hold.
  1. the event corresponding to the return of *op1* occurs before (i.e., precedes) the event corresponding to the invocation of *op2*;
  2. the operations are invoked by the same process and the event corresponding to the invocation of *op2* occurs after the event corresponding to the invocation of *op1*.

It is important to note here that, for an operation *op1*, invoked by some process p_1 to *precede* an operation *op2* invoked by the same process, *op1* does not need to be complete. In this case, a process might have invoked *op1*, crashed, recovered, and invoked *op2*. This was clearly not possible in a crash-no-recovery model.

4.5.2 Specification

The interface and properties of a $(1, N)$ regular register in a fail-recovery model, called a *logged register* here, are given in Module 4.4. Logged atomic registers ($(1, N)$ and (N, N)) can be specified accordingly.

Module 4.4 Interface and properties of a $(1, N)$ logged regular register

Module:

    Name: $(1, N)$LoggedRegularRegister (on-log-rreg).

Events:

    Request: ⟨ *on-log-rregRead* | *reg* ⟩: Used to invoke a read operation on register *reg*.

    Request: ⟨ *on-log-rregWrite* | *reg, v* ⟩: Used to invoke a write operation of value *v* on register *reg*.

    Confirmation: ⟨ *on-log-rregReadReturn* | *reg, v* ⟩: Used to return *v* as a response to the read invocation on register *reg* and confirms that the operation is complete.

    Confirmation: ⟨ *on-log-rregWriteReturn* | *reg* ⟩: Confirms that the write operation is complete.

Properties:

    LRR1: *Termination:* If a process invokes an operation and does not crash,, the process eventually receives the corresponding confirmation.

    LRR2: *Validity:* A read returns the last value written, or the value concurrently written.

The *termination* property is similar to what we considered before, though expressed here in a different manner. Indeed the notion of correctness used in earlier register specifications has a different meaning here. It does not make much sense to require that a process that invokes some operation, that crashes, and then recovers, still gets back a reply to the operation. Our *termination* property requires, however, that if a process invokes an operation and does not crash, it eventually gets a reply.

On the other hand, the *validity* property is expressed as in earlier specifications, but now has a different meaning. Assume the writer p_1 crashes before completing the writing of some value X (no write was invoked before), then recovers and invokes the writing of value Y. Assume that p_2 concurrently invokes a read operation on the same register. It is valid that this read operation returns 0: value X is not considered to have been written. Now assume that p_2 invokes another read operation that is still concurrent with the writing of Y. It is no longer valid for p_2 to return X. In other words, there is only one last value written before Y: this can be either 0 or X, but not both.

4.5.3 Fail-Recovery Algorithm: Logged-Majority-Voting

Considering a fail-recovery model where all processes can crash, it is easy to see that even a $(1, 1)$ regular register algorithm cannot be implemented unless the processes have access to stable storage and a majority is correct. We thus make the following assumptions.

1. Every process has access to a local stable storage. This is supposed to be accessible through the primitives *store*, which atomically logs information in the stable storage, and *retrieve*, which gets back that information from the storage. Information that is logged in the stable storage is not lost after a crash.

2. A majority of the processes are correct. Remember that a correct process in a fail-recovery model is one that either never crashes, or eventually recovers and never crashes again.

Intuitively, we might consider transforming our "Majority Voting" regular register algorithm (i.e., Algorithm 4.2–4.3) to deal with process crashes and recoveries simply by logging every new value of any local variable to stable storage upon modification of that variable, and then retrieving all variables upon recovery. This would include messages to be delivered, i.e., the act of delivering a message would coincide with the act of storing it in stable storage. However, as we discussed earlier in this book, one should be careful with such an automatic transformation because access to stable storage is an expensive operation and should only be used when necessary.

In particular, we describe an algorithm (Algorithm 4.16–4.17), called "Logged Majority Voting" algorithm, that implements an array of $(1, N)$ logged regular registers. The algorithm logs the variables that are persistent across invocations (e.g., the value of the register at a given process and the associated timestamp), in one atomic operation, and retrieves these variables upon recovery. We discuss the need of logging atomicity through an exercise (at the end of the chapter).

The algorithm makes use of stubborn communication channels and stubborn broadcast communication abstractions. Remember that stubborn communication primitives ensure that, roughly speaking, if a message is sent to a correct process (in the fail-recovery sense), the message is delivered an infinite number of times, unless the sender crashes. This ensures that the process, even if it crashes and recovers a finite number of times, will eventually process every message sent to it.

Note that, upon recovery, every process first executes its initialization procedure and then its recovery one. Note also that we do not log the variables that are only persistent across events, e.g., the variable that counts the number of acknowledgments that a writer has received. The communication pattern of Algorithm 4.16–4.17 is similar to the one of the "Majority Voting" algorithm that implements a regular register for the fail-silent model (Algorithm 4.2–4.3). What we, furthermore, add here are logs. For every write operation, the writer logs the new timestamp and the value to be written, and then a majority of the processes logs the new value with its timestamp.

Correctness. The *termination* property follows from the properties of the underlying stubborn communication abstractions and the assumption of a majority of the correct processes.

Algorithm 4.16 Logged Majority Voting (init/recovery)

Implements:
  (1, N)LoggedRegularRegister (on-logrreg)
Uses:
  StubbornBestEffortBroadcast (sbeb);
  StubbornPointToPointLinks (sp2p).

upon event ⟨ *Init* ⟩ **do**
    forall r **do**
        sn[r] := 0;
        v[r] := 0;
        acks[r] := 0;
        reqid[r] := 0;
        readSet[r] := ∅;
        writing[r] = false;

upon event ⟨ *Recovery* ⟩ **do**
    retrieve (reqid, sn, v, writing);
    forall r **do**
        if writing[r] = true **then**
            acks[r] := 0;
            reqid[r] := reqid[r] + 1;
            trigger ⟨ *sbebBroadcast* | [WRITE, r, reqid[r], ts[r], v[r]] ⟩;

Consider now *validity*. Consider first the case of a read that is not concurrent with any write. Assume, furthermore, that a read is invoked by some process p_i and the last value written by p_1, say, v, has timestamp sn_1 at p_1. Because the writer logs every timestamp and increments the timestamp for every write, at the time when the read is invoked, a majority of the processes have logged v and timestamp sn_1 and there is no larger timestamp in the system. Before reading a value, i.e., returning from the read operation, p_i consults a majority of the processes and hence gets at least one value with timestamp sn_1. Process p_i hence returns value v with timestamp sn_1, which is indeed the last value written.

Consider now the case where the read is concurrent with some write of value v and timestamp sn_1, and the previous write was value v' and timestamp $sn_1 - 1$. If the latter write had failed before p_1 logged v' then no process will ever see v'. Otherwise, p_1 would have first completed the writing of v' upon recovery. If any process returns sn_1 to p_i, p_i will return v, which is a valid reply. Otherwise, at least one process will return $sn_1 - 1$ and p_i will return v', which is also a valid reply.

Performance. Every write operation requires two communication steps between p_1 and a majority of the processes. Similarly, every read requires two communication steps between the reader process and a majority of the processes. In both cases, at most $2N$ messages are exchanged. Every write re-

---

Algorithm 4.17 Logged Majority Voting (read/write)

---

upon event $\langle$ *on-logrregWrite* | r, val $\rangle$ $\wedge$ ¬writing[r] **do**
    sn[r] := sn[r] + 1;
    v[r] := val;
    acks[r] := 1;
    reqid[r] := reqid[r] + 1;
    writing[r] := true;
    store (sn[r], reqid[r], v[r], writing[r]);
    trigger $\langle$ *sbebBroadcast* | [WRITE, r, reqid[r], ts[r], v[r]] $\rangle$;

upon event $\langle$ *sbebDeliver* | p_j, [WRITE, r, id, t, val] $\rangle$ **do**
    if t > sn[r] **then**
        v[r] := val;
        sn[r] := t;
        store(sn[r], v[r]);
    trigger $\langle$ *sbp2pSend* | p_j, [ACK, r, id] $\rangle$;

upon event $\langle$ *sbp2pDeliver* | p_j, [ACK, r, id] $\rangle$ **do**
    if id = reqid[r] **then**
        acks[r] := acks[r]+1;

upon exists r **such that** acks[r] > N/2 **do**
    writing[r] = false;
    store(writing[r]);
    $\langle$ *on-logrregWriteReturn* | r $\rangle$;

upon event $\langle$ *on-logrregRead* | r $\rangle$ **do**
    reqid[r] := reqid[r]+1;
    readSet[r] := ∅;
    trigger $\langle$ *sbebBroadcast* | [READ, r, id] $\rangle$;

upon event $\langle$ *sbebDeliver* | p_j, [READ, r, id] $\rangle$ **do**
    trigger $\langle$ *sp2pSend* | p_j, [READVALUE, r, id, sn[r], v[r]] $\rangle$;

upon event $\langle$ *sp2pDeliver* | p_j, [READVALUE, r, id, snb, val] $\rangle$ **do**
    if id = reqid[r] **then**
        readSet[r] := readSet[r] ∪ { (snb, val) };

upon exists r **such that** | readSet[r]| > N/2 **do**
    (ts, v) := *highest*(readSet[r]);
    v[r] := v;
    sn[r] := ts;
    trigger $\langle$ *on-logrregReadReturn* | r, v $\rangle$;

---

quires one log at p_1, and then at least a majority of *logs* (possibly parallel ones). Thus, every write requires two causally related logs.

It is important to note that stubborn channels are implemented by retransmitting messages periodically, and this retransmission can be stopped by a writer and a reader that receives a reply of some process or receives enough replies to complete its operation.

Interestingly, Algorithm 4.9–4.10 ("Read-Impose Write-Majority") and Algorithm 4.14–4.15 ("Read-Impose Write-Consult-Majority") can easily be adapted to implement, respectively, a $(1, N)$ and an (N, N) atomic registers in a fail-recovery model, pretty much like "Logged Majority Voting" extends "Majority Voting."

4.6 Hands-On

4.6.1 $(1, N)$ Regular Register

The $(1, N)$ Regular Register algorithm implemented was the "Read-One Write-All." The communication stack used to implement this protocol is the following:

Application
$(1, N)$**RegularRegister** **(implemented by Read-One Write-All)**
Perfect Failure Detector (implemented by TcpBasedPFD)
Best-Effort Broadcast (implemented by Basic Broadcast)
Perfect Point-to-Point Links (implemented by TcpBasedPerfectP2P)

This implementation uses two different *Appia* channels because the algorithm uses the *best-effort broadcast* (which in turn is based on *perfect point-to-point links*) also the *perfect point-to-point links* directly (without best-effort reliability).

The protocol implementation is depicted in Listing 4.1. It follows Algorithm 4.1 very closely. The only significant difference is that values are generic instead of integers, thus allowing registers to contain *strings*.

Listing 4.1. Read-One Write-All $(1, N)$ Regular Register implementation

```
package appia.protocols.tutorialDA.readOneWriteAll1NRR;

public class ReadOneWriteAll1NRRSession extends Session {
    public static final int NUM_REGISTERS=20;

    public ReadOneWriteAll1NRRSession(Layer layer) {
        super(layer);
    }

    private Object[] value=new Object[NUM_REGISTERS];
    private HashSet[] writeSet=new HashSet[NUM_REGISTERS];
    private ProcessSet correct=null;

    private Channel mainchannel=null;
    private Channel pp2pchannel=null;
    private Channel pp2pinit=null;
```

```
public void handle(Event event) {
    if (event instanceof ChannelInit)
        handleChannelInit((ChannelInit)event);
    else if (event instanceof ProcessInitEvent)
        handleProcessInit((ProcessInitEvent)event);
    else if (event instanceof Crash)
        handleCrash((Crash)event);
    else if (event instanceof SharedRead)
        handleSharedRead((SharedRead)event);
    else if (event instanceof SharedWrite)
        handleSharedWrite((SharedWrite)event);
    else if (event instanceof WriteEvent)
        handleWriteEvent((WriteEvent)event);
    else if (event instanceof AckEvent)
        handleAckEvent((AckEvent)event);
    else {
        event.go();
    }
}

public void pp2pchannel(Channel c) {
    pp2pinit=c;
}

private void handleChannelInit(ChannelInit init) {
    if (mainchannel == null) {
        mainchannel=init.getChannel();
        pp2pinit.start();
    } else {
        if (init.getChannel() == pp2pinit) {
            pp2pchannel=init.getChannel();
        }
    }

    init.go();
}

private void handleProcessInit(ProcessInitEvent event) {
    correct=event.getProcessSet();
    init();
    event.go();
}

private void init() {
    int i;
    for (i=0 ; i < NUM_REGISTERS ; i++) {
        value[i]=null;
        writeSet[i]=new HashSet();
    }
}

private void handleCrash(Crash event) {
    correct.setCorrect(event.getCrashedProcess(), false);
    event.go();

    allCorrect();
}

private void handleSharedRead(SharedRead event) {
    SharedReadReturn ev=new SharedReadReturn(mainchannel, Direction.UP, this);
    ev.reg=event.reg;
    ev.value=value[event.reg];
    ev.go();
}

private void handleSharedWrite(SharedWrite event) {
```

```
        WriteEvent ev=new WriteEvent(mainchannel, Direction.DOWN, this);
        ev.getExtendedMessage().pushObject(event.value);
        ev.getExtendedMessage().pushInt(event.reg);
        ev.go();
    }

    private void handleWriteEvent(WriteEvent event) {
        int reg=event.getExtendedMessage().popInt();
        Object val=event.getExtendedMessage().popObject();

        value[reg]=val;

        AckEvent ev=new AckEvent(pp2pchannel, Direction.DOWN, this);
        ev.getExtendedMessage().pushInt(reg);
        ev.dest=event.source;
        ev.go();
    }

    private void handleAckEvent(AckEvent event) {
        SampleProcess p_j=correct.getProcess((InetWithPort)event.source);
        int reg=event.getExtendedMessage().popInt();

        writeSet[reg].add(p_j);

        allCorrect();
    }

    private void allCorrect() {
        int reg;
        for (reg=0 ; reg < NUM_REGISTERS ; reg++) {
            boolean allAcks=true;
            int i;
            for (i=0 ; (i < correct.getSize()) && allAcks ; i++) {
                SampleProcess p=correct.getProcess(i);
                if (p.isCorrect() && !writeSet[reg].contains(p))
                    allAcks=false;
            }
            if (allAcks) {
                writeSet[reg].clear();

                SharedWriteReturn ev=new SharedWriteReturn(mainchannel, Direction.UP, this);
                ev.reg=reg;
                ev.go();

            }
        }
    }
}
```

Try It

1. Setup
   a) Open three shells/command prompts.
   b) In each shell go to the directory where you have placed the supplied code.
   c) In each shell launch the test application, *SampleAppl*, giving a different *n* value (0, 1, or 2) and specifying the *qos* as **r1nr**.
      - In shell 0, execute

        ```
        java demo/tutorialDA/SampleAppl \
            -f demo/tutorialDA/procs \
        ```

```
                    -n 0 \
                    -qos r1nr
```

- In shell 1, execute

```
        java demo/tutorialDA/SampleAppl \
            -f demo/tutorialDA/procs \
            -n 1 \
            -qos r1nr
```

- In shell 2, execute

```
        java demo/tutorialDA/SampleAppl \
            -f demo/tutorialDA/procs
            -n 2 \
            -qos r1nr
```

   d) If the error NoClassDefError has appeared, confirm that you are at the root of the supplied code.

   e) Start the *prefect failure detector* by writing **startpfd** in each shell.

2. Run: Now that processes are launched and running, let us try the following execution:

   a) In shell 0, write the value **S1** to register **2** (type **write 2 S1** and press Enter).

   b) In shell 1, read the value stored in register **2** (type **read 2** and press enter).

- The shell displays that the value S1 is stored in register 2.

   c) In shell 0, write the value **S2** to register **5** (type **write 5 S2** and press Enter).

   d) In shell 1, write the value **S5** to register **5** (type **write 5 S5** and press Enter).

   e) In shell 0, read the value stored in register **5** (type **read 5** and press Enter).

- Despite the fact that process 0 has written the value S2, the displayed content of register 5 is S5 because process 1 has afterward written to that register, .

4.6.2 $(1, N)$ Atomic Register

The $(1, N)$ Atomic Register algorithm implemented was the *Read-Impose Write-All*. The communication stack used to implement this protocol is the following:

Application
$(1, N)$**AtomicRegister**   **(implemented by Read-Impose Write-All)**
Perfect Failure Detector   (implemented by TcpBasedPFD)
Best-Effort Broadcast   (implemented by Basic Broadcast)
Perfect Point-to-Point Links   (implemented by TcpBasedPerfectP2P)

The protocol implementation is depicted in Listing 4.2. It follows the Algorithm 4.7–4.8 very closely. The only significant difference is that values are again generic instead of integers, thus allowing the registers to contain *strings*.

Listing 4.2. Read-Impose Write-All $(1, N)$ Atomic Register implementation

```
package appia.protocols.tutorialDA.readImposeWriteAll1NAR;

public class ReadImposeWriteAll1NARSession extends Session {
    public static final int NUM_REGISTERS = 20;

    public ReadImposeWriteAll1NARSession(Layer layer) {
        super(layer);
    }

    private Object[] v = new Object[NUM_REGISTERS];
    private int[] ts = new int[NUM_REGISTERS];
    private int[] sn = new int[NUM_REGISTERS];
    private Object[] readval = new Object[NUM_REGISTERS];
    private int[] rqid = new int[NUM_REGISTERS];
    private boolean[] reading = new boolean[NUM_REGISTERS];
    private HashSet[] writeSet = new HashSet[NUM_REGISTERS];
    private ProcessSet correct = null;
    private Channel mainchannel = null;
    private Channel pp2pchannel = null;
    private Channel pp2pinit = null;

    public void handle(Event event) {
        if (event instanceof ChannelInit)
            handleChannelInit((ChannelInit) event);
        else if (event instanceof ProcessInitEvent)
            handleProcessInit((ProcessInitEvent) event);
        else if (event instanceof Crash)
            handleCrash((Crash) event);
        else if (event instanceof SharedRead)
            handleSharedRead((SharedRead) event);
        else if (event instanceof SharedWrite)
            handleSharedWrite((SharedWrite) event);
        else if (event instanceof WriteEvent)
            handleWriteEvent((WriteEvent) event);
        else if (event instanceof AckEvent)
            handleAckEvent((AckEvent) event);
        else {
            event.go();
        }
    }

    public void pp2pchannel(Channel c) {
        pp2pinit = c;
    }
```

```
private void handleChannelInit(ChannelInit init) {
    if (mainchannel == null) {
        mainchannel = init.getChannel();
        pp2pinit.start ();
    } else {
        if ( init .getChannel() == pp2pinit) {
            pp2pchannel = init.getChannel();
        }
    }

    init .go ();
}

private void handleProcessInit(ProcessInitEvent event) {
    correct = event.getProcessSet();
    init ();
    event.go ();
}

private void init() {
    int r;
    for (r = 0; r < NUM_REGISTERS; r++) {
        v[r] = readval[r] = null;
        ts [r] = sn[r] = rqid [r] = 0;
        reading[r] = false;
        writeSet[r] = new HashSet();
    }
}

private void handleCrash(Crash event) {
    correct .setCorrect(event.getCrashedProcess(), false);
    event.go ();

    allCorrect ();
}

private void handleSharedRead(SharedRead event) {
    rqid [event.reg]++;
    reading[event.reg] = true;
    readval [event.reg] = v[event.reg];

    WriteEvent ev = new WriteEvent(mainchannel, Direction.DOWN, this);
    ev.getExtendedMessage().pushObject(v[event.reg]);
    ev.getExtendedMessage().pushInt(sn[event.reg]);
    ev.getExtendedMessage().pushInt(rqid[event.reg]);
    ev.getExtendedMessage().pushInt(event.reg);
    ev.go ();
}

private void handleSharedWrite(SharedWrite event) {
    rqid [event.reg]++;
    ts [event.reg]++;

    WriteEvent ev = new WriteEvent(mainchannel, Direction.DOWN, this);
    ev.getExtendedMessage().pushObject(event.value);
    ev.getExtendedMessage().pushInt(ts[event.reg]);
    ev.getExtendedMessage().pushInt(rqid[event.reg]);
    ev.getExtendedMessage().pushInt(event.reg);
    ev.go ();
}

private void handleWriteEvent(WriteEvent event) {
    int r = event.getExtendedMessage().popInt();
    int id = event.getExtendedMessage().popInt();
    int tstamp = event.getExtendedMessage().popInt();
```

```
        Object val = event.getExtendedMessage().popObject();

        if (tstamp > sn[r]) {
            v[r] = val;
            sn[r] = tstamp;
        }

        AckEvent ev = new AckEvent(pp2pchannel, Direction.DOWN, this);
        ev.getExtendedMessage().pushInt(id);
        ev.getExtendedMessage().pushInt(r);
        ev.dest = event.source;
        ev.go();
    }

    private void handleAckEvent(AckEvent event) {
        SampleProcess p_j = correct.getProcess((InetWithPort) event.source);
        int r = event.getExtendedMessage().popInt();
        int id = event.getExtendedMessage().popInt();

        if (id == rqid[r]) {
            writeSet[r].add(p_j);

            allCorrect();
        }
    }

    private void allCorrect() {
        int reg;
        for (reg = 0; reg < NUM_REGISTERS; reg++) {
            boolean allAcks = true;
            int i;
            for (i = 0; (i < correct.getSize()) && allAcks; i++) {
                SampleProcess p = correct.getProcess(i);
                if (p.isCorrect() && !writeSet[reg].contains(p))
                    allAcks = false;
            }
            if (allAcks) {
                writeSet[reg].clear();

                if (reading[reg]) {
                    reading[reg] = false;

                    SharedReadReturn ev =
                        new SharedReadReturn(mainchannel, Direction.UP, this);
                    ev.reg = reg;
                    ev.value = readval[reg];
                    ev.go();
                } else {
                    SharedWriteReturn ev =
                        new SharedWriteReturn(mainchannel, Direction.UP, this);
                    ev.reg = reg;
                    ev.go();
                }
            }
        }
    }
}
```

Try It Perform the same steps as suggested for the Regular $(1, N)$ Register. Please note that you should now specify the *qos* as **a1nr**.

4.6.3 (N, N) Atomic Register

The (N, N) Atomic Register algorithm implemented was the "Read-Impose Write-Consult." The communication stack used to implement this protocol is the following:

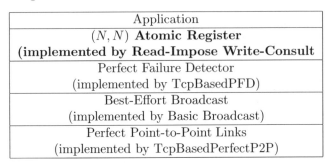

Application
(N, N) **Atomic Register**
(implemented by Read-Impose Write-Consult
Perfect Failure Detector
(implemented by TcpBasedPFD)
Best-Effort Broadcast
(implemented by Basic Broadcast)
Perfect Point-to-Point Links
(implemented by TcpBasedPerfectP2P)

The protocol implementation is depicted in Listing 4.3. It follows Algorithm 4.12–4.13 very closely. The only significant difference is that values are again generic instead of integers.

Listing 4.3. Read-Impose Write-Consult (N, N) Atomic Register implementation

```
package appia.protocols.tutorialDA.readImposeWriteConsultNNAR;

public class ReadImposeWriteConsultNNARSession extends Session {
    public static final int NUM_REGISTERS = 20;

    public ReadImposeWriteConsultNNARSession(Layer layer) {
        super(layer);
    }

    private ProcessSet correct = null;
    private int i = -1;
    private HashSet[] writeSet = new HashSet[NUM_REGISTERS];
    private boolean[] reading = new boolean[NUM_REGISTERS];
    private int[] reqid = new int[NUM_REGISTERS];
    private Object[] readval = new Object[NUM_REGISTERS];
    private Object[] v = new Object[NUM_REGISTERS];
    private int[] ts = new int[NUM_REGISTERS];
    private int[] mrank = new int[NUM_REGISTERS];

    private Channel mainchannel = null;
    private Channel pp2pchannel = null;
    private Channel pp2pinit = null;

    public void handle(Event event) {
        if (event instanceof ChannelInit)
            handleChannelInit((ChannelInit) event);
        else if (event instanceof ProcessInitEvent)
            handleProcessInit((ProcessInitEvent) event);
        else if (event instanceof Crash)
            handleCrash((Crash) event);
        else if (event instanceof SharedRead)
            handleSharedRead((SharedRead) event);
        else if (event instanceof SharedWrite)
            handleSharedWrite((SharedWrite) event);
        else if (event instanceof WriteEvent)
            handleWriteEvent((WriteEvent) event);
        else if (event instanceof AckEvent)
```

```
            handleAckEvent((AckEvent) event);
        else {
            event.go ();
}
    }

    public void pp2pchannel(Channel c) {
        pp2pinit = c;
    }

    private void handleChannelInit(ChannelInit init) {
        if (mainchannel == null) {
            mainchannel = init.getChannel();
            pp2pinit. start ();
        } else {
            if ( init .getChannel() == pp2pinit) {
                pp2pchannel = init.getChannel();
            }
        }
        init .go ();
    }

    private void handleProcessInit(ProcessInitEvent event) {
        correct = event.getProcessSet ();
        init ();
        event.go ();
    }

    private void init() {
        i=correct.getSelfRank();

        int r;
        for (r = 0; r < NUM_REGISTERS; r++) {
            writeSet[r] = new HashSet();
            reqid [r] = ts [r] = 0;
            mrank[r] = −1;
            readval [r] = null;
            v[r] = null;
            reading[r] = false;
        }
    }

    private void handleCrash(Crash event) {
        correct .setCorrect(event.getCrashedProcess(), false);
        event.go ();

        allAcked();
    }

    private void handleSharedRead(SharedRead event) {
        reqid [event.reg]++;
        reading[event.reg] = true;
        writeSet [event.reg]. clear ();
        readval [event.reg] = v[event.reg];

        WriteEvent ev = new WriteEvent(mainchannel, Direction.DOWN, this);
        ev.getExtendedMessage().pushObject(v[event.reg]);
        ev.getExtendedMessage().pushInt(mrank[event.reg]);
        ev.getExtendedMessage().pushInt(ts[event.reg]);
        ev.getExtendedMessage().pushInt(reqid[event.reg]);
        ev.getExtendedMessage().pushInt(event.reg);
        ev.go ();
    }

    private void handleSharedWrite(SharedWrite event) {
        reqid [event.reg]++;
```

```
            writeSet[event.reg]. clear ();

            WriteEvent ev = new WriteEvent(mainchannel, Direction.DOWN, this);
            ev.getExtendedMessage().pushObject(event.value);
            ev.getExtendedMessage().pushInt(i);
            ev.getExtendedMessage().pushInt(ts[event.reg]+1);
            ev.getExtendedMessage().pushInt(reqid[event.reg]);
            ev.getExtendedMessage().pushInt(event.reg);
            ev.go();
    }

    private void handleWriteEvent(WriteEvent event) {
        int r = event.getExtendedMessage().popInt();
        int id = event.getExtendedMessage().popInt();
        int t = event.getExtendedMessage().popInt();
        int j = event.getExtendedMessage().popInt();
        Object val = event.getExtendedMessage().popObject();

        if ((t > ts[r ]) || (( t == ts[r]) && (j < mrank[r]))) {
            v[r]=val;
            ts [r]=t;
            mrank[r]=j;
        }

        AckEvent ev = new AckEvent(pp2pchannel, Direction.DOWN, this);
        ev.getExtendedMessage().pushInt(id);
        ev.getExtendedMessage().pushInt(r);
        ev.dest = event.source;
        ev.go();
    }

    private void handleAckEvent(AckEvent event) {
        SampleProcess p_j = correct.getProcess((InetWithPort) event.source);
        int r = event.getExtendedMessage().popInt();
        int id = event.getExtendedMessage().popInt();

        if (id == reqid[r]) {
            writeSet[r].add(p_j);

            allAcked();
        }
    }

    private void allAcked() {
        int reg;
        for (reg = 0; reg < NUM_REGISTERS; reg++) {
            boolean allAcks = true;
            int i;
            for (i = 0; (i < correct.getSize()) && allAcks; i++) {
                SampleProcess p = correct.getProcess(i);
                if (p.isCorrect() && !writeSet[reg].contains(p))
                    allAcks = false;
            }
            if (allAcks) {
                writeSet[reg]. clear ();

                if (reading[reg]) {
                    reading[reg] = false;

                    SharedReadReturn ev =
                        new SharedReadReturn(mainchannel, Direction.UP, this);
                    ev.reg = reg;
                    ev.value = readval[reg];
                    ev.go();
                } else {
                    SharedWriteReturn ev =
```

```
                new SharedWriteReturn(mainchannel, Direction.UP, this);
                ev.reg = reg;
                ev.go();
            }
        }
    }
}
}
```

Try It Perform the same steps as suggested for the Regular $(1, N)$ Register. Please note that you should now specify the *qos* as **a1nnr**.

4.7 Exercises

Exercise 4.1 *Explain why every process needs to maintain a copy of the register value in the "Read-One Write-All" algorithm (Algorithm 4.1) as well as in the "Majority Voting" algorithm (Algorithm 4.2–4.3).*

Exercise 4.2 *Use the idea of the tranformation from $(1, N)$ regular to $(1, 1)$ atomic registers (Algorithm 4.4) to adapt the "Read-One Write-All" algorithm (i.e., Algorithm 4.1) to implement a $(1, 1)$ Atomic Register.*

Exercise 4.3 *Use the idea of the tranformation from $(1, N)$ regular to $(1, 1)$ atomic registers (Algorithm 4.4) to adapt the "Majority Voting" algorithm (Algorithm 4.2–4.3) to implement a $(1, 1)$ Atomic Register.*

Exercise 4.4 *Explain why a timestamp is needed in the "Majority Voting" algorithm (Algorithm 4.2–4.3) but not in the "Read-One Write-All" algorithm (Algorithm 4.1).*

Exercise 4.5 *Give an algorithm that implements a $(1, 1)$ atomic register algorithm in a fail-silent model and that is more efficient than the "Read-Impose Write-Majority" algorithm (itself implementing a $(1, N)$ atomic register in fail-silent model (Algorithm 4.9–4.10)).*

Exercise 4.6 *Does any implementation of a regular register require a majority of the correct processes in a fail-silent model with no failure detector? What if an eventually perfect failure detector is available?*

Exercise 4.7 *Would the "Majority Voting" algorithm still be correct if a process p_j that receives a WRITE message from the writer p_1 with a value v and timestamp ts does not reply back (with an ACK message) if ts is not strictly larger that the timestamp already kept by p_i (associated with a previously received WRITE message with a more recent value). Explain what happens in the same situation if we consider the "Read-Impose Write-Majority" and then the "Read-Impose Write-Consult-Majority" algorithms.*

Exercise 4.8 *Assume that some algorithm A implements a regular register in a system where up to $N - 1$ processes can crash. Can we implement a perfect failure detector out of A?*

Exercise 4.9 *Explain why, in the "Logged Majority Voting" algorithm (Algorithm 4.16–4.17), if the store primitive is not atomic, it is important not to log the timestamp without having logged the value. Explain what happens if the value is logged without having logged the timestamp.*

Exercise 4.10 *Explain why, in the "Logged Majority Voting" algorithm (Algorithm 4.16–4.17), the writer needs to store its timestamp in stable storage.*

4.8 Solutions

Solution 4.1 We discuss each algorithm separately.

Algorithm 4.1 ("Read-One Write-All"). In this algorithm, a copy of the register value needs to be stored at every process because we assume that any number of processes can crash and any process can read. Assume that the value is not stored at some process p_k. It is easy to see that after some write operation, all processes might crash except for p_k. In this case, there is no way for p_k to return the last value written.

Algorithm 4.2–4.3 ("Majority Voting"). In this algorithm, a copy of the register value also needs to be maintained at all processes, even if we assume only one reader. Assume that some process p_k does not maintain a copy. Assume, furthermore, that the writer updates the value of the register: it can do so only by accessing a majority of the processes. If p_k is in that majority, then the writer would have stored the value in a majority of the processes minus one. It might happen that all processes in that majority, except for p_k, crash: the rest of the processes, plus p_k, also constitutes a majority. A subsequent read in this majority might not get the last value written. □

Solution 4.2 The "Read-One Write-All" algorithm (i.e., Algorithm 4.1) does not need to be transformed to implement an atomic register if we consider only *one* reader: indeed the scenario of Figure 4.4, which violates *ordering*, involves two readers. As is, the algorithm implements a $(1, 1)$ atomic register where any process can write and one specific process, say, p_2, can read. In fact, if we assume a single reader, say p_2, the algorithm can even be optimized in such a way that the writer simply tries to store its value in p_2, and gives up if detects the crash of p_2. Basically, only the reader p_2 needs to maintain the register value, and the writer p_1 would not need to send any message to all processes. □

Algorithm 4.18 Adapted Majority Voting

Implements:
  $(1, 1)$AtomicRegister (oo-areg).
Uses:
  BestEffortBroadcast (beb);
  perfectPointToPointLinks (pp2p).

upon event $\langle$ *Init* $\rangle$ **do**
  forall r **do**
    $sn[r] := v[r] := acks[r] := reqid[r] := 0;$ $readSet[r] := \emptyset;$

upon event $\langle$ *oo-aregWrite* | r, val $\rangle$ **do**
  $sn[r] := sn[r] + 1;$ $v[r] := val;$ $acks[r] := 1;$ $reqid[r] := reqid[r] + 1;$
  trigger $\langle$ *bebBroadcast* | [WRITE, r, reqid[r], ts[r], val] $\rangle$;

upon event $\langle$ *bebDeliver* | p_j, [WRITE, r, id, tstamp, val] $\rangle$ **do**
  if tstamp $>$ sn[r] **then** $v[r] := val;$ $sn[r] := tstamp;$
  trigger $\langle$ *pp2pSend* | p_j, [ACK, r,id] $\rangle$;

upon event $\langle$ *pp2pDeliver* | p_j, [ACK, r, id] $\rangle$ **do**
  if id=reqid[r] **then** $acks[r] := acks[r] + 1;$

upon exists r **such that** $acks[r] > N/2$ **do**
  trigger $\langle$ *oo-aregWriteReturn* | r $\rangle$;

upon event $\langle$ *oo-aregRead* | r $\rangle$ **do**
  $readSet[r] := \emptyset;$ $reqid[r] := reqid[r] +1;$
  trigger $\langle$ *bebBroadcast* | [READ, r, reqid[r]] $\rangle$;

upon event $\langle$ *bebDeliver* | p_j, [READ, r, id] $\rangle$ **do**
  trigger $\langle$ *pp2pSend* | p_j,[READVALUE, r, id, sn[r], v[r]] $\rangle$;

upon event $\langle$ *pp2pDeliver* | p_j, [READVALUE, r, id, snb,val] $\rangle$ **do**
  if id=reqid[r] **then** $readSet[r] := readSet[r] \cup \{(snb, val)\};$

upon exists r **such that** $|readSet[r]| > N/2$ **do**
  $(ts, v) :=$ highest(readSet[r]); $v[r] := v;$ $sn[r] := ts;$
  trigger $\langle$ *oo-aregReadReturn* | r, v $\rangle$;

Solution 4.3 Consider our "Majority Voting" algorithm, i.e., Algorithm 4.2–4.3. This algorithm does not implement a $(1, 1)$ atomic register but can easily be extended to do so by satisfying the *ordering* property. The idea is to add a simple local computation at the reader p_2 which requires for it to update its value and timestamp whenever p_2 selects the value with the largest timestamp before returning it. Then p_2 has simply to make sure that it includes its own value in the set (read majority) from which it selects new values. (The problematic scenario of Figure 4.5 occurs precisely because the reader has no memory of the previous value read.)

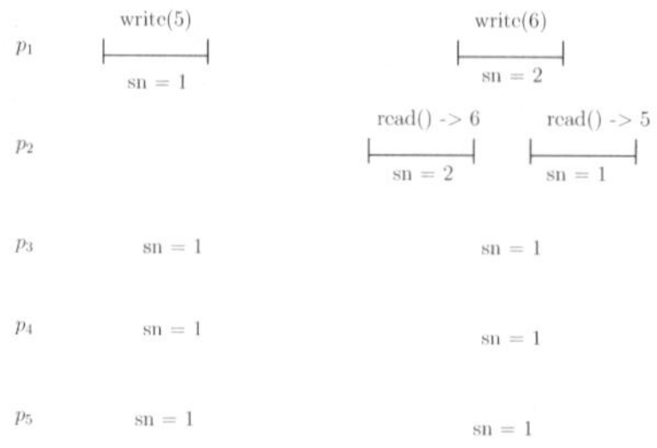

Fig. 4.7: Violation of ordering

A solution is depicted in Algorithm 4.18, an adaption of Algorithm 4.2–4.3 ("Majority Voting") that implements a $(1, 1)$ atomic register. We assume here that the reader includes itself in every read majority. Note that, in this case, we assume that the function *select* returns a pair *(timestamp, value)* (with the highest timestamp), rather than simply a value. With this algorithm, the scenario of Figure 4.5 cannot occur, whereas the scenario depicted in Figure 4.6 could. As in the original "Majority Voting" algorithm (Algorithm 4.2–4.3), every write operation requires one communication roundtrip between p_1 and a majority of the processes, and every read requires one communication roundtrip between p_2 and a majority of the processes. In both cases, $2N$ messages are exchanged. □

Solution 4.4 The timestamp of Algorithm 4.2–4.3 ("Majority Voting") is needed precisely because we do not make use of a perfect failure detector. Without the use of any timestamp, reader p_2 would not have any means to compare different values from any read majority.

In particular, if p_1 writes a value v and then a value v', and p_1 does not access the same majority in both cases, then p_2, which is supposed to return v', might not figure out which one is the latest. The timestamp is used to date the values and help the reader figures out which is the latest.

Such a timestamp is not needed in Algorithm 4.1 ("Read-One Write-All"). This is because the writer accesses all processes that did not crash. The writer can do so because of its relying on a perfect failure detector. The reader would not find different values as in the "Majority Voting" algorithm. □

Solution 4.5 Algorithm 4.18 requires one communication roundtrip for every operation. It is important to note that the reader p_2 needs always include its own value and timestamp when selecting a majority.

Unless it includes its own value and timestamp when selecting a majority, the reader p_2 might violate the *ordering* property as depicted in the scenario of Figure 4.7. This is because, in its first read, p_2 accesses the writer, p_1, which has the latest value. In its second read, p_2 accesses a majority with timestamp 1 and old value 5. □

Solution 4.6 Assume by contradiction that the correct majority assumption is not needed to implement a regular register in a fail-silent model.

The argument we use here is a *partitioning* argument and it is similar to the argument used earlier in this book to explain why uniform reliable broadcast requires a majority of the correct processes even if the system is augmented with an eventually perfect failure detector.

We partition the system into two disjoint sets of processes, X and Y, such that $\mid X \mid = \lceil n/2 \rceil$; p_1, the writer of the register, is in X, and p_2, the reader of the register, is in Y. The assumption that there is no correct majority means here that there are executions where all processes of X crash and executions where all processes of Y crash.

Basically, the writer p_1 might return from having written a value, say, v, even if none of the processes in Y has witnessed this value. The other processes, including p_2, were considered to have crashed, even if they did not. If the processes of X which might have witnessed v later crash, the reader, p_2, has no way of knowing about v and might not return the last value written.

Note that assuming an eventually perfect detector does not lead to circumventing the majority assumption. This is because, even with such a failure detector, the processes of X, including the writer p_1, might return from having written a value, say, v, even if no process in Y has witnessed v. The processes of Y might have been falsely suspected, and there is no way to know whether the suspicions are true or false. □

Solution 4.7 Consider a variant of the "Majority Voting" algorithm where a process p_j that receives a WRITE message from the writer p_1 with a value v and timestamp ts does not reply back (with an ACK message) to p_1 if ts is not strictly larger that the timestamp already kept by p_i (associated with a previously received WRITE message with a more recent value v').

clearly, the only risk here is to violate liveness and prevent p_1 from completing the writing of v. However, given that p_i has already stored a more recent value than v, i.e., v', this means that p_1 has already completed v. (Remember that the processes are sequential and, in particular, p_1 does not issue a new operation before completing the current one).

The same argument holds for the "Read-Impose Write-Majority" algorithm because a single writer (i.e., p_1) is involved and it is sequential.

The situation is however different with the "Read-Impose Write-Consult-Majority" algorithm. This is because of the possibility of multiple writers. Consider two writers p_1 and p_2, both sending WRITE messages to some process p_i, with different values v and v' respectively such that v' is more recent than v (v' has a larger timestamp than v). Assume p_i receives v' first from p_2 and does not reply back to p_1. It might happen in this case that p_1 does not complete its write operation. □

Solution 4.8 The answer is yes, and this means that a perfect failure detector is needed to implement a regular register if $N - 1$ processes can crash.

We sketch the idea of an algorithm A' that uses A to implement a perfect failure detector, i.e., to emulate its behavior within a distributed variable $v[P]$. Every process p_i has a copy of this variable, denoted by $v[P]_i$. The variable $v[P]_i$ is supposed to contain a set of processes suspected by p_i according to the *strong completeness* and *strong accuracy* properties of the perfect failure detector P. The variable is initially empty at every process and the processes use algorithm A, and the register they can build out of A, to update the variable.

The principle of algorithm A' is the following. It uses N regular $(1, N)$ registers: every process is the writer of exactly one register (we say *its* register). Every process p_i holds a counter that p_i keeps on incrementing and writing in its register. For a value k of the counter, p_i triggers an instance of algorithm A, which itself triggers an exchange of messages among processes. Whenever a process p_j receives such a message, it tags it with k and its identity. When p_i receives, in the context of its instance k of A, a message tagged with p_j and k, p_i remembers p_j as one of the processes that participated in its kth writing. When the write terminates, p_i adds to $v[P]_i$ all processes that did not participate in the kth writing and never removes them from $v[P]_i$.

It is easy to see that variable $v[P]$ ensures *strong completeness*. Any process that crashes stops participating in the writing and will be permanently suspected by every correct process. We argue now that it also ensures *strong accuracy*. Assume by contradiction that some process p_j is falsely suspected. In other words, process p_j does not participate in the k'th writing of some process p_i in the register. Given that $N - 1$ processes can crash, right after p_i terminates its k't writing, all processes can crash except p_j. The latter has no way of distinguishing a run where p_i did write the value k from a run where p_i did not write such a value. Process p_j might hence violate the *validity* property of the register. □

Solution 4.9 Assume p_1 writes a value v, then a value v', and then a value v''. While writing v, assume p_1 accesses some process p_k and not p'_k whereas, while writing v', p_1 accesses p'_k and not p_k. While writing v'', p_1 also accesses p_k, which logs first the timestamp and then crashes without logging the associated value, and then recovers. When reading, process p_2 might select the old value v because it has a larger timestamp, violating *validity*.

On the other hand, logging the timestamp without logging the value is not necessary (although desirable to minimize accesses to stable storage). In the example depicted above, p_2 would not be able to return the new value because it still has an old timestamp. But that is okay because the value was not completely written and there is no obligation to return it. □

Solution 4.10 The reason for the writer to log its timestamp in Algorithm 4.16–4.17 is the following. If it crashes and recovers, the writer should not use a smaller timestamp than the one associated with the current value of the register. Otherwise, the reader might return an old value and violate the *validity* property of the register. □

4.9 Historical Notes

- Register specifications were first given by Lamport (Lamport 1977; Lamport 1986a; Lamport 1986b), for the case of a concurrent but failure-free system with one writer. The original notion of atomic register was close to the one we introduced here. There is a slight difference, however, in the way we gave our definition because we had to take into account the possibility for the processes to fail independently of each other, which is typical in a message passing system. (The original definition was given in the context of a multiprocessor machine where processes are sometimes not assumed to fail independently.) We had thus to deal explicitly with the notion of failed operations, and, in particular, failed writes.
- In the fail-stop model, our notion of atomicity is similar to the notion of linearizability (Herlihy and Wing 1990). In the fail-recovery model, we had to consider a slightly different notion to take into account the fact that a write operation that was interrupted by a failure has to appear as if it was never invoked or as if it was completed before the next invocation of the same process, which might have recovered, took place (Guerraoui and Levy 2004).
- Our notion of regular register also corresponds to the notion of initially introduced by Lamport (Lamport 1977; Lamport 1986a; Lamport 1986b). For the case of multiple writers, the notion of regular register was generalized in three different ways (Shao, Pierce, and Welch 2003), all stronger than our notion of regular register.
- A strictly weaker notion of register than the regular one was also considered in the literature: the *safe* register (Lamport 1977; Lamport 1986a; Lamport 1986b). A safe register is similar to a regular one when there is no concurrency: the read should return the last value written. When there is concurrency, a safe register can return an arbitrary value. This value does not need to be some value that a process has written, or tried to write (i.e., an input parameter or a write invocation). It does not even need to be the initial value of the register. Again, this difference reflects the case where concurrent accesses to a hardware device might lead to an arbitrary output. In the message passing model we consider, a value cannot simply

be invented out of thin air and needs to be communicated through message passing, which we assume not to be able to alter or create messages.

- In this chapter, we considered registers that can contain integer values, and we did not make any assumption on the possible range of these values. Registers with values of a limited range have also been considered (Lamport 1977), i.e., the value in the register cannot be greater than some specific value V. Several transformation algorithms were also invented, including some to emulate a register with a given range value into a register with a larger range value (Lamport 1977; Peterson 1983; Vitanyi and Awerbuch 1986; Vidyasankar 1988; Vidyasankar 1990; Israeli and Li 1993).

- Fail-silent register implementations over a crash-stop message passing system and assuming a correct majority were first given for the case of a single writer (Attiya, Bar-Noy, and Dolev 1995). They were later generalized for the case of multiple writers (Lynch and Shvartsman 1997; Lynch and Shvartsman 2002). Implementations in the fail-recovery model were given more recently (Boichat, Dutta, Frolund, and Guerraoui 2001; Guerraoui and Levy 2004).

- Failure detection lower bounds for registers have constituted an active area of research (Delporte-Gallet, Fauconnier, and Guerraoui 2002; Delporte-Gallet, Fauconnier, Guerraoui, Hadzilacos, Kouznetsov, and Toueg 2004; Delporte-Gallet, Fauconnier, and Guerraoui 2005). In particular, and as we discussed through an exercise, in a system where any number of processes can crash and failures cannot be predicted, the weakest failure detector to implement a (regular or atomic) register abstraction is the *Perfect* one.

- We considered in this chapter implementations of shared memory abstractions assuming that processes do not behave maliciously. That is, we assumed that processes can simply deviate from the algorithms assigned to them by crashing and halting their activities. Several researchers have studied shared memory abstractions with underlying malicious processes, bridging the gap between distributed computing and security (Malkhi and Reiter 1997; Martin and Alvisi 2004).

5. Consensus

> *Life is what happens to you while you are making other plans.*
> (John Lennon)

This chapter considers the *consensus* abstraction. The processes use this abstraction to agree on a common value out of values they initially propose. We consider four variants of this abstraction: *regular, uniform, logged,* and *randomized.* We will show later in this book (Chapter 6) how consensus abstractions can be used to build more sophisticated forms of agreements.

5.1 Regular Consensus

5.1.1 Specification

Consensus is specified in terms of two primitives: *propose* and *decide*. Each process has an initial value that it proposes for the agreement, through the primitive *propose*.

The proposed values are private to the processes and the act of proposing is local. This act typically triggers broadcast events through which the processes exchange their proposed values in order to eventually reach agreement. All correct processes have to decide on a single value, through the primitive *decide*. This decided value has to be one of the proposed values. Consensus, in its regular form, satisfies the properties C1–C4 listed in Module 5.1.

In the following, we present two different algorithms to implement consensus. Both algorithms are fail-stop: they rely on a perfect failure detector abstraction. The first algorithm uses a small number of communication steps but a large number of messages. The second, uses fewer messages but more communication steps.

Module 5.1 Interface and properties of consensus

Module:

    Name: (regular) Consensus (c).

Events:

    Request: $\langle$ *cPropose* | v $\rangle$: Used to propose a value for consensus.

    Indication: $\langle$ *cDecide* | v $\rangle$: Used to indicate the decided value for consensus.

Properties:

    C1: *Termination:* Every correct process eventually decides some value.

    C2: *Validity:* If a process decides v, then v was proposed by some process.

    C3: *Integrity:* No process decides twice.

    C4: *Agreement:* No two correct processes decide differently.

5.1.2 Fail-Stop Algorithm: Flooding Consensus

Our first consensus algorithm, Algorithm 5.1, called "Flooding Consensus" uses, besides a perfect failure detector, a best-effort broadcast communication abstraction. The basic idea of the algorithm is the following. The processes execute sequential rounds. Each process maintains the set of proposed values (proposals) it has seen, and this set is typically augmented when moving from one round to the next (and new proposed values are encountered). In each round, every process disseminates its set to all processes using the best-effort broadcast abstraction, i.e., the process floods the system with all proposals it has seen in previous rounds. When a process receives a proposal set from another process, it merges this set with its own. That is, in each round, every process computes the union of all sets of proposed values it received so far.

Roughly speaking, a process decides a specific value in its set when it knows it has gathered all proposals that will ever possibly be seen by any correct process. We explain, in the following, (1) when a round terminates and a process moves from one round to the next, (2) when a process knows it is safe to decide, and (3) how a process selects the value to decide.

1. Every message is tagged with the round number in which the message was broadcast. A round terminates at a given process p_i when p_i has received a message from every process that has not been detected to have crashed by p_i in that round. That is, a process does not leave a round unless it receives messages, tagged with that round, from all processes that have not been detected to have crashed.

2. A consensus decision is reached when a process knows it has seen all proposed values that will be considered by correct processes for possible decision. In a round where a new failure is detected, a process p_i is not sure of having exactly the same set of values as the other processes. This

---

Algorithm 5.1 Flooding Consensus

Implements:
    Consensus (c).

Uses:
    BestEffortBroadcast (beb);
    PerfectFailureDetector ($\mathcal{P}$).

upon event $\langle$ *Init* $\rangle$ **do**
    correct := correct-this-round[0] := Π;
    decided := $\bot$; round := 1;
    for $i = 1$ **to** N **do**
        correct-this-round[i] := proposal-set[i] := $\emptyset$;

upon event $\langle$ *crash* $\mid p_i$ $\rangle$ **do**
    correct := correct $\setminus \{p_i\}$;

upon event $\langle$ *cPropose* $\mid v$ $\rangle$ **do**
    proposal-set[1] := proposal-set[1] $\cup \{v\}$;
    trigger $\langle$ *bebBroadcast* $\mid$ [MySET, 1, proposal-set[1]] $\rangle$;

upon event $\langle$ *bebDeliver* $\mid p_i$, [MySET, r, set] $\rangle$ **do**
    correct-this-round[r] := correct-this-round[r] $\cup \{p_i\}$;
    proposal-set[r] := proposal-set[r] $\cup$ set;

upon correct $\subset$ correct-this-round[round] $\wedge$ (decided = $\bot$) **do**
    if (correct-this-round[round] = correct-this-round[round-1]) **then**
        decided := *min* (proposal-set[round]);
        trigger $\langle$ *cDecide* $\mid$ decided $\rangle$;
        trigger $\langle$ *bebBroadcast* $\mid$ [DECIDED, decided] $\rangle$;
    else
        round := round +1;
        trigger $\langle$ *bebBroadcast* $\mid$ [MySET, round, proposal-set[round-1]] $\rangle$;

upon event $\langle$ *bebDeliver* $\mid p_i$, [DECIDED, v] $\rangle$ $\wedge$ $p_i \in$ correct $\wedge$ (decided = $\bot$) **do**
    decided := v;
    trigger $\langle$ *cDecide* $\mid$ v $\rangle$;
    trigger $\langle$ *bebBroadcast* $\mid$ [DECIDED, decided] $\rangle$;

---

might happen because the crashed process(es) may have broadcast some value(s) to the other processes but not to p_i. In order to know when it is safe to decide, each process keeps a record of the processes it did not detect to have crashed in the previous round, and from how many processes it has received a proposal in the current round. If a round terminates with the same number of undetected crashed processes as in the previous round, a decision can be made. (No new failure is detected in that round). In a sense, all the messages broadcast by all processes that moved to the current round did reach their destination.

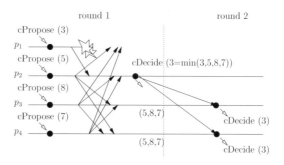

Fig. 5.1: Sample execution of flooding consensus

3. To make a decision, a process can apply any deterministic function to the set of accumulated values, provided this function is the same at all processes (i.e., it is agreed upon by all processes in advance). In our case, the process decides the minimum value (through function *min* in the algorithm); we implicitly assume here that the set of all possible proposals is totally ordered and the order is known by all processes. (The processes could also pick the value proposed by the process with the lowest identity, for instance.) A process that decides disseminates the decision to all processes using the best-effort broadcast abstraction.

An execution of the "Flooding Consensus" algorithm is illustrated in Figure 5.1. Process p_1 crashes during the first round (round 1) after broadcasting its proposal. Only p_2 sees that proposal. No other process crashes. Therefore, p_2 sees the proposals of all processes and can decide. This is because the set of processes from which it receives proposals in the first round is the same as the initial set of processes which start the algorithm (round 0). Process p_2 selects the *min* of the proposals and decides value 3. Processes p_3 and p_4 detect the crash of p_1 and cannot decide. So they advance to the next round, namely, round 2.

Note that if any of these processes (p_3 and p_4) decided the *min* of the proposals it had after round 1, it would have decided differently, i.e., value 5. Since p_2 has decided, p_2 disseminates its decision through a best-effort broadcast. When the decision is delivered, processes p_3 and p_4 also decide 3.

Correctness. *Validity* and *integrity* follow from the algorithm and the properties of the communication abstractions.

Termination follows from the fact that at round N, at the latest, all processes decide. This is because (1) processes that do not decide keep moving from round to round due to the *completeness* property of the failure detector, (2) at least one process needs to fail per round, in order to force the execution of a new round without decision, and (3) there are only N processes in the system.

Consider now *agreement*. Let r be the smallest round in which some correct process p_i decides and v be the value it decides. There are two cases to consider. (1) Assume that process p_i decides after observing two similar sets of undetected (to have crashed) processes $(correct - this - round[round])$ in the two consecutive rounds $r - 1$ and r. Due to the *accuracy* property of the failure detector, no process that reaches the end of round r sees a smaller value than v. Let p_j be any of those processes. Either p_j detects no failure in round r, in which case it also decides v, or p_j detects some failure and it decides v in round $r + 1$ after delivering a DECIDED message from p_i. (2) Assume that p_i decides after delivering a DECIDED message from some process p_k which crashed in round r. Processes that detect the crash of p_k do not decide in round r but in round $r + 1$, after delivering a DECIDED message from p_i.

Performance. If there are no failures, then the algorithm requires a single communication step: all processes decide at the end of round 1. Each failure may cause at most one additional communication step. Therefore, in the worst case, the algorithm requires N steps, if $N - 1$ processes crash in sequence.

If there are no failures, N^2 messages are exchanged before a decision is reached (N^2 DECIDED messages are also exchanged after the decision). There are an additional N^2 message exchanges for each round where a process crashes.

5.1.3 Fail-Stop Algorithm: Hierarchical Consensus

Algorithm 5.2, called "Hierarchical Consensus", is an alternative way to implement regular consensus. This algorithm is interesting because it uses less messages than our "Flooding Consensus" algorithm and enables one process to decide before exchanging any messages with the rest of the processes (0-latency). However, to reach a global decision, i.e., for all correct processes to decide, the algorithm requires N communication steps, even in situations where no failure occurs. Algorithm 5.2 is particularly adequate if consensus is used as a service implemented by a set of server processes where the clients are happy to get a value as fast as possible, even if the servers did not all decide that value yet.

"Hierarchical Consensus" (Algorithm 5.2) makes use of the fact that processes can be ranked according to their identity, and this rank is used to totally order them a priori, i.e., $p_1 > p_2 > p_3 > .. > p_N$. In short, the algorithm ensures that the correct process with the highest rank in the hierarchy, i.e., the process with the lowest identity, imposes its value on all the other processes.

Basically, if p_1 does not crash, then p_1 will impose its value on all processes: every correct process will decide the value proposed by p_1. If p_1 crashes initially and p_2 is correct, then the algorithm ensures that p_2's proposal will be accepted. A nontrivial issue that the algorithm handles is the case where

---

Algorithm 5.2 Hierarchical Consensus

Implements:
    Consensus (c).

Uses:
    BestEffortBroadcast (beb);
    PerfectFailureDetector ($\mathcal{P}$).

upon event ⟨ *Init* ⟩ **do**
    detected := ∅; round := 1;
    proposal := ⊥; proposer :=0;
    for i = 1 **to** N **do**
        delivered[i] := broadcast[i] := false;

upon event ⟨ *crash* | p_i ⟩ **do**
    detected := detected ∪ {$rank(p_i)$};

upon event ⟨ *cPropose* | v ⟩ ∧ (proposal = ⊥) **do**
    proposal := v;

upon (round = *rank* (self)) ∧ (proposal ≠ ⊥) ∧ (broadcast[round] = false) **do**
    broadcast[round] := true;
    trigger ⟨ *cDecide* | proposal ⟩;
    trigger ⟨ *bebBroadcast* | [DECIDED, round, proposal] ⟩;

upon (round ∈ detected) ∨ (delivered[round] = true) **do**
    round := round + 1;

upon event ⟨ *bebDeliver* | p_i, [DECIDED, r, v] ⟩ **do**
    if (r < *rank* (self)) ∧ (r > proposer) **then**
        proposal := v;
        proposer := r;
    delivered[r] := true;

---

p_1 is faulty, but does not initially crash, whereas p_2 is correct. The issue has to do with the fact that p_1's decision message might only reach process p_3 but not p_2.

"Hierarchical Consensus" works in rounds and uses a best-effort broadcast abstraction. In the kth round, process p_k decides its proposal, and broadcasts it to all processes: all other processes in round k wait to deliver the message of p_k or to suspect p_k. None of these processes broadcast any message in this round. When a process p_k receives the proposal of p_i, in round $i < k$, p_k adopts this proposal as its own new proposal.

Consider the example depicted in Figure 5.2. Process p_1 decides 3 and broadcasts its proposal to all processes, but crashes. Processes p_2 and p_3 detect the crash before they deliver the proposal of p_1 and advance to the next round. Process p_4 delivers the value of p_1 and changes its own proposal accordingly, i.e., p_4 adopts p_1's value. In round 2, process p_2 decides and

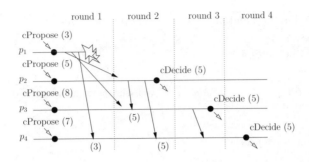

Fig. 5.2: Sample execution of hierarchical consensus

broadcasts its own proposal. This causes p_4 to change its proposal again, i.e., now p_4 adopts p_2's value. From this point on, there are no further failures and the processes decide in sequence the same value, namely, p_2's value (5).

Correctness. The *validity* and *integrity* properties follow from the algorithm and the use of an underlying best-effort broadcast abstraction. *Termination* follows from the *completeness* property of the perfect failure detector and the *validity* property of best-effort broadcast: no process will remain indefinitely blocked in a round and every correct process p_i will eventually reach round i and decide in that round.

Consider now *agreement*; let p_i be the correct process with the highest rank which decides some value v. According to the algorithm, every process p_j, such that $j > i$, decides v: no process will suspect p_i because p_i is correct. This is guaranteed by the *accuracy* property of the perfect failure detector. Hence, every process will adopt and decide p_i's decision.

Performance. The algorithm requires N communication steps to terminate. The algorithm exchanges N messages in each round and can clearly be optimized to use fewer messages: a process does not need to send a message to processes with a higher rank. No process p_i ever uses the value broadcast from any process p_j such that $i \geq j$.

5.2 Uniform Consensus

5.2.1 Specification

As with reliable broadcast, we can define a uniform variant of consensus. The uniform specification is presented in Module 5.2: correct processes decide a value that must be consistent with values decided by processes that might have decided before crashing. In short, uniform consensus ensures that no two processes decide different values, whether they are correct or not.

None of the consensus algorithms we presented so far ensure uniform agreement. Roughly speaking, this is because some of the processes decide

---

Module 5.2 Interface and properties of uniform consensus

Module:

   Name: UniformConsensus (uc).

Events:

   $\langle$ *ucPropose* $\mid v$ $\rangle$, $\langle$ *ucDecide* $\mid v$ $\rangle$: with the same meaning and interface as the consensus interface.

Properties:

   C1–C3: from consensus.

   C4': *Uniform Agreement:* No two processes decide differently.

---

too early: without making sure that their decision has been seen by enough processes. Should the deciding processes crash, other processes might have no choice but to decide a different value.

To illustrate the issue in our "Flooding Consensus" algorithm, i.e., Algorithm 5.1, consider a scenario where process p_1, at the end of round 1, receives messages from all processes. Assume, furthermore, that p_1 decides its own value as this turns out to be the smallest value. Assume, however, that p_1 crashes after deciding and its message does not reach any other process. The rest of the processes move to round 2 without having received p_1's message. Again, the processes are likely to decide some other value.

To illustrate this issue in our "Hierarchical Consensus" algorithm, i.e., Algorithm 5.2, remember that process p_1 decides its own proposal in a unilateral way, without making sure its proposal is seen by any other process. Hence, if process p_1 crashes immediately after deciding, it is likely that the other processes decide a different value.

In the following, we present two uniform consensus algorithms for the fail-stop model. Each algorithm can be viewed as a uniform variant of one of our regular consensus algorithms above: "Flooding Consensus" and "Hierarchical Consensus", respectively. We simply call them "Uniform Flooding Consensus" and "Uniform Hierarchical Consensus", respectively. Subsequently, we also present an algorithm for the fail-noisy model.

5.2.2 Fail-Stop Algorithm: Flooding Uniform Consensus

Algorithm 5.3 implements uniform consensus. The processes follow sequential rounds. As in our "Flooding Consensus" algorithm, each process gathers a set of proposals that it has seen and disseminates its own set to all processes using a best-effort broadcast primitive. The main difference with Algorithm 5.3 is that all processes wait for round N before deciding.

Correctness. Validity and *integrity* follow from the algorithm and the properties of best-effort broadcast. *Termination* is ensured here because all correct processes reach round N and decide in that round. This is ensured by the

---

Algorithm 5.3 Flooding Uniform Consensus

Implements:
    UniformConsensus (uc).

Uses:
    BestEffortBroadcast (beb);
    PerfectFailureDetector ($\mathcal{P}$).

upon event $\langle$ *Init* $\rangle$ **do**
    correct := Π; round := 1; decided := $\perp$; proposal-set := $\emptyset$;
    for $i = 1$ **to** N **do** delivered[i] := $\emptyset$;

upon event $\langle$ *crash* $\mid p_i$ $\rangle$ **do**
    correct := correct $\setminus \{p_i\}$;

upon event $\langle$ *ucPropose* $\mid v$ $\rangle$ **do**
    proposal-set := proposal-set $\cup \{v\}$;
    trigger $\langle$ *bebBroadcast* $\mid$ [MYSET, 1, proposal-set] $\rangle$;

upon event $\langle$ *bebDeliver* $\mid p_i$, [MYSET, r, newSet] $\rangle$ **do**
    proposal-set := proposal-set $\cup$ newSet;
    delivered[r] := delivered[r] $\cup \{p_i\}$;

upon (correct $\subseteq$ delivered[round]) $\wedge$ (decided $= \perp$) **do**
    if round $= N$ **then**
        decided := *min* (proposal-set);
        trigger $\langle$ *ucDecide* $\mid$ decided) $\rangle$;
    else
        round := round + 1;
        trigger $\langle$ *bebBroadcast* $\mid$ [MYSET, round, proposal-set] $\rangle$;

---

completeness property of the failure detector. *Uniform agreement* is ensured because all processes that reach round N have the same set of values.

Performance. The algorithm requires N communication steps and N^3 messages for all correct processes to decide.

5.2.3 Fail-Stop Algorithm: Hierarchical Uniform Consensus

Algorithm 5.4 is round-based, hierarchical, and is in this sense similar to our "Hierarchical Consensus" algorithm. Algorithm 5.4 uses both a best-effort broadcast abstraction to exchange messages and a reliable broadcast abstraction to disseminate the decision. We explain the need for the latter after an overview of the algorithm.

Every round has a leader: process p_i is the leader of round i. Unlike our "Hierarchical Consensus" algorithm, however, a round here consists of two communication steps: within the same round, the leader broadcasts a message to all processes, trying to impose its value, and then expects to get an acknowledgment from all. Processes that get a proposal from the leader of the round adopt this proposal as their own and send an acknowledgment back to the leader of the round. If it succeeds in collecting an acknowledgment from all correct processes, the leader disseminates the value decided on using a reliable broadcast communication abstraction.

If the leader of a round fails, the correct processes detect this and proceed to the next round with a new leader, unless they have already delivered the decision through the reliable broadcast abstraction. Note that even if the leader fails after disseminating the decision, the reliable broadcast abstraction ensures that, if any process decides and stops taking any leadership action, then all correct processes will also decide. This property would not be guaranteed by a best-effort broadcast abstraction. (An alternative would have been to use a best-effort broadcast but have processes continue the algorithm even if they receive a decision message.)

Correctness. *Validity* and *integrity* follow trivially from the algorithm and the properties of the underlying communication abstractions.

Consider *termination*. If some correct process decides, it decides through the reliable broadcast abstraction, i.e., by rbDelivering a decision message. Due to the properties of this broadcast abstraction, every correct process rb-Delivers the decision message and decides. Hence, either all correct processes decide or no correct process decides. Assume by contradiction that there is at least one correct process, and no correct process decides. Let p_i be the correct process with the highest rank. Due to the *completeness* property of the perfect failure detector, every correct process detects the crashes of the processes with higher ranks than p_i (or bebDelivers their message). Hence, all correct processes reach round i and, due to the *accuracy* property of the failure detector, no process detects the crash of process p_i or moves to a higher round, i.e., all correct processes wait until a message from p_i is bebDelivered. In this round, process p_i hence succeeds in collecting acknowledgments from all correct processes and deciding.

Consider now *agreement*, and assume that two processes decide differently. This can only be possible if two processes rbBroadcast two decision messages with two propositions. Consider any two processes p_i and p_j, such that $j > i$ and p_i and p_j rbBroadcast two decision values v and v'. Because of the *accuracy* property of the failure detector, process p_j must have adopted v before reaching round j.

Performance. If there are no failures, the algorithm terminates in three communication steps: two steps for the first round and one step for the reliable broadcast. The algorithm exchanges $3N$ messages. Each failure of a leader adds two additional communication steps and $2N$ additional messages.

Algorithm 5.4 Hierarchical Uniform Consensus

Implements:
UniformConsensus (uc).

Uses:
ReliableBroadcast (rb);
BestEffortBroadcast (beb);
PerfectPointToPointLinks (pp2p);
PerfectFailureDetector ($\mathcal{P}$).

upon event $\langle$ *Init* $\rangle$ **do**
proposal := decided := $\bot$; round := 1;
detected := ack-set := $\emptyset$;
for i = 1 **to** N **do** proposed[i] := $\bot$;

upon event $\langle$ *crash* $\mid p_i$ $\rangle$ **do**
detected := detected $\cup$ { $rank(p_i)$ };

upon event $\langle$ *ucPropose* $\mid v$ $\rangle \wedge$ (proposal = $\bot$) **do**
proposal := v;

upon (round = $rank$(self)) $\wedge$ (proposal $\neq \bot$) $\wedge$ (decided = $\bot$) **do**
trigger $\langle$ *bebBroadcast* $\mid$ [PROPOSE, round, proposal] $\rangle$;

upon event $\langle$ *bebDeliver* $\mid p_i$, [PROPOSE, r, v] $\rangle$ **do**
proposed[r] = v;
if r $\geq$ round **then**
trigger $\langle$ *pp2pSend* $\mid p_i$, [ACK, r] $\rangle$;

upon round $\in$ detected **do**
if proposed[round] $\neq \bot$ **then**
proposal := proposed[round];
round := round + 1;

upon event $\langle$ *pp2pDeliver* $\mid p_i$, [ACK, r] $\rangle$ **do**
ack-set := ack-set $\cup$ {$rank(p_i)$};

upon |ack-set $\cup$ detected| = N **do**
trigger $\langle$ *rbBroadcast* $\mid$ [DECIDED, proposal] $\rangle$;

upon event $\langle$ *rbDeliver* $\mid p_i$, [DECIDED, v] $\rangle \wedge$ (decided = $\bot$) **do**
decided := v;
trigger $\langle$ *ucDecide* $\mid$ v $\rangle$;

5.3 Abortable Consensus

5.3.1 Overview

All the consensus and uniform consensus algorithms we have given so far
assume a fail-stop model: they rely on the assumption of a perfect failure

detector. It is easy to see that, in any of those algorithms, a false failure suspicion (i.e., a violation of the *accuracy* property of the failure detector) might lead to the violation of the *agreement* property of consensus (see the exercice part at the end of this chapter). That is, if a process is detected to have crashed while it is actually correct, then two correct processes might decide differently. On the other hand, in any of those algorithms, not suspecting a crashed process (i.e., violating the *completeness* property of the failure detector) might lead to the violation of the *termination* property of consensus.

In fact, there is no solution to consensus in a fail-silent model if at least one process can crash. Note that this does not mean that a perfect failure detector is always necessary. As we will describe below, there is a consensus algorithm based on an eventual leader detector (which can itself be implemented assuming an eventually perfect failure detector), i.e., assuming a fail-noisy model. This solution is however quite involved. To simplify its presentation, we introduce here an intermediate abstraction, which we call *abortable consensus*. Roughly speaking, this abstraction is weaker than consensus because processes do not always need to decide: they can abort in case of contention.

Abortable consensus can be implemented in a fail-silent model, provided a majority of the processes are correct. We will later show how, given such abstraction, (uniform) consensus can be obtained in a fail-noisy model. In the exercise section, we will also show that any fail-noisy algorithm that solves consensus also solves uniform consensus, and no fail-silent algorithm can solve abortable consensus (respectively, no fail-noisy algorithm can solve consensus) without a correct majority of the processes.

5.3.2 Specification

Just like consensus, abortable consensus has a single *propose* operation. This operation takes one input parameter, i.e., a proposal for a consensus decision. The operation is also supposed to return a value. Unlike consensus, however, the value returned is not necessarily a value that was proposed by some process. It could also be a specific indication $\perp$, meaning that consensus has aborted. It is important to note that the specific value $\perp$ is not a value that could be proposed to consensus. We use the following terminology to define the abortable consensus abstraction.

- When a process invokes the propose operation with v as an argument, we say that the process *proposes* v.
- When a process returns from the invocation with $v \neq \perp$, we say that the process *decides* v.
- When a process returns from the invocation with $\perp$, we say that the process aborts.

Module 5.3 Interface and properties of abortable consensus

Module:

   Name: Abortable Consensus (ac).

Events:

   Request: ⟨ *acPropose* | *v* ⟩: Used to propose a value *v*.

   Indication: ⟨ *acReturn* | x ⟩: Used to return x, either a decision value or
   ⊥, as a response to the proposition.

Properties:

   AC1: *Termination:* Every correct process that proposes eventually decides
   or aborts.

   AC2: *Decision:* If a single process proposes infinitely often, it eventually
   decides.

   AC3: *Agreement:* No two processes decide differently.

   AC4: *Validity:* Any value decided must have been proposed.

With consensus, we require, when a process decides v that v have been proposed by some process: v cannot be invented out of thin air. Furthermore,
once a process has decided a value v, no other process can decide a different
value v'. We explain now intuitively when a process can abort and when it
has to decide. Roughly speaking;

- A process might abort if another process tries concurrently to propose a
  value.
- If only one process keeps proposing, then this process eventually decides.
  Underlying this idea lies the very fact that abortable consensus is typically
  an abstraction that processes might (need to) use in a repeated fashion.

Module 5.3 describes the interface and specification of abortable consensus.

5.3.3 Fail-Silent Algorithm: RW Abortable Consensus

We describe here a fail-silent algorithm that implements abortable consensus.
The algorithm assumes a majority of the correct processes. We do not make
use of any failure detection scheme.

   In short, the idea underlying the algorithm is the following. Each process
stores an estimate of the proposal value as well as a corresponding timestamp.
A process p_i that proposes a value first determines a timestamp to associate
with that value: this is simply done by having the process increment its
previous timestamp with the value N. Then the process proceeds in two
phases: a *read* and then a *write* phase. Hence the name of the algorithm:
"RW Abortable Consensus."

   The aim of the *read* phase is to check if there already is some estimate of
the decision in the system, whereas the aim of the *write* phase is to reach a

decision. Any of these phases can abort, in which case the process returns back
the abort value $\perp$. The other processes act during these phases as witnesses.

We describe below the two phases of the algorithm for the process that is
proposing a value, say, p_i, as well as the tasks of the witness processes.

- **Read**. The aim of this phase, described in Algorithm 5.5, is twofold.
    1. First, the aim is for p_i to check, from a majority of the witness processes,
       the estimates already stored in the processes, and the timestamps that
       those processes have already seen. If any of those timestamps is largest
       than the timestamp that p_i is proposing, then p_i aborts. Otherwise, p_i
       selects the value with the largest timestamp, or its own proposal if no
       such value has been stored, and then proceeds to the *write* phase. We
       make use here of a function *highest* that returns the estimate value with
       the largest timestamp from a set of (timestamp, value) pairs.
    2. The second aim is for p_i to get a promise from a majority of the processes
       that no other process will succeed in a *read* or *write* phase with a smaller
       timestamp.
- **Write**. The aim of this phase, described in Algorithm 5.6, is also twofold.
    1. The first aim is for p_i to store an estimate value in a majority of the
       witness processes, and then decide that value. While doing so, p_i might
       figure out that some process in the majority has seen a larger timestamp
       than the one p_i is proposing. In this case, p_i simply aborts. Otherwise,
       p_i decides.
    2. The second aim is for p_i to get a promise from a majority of processes
       that no other process will succeed in a read or write phase with a strictly
       smaller timestamp.

Correctness. The *termination* and *validity* properties follow from the properties of the channels and the assumption that a majority of the correct
processes exists.

Consider now the *decision* property. Let p_i be the process that keeps on
proposing infinitely often, and let t be the time after which no other process
proposes a value. Assume by contradiction that no process decides. According
to the algorithm, p_i keeps on incrementing its timestamp until it gets to a
timestamp no process has ever used. Due to the properties of the channels
and the algorithm, there is a time t' higher than t after which p_i decides. A
contradiction.

Consider now *agreement*. Let p_i be the process which decides with the
smallest timestamp t_i. Assume p_i decides value v_i. By induction on the timestamp, any process that decides with a larger timestamp t_j, does so on value
v_i. Clearly, $t_j \neq t_i$, otherwise, according to the algorithm and the use of a
majority, some process will abort the *read* phase of p_i or p_j. Assume the
induction property up to some timestamp $t_j > t_i$, and consider $t_j + 1$. According to the algorithm, p_j selects the value with the largest timestamp from
a majority, and this must be v_i in a majority, with the largest timestamp.

Algorithm 5.5 RW Abortable Consensus: Read Phase

Implements:
    Abortable Consensus (ac).

Uses:
    BestEffortBroadcast (beb);
    PerfectPointToPointLinks (pp2p).

upon event ⟨ *Init* ⟩ **do**
    tempValue := val := ⊥;
    wAcks := rts := wts := 0;
    tstamp := *rank*(self);
    readSet := ∅;

upon event ⟨ *acPropose* | v ⟩ **do**
    tstamp := tstamp+N;
    tempValue := v;
    trigger ⟨ *bebBroadcast* | [READ, tstamp] ⟩;

upon event ⟨ *bebDeliver* | p_j,[READ, ts] ⟩ **do**
    if rts ≥ ts **or** wts ≥ ts **then**
        trigger ⟨ *pp2pSend* | p_j, [NACK] ⟩;
    else
        rts := ts;
        trigger ⟨ *pp2pSend* | p_j, [READACK, wts, val] ⟩;

upon event ⟨ *pp2pDeliver* | p_j, [NACK] ⟩ **do**
    trigger ⟨ *acReturn* | ⊥ ⟩;

upon event ⟨ *p2pDeliver* | p_j, [READACK, ts, v] ⟩ **do**
    readSet := readSet ∪ {(ts, v)}

upon (|readSet| > $N/2$) **do**
    (ts, v) := *highest*(readSet);
    if v ≠ ⊥ **then** tempValue := v;
    trigger ⟨ *bebBroadcast* | [WRITE, tstamp, tempValue] ⟩;

Performance. Every propose operation requires two communication round-trips between the process that is proposing a value and a majority of the processes (four communication steps). Hence, at most $4N$ messages are exchanged.

Variant. It is easy to see how our abortable consensus algorithm can be transformed to alleviate the need for a majority of the correct processes if a perfect failure detector is available (i.e., in a fail-stop model). Roughly speaking, instead of relying on a majority to read and write a value, a process would do so at all processes that it did not suspect to have crashed. Later in this chapter, we will give an algorithm that implements abortable consensus in a fail-recovery model.

Algorithm 5.6 RW Abortable Consensus: Write Phase

Implements:
    Abortable Consensus (ac).

upon event ⟨ *bebDeliver* | p_j, [WRITE, ts, v] ⟩ **do**
    if rts > ts **or** wts > ts **then**
        trigger ⟨ *pp2pSend* | p_j,[NACK] ⟩;
    else
        val := v;
        wts := ts;
        trigger ⟨ *pp2pSend* | p_j, [WRITEACK] ⟩;

upon event ⟨ *pp2pDeliver* | p_j, [NACK] ⟩ **do**
    trigger ⟨ *acReturn* | ⊥ ⟩;

upon event ⟨ *pp2pDeliver* | p_j, [WRITEACK] ⟩ **do**
    wAcks := wAcks+1;

upon (wAcks > $N/2$) **do**
    readSet := ∅;
    wAcks := 0;
    trigger ⟨ *acReturn* | tempValue ⟩;

5.3.4 Fail-Noisy Algorithm: From Abortable Consensus to Consensus

Algorithm 5.7 implements uniform consensus. It uses, besides an eventual leader election abstraction and a best-effort broadcast communication abstraction, abortable consensus.

Intuitively, the value that is decided in the consensus algorithm is the value that is decided in the underlying abortable consensus. Two processes that concurrently propose values to abortable consensus might abort. If only one process keeps proposing for sufficiently long, however, this process will succeed. This will be ensured in our algorithm by having only leaders propose values. Eventually, only one leader is elected and this leader will be able to successfully propose and decide a value. Once this is done, the leader broadcasts a message to all processes informing them of the decision.

Correctness. *Validity* and *integrity* follow from the algorithm and the properties of the underlying communication abstractions.

Consider *termination* and assume some process is correct. According to the algorithm, only a process that is leader can propose a value to abortable consensus. Due to the assumption of the underlying eventually perfect leader election, there is a time after which exactly one correct process is eventually elected and remains leader forever. Let p_i be that process. Process p_i will permanently keep on proposing values. Due to the properties of abortable consensus, p_i will decide and broadcast the decision. Due to the properties

---

Algorithm 5.7 From Abortable Consensus to Consensus

Implements:
    UniformConsensus (uc).

Uses:
    AbortableConsensus (ac);
    BestEffortBroadcast (beb);
    EventualLeaderDetector (Ω).

upon event $\langle$ *Init* $\rangle$ **do**
    proposal := $\perp$;
    leader := proposed := decided := false;

upon event $\langle$ *trust* $\mid p_i$ $\rangle$ **do**
    if p_i = self **then** leader := true;
    else leader := false;

upon event $\langle$ *ucPropose* $\mid$ v $\rangle$ **do**
    proposal := v;

upon (leader = true) $\wedge$ (proposed = false) $\wedge$ (proposal $\neq \perp$) **do**
    proposed := true;
    trigger $\langle$ *acPropose* $\mid$ proposal $\rangle$;

upon event $\langle$ *acReturn* $\mid$ result $\rangle$ **do**
    if result $\neq \perp$ **then**
        trigger $\langle$ *bebBroadcast* $\mid$ [DECIDED, result] $\rangle$;
    else
        proposed := false;

upon event $\langle$ *bebDeliver* $\mid p_i$, [DECIDED, v] $\rangle$ $\wedge$ (decided = false) **do**
    decided := true;
    trigger $\langle$ *ucDecide* $\mid$ v $\rangle$;

---

of the best-effort communication primitive, all correct processes eventually deliver the decision message and decide.

Consider now *agreement* and assume that some process p_i decides some value v. This means that v was decided in the underlying abortable consensus. Duw to the properties of abortable consensus, no other process can decide any different value. Any other process p_j that decides, necessarily decides v.

Performance. We consider here our implementation of abortable consensus assuming a majority of the correct processes. If there is a single leader and this leader does not crash, then four communication steps and $4N$ messages are needed for this leader to decide. Therefore, five communication steps and $5N$ messages are needed for all correct processes to decide.

Module 5.4 Interface and properties of logged abortable consensus

Module:

    Name: Logged Abortable Consensus (lac).

Events:

    Request: $\langle$ *lacPropose* | v $\rangle$: Used to propose a value v.

    Indication: $\langle$ *lacReturn* | x $\rangle$: Used to return x, either a decision value or $\perp$, as a response to the proposition.

Properties:

    LAC1: *Termination:* If a process proposes and does not crash, it eventually decides or aborts.

    LAC2: *Decision:* If a single correct process proposes infinitely often, it eventually decides.

    LAC3: *Agreement:* No two processes decide differently.

    LAC4: *Validity:* Any value decided must have been proposed.

Module 5.5 Interface and properties of logged consensus

Module:

    Name: LoggedConsensus (lc).

Events:

    Request: $\langle$ *lcPropose* | v $\rangle$: Used to propose a value for logged consensus.

    Indication: $\langle$ *lcDecide* | v $\rangle$: Used to indicate the decided value for logged consensus.

Properties:

    C1: *Termination:* Unless it crashes, every process eventually decides some value.

    C2: *Validity:* If a process decides v, then v was proposed by some process.

    C3: *Agreement:* No two processes decide differently.

5.4 Logged Abortable Consensus and Logged Consensus

We consider here the fail-recovery model and we introduce the abortable logged consensus and logged abortable consensus abstractions in Module 5.4 and Module 5.5, respectively.

5.4.1 Fail-Recovery Algorithm: Logged Abortable Consensus

We give now an algorithm that implements logged abortable consensus. The algorithm we describe here is also composed of two parts (as in the fail-silent model): Algorithm 5.8 and Algorithm 5.9, which are similar to Algorithm 5.5 and Algorithm 5.6, respectively, with three major differences.

Algorithm 5.8 RW Logged Abortable Consensus: read phase

Implements:
    LoggedAbortableConsensus (lac).

Uses:
    StubbornBroadcast (sb);
    StubbornPointToPointLinks (sp2p).

upon event ⟨ *Init* ⟩ **do**
    tempValue := val := ⊥;
    wAcks := tstamp := rts := wts := 0;
    readSet := ∅;

upon event ⟨ *Recovery* ⟩ **do**
    retrieve(rts, wts, val);

upon event ⟨ *lacPropose* | v ⟩ **do**
    tstamp := tstamp+N;
    tempValue := v;
    trigger ⟨ *sbBroadcast* | [READ, tstamp] ⟩;

upon event ⟨ *sbDeliver* | p_j, [READ, ts] ⟩ **do**
    if rts ≥ ts **or** wts ≥ ts **then**
        trigger ⟨ *sp2pSend* | p_j, [NACK] ⟩;
    else
        rts := ts; *store*(rts);
        trigger ⟨ *sp2pSend* | p_j, [READACK, wts, val] ⟩;

upon event ⟨ *sp2pDeliver* | p_j, [NACK] ⟩ **do**
    trigger ⟨ *lacReturn* | ⊥ ⟩;

upon event ⟨ *sp2pDeliver* | p_j, [READACK, ts,v] ⟩ **do**
    readSet := readSet ∪ {(ts, v)};

upon (|readSet| > $N/2$) **do**
    (ts, v) := *highest*(readSet);
    if v ≠ ⊥ **then** tempValue := v;
    trigger ⟨ *sbBroadcast* | [WRITE, tstamp, tempValue] ⟩;

---

1. We use stubborn links and stubborn broadcast instead of perfect links and best-effort broadcast.
2. We also assume a majority of the correct processes; remember however that the notion of correct is different in a fail-recovery model: a process is said to be correct in this case if eventually it is permanently up.
3. The updates of the timestamps and estimate values are now logs, i.e., on stable storage. The timestamps and estimate values are retreived upon recovery.

Algorithm 5.9 RW Logged Abortable Consensus: write phase

Implements:
    LoggedAbortableConsensus (lac).

upon event ⟨ *sbDeliver* | p_j,[WRITE, ts,v] ⟩ **do**
    if rts > ts **or** wts > ts **then**
        trigger ⟨ *sp2pSend* | p_j, [NACK] ⟩;
    else
        val := v; wts := ts; *store*(val, wts);
        trigger ⟨ *sp2pSend* | p_j, [WRITEACK] ⟩;

upon event ⟨ *sp2pDeliver* | p_j, [NACK] ⟩ **do**
    trigger ⟨ *lacReturn* | ⊥ ⟩;

upon event ⟨ *sp2pDeliver* | p_j, [WRITEACK] ⟩ **do**
    wAcks := wAcks+1;

upon (wAcks > $N/2$) **do**
    readSet := ∅; wAcks := 0;
    trigger ⟨ *lacReturn* | tempValue ⟩;

Interestingly, assuming a logged abortable consensus instead of abortable consensus, Algorithm 5.7 directly implements logged consensus (instead of uniform consensus).

5.5 Randomized Consensus

In this section, we discuss how randomization can be used to solve a probabilistic variant of consensus without resorting to a failure detector. This variant of consensus, which we call *randomized consensus*, ensures *integrity*, *(uniform) agreement*, and *validity* properties of (uniform) consensus, plus the *termination* properties which stipulates that, with probability 1, every correct process eventually decides.

5.5.1 Specification

Each process has an initial value that it proposes through the primitive *rcPropose* (we simply write *propose* when there is no confusion). All correct processes have to decide on a single value that has to be one of the proposed values: the decision primitive is denoted by *rcDecide*) (we simply write *decide* when there is no confusion). Randomized consensus ensures the properties RC1–RC4 listed in Module 5.6.

Module 5.6 Interface and properties of probabilistic consensus

Module:

   Name: RandomizedConsensus (rc).

Events:

   Request: $\langle$ *rcPropose* | *v* $\rangle$: Used to propose a value for consensus.

   Indication: $\langle$ *rcDecide* | *v* $\rangle$: Used to indicate the decided value for consensus.

Properties:

   RC1: *Termination:* With probability 1, every correct process decides some value.

   RC2: *Validity:* If a process decides v, then v was proposed by some process.

   RC3: *Integrity:* No process decides twice.

   RC4: *Agreement:* No two correct processes decide differently.

5.5.2 Randomized Algorithm: Probabilistic Consensus

The randomized consensus algorithm described here operates in (asynchronous) rounds where, in each round, the processes try to ensure that the same value is proposed by a majority of the processes. If there is no such value, the processes use randomization to select which of the initial values they will propose in the next round. The probability that processes agree in a given round is strictly greater than zero. Therefore, if the algorithm continues to execute rounds, eventually it terminates with probability 1.

Algorithm 5.10–5.11 is randomized and requires a majority of the correct processes to make progress. Initially, each process uses reliable broadcast to disseminate its own initial value to every other correct process. Therefore, eventually, all correct processes will have all initial values from every other correct process.

As we pointed out, the algorithm operates in rounds. Each round consists of two phases. In the first phase every correct process proposes a value. If a process observes that a majority of the processes have proposed the same value in the first phase, then it proposes that value for the second phase. If a process is unable to observe a majority of proposals for the same value in the first phase, the process simply proposes ⊥ for the second phase. Note that, as a result of this procedure, if two processes propose a value (different from ⊥) for the second phase, they propose exactly the same value. Let this value be called *majph1*.

The purpose of the second phase is to verify if *majph1* was observed by a majority of the processes. In this case, *majph1* is the decided value. A process that receives *majph1* in the second phase but is unable to collect a majority of *majph1* in that phase, starts a new round with *majph1* as its estimate.

Algorithm 5.10 Probabilistic Consensus (phase 1)

Implements:
    RandomizedConsensus (rc).

Uses:
    ReliableBroadcast (rb);
    BestEffortBroadcast (beb).

upon event ⟨ *Init* ⟩ **do**
        decided := ⊥;
        estimate := ⊥;
        round := 0;
        val := ∅;
        forall r **do**
            phase1[r] := ∅;
            phase2[r] := ∅;

upon event ⟨ *rcPropose* | v ⟩ **do**
        trigger ⟨ *bebBroadcast* | [INIVAL, v] ⟩;
        estimate := v;
        round := round +1;
        val := val ∪ {v};
        trigger ⟨ *bebBroadcast* | [PHASE1, round, v] ⟩;

upon event ⟨ *bebDeliver* | p_i, [INIVAL, v] ⟩ **do**
        val:= val ∪ {v};

upon event ⟨ *bebDeliver* | p_i, [PHASE1, r, v] ⟩ **do**
        phase1[r] := phase1[r] ∪ {v};

Finally, it is possible that a process does not receive *majph1* in the second phase (either because no such value was found in phase 1 or simply because it has received a majority of ⊥ in the second phase). In this case, the process has to start a new round, with a new estimate. To ensure that there is some probability of obtaining a majority in the new round, the process selects, at random, one of the initial values it has seen, and uses this value as its proposal for the first phase of the next round.

Figure 5.3 illustrates the idea underlying the algorithm. At first glance, it may seem that a deterministic decision would allow a majority in the first phase to be reached faster. For instance, if a process would receive a majority of ⊥ in the second phase of a round, it could deterministically select the first non-⊥ initial value instead of selecting a value at random. Unfortunately, a deterministic choice allows executions where the algorithm never terminates.

In the example of Figure 5.3, we have three processes, p_1, p_2 and p_3, with initial values of 1, 2, and 2, respectively. Each process proposes its own value for the first phase of the round. Consider the following execution for the first phase:

Algorithm 5.11 Probabilistic Consensus (phase 2)

---

upon (decided $= \perp \wedge$ |phase1[round]| $> N/2$) **do**
    if exists v **such that** $\forall x \in$ phase1[round]: $x = v$ **then** estimate $:= v$;
    else estimate $:= \perp$;
    trigger $\langle$ *bebBroadcast* | [PHASE2, round, estimate] $\rangle$;

upon event $\langle$ *bebDeliver* | p_i, [PHASE2, r, v] $\rangle$ **do**
    phase2[r] $:=$ phase2[r] $\cup \{v\}$;

upon (decided $= \perp \wedge$ |phase2[round]| $> N/2$) **do**
    if exists $v \neq \perp$ **such that** $\forall x \in$ phase2[round]: $x = v$ **then**
        decided $:= v$;
        trigger $\langle$ *rbBroadcast* | [DECIDED, round, decided] $\rangle$;
    else
        if exists $v \in$ phase2[round] **such that** $v \neq \perp$ **then** estimate $:= v$;
        else estimate $:=$ random(val);
        round $:=$ round $+1$; // start one more round
        trigger $\langle$ *rbBroadcast* | [PHASE1, round, estimate] $\rangle$;

upon event $\langle$ *rbDeliver* | p_i, [DECIDED, r, v] $\rangle$ **do**
    decided $:= v$;
    trigger $\langle$ *rcDecide* | decided $\rangle$;

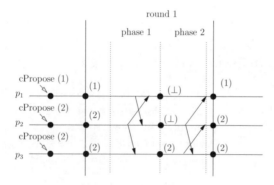

Fig. 5.3: Role of randomization

- Process p_1 receives the value from p_2. Since both values differ, p_1 proposes $\perp$ for the second phase.
- Process p_2 receives the value from p_1. Since both values differ, p_2 proposes $\perp$ for the second phase.
- Process p_3 receives the value from p_2. Since both values are the same, p_3 proposes 2 for the second phase.

Now consider the following execution for the second phase:

- Process p_1 receives the value from p_2. Since both values are $\perp$, p_1 deterministically selects value 1 for the first phase of the next round.

- Process p_2 receives the value from p_3. Since one of the values is 2, p_2 proposes 2 for the first phase of the next round.
- Process p_3 receives the value from p_2. Since one of the values is 2, p_3 proposes 2 for the first phase of the next round.

This execution is clearly possible. Note that in this example no messages is lost; some messages are delayed as processes move to the next round as soon as they receive a majority of messages. Unfortunately, the result of this execution is that the input values for the next round are exactly the same as for the previous round. The same execution sequence could be repeated indefinitely. Randomization prevents this infinite executions from occurring since there would be a round where p_1 would also propose 2 as the input value for the next round.

5.6 Hands-On

5.6.1 Flooding Regular Consensus Protocol

The communication stacks used to implement the regular *flooding* consensus protocol is depicted in the following:

Application
Consensus   **(implemented by Flooding Consensus)**
Perfect Failure Detector   (implemented by TcpBasedPFD)
Best-Effort Broadcast   (implemented by Basic Broadcast)
Perfect Point-to-Point Links   (implemented by TcpBasedPerfectP2P)

The FloodingConsensus layer implements the flooding consensus algorithm. It follows Algorithm 5.1 very closely. It operates in rounds, and in each round it tries to gather the proposals from all correct members. This is achieved by each member sending all the proposals he knows. If a member fails, it advances to the next round. If in a round it gathers messages from all other correct processes, it decides by choosing in a deterministic way. In the implementation, all proposals must derive from the Proposal class, which forces the proposals to implement the int compareTo(Object o) method that allows comparison between proposals. The implemented algorithm chooses the lowest proposal. For instance, the proposal sent by the test application consists of a String, and therefore the algorithm chooses the one with the lowest lexicographical value. When the decision is made, it is also broadcasted by all members.

The protocol implementation is depicted in Listing 5.1.

Listing 5.1. Flooding Regular Consensus implementation

```
package appia.protocols.tutorialDA.floodingConsensus;

public class FloodingConsensusSession extends Session {

    public FloodingConsensusSession(Layer layer) {
        super(layer);
    }

    private int round=0;
    private ProcessSet correct=null;
    private Comparable decided=null;
    private HashSet[] correct_this_round=null;
    private HashSet[] proposal_set=null;

    public void handle(Event event) {
        if (event instanceof ProcessInitEvent)
            handleProcessInit((ProcessInitEvent)event);
        else if (event instanceof Crash)
            handleCrash((Crash)event);
        else if (event instanceof ConsensusPropose)
            handleConsensusPropose((ConsensusPropose)event);
        else if (event instanceof MySetEvent)
            handleMySet((MySetEvent)event);
        else if (event instanceof DecidedEvent)
            handleDecided((DecidedEvent)event);
        else {
            event.go();
        }
    }

    private void init() {
        int max_rounds=correct.getSize()+1;
        correct_this_round=new HashSet[max_rounds];
        proposal_set=new HashSet[max_rounds];
        int i;
        for (i=0 ; i < max_rounds ; i++) {
            correct_this_round[i]=new HashSet();
            proposal_set[i]=new HashSet();
        }
        for (i=0 ; i < correct.getSize () ;  i++) {
            SampleProcess p=correct.getProcess(i);
            if (p.isCorrect ())
                correct_this_round [0].add(p);
        }
        round=1;
        decided=null;

        count_decided=0;
    }

    private void handleProcessInit(ProcessInitEvent event) {
        correct=event.getProcessSet();
        init ();
        event.go();
    }

    private void handleCrash(Crash crash) {
        correct.setCorrect(crash.getCrashedProcess(),false);
        crash.go();

        decide(crash.getChannel());
    }

    private void handleConsensusPropose(ConsensusPropose propose) {
        proposal_set [round].add(propose.value);
```

```
        MySetEvent ev=new MySetEvent(propose.getChannel(),Direction.DOWN,this);
        ev.getExtendedMessage().pushObject(proposal_set[round]);
        ev.getExtendedMessage().pushInt(round);
        ev.go();

        decide(propose.getChannel());
    }

    private void handleMySet(MySetEvent event) {
        SampleProcess p_i=correct.getProcess((InetWithPort)event.source);
        int r=event.getExtendedMessage().popInt();
        HashSet set=(HashSet)event.getExtendedMessage().popObject();

        correct_this_round [r]. add(p_i);
        proposal_set [r]. addAll(set);

        decide(event.getChannel());
    }

    private void decide(Channel channel) {
        int i;

        if (decided != null)
            return;

        for (i=0 ; i < correct. getSize () ; i++) {
            SampleProcess p=correct.getProcess(i);
            if ((p != null) && p.isCorrect() && !correct_this_round[round].contains(p))
                return;
        }

        if ( correct_this_round [round].equals( correct_this_round [round−1])) {
            Iterator  iter =proposal_set[round]. iterator ();
            while (iter .hasNext()) {
                Comparable proposal=(Comparable)iter.next();
                if (decided == null)
                    decided=proposal;
                else
                    if (proposal.compareTo(decided) < 0)
                        decided=proposal;
            }

            ConsensusDecide ev=new ConsensusDecide(channel,Direction.UP,this);
            ev. decision=(Proposal)decided;
            ev.go();

            DecidedEvent ev=new DecidedEvent(channel,Direction.DOWN,this);
            ev.getExtendedMessage().pushObject(decided);
            ev.go();
        } else {
            round++;
            proposal_set [round].addAll(proposal_set[round−1]);

            MySetEvent ev=new MySetEvent(channel,Direction.DOWN,this);
            ev.getExtendedMessage().pushObject(proposal_set[round]);
            ev.getExtendedMessage().pushInt(round);
            ev.go();

            count_decided=0;
        }
    }

    private void handleDecided(DecidedEvent event) {
        // Counts the number os Decided messages received and reinitiates the algorithm
        if ((++count_decided >= correctSize()) && (decided != null)) {
```

```
            init ();
            return;
        }

    if (decided != null)
            return;

    SampleProcess p_i=correct.getProcess((InetWithPort)event.source);
    if (! p_i.isCorrect())
            return;

    decided=(Comparable)event.getExtendedMessage().popObject();

    ConsensusDecide ev=new ConsensusDecide(event.getChannel(),Direction.UP,this);
    ev.decision=(Proposal)decided;
    ev.go();

    DecidedEvent ev=new DecidedEvent(event.getChannel(),Direction.DOWN,this);
    ev.getExtendedMessage().pushObject(decided);
    ev.go();

    round=0;
    }
    // Used to count the number of Decided messages received, therefore determining when
    // all processes have decided and therefore allow a new decision process.
    private int count_decided;
    private int correctSize() {
        int size=0,i;
        SampleProcess[] processes=correct.getAllProcesses();
        for (i=0 ; i < processes.length ; i++) {
            if ((processes[i] != null) && processes[i].isCorrect())
                ++size;
        }
        return size;
    }
}
```

Try It

1. Setup
    a) Open three shells/command prompts.
    b) In each shell, go to the directory where you have placed the supplied code.
    c) In each shell, launch the test application, *SampleAppl*, giving a different n value (0, 1, or 2) and specifying the *qos* as **fc**.
        • In shell 0, execute

```
java demo/tutorialDA/SampleAppl \
        -f demo/tutorialDA/procs \
        -n 0 \
        -qos fc
```

        • In shell 1, execute

```
java demo/tutorialDA/SampleAppl \
        -f demo/tutorialDA/procs \
        -n 1 \
```

```
-qos fc
```

- In shell 2, execute

```
java demo/tutorialDA/SampleAppl \
    -f demo/tutorialDA/procs \
    -n 2 \
    -qos fc
```

   d) If the error NoClassDefError has appeared, confirm that you are at the root of the supplied code.

   e) Start the *prefect failure detector* by writing **startpfd** in each shell.

2. Run: Now that the processes are launched and running, let us try this execution:

   a) In shell 0, propose the value **B** (type **consensus B** and press Enter).

   b) In shell 1, propose the value **C** (type **consensus C** and press Enter).

   c) In shell 2, propose the value **D** (type **consensus D** and press Enter).

   d) All processes display that a decision was made and that it is **B**.

   e) Wait a while to ensure that all messages related to the last decision are sent and received, and do not interfere with the next decision.

   f) In shell 0, propose the value **E**.

   g) In shell 1, propose the value **F**.

   h) Note that a decision has not been made yet.

   i) In shell 2, kill the test process.

   j) The remaining processes display that a decision was made and that it is **E**. When the failure notification reaches them they start another round without the failed process.

5.6.2 Hierarchical Regular Consensus Protocol

The communication stacks used to implement the regular *hierarchical* consensus protocol is depicted in the following:

Application
Consensus **(implemented by Hierarchical Consensus)**
Perfect Failure Detector (implemented by TcpBasedPFD)
Best-Effort Broadcast (implemented by Basic Broadcast)
Perfect Point-to-Point Links (implemented by TcpBasedPerfectP2P)

The HierarchicalConsensus layer implements the hierarchical consensus algorithm. It follows Algorithm 5.2 very closely. It also operates in rounds, and in each round one of the members chooses a proposal, either the one chosen in the previous round, if such a choice was made, or is own proposal. The process that chooses in each round is the one with its *rank* equal to the round. For this reason the first round is round 0. The protocol implementation is depicted in Listing 5.2.

Listing 5.2. Hierarchical Regular Consensus implementation

```
package appia.protocols.tutorialDA.hierarchicalConsensus;

public class HierarchicalConsensusSession extends Session {

    public HierarchicalConsensusSession(Layer layer) {
        super(layer);
    }

    private int round=-1;
    private int prop_round=-1;
    private ProcessSet processes=null;
    private HashSet suspected=new HashSet();
    private boolean[] broadcast=null;
    private boolean[] delivered=null;
    private Comparable proposal=null;

    public void handle(Event event) {
        if (event instanceof ProcessInitEvent)
            handleProcessInit((ProcessInitEvent)event);
        else if (event instanceof Crash)
            handleCrash((Crash)event);
        else if (event instanceof ConsensusPropose)
            handleConsensusPropose((ConsensusPropose)event);
        else if (event instanceof DecidedEvent)
            handleDecided((DecidedEvent)event);
        else {
            event.go();
        }
    }

    private void init() {
        int max_rounds=processes.getSize();

        //suspected
        round=0;
        proposal=null;
        prop_round=-1;

        delivered=new boolean[max_rounds];
        Arrays.fill(delivered,false);
        broadcast=new boolean[max_rounds];
        Arrays.fill(broadcast,false);
    }

    private void handleProcessInit(ProcessInitEvent event) {
        processes=event.getProcessSet();
        init();
        event.go();
    }

    private void handleCrash(Crash crash) {
        processes.setCorrect(crash.getCrashedProcess(),false);
        suspected.add(new Integer(crash.getCrashedProcess()));
        crash.go();

        suspected_or_delivered();
        decide(crash.getChannel());
    }
```

```
private void handleConsensusPropose(ConsensusPropose propose) {
    if (proposal != null)
        return;

    proposal=propose.value;

    decide(propose.getChannel());
}

private void decide(Channel channel) {
    if (broadcast[round])
        return;
    if (proposal == null)
        return;
    if (round != processes.getSelfRank())
        return;

    broadcast[round]=true;
    ConsensusDecide ev=new ConsensusDecide(channel,Direction.UP,this);
    ev.decision=(Proposal)proposal;
    ev.go();

    DecidedEvent ev=new DecidedEvent(channel,Direction.DOWN,this);
    ev.getExtendedMessage().pushObject(proposal);
    ev.getExtendedMessage().pushInt(round);
    ev.go();
}

private void suspected_or_delivered() {
    if (suspected.contains(new Integer(round)) || delivered[round])
        round++;

    if (round >= delivered.length) {
        init ();
    }
}

private void handleDecided(DecidedEvent event) {
    SampleProcess p_i=processes.getProcess((InetWithPort)event.source);
    int r=event.getExtendedMessage().popInt();
    Comparable v=(Comparable)event.getExtendedMessage().popObject();

    if ((r < processes.getSelfRank()) && (r > prop_round)) {
        proposal=v;
        prop_round=r;
    }
    delivered[r]=true;

    suspected_or_delivered ();
    decide(event.getChannel());
}
}
```

Try It

1. Setup

    a) Open three shells/command prompts.

    b) In each shell, go to the directory where you have placed the supplied code.

    c) In each shell, launch the test application, *SampleAppl*, as with the flooding algorithm, but specifying the *qos* as **hc**.

- In shell 0, execute

```
java demo/tutorialDA/SampleAppl \
    -f demo/tutorialDA/procs \
    -n 0 \
    -qos hc
```

- In shell 1, execute

```
java demo/tutorialDA/SampleAppl \
    -f demo/tutorialDA/procs \
    -n 1 \
    -qos hc
```

- In shell 2, execute

```
java demo/tutorialDA/SampleAppl \
    -f demo/tutorialDA/procs \
    -n 2 \
    -qos hc
```

d) If the error NoClassDefError has appeared, confirm that you are at the root of the supplied code.

e) Start the *prefect failure detector* by typing **startpfd** in each shell.

2. Run: Now that the processes are launched and running, let us try this execution:

a) In shell 0, propose the value **B** (type **consensus B** and press Enter).

b) Note that all processes decide **B**. Because the proposal came from the process with the lowest rank, a decision is almost immediate.

c) In shell 2, propose the value **G**.

d) Note that no decision as yet been made.

e) In shell 1, propose the value **H**.

f) Again, note that no decision as yet been made.

g) In shell 0, propose the value **I**.

h) All processes decide **I**.

i) In shell 1, propose the value **J**.

j) No decision has yet been made.

k) In shell 0, kill the test process.

l) The remaining processes display that a decision was made and that it is **J**. Because **J** was proposed by the living process with the lowest rank, as soon as it is detected that all other processes with lower ranks have failed, the proposal becomes a decision.

5.6.3 Flooding Uniform Consensus

The communication stack used to implement the flooding uniform consensus protocol is depicted in the following:

SampleAppl
Uniform Consensus   **(implemented by Flooding UC)**
Perfect Failure Detector   (implemented by TcpBasedPFD)
Best-Effort Broadcast   (implemented by Basic Broadcast)
Perfect Point-To-Point Links   (implemented by TcpBasedPerfectP2P)

The *FloodingUniformConsensus* implements the uniform flooding consensus algorithm. It follows the Algorithm 5.3 very closely. Its main difference when compared with the regular flooding algorithm is that it runs through N rounds, N being the number of processes. Due to this, it is not necessary to broadcast the decision. The protocol implementation is depicted in Listing 5.3.

Listing 5.3. Flooding Uniform Consensus implementation

```
package appia.protocols.tutorialDA.floodingUniformConsensus;

public class FloodingUniformConsensusSession extends Session {
    public FloodingUniformConsensusSession(Layer layer) {
        super(layer);
    }

    private int round=-1;
    private ProcessSet correct=null;
    private Comparable decided=null;
    private HashSet[] delivered=null;
    private HashSet proposal_set=null;

    public void handle(Event event) {
        if (event instanceof ProcessInitEvent)
            handleProcessInit((ProcessInitEvent)event);
        else if (event instanceof Crash)
            handleCrash((Crash)event);
        else if (event instanceof ConsensusPropose)
            handleConsensusPropose((ConsensusPropose)event);
        else if (event instanceof MySetEvent)
            handleMySet((MySetEvent)event);
        else {
            event.go();
        }
    }

    private void init() {
        int max_rounds=correct.getSize();
        delivered=new HashSet[max_rounds];
        proposal_set=new HashSet();
        int i;
        for (i=0 ; i < max_rounds ; i++) {
            delivered[i]=new HashSet();
        }
        round=0;
        decided=null;
    }

    private void handleProcessInit(ProcessInitEvent event) {
        correct=event.getProcessSet();
```

```
        init ();
        event.go ();
    }

    private void handleCrash(Crash crash) {
        correct.setCorrect(crash.getCrashedProcess(),false);
        crash.go ();

        decide(crash.getChannel());
    }

    private void handleConsensusPropose(ConsensusPropose propose) {
        proposal_set.add(propose.value);

        MySetEvent ev=new MySetEvent(propose.getChannel(),Direction.DOWN,this);
        ev.getExtendedMessage().pushObject(proposal_set);
        ev.getExtendedMessage().pushInt(round);
        ev.go ();
    }

    private void handleMySet(MySetEvent event) {
        SampleProcess p_i=correct.getProcess((InetWithPort)event.source);
        int r=event.getExtendedMessage().popInt();
        HashSet newSet=(HashSet)event.getExtendedMessage().popObject();

        proposal_set.addAll(newSet);
        delivered[r].add(p_i);

        decide(event.getChannel());
    }

    private void decide(Channel channel) {
        int i;

        if (decided != null)
            return;

        for (i=0 ; i < correct.getSize () ; i++) {
            SampleProcess p=correct.getProcess(i);
            if ((p != null) && p.isCorrect() && !delivered[round].contains(p))
                return;
        }

        if (round == delivered.length-1) {
            Iterator iter=proposal_set.iterator ();
            while (iter.hasNext()) {
                Comparable proposal=(Comparable)iter.next();
                if (decided == null)
                    decided=proposal;
                else
                    if (proposal.compareTo(decided) < 0)
                        decided=proposal;
            }

            ConsensusDecide ev=new ConsensusDecide(channel,Direction.UP,this);
            ev.decision=(Proposal)decided;
            ev.go ();

            init ();
        } else {
            round++;

            MySetEvent ev=new MySetEvent(channel,Direction.DOWN,this);
            ev.getExtendedMessage().pushObject(proposal_set);
            ev.getExtendedMessage().pushInt(round);
            ev.go ();
```

```
        }
      }
    }
  }
```

Try It The same executions suggested for flooding regular consensus can be experimented with. Remember to specify the *qos* as **ufc**.

5.6.4 Hierarchical Uniform Consensus

The communication stack used to implement the uniform hierarchical consensus protocol is depicted in the following:

Application
Uniform Consensus   **(implemented by Hierarchical UC)**
Perfect Failure Detector   (implemented by TcpBasedPFD)
Best-Effort Broadcast   (implemented by Basic Broadcast)
Perfect Point-to-Point Links   (implemented by TcpBasedPerfectP2P)

This implementation uses two different *Appia* channels because it requires *best-effort broadcast* and *perfect point-to-point links*, and each channel can only offer one of those properties, despite the fact that best-effort broadcast uses perfect point-to-point links. The *HierarchicalUniformConsensus* layer implements the uniform hierarchical consensus algorithm. It follows Algorithm 5.4 very closely. The protocol implementation is depicted in Listing 5.4.

Listing 5.4. Hierarchical Uniform Consensus implementation

```
package appia.protocols.tutorialDA.hierarchicalUniformConsensus;

public class HierarchicalUniformConsensusSession extends Session {
    public HierarchicalUniformConsensusSession(Layer layer) {
        super(layer);
    }

    private Comparable proposal=null;
    private Comparable decided=null;
    private int round=-1;
    private HashSet suspected=new HashSet();
    private HashSet ack_set=new HashSet();
    private int prop_round=-1;
    private ProcessSet processes=null;

    private Channel mainchannel=null;
    private Channel rbchannel=null;
    private Channel rbinit=null;

    public void handle(Event event) {
        if (event instanceof ChannelInit)
            handleChannelInit((ChannelInit)event);
        else if (event instanceof ProcessInitEvent)
```

```
                handleProcessInit((ProcessInitEvent)event);
        else if (event instanceof Crash)
                handleCrash((Crash)event);
        else if (event instanceof ConsensusPropose)
                handleConsensusPropose((ConsensusPropose)event);
        else if (event instanceof ProposeEvent)
                handleProposeEvent((ProposeEvent)event);
        else if (event instanceof DecidedEvent)
                handleDecided((DecidedEvent)event);
        else {
                event.go();
        }
}

public void rbchannel(Channel c) {
        rbinit=c;
}

private void handleChannelInit(ChannelInit init) {
        if (mainchannel == null) {
                mainchannel=init.getChannel();
                rbinit.start();
        } else {
                if (init.getChannel() == rbinit) {
                        rbchannel=init.getChannel();

                        if (processes != null) {
                                ProcessInitEvent ev=new ProcessInitEvent(rbchannel,Direction.DOWN,this);
                                ev.setProcessSet(processes);
                                ev.go();
                        } catch (AppiaEventException ex) {
                                ex.printStackTrace();
                        }
                }
        }

        init.go();
}

private void handleProcessInit(ProcessInitEvent event) {
        processes=event.getProcessSet();
        init();
        event.go();

        if (rbchannel != null) {
                ProcessInitEvent ev=new ProcessInitEvent(rbchannel,Direction.DOWN,this);
                ev.setProcessSet(processes);
                ev.go();
        }
}

private void init() {
        int max_rounds=processes.getSize();

        proposal=null;
        decided=null;
        round=0;
        //suspected
        ack_set=new HashSet();
        prop_round=-1;

        count_decided=0;
}

private void handleCrash(Crash crash) {
        processes.setCorrect(crash.getCrashedProcess(),false);
```

```
            suspected.add(new Integer(crash.getCrashedProcess()));

            crash.go();

            suspected_or_acked();
            propose();
            decide();
    }

    private void handleConsensusPropose(ConsensusPropose propose) {
            if (proposal != null)
                return;

            proposal=propose.value;

            propose();
    }

    private void propose() {
            if (decided != null)
                return;
            if (proposal == null)
                return;
            if (round != processes.getSelfRank())
                return;

            ProposeEvent ev=new ProposeEvent(mainchannel,Direction.DOWN,this);
            ev.getExtendedMessage().pushObject(proposal);
            ev.getExtendedMessage().pushInt(round);
            ev.go();
    }

    private void handleProposeEvent(ProposeEvent event) {
            int p_i_rank=processes.getRank((InetWithPort)event.source);
            int r=event.getExtendedMessage().popInt();
            Comparable v=(Comparable)event.getExtendedMessage().popObject();

            ack_set.add(new Integer(p_i_rank));
            if ((r < processes.getSelfRank()) && (r > prop_round)) {
                proposal=v;
                prop_round=r;
            }

            suspected_or_acked();
            propose();
            decide();
    }

    private void suspected_or_acked() {
            if (suspected.contains(new Integer(round)) || ack_set.contains(new Integer(round)))
                round++;
    }

    private void decide() {
            int i;
            for (i=0 ; i < processes.getSize() ; i++) {
                int p_i_rank=processes.getProcess(i).getProcessNumber();
                if (!suspected.contains(new Integer(p_i_rank)) &&
                    !ack_set.contains(new Integer(p_i_rank))) {
                    return;
                }
            }

            DecidedEvent ev=new DecidedEvent(rbchannel,Direction.DOWN,this);
            ev.getExtendedMessage().pushObject(proposal);
            ev.go();
```

```
    }

    private void handleDecided(DecidedEvent event) {
        // Counts the number os Decided messages received and reinitiates the algorithm
        if ((++count_decided >= correctSize()) && (decided != null)) {
            init ();
            return;
        }

        if (decided != null)
            return;

        decided=(Comparable)event.getExtendedMessage().popObject();

        ConsensusDecide ev=new ConsensusDecide(mainchannel,Direction.UP,this);
        ev. decision=(Proposal)decided;
        ev.go ();
    }

    // Used to count the number of Decided messages received, therefore determining when
    // all processes have decided and therefore allow a new decision process.
    private int count_decided;
    private int correctSize() {
        int size=0,i;
        for (i=0 ; i < processes.getSize () ; i++) {
            if ((processes.getProcess(i) != null) && processes.getProcess(i). isCorrect ())
                ++size;
        }
        return size;
    }
}
```

Try It The same executions suggested for hierarchical regular consensus can be experimented with. Remember to specify the *qos* as **uhc**.

5.7 Exercises

Exercise 5.1 *Improve our "Hierarchical Consensus" algorithm to save one communication step. The "Hierarchical Consensus" algorithm we presented requires N communication steps for all correct processes to decide. By a slight modification, it can run in $N - 1$ steps: suggest such a modification.*

Exercise 5.2 *Explain why none of our regular consensus algorithms ("Hierarchical Consensus"and "Flooding Consensus") ensure uniform consensus.*

Exercise 5.3 *Can we optimize our "Flooding Uniform Consensus" algorithm to save one communication step, i.e., such that all correct processes always decide after $N - 1$ communication steps? Consider simply the case of a system of two processes.*

Exercise 5.4 *What would happen in our "Flooding Uniform Consensus" algorithm if*

1. we did not use set[round] but directly updated proposedSet in **upon event** bebDeliver?
2. we accepted any bebDeliver event, even if $p_i \notin correct$?

Exercise 5.5 *Consider all our fail-stop consensus algorithms ("Hierarchical (Uniform) Consensus"and "Flooding (Uniform) Consensus"). Explain why none of those algorithms would be correct if the failure detector turns out not to be perfect.*

Exercise 5.6 *Explain why any fail-noisy consensus algorithm actually solves uniform consensus.*

Exercise 5.7 *Explain why any fail-noisy consensus (or abortable consensus) algorithm requires a majority of the correct processes.*

Exercise 5.8 *Give a fail-noisy consensus algorithm that assumes a correct majority of the processes and uses an eventually perfect failure detector abstraction in such a way that (1) in any execution where p_1 is never suspected, it imposes its proposed value as the consensus decision, (2) in any execution where p_1 crashes initially and p_2 is never suspected, p_2 imposes its proposal, ..., (k) if p_1, p_2, ... p_k all initially crash, then p_{k+1} imposes its proposal if it is not suspected;and so on.*

Exercise 5.9 *Give a fail-recovery logged consensus algorithm which uses the eventual leader detector and ensures the following property: if p_1 does not crash and is the only leader from the beginning of the execution, only three communication steps, $3N$ messages, and one log at each process of a majority is needed for all correct processes to decide.*

5.8 Solutions

Solution 5.1 The last process (p_N) does not need to broadcast its message. Indeed, the only process that uses p_N's broadcast value is p_N itself, and p_N decides its proposal just *before* it broadcasts it (not when it delivers it). □

Solution 5.2 Consider first our "Flooding Consensus" algorithm and the scenario of Figure 5.1. Assume that p_1's message has reached only p_2. At the end of the first round, p_2 has not detected any process to have crashed and can thus decide 3. However, if p_2 crashes after deciding 3, p_3 and p_4 might decide 5.

Now consider our "Hierarchical Consensus" algorithm and the scenario of Figure 5.2. In the case where p_1 decides and crashes, and no other process sees p_1's proposal (i.e., 3), then p_1 decides differently from the other processes. □

Solution 5.3 In the case of two processes, our "Flooding Uniform Consensus" needs two communication steps. We argue here that a decision cannot be reached by al correct processes after simply one step. (The interested reader will extend this argument beyond this case to the general case of any N.)

Consider a system made of two processes, p_1 and p_2. We exhibit an execution where the processes do not reach uniform agreement after one round; thus they need at least two rounds. More precisely, consider the execution where p_1 and p_2 propose two different values, respectively, v_1 and v_2. Without loss of generality, assume that $v_1 < v_2$. We shall consider the following execution, where p_1 is faulty.

During round 1, p_1 and p_2 send their message to each other. Process p_1 receives its own value and p_2's message (p_2 is correct), and decides. Assume that p_1 decides its own value v_1, which is different from p_2's value, and then crashes. Now, assume that the message p_1 sent to p_2 in round 1 is arbitrarily delayed. There is a time after which p_2 permanently suspects p_1 because of the *completeness* property of the perfect failure detector. As p_2 does not know that p_1 did send a message, p_2 decides at the end of round 1 on its own value v_2. Hence the violation of *uniform agreement*.

Note that if we allow processes to decide only after two rounds, the above scenario does not occur. This is because p_1 crashes *before* deciding (i.e., it never decides), and, later on, p_2 decides v_2. □

Solution 5.4 Consider a variant of our "Flooding Uniform Consensus" where we would not use *set[round]* but directly update *proposedSet* in **upon event** bebDeliver. The resulting algorithm would also be correct. In this algorithm, the processes would also need to execute N rounds before deciding. Thus, unless all processes crash, there exists a round r during which no process crashes. This is because, at each round, every process broadcasts the values it knows from the previous rounds. After executing round r, all processes that have not crashed know exactly the same information. If we now update *proposedSet* *before* the beginning of the next round (and, in particular, before the beginning of round r), the processes will still have the information on time. In short, the fact they get the information earlier is not a problem since they must execute N rounds anyway.

Consider now a variant of our "Flooding Uniform Consensus" where would accept any bebDeliver event, even if $p_i \notin correct$. The resulting algorithm would be wrong. In the following, we exhibit an execution that leads to disagreement. More precisely, consider a system made of three processes, p_1, p_2, and p_3. The processes propose 0, 1, and 1, respectively. During the first round, the messages of p_1 are delayed, and p_2 and p_3 never see them. Process p_1 crashes at the end of round 2, but p_2 still sees p_1's round 2 message (the set $\{0,1\}$) in round 2). Process p_3 does not receive p_1's message in round 2, though. In round 3, the message from p_2 to p_3 (the set $\{0,1\}$) is delayed and process p_2 crashes at the end of round 3, so that p_3 never sees p_2's message. Before crashing, p_2 decides on value 0, whereas p_3 decides on 1. Hence the disagreement. □

Solution 5.5 In all our fail-stop algorithms, there is at least one critical point where a process p waits to deliver a message from a process q or to detect the crash of process q. Should q crash and p never detect the crash of q, p would remain blocked forever and never decide. In short, in any of our algorithms using a perfect failure detector, a violation of *strong completeness* could lead to the violation of the *termination* property of consensus.

Consider now *strong accuracy*. Consider, for instance, our "Flooding Consensus" algorithm and the scenario of Figure 5.1: if p_2 crashes after deciding 3, and p_1 is falsely suspected to have crashed by p_3 and p_4, then p_3 and p_4 will decide 5. A similar scenario can occur for "Hierarchical Consensus." □

Solution 5.6 Consider any fail-noisy consensus algorithm that implements consensus but not uniform consensus. This means that there is an execution where two processes p_i and p_j decide differently and one of them crashes: the algorithm violates *uniform agreement*. Assume that process p_i crashes. With an eventually perfect failure detector, it might be the case that p_i has not crashed but is falsely suspected to have crashed by all other processes. Process p_j would decide the same as in the previous execution, and the algorithm would even violate *(non-uniform) agreement*. □

Solution 5.7 We explain this for the case of a system of four processes $\{p_1, p_2, p_3, p_4\}$. Assume by contradiction that there is a fail-noisy consensus algorithm that tolerates the crash of two processes. Assume that p_1 and p_2 propose a value v whereas p_3 and p_4 propose a different value v'. Consider an execution E_1 where p_1 and p_2 crash initially: in this execution, p_3 and p_4 decide v' to respect the *validity* property of consensus. Consider also an execution E_2 where p_3 and p_4 crash initially: in this scenario, p_1 and p_2 decide v. With an eventually perfect failure detector, a third execution E_3 is possible: the one where no process crashes, p_1 and p_2 falsely suspect p_3 and p_4, and p_3 and p_4 falsely suspect p_1 and p_2. In this execution, E_3, p_1 and p_2 decide v, just as in execution E_1 (they execute the same steps as in E_1, and cannot distinguish E_3 from E_1 up to the decision point), whereas p_3 and p_4 decide v', just as in execution E_2 (they execute the same steps as in E_2, and cannot distinguish E_3 from E_2 up to the decision point). *Agreement* would hence be violated.

A similar argument applies to abortable consensus. □

Solution 5.8 It is first important to note that, in Algorithm 5.7, the process that imposes its proposal is the one chosen by the eventual leader detector abstraction. We give here a "Rotating Coordinator" algorithm where if p_1, p_2, ... p_k all initially crash, then $p_k + 1$ imposes its proposal if it is not suspected.

The "Rotating Coordinator" algorithm we give here is round-based and the processes play two roles: the role of a leader, described in Algorithm 5.12, and the role of a witness, described in Algorithm 5.13. Every process goes sequentially from round i to round $i + 1$: no process ever jumps from one round k to another round $k' < k + 1$. Every round has a leader determined a priori: the leader of round i is process $p_{(i-1) \mod (N+1)}$, e.g., p_2 is the leader of rounds 2, $N + 2$, $2N + 2$, and so on.

The process that is the leader in a round computes a new proposal and tries to impose that proposal on all processes; every process that gets the proposal from the current leader adopts this proposal and assigns it the current round number as a timestamp. Then it acknowledges that proposal back to the leader. If the leader gets a majority of acknowledgments, it decides and disseminates that decision using a reliable broadcast abstraction.

There is a critical point where processes need the input of their failure detector in every round. When the processes are waiting for a proposal from the leader of that round, the processes should not wait indefinitely if the leader has crashed without having broadcast its proposal. In this case, the processes consult their failure detector module to get a hint on whether the leader process has crashed.

Given that an eventually perfect detector ensures that, every crashed process is eventually permanently suspected by every correct process, the process that is waiting for a crashed leader will eventually suspect it. In this case, the process sends a specific message *Nack* to the leader, and then moves to the next round. In fact, a leader that is waiting for acknowledgments might get some *Nacks* (if some processes falsely suspected it); in this case, the leader moves to the next round without deciding.

Note also that processes after acknowledging a proposal move to the next round directly: they do not need to wait for a decision. They might deliver the decision through the reliable broadcast dissemination phase. In that case, they will simply stop their algorithm.

Correctness. Validity and *integrity* follow from the algorithm and the properties of the underlying communication abstractions. Consider *termination*. If some correct process decides, it decides through the reliable broadcast abstraction, i.e., by rbDelivering a decision message. Due to the properties of this broadcast abstraction, every correct process rbDelivers the decision message and decides. Assume by contradiction that there is at least one correct process and no correct process decides. Consider the time t after which all faulty processes crashed, all faulty processes are suspected by every correct process, forever and no correct process is ever suspected. Let p_i be the first correct process that is the leader after time t and let r denote the round at

---

Algorithm 5.12 Rotating Coordinator: leader role

Uses:
    PerfectPointToPointLinks (pp2p);
    ReliableBroadcast (rb);
    BestEffortBroadcast (beb);
    EventuallyPerfectFailureDetector ($\Diamond \mathcal{P}$).

function leader (r) **returns** processid **is**
    return p_i: ($rank(p_i) = $ (r mod $N + 1$));

upon event $\langle$ *Init* $\rangle$ **do**
    round := 1; decided := $\perp$;
    (ts, proposal) := ($\perp$, $\perp$);
    suspected:= estimate-set[] := ack-set[] := nack-set[] := $\emptyset$;
    forall r **do** estimate[r] := ack[r] := false; proposed[r] := $\perp$

upon event $\langle$ *ucPropose* $\mid v$ $\rangle$ $\wedge$ proposal $\neq \perp$ **do**
    (ts, proposal) := (0, v);

upon event $\langle$ *pp2pDeliver* $\mid p_i$, [ESTIMATE, r, e] $\rangle$ **do**
    estimate-set[r] := estimate-set[r] $\cup$ {e};

upon (leader(round)=self) $\wedge$ (|estimate-set[round]| > N/2$) **do**
    (ts, proposal) := *highest*(estimate-set[round]);
    trigger $\langle$ *bebBroadcast* $\mid$ [PROPOSE, round, (round, proposal)] $\rangle$;

upon event $\langle$ *pp2pDeliver* $\mid p_i$, [ACK, r] $\rangle$ **do**
    ack-set[r] := ack-set[r] $\cup$ {p_i};

upon event $\langle$ *pp2pDeliver* $\mid p_i$, [NACK, r] $\rangle$ **do**
    nack-set[r] := nack-set[r] $\cup$ {p_i};

upon (leader(round)=self) $\wedge$ nack-set[round] $\neq \emptyset$ **do**
    round := round + 1;

upon (leader(round)=self) $\wedge$ (|ack-set[round]| > N/2$) **do**
    trigger $\langle$ *rbBroadcast* $\mid$ [DECIDE, proposal] $\rangle$;

---

which that process is leader. If no process has decided, then all correct processes reach round r, and p_i eventually reaches a decision and rbBroadcasts that decision.

Consider now *agreement*. Assume by contradiction any two rounds i and j, where j is the closest integer to i such that $j > i$, and $p_{i \ mod \ (N+1)}$, and $p_{j \ mod \ (N+1)}$, proposed two different decision values v and v' respectively. Process $p_{j \ mod \ (N+1)}$ must have adopted v before reaching round j. This is because $p_{j \ mod \ (N+1)}$ selects the value with the largest timestamp and $p_{j \ mod \ (N+1)}$ cannot miss the value of $p_{i \ mod \ (N+1)}$: any two majorities always

---

Algorithm 5.13 Rotating Coordinator: witness role

---

upon event (proposal $\neq \perp$) $\wedge$ (estimate[round] = false) **do**
    estimate[round] := true;
    trigger $\langle$ pp2pSend | leader(round), [ESTIMATE, round, proposal] $\rangle$;

upon event $\langle$ bebDeliver | p_i, [PROPOSE, r, (ts, v)] $\rangle$ **do**
    proposed[r] := (ts, v);

upon event (proposed[round]$\neq \perp$) $\wedge$ (ack[round] = false) **do**
    (ts, proposal) := proposed[round];
    ack[round] := true;
    trigger $\langle$ pp2pSend | leader(round), [ACK, round] $\rangle$;
    round := round + 1;

upon event (leader(round) $\in$ suspected) $\wedge$ (ack[round] = false) **do**
    ack[round] := true;
    trigger $\langle$ pp2pSend | leader(round), [NACK, round] $\rangle$;
    round := round + 1;

upon event $\langle$ rbDeliver | p_i, [DECIDED, v] $\rangle$ $\wedge$ (decided = $\perp$) **do**
    decided := v;
    trigger $\langle$ ucDecide | v $\rangle$;

upon event $\langle$ suspect | p_i $\rangle$ **do**
    suspected := suspected $\cup$ {p_i};

upon event $\langle$ restore | p_i $\rangle$ **do**
    suspected := suspected $\setminus$ {p_i};

---

intersect. Given that j is the closest integer to i such that some process proposed v' different from v, after v was proposed, we have a contradiction.

Performance. If no process fails or is suspected to have failed, then four communication steps and $4N$ messages are required for all correct processes to decide. $\square$

Solution 5.9 The algorithm is a variant of our "Logged Consensus" algorithm where the underlying logged abortable consensus abstraction is opened for optimization purposes. In the case where p_1 is initially elected leader, p_1 directly tries to impose its decision, i.e., without consulting the other processes. In a sense, it skips the read phase of the underlying logged abortable consensus. This computation phase is actually only needed to make sure that the leader will propose any value that might have been proposed. For the case where p_1 is initially the leader, p_1 is sure that no decision has been made in a previous round (there cannot be any previous round), and can save one communication phase by directly making its own proposal. This also leads to saving the first access to stable storage and one communication round-trip. $\square$

5.9 Historical Notes

- The consensus problem was defined in 1982 (Lamport, Shostak, and Pease 1982).
- It was proved in 1985 that consensus is impossible to solve with a deterministic algorithm in a fail-silent model even if only one process fails (Fischer, Lynch, and Paterson 1985).
- Later on, in 1988, intermediate models between the synchronous and the asynchronous model were introduced to circumvent the consensus impossibility (Dwork, Lynch, and Stockmeyer 1988).
- The notion of failure detection was then considered an elegant way to encapsulate partial synchrony assumptions (Chandra and Toueg 1996).
- The "Rotating Coordinator" fail-noisy consensus algorithm (presented in the exercise section) was introduced in 1996 (Chandra and Toueg 1996) whereas the "Abortable Consensus" based fail-noisy consensus algorithm was introduced in 1989 in the context of the Paxos algorithm (Lamport 1989). The abortable consensus abstraction was made precise in 2003 (Boichat, Dutta, Frolund, and Guerraoui 2003a; Boichat, Dutta, Frolund, and Guerraoui 2003b).
- It was shown in 1996 (Chandra and Toueg 1996; Guerraoui 2000) that any fail-noisy consensus algorithm (using an unreliable failure detector) requires a majority of the correct processes.
- It was shown in 2000 (Guerraoui 2000) that any fail-noisy algorithm that solves regular consensus also solves uniform consensus.
- The randomized consensus algorithm presented in this chapter is from 2001 (Ezhilchelvan, Mostefaoui, and Raynal 2001), and is a generalization of an older binary randomized consensus algorithm (Ben-Or 1983).
- Failure detector lower bounds for consensus were first given in 1996 (Chandra, Hadzilacos, and Toueg 1996) and refined later (Delporte-Gallet, Fauconnier, and Guerraoui 2002; Delporte-Gallet, Fauconnier, Guerraoui, Hadzilacos, Kouznetsov, and Toueg 2004).
- Algorithms that implement consensus assuming asynchronous periods and underlying malicious processes have also constituted an active area of research (Yin, Martin, Venkataramani, Alvisi, and Dahlin 2003; Baldoni, Hélary, Raynal, and Tangui 2003; Abraham, Chockler, Keidar, and Malkhi 2004; Avoine, Gärtner, Guerraoui, and Vukolic 2005; Doudou, Garbinato, and Guerraoui 2005).

6. Consensus Variants

God does not often clap his hands. When he does, everybody should dance.
(African Proverb)

This chapter describes variants of the consensus abstraction which we studied in the previous chapter. These variants are motivated by applications of consensus in areas like replication and distributed databases.

In the variants we consider here, just like in consensus, the processes need to make consistent decisions, e.g., decide on common values. Unlike in consensus, however, the decisions here cannot be any values proposed by the processes. They, rather, need to obey specific coordination requirements driven by the upper layer application.

The abstractions we will study here include *total order broadcast, terminating reliable broadcast, (non-blocking) atomic commitment, group membership,* and *view synchrony.* We will focus here on fail-stop algorithms that implement these abstractions. Excluding the total order abstraction (of which we will discuss several variants in the exercise section), determining adequate means to specify and implement these consensus variants for other models is an open area of research.

6.1 Total Order Broadcast

6.1.1 Overview

Earlier in the book (Section 3.9), we discussed the causal order broadcast abstraction and its implementation. Causal order broadcast enforces a global ordering for all messages that causally depend on each other: such messages need to be delivered in the same order and this order must respect causality. Messages that are not causally related are said to be *concurrent*. Causal order broadcast does not enforce any ordering among concurrent messages.

In particular, if a process p_1 broadcasts a message m_1 whereas a process p_2 concurrently broadcasts a message m_2, then the messages might be delivered in different orders by the processes. For instance, p_1 might deliver first m_1 and then m_2, whereas p_2 might deliver first m_2 and then m_1.

A *total order broadcast* abstraction orders all messages, even those that are not causally related. More precisely, total order broadcast is a reliable broadcast communication abstraction which ensures that all processes deliver messages in the same order. Whereas reliable broadcast ensures that processes agree on the same *set* of messages they deliver, total order broadcast ensures that they agree on the same *sequence* of messages, i.e., the set is now ordered.

The total order broadcast abstraction is sometimes also called *atomic broadcast* because the message delivery occurs as if the broadcast were an indivisible primitive (i.e., atomic): the message is delivered to all or to none of the processes and, if the message is delivered, every other message is ordered either before or after this message.

Total order broadcast is a very convenient abstraction to maintain the consistency of replicas of a deterministic service whose behavior can be captured by a state machine. A state machine consists of state variables and commands that update these variables and may produce some output. Commands consist of *deterministic* programs, such that the outputs of the state machine are solely determined by the initial state and the sequence of commands previously executed. The service modeled by the state machine can be made fault-tolerant by replicating it on different processes. Total order broadcast ensures that all the replicas deliver concurrent commands from different clients in the same order, and hence maintain the same state.

This approach can, for instance, be applied to implement highly available shared objects of arbitrary types in a distributed system, i.e., beyond the read-write (register) objects studied earlier in the book (Chapter 4). Each process would host a replica of the object and invocations to the object would be broadcast to all replicas using the total order broadcast primitive. This will ensure that all replicas keep the same state and ensure that the responses are consistent. In short, the use of total order broadcast ensures that the object is highly available, yet it appears as if it were a single logical entity accessed in a sequential and failure-free manner, i.e., it is atomic. We will return to this topic in the exercise section.

6.1.2 Specifications

Many specifications of the total order broadcast abstraction can be considered. We focus here on two variants, which are both extensions of reliable broadcast abstractions. The first is a regular variant that ensures total ordering only among the correct processes. The second is a uniform variant that ensures total ordering with regard to all processes, including the faulty processes as well. The first specification, depicted in Module 6.1, is captured by property TO, together with properties RB1–RB4 (from Section 3.3), whereas

---

Module 6.1 Interface and properties of regular total order broadcast

Module:

    Name: TotalOrder (to).

Events:

    Request: ⟨ *toBroadcast* | m ⟩: Used to broadcast message m to Π.

    Indication: ⟨ *toDeliver* | src, m ⟩: Used to deliver message m sent by process *src*.

Properties:

    TO: *Total order:* Let m_1 and m_2 be any two messages. Let p_i and p_j be any two correct processes that deliver m_1 and m_2. If p_i delivers m_1 before m_2, then p_j delivers m_1 before m_2.

    RB1: *Validity:* If a correct process p_i broadcasts a message m, then p_i eventually delivers m.

    RB2: *No duplication:* No message is delivered more than once.

    RB3: *No creation:* If a message m is delivered by some process p_j, then m was previously broadcast by some process p_i.

    RB4: *Agreement:* If a message m is delivered by some correct process p_i, then m is eventually delivered by every correct process p_j.

Module 6.2 Interface and properties of uniform total order broadcast

Module:

    Name: UniformTotalOrder (uto).

Events:

    ⟨ *utoBroadcast* | m ⟩, ⟨ *utoDeliver* | src, m ⟩: with the same meaning and interface of the total order broadcast interface.

Properties:

    UTO: *Uniform total order:* Let m_1 and m_2 be any two messages. Let p_i and p_j be any two processes that deliver m_2. If p_i delivers m_1 before m_2, then p_j delivers m_1 before m_2.

    RB1–RB3: Same as in regular total order broadcast.

    URB4: *Uniform Agreement:* If a message m is delivered by some process p_i (whether correct or faulty), then m is also eventually delivered by every other correct process p_j.

---

the second specification, depicted in Module 6.2, is captured by property UTO, together with properties RB1–RB3 and URB4 (from Section 3.4).

    Other combinations of TO or UTO with reliable and uniform reliable broadcast properties lead to slightly different specifications. For conciseness, we omit describing all the corresponding modules.

It is important to note that the total order property is orthogonal to the causal order property discussed in Section 3.9. It is possible to have a total order abstraction that does not respect causal order. On the other hand, and as we pointed out, a causal order abstraction does not enforce total order: the processes may deliver concurrent messages in different order to different processes. Of course, it is also possible to build a total order abstraction on top of a causal order primitive. We omit the interface of the resulting module in this case.

6.1.3 Algorithm: Consensus-Based Total Order Broadcast

In the following, we give a total order broadcast algorithm, implementing the interface of Module 6.1. The algorithm (Algorithm 6.1), called "Consensus-Based Total Order", ensures the properties of reliable broadcast plus the total order (TO) property. It uses a reliable broadcast and a regular consensus abstraction as underlying building blocks.

The intuitive idea underlying Algorithm 6.1 is the following. Messages are first disseminated using a reliable (but possibly unordered) broadcast primitive. Messages delivered this way are stored in a bag of unordered messages at every process. The processes then use the consensus abstraction to order the messages in this bag.

More precisely, the algorithm works in consecutive rounds. As long as new messages are broadcast, the processes keep on moving sequentially from one round to the other: $1, 2, \ldots, k, k+1, \ldots$. There is one consensus instance per round. The consensus instance of a given round is used to have the processes agree on a set of messages to assign to that round number. The messages are then delivered in that round, according to some deterministic order, hence ensuring total order. For instance, the first round decides which messages are assigned sequence number 1, i.e., which messages are delivered in round 1. The second round decides which messages are assigned sequence number 2, and so on. All messages that are assigned round number k are delivered after the messages assigned round number $k-1$. Messages with the same sequence number are delivered according to some deterministic order agreed upon by the processes in advance, e.g., based on message identifiers; that is, once the processes have agreed on a set of messages for a given round, they simply apply a deterministic function to sort the messages of the same set.

In each instance of consensus, every process proposes a (possibly different) set of messages to be ordered. Each process simply proposes the set of messages it has seen (i.e., it has rbDelivered) and not yet delivered according to the total order semantics (i.e., it has not yet toDelivered). The properties of consensus ensure that all processes decide the same set of messages for that sequence number. In Algorithm 6.1, the *wait* flag is used to ensure that a new round is not started before the previous round has terminated.

An execution of the algorithm is illustrated in Figure 6.1. The figure is unfolded into two parallel flows: that of the reliable broadcasts, used to dis-

---

Algorithm 6.1 Consensus-Based Total Order Broadcast

Implements:
    TotalOrder (to).

Uses:
    ReliableBroadcast (rb);
    Consensus (c).

upon event ⟨ *Init* ⟩ **do**
    unordered := delivered := ∅;
    sn := 1;
    wait := false;

upon event ⟨ *toBroadcast* | m ⟩ **do**
    trigger ⟨ *rbBroadcast* | m ⟩;

upon event ⟨ *rbDeliver* | s_m, m ⟩ **do**
    if $m \notin$ delivered **then**
        unordered := unordered ∪ {(s_m, m)};

upon (unordered ≠ ∅) ∧ (wait = false) **do**
    wait := true;
    trigger ⟨ *cPropose* | sn, unordered ⟩;

upon event ⟨ *cDecided* | sn, decided ⟩ **do**
    delivered := delivered ∪ decided;
    unordered := unordered \ decided;
    decided := sort (decided); // some deterministic order;
    forall $(s_m, m) \in$ decided **do**
        trigger ⟨ *toDeliver* | s_m, m ⟩; // following the deterministic order
    sn := sn +1;
    wait := false;

---

seminate the messages, and that of the consensus instances, used to order the messages. Messages received from the reliable broadcast module are proposed to the next instance of consensus. For instance, process p_4 proposes message m_2 to the first instance of consensus. Since the first instance of consensus decides message m_1, process p_4 resubmits m_2 (along with m_3 that was received meanwhile) to the second instance of consensus.

Correctness. The *no creation* property follows from (1) the *no creation* property of the reliable broadcast abstraction and (2) the *validity* property of consensus. The *no duplication* property follows from (1) the *no duplication* property of the reliable broadcast abstraction, and (2) the *integrity* property of consensus and the use of the variable *delivered*.

Consider the *agreement* property. Assume that some correct process p_i toDelivers some message m. According to the algorithm, p_i must have decided a batch of messages with m inside that batch. Every correct process

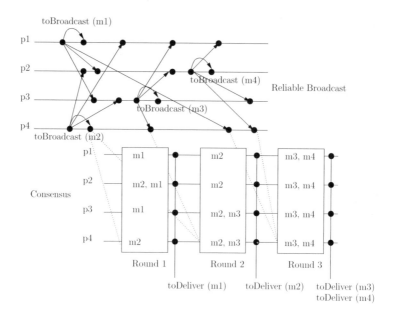

Fig. 6.1: Sample execution of the consensus-based total order broadcast algorithm

eventually decides that batch because of the algorithm and the *termination* property of consensus, and then toDelivers m.

Consider the *validity* property of total order broadcast, and let p_i be some correct process that toBroadcasts a message m. Assume by contradiction that p_i never toDelivers m. This means that m is never included in a batch of messages that some correct process decides. Due the *validity* property of reliable broadcast, every correct process eventually rbDelivers and proposes m in a batch of messages to consensus. Due the *validity* property of consensus, p_i eventually decides a batch of messages including m and toDelivers m.

Consider now the *total order* property. Let p_i and p_j be any two correct processes that toDeliver some message m_2. Assume that p_i toDelivers some message m_1 before m_2. If p_i toDelivers m_1 and m_2 in the same batch (i.e., the same round number), then due to the *agreement* property of consensus, p_j must have also decided the same batch. Thus, p_j must toDeliver m_1 before m_2 since we assume a deterministic function to order the messages for the same batch before their toDelivery. Assume that m_1 is from a previous batch at p_i. Due to the *agreement* property of consensus, p_j must have decided the batch of m_1 as well. Given that processes proceed sequentially from one round to the other, p_j must have toDelivered m_1 before m_2.

Performance. To toDeliver a message when no failures occur, and by merging fail-stop reliable broadcast and consensus algorithms presented in previous chapters, three communication steps and $3N$ messages are required.

Variant. By replacing the regular consensus abstraction with a uniform one, Algorithm 6.1 implements a uniform total order broadcast abstraction.

6.2 Terminating Reliable Broadcast

6.2.1 Overview

The goal of the reliable broadcast abstraction introduced earlier in the book (Section 3.3) is to ensure that if a message is delivered to a process, then it is delivered to all correct processes (uniform definition).

As its name indicates, *terminating reliable broadcast* is a form of reliable broadcast with a specific termination property. To explain the underlying intuition, consider the case where a given process p_i is known to have the obligation of broadcasting some message to all processes in the system. In other words, p_i is an expected source of information in the system and all processes must perform some specific processing according to the message m to be delivered from the source p_i. All the remaining processes are thus waiting for p_i's message. If p_i uses a best-effort broadcast and does not crash, then its message m will indeed be delivered by all correct processes.

Consider now the case where p_i crashed and some process p_j detects that p_i has crashed without having seen m. Does this mean that m was not broadcast? Not really. It is possible that p_i crashed while broadcasting m. In fact, some processes might have delivered m whereas others might never do so. This might be problematic for some applications. In our example, process p_j might need to know whether it should keep on waiting for m, or if it can know at some point that m will never be delivered by any process.

At this point, one may think that the problem could have been avoided if p_i had used a uniform reliable broadcast primitive to broadcast m. Unfortunately, this is not the case. Consider process p_j in the example above. The use of a uniform reliable broadcast primitive would ensure that, if some other process p_k delivered m, then p_j would eventually also deliver m. However, p_j cannot decide if it should wait for m or not. Process p_j has no means to distinguish the case where some process has delivered m, and where p_j can indeed wait for m, from the case where no process will ever deliver m, in which case p_j should definitely not keep waiting for m.

The terminating reliable broadcast (TRB) abstraction ensures precisely that every process p_j either delivers the message m or some indication F that m will never be delivered (by any process). This indication is given in the form of a specific message to the processes: it is, however, assumed that the indication is not like any other message, i.e., it does not belong to the set of possible messages that processes broadcast. The TRB abstraction is a variant of consensus because all processes deliver the same message, i.e., either message m or message F.

Module 6.3 Interface and properties of terminating reliable broadcast

Module:

    Name: TerminatingReliableBroadcast (trb).

Events:

    Request: $\langle$ *trbBroadcast* | src, m $\rangle$: Used to initiate a terminating reliable broadcast for process *src*. Note that if *src* $\neq$ self then $m = \perp$.

    Indication: $\langle$ *trbDeliver* | src, m $\rangle$: Used to deliver message m broadcast by process *src* (or F in the case *src* crashes).

Properties:

    TRB1: *Termination:* Every correct process eventually delivers exactly one message.

    TRB2: *Validity:* If the sender *src* is correct and broadcasts a message m, then *src* eventually delivers m.

    TRB3: *Integrity:* If a correct process delivers a message m then either $m = F$ or m was previously broadcast by *src*.

    TRB4: *Uniform Agreement:* If any process delivers a message m, then every correct process eventually delivers m.

6.2.2 Specification

The properties of terminating reliable broadcast are depicted in Module 6.3. It is important to note that the abstraction is defined for a specific originator process, denoted by *src* in Module 6.3, and known to all processes in advance. A process declares itself as the originator by broadcasting a message m and indicating itself as the source. For presentation uniformity, we also assume that a process indicates that it participates in the terminating reliable broadcast by broadcasting an empty message.

    We consider here the uniform variant of the problem where agreement is uniformly required among any pair of processes, be they correct or faulty.

6.2.3 Algorithm: Consensus-Based TRB

Algorithm 6.2, called "Consensus-Based TRB", implements TRB using three underlying abstractions: a perfect failure detector, a uniform consensus, and a best-effort broadcast abstraction.

    Algorithm 6.2 works by having the source of the message m disseminate m to all processes using a best-effort broadcast. Every process waits until it either gets the message broadcast by the sender process or detects the crash of the originator process. The assumption of a perfect failure detector and the *validity* property of the broadcast ensure that the process does not wait forever.

    Then all processes run a consensus instance to agree on whether to deliver m or to deliver the failure notification F. The value that is proposed to the

---

Algorithm 6.2 Consensus-Based TRB

Implements:
    TerminatingReliableBroadcast (trb).

Uses:
    BestEffortBroadcast (beb);
    UniformConsensus (uc);
    PerfectFailureDetector ($\mathcal{P}$).

upon event ⟨ *Init* ⟩ **do**
    src := ⊥;
    proposal := ⊥;
    correct := Π;

upon event ⟨ *crash* | p_i ⟩ **do**
    correct := correct \ $\{p_i\}$;

upon event ⟨ *trbBroadcast* | p_i, m ⟩ **do**
    src := p_i;
    if (src = self) **then**
        trigger ⟨ *bebBroadcast* | m ⟩;

upon event ⟨ *bebDeliver* | src, m ⟩ ∧ (proposal = ⊥) **do**
    proposal := m;
    trigger ⟨ *ucPropose* | proposal ⟩;

upon (src ∉ correct) ∧ (src ≠ ⊥) ∧ (proposal = ⊥) **do**
    proposal := F_{src};
    trigger ⟨ *ucPropose* | proposal ⟩;

upon event ⟨ *ucDecide* | decided ⟩ **do**
    trigger ⟨ *trbDeliver* | src, decided ⟩

---

consensus instance depends on whether the process delivered m or detected the crash of the sender. The result of the consensus is then delivered by the TRB algorithm.

An execution of the algorithm is illustrated in Figure 6.2. Process p_1 crashes while broadcasting m. Therefore p_2 and p_3 get m but p_4 does not. The remaining processes use the consensus module to decide which value must be delivered. In the example of the figure, the processes decide to deliver m, but F could be also a possible outcome (since p_1 has crashed).

Correctness. The *integrity* property of best-effort broadcast, together with the *validity* property of consensus, ensure that if a process trbDelivers a message m, then either m is F or m was trbBroadcast by *src*.

The *no duplication* property of best-effort broadcast and the *integrity* property of consensus ensure that no process trbDelivers more than one message. The *completeness* property of the failure detector, the *validity* property

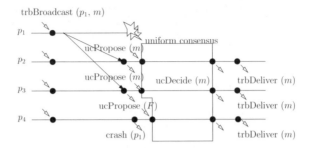

Fig. 6.2: Sample execution of consensus-based terminating reliable broadcast

of best-effort broadcast, and the *termination* property of consensus, ensure that every correct process eventually trbDelivers a message.

The *(uniform) agreement* property of (uniform) consensus ensures uniformity of terminating reliable broadcast.

Consider now the *validity* property of terminating reliable broadcast. Assume that *src* does not crash and trbBroadcasts a message $m \neq F$. Due the *accuracy* property of the failure detector, no process detects the crash of *src*. Due to the *validity* property of best-effort broadcast, every correct process bebDelivers *m* and proposes *m* to consensus. By the *termination* property of consensus, all correct processes, including *src*, eventually decide and trbDeliver a message *m*.

Performance. The algorithm requires the execution of the uniform consensus abstraction. In addition to the cost of uniform consensus, the algorithm exchanges N messages and requires one additional communication step (for the initial best-effort broadcast).

Variant. Our TRB specification has a *uniform agreement* property. As for reliable broadcast, we could specify a regular variant of TRB with a regular *agreement* property. In that case, the underlying uniform consensus abstraction could be replaced by a regular one.

6.3 Non-blocking Atomic Commit

6.3.1 Overview

The unit of data processing in a distributed information system is the *transaction*. This can be viewed as a portion of a program delimited by two primitives: *begin* and *end*. The transaction is typically expected to be *atomic* in two senses, namely,

Concurrency atomicity: transactions appear to execute one after the other and this *serializability* is usually guaranteed using some form of *distributed locking* or some form of *optimistic concurrency control*.

Failure atomicity: every transaction appears to execute either completely (it is said to *commit*) or not at all (it is said to *abort*).

Ensuring these two forms of atomicity in a distributed environment is not trivial because the transaction might be accessing information on different processes (i.e., different data managers), which might have different opinions on whether the transaction should commit or not. For instance, some data managers might detect concurrency control conflicts whereas others might not. Similarly, some data managers might detect problems that prevent a transaction from committing, either logical or physical ones, as we discuss below. Despite differences in opinions, all data managers need to make sure that they discard the new updates in case the transaction aborts, or make them visible in case the transaction commits. In other words, all data managers need to agree on the same outcome for the transaction.

The *non-blocking atomic commit* (NBAC) abstraction is used precisely to solve this problem in a reliable way. The processes, each representing a data manager, agree on the outcome of a transaction. The outcome is either to *commit* the transaction, say, to decide 1, or to *abort* the transaction, say to decide 0. The outcome depends of the initial proposals of the processes. Every process proposes an initial vote for the transaction: 0 or 1. Voting 1 for a process means that the process is willing and able to commit the transaction.

- Typically, by voting 1, a process witnesses the absence of any problem during the execution of the transaction. Furthermore, the process promises to make the update of the transaction permanent. This, in particular, means that the process has stored the temporary update of the transaction in stable storage: should it crash and recover, it can install a consistent state including all updates of the committed transaction.
- By voting 0, a data manager process vetos the commitment of the transaction. As we pointed out above, this can occur if the process cannot commit the transaction for an application-related reason, e.g., not enough money for a bank transfer in a specific node, for a concurrency control reason, e.g., there is a risk of violating serializability in a database system, or a storage reason, e.g., the disk is full and there is no way to guarantee the durability of the transaction's updates.

6.3.2 Specification

NBAC is characterized by the properties listed in Module 6.4. At first glance, the problem looks like uniform consensus: the processes propose 0 or 1 and need to decide on a common final value of 0 or 1. There is, however, a fundamental difference: in consensus, any proposed value can be decided. In the atomic commit problem, the decision 1 cannot be taken if any of the processes has proposed 0 (this would mean that some data managers can indeed

---

Module 6.4 Interfaces and properties of NBAC

Module:

   Name: Non-BlockingAtomicCommit (nbac).

Events:

   Request: ⟨ *nbacPropose* | *v* ⟩: Used to propose a value for the commit (0 or 1).

   Indication: ⟨ *nbacDecide* | *v* ⟩: Used to indicate the decided value for nbac.

Properties:

   NBAC1: *Uniform Agreement:* No two processes decide different values.

   NBAC2: *Integrity:* No process decides two values.

   NBAC3: *Abort-Validity:* 0 can only be decided if some process proposes 0 or crashes.

   NBAC4: *Commit-Validity:* 1 can only be decided if no process proposes 0.

   NBAC5: *Termination:* Every correct process eventually decides.

---

commit the transaction and ensure its durability whereas others cannot). It is indeed a veto right that is expressed with a 0 vote.

6.3.3 Algorithm: Consensus-Based NBAC

Algorithm 6.3 implements NBAC using three underlying abstractions: a perfect failure detector, a uniform consensus, and a best-effort broadcast. To distinguish the value proposed to the NBAC abstraction (to be implemented) and the one proposed to the underlying consensus abstraction, we call the first a *vote* and the second a *proposal*.

   The algorithm works as follows. Every process p_i broadcasts its initial vote (0 or 1) to all other processes, and waits, for every process p_j, either to get the vote of p_j or to detect the crash of p_j. If p_i detects the crash of any process or gets a vote 0 from any process, then p_i directly (without waiting for more messages) invokes consensus with 0 as its proposal. If p_i gets the vote 1 from all processes, then p_i invokes consensus with 1 as its proposal. Then the processes decide for NBAC according to the outcome of consensus.

Correctness. The *agreement* property of NBAC directly follows from that of consensus. The *no duplication* property of best-effort broadcast and the *integrity* property of consensus ensure that no process nbacDecides two different values. The *termination* property of NBAC follows from the *validity* property of best-effort broadcast, the *termination* property of consensus, and the *completeness* property of the failure detector.

Algorithm 6.3 Consensus-Based NBAC

Implements:
    NonBlockingAtomicCommit (nbac).

Uses:
    BestEffortBroadcast (beb);
    UniformConsensus (uc);
    PerfectFailureDetector ($\mathcal{P}$).

upon event ⟨ *Init* ⟩ **do**
    voted := ∅;
    correct := Π;
    proposed := false;

upon event ⟨ *crash* | p_i ⟩ **do**
    correct := correct \ $\{p_i\}$;

upon event ⟨ *nbacPropose* | v ⟩ **do**
    trigger ⟨ *bebBroadcast* | v ⟩;

upon event ⟨ *bebDeliver* | p_i, v ⟩ **do**
    if $(v = 0)$ ∧ (proposed = false) **then**
        trigger ⟨ *ucPropose* | 0 ⟩;
        proposed := true;
    else
        voted := voted ∪ $\{p_i\}$;

upon (correct \ voted = ∅) ∧ (proposed = false) **do**
    if correct ≠ Π **then**
        trigger ⟨ *ucPropose* | 0 ⟩;
    else
        trigger ⟨ *ucPropose* | 1 ⟩;
    proposed := true;

upon event ⟨ *ucDecide* | decided ⟩ **do**
    trigger ⟨ *nbacDecide* | decided ⟩

Consider now the *validity* properties of NBAC. The *commit-validity* property requires that 1 is decided only if all processes propose 1. Assume by contradiction that some process p_i nbacProposes 0 whereas some process p_j nbacDecides 1. According to the algorithm, for p_j to nbacDecide 1, it must have decided 1, i.e., through the consensus abstraction. Due to the *validity* property of consensus, some process p_k must have proposed 1 to the consensus abstraction. Due to the *validity* property of best-effort broadcast, there are two cases to consider: either (1) p_i crashes before p_k bebDelivers p_i's proposal or (2) p_k bebDelivers p_i's proposal. In both cases, according to the algorithm, p_k proposes 0 to consensus: a contradiction. Consider now the *abort-validity* property of NBAC. This property requires that 0 is decided only if some process nbacProposes 0 or crashes. Assume by contradiction that all processes nbacPropose 1 and no process crashes, whereas some process p_i nbacDecides 0. For p_i to nbacDecide 0, due the *validity* property of consensus, some process p_k must propose 0. According to the algorithm and the *accuracy* property of the failure detector, p_k would only propose 0 if some process nbacProposes 0 or crashes: a contradiction.

Performance. The algorithm requires the execution of the consensus abstraction. In addition to the cost of consensus, the algorithm exchanges N^2 messages and requires one additional communication step for the initial best-effort broadcast.

Variant. One could define a nonuniform variant of NBAC, i.e., by requiring only *agreement* and not *uniform agreement*. However, this abstraction would not be useful in a practical setting to coordinate the termination of a transaction in a distributed database system. Indeed, the very fact that some process has decided to commit a transaction might trigger an external action: say, the process has delivered some cash through an ATM. Even if that process has crashed, its decision is important and other processes should reach the same outcome.

6.4 Group Membership

6.4.1 Overview

In the previous sections, our algorithms were required to make decisions based on the information about which processes were operational or crashed. At any point in the computation, every process has a view of what processes in the system are up and running. In the algorithms we considered, this information is provided by the failure detector module available at each process. According to the underlying failure detector, the view might or not accurately reflect the actual status of the crashes in the system. In any case, the outputs of failure detector modules at different processes are not coordinated. In particular, different processes may get notifications of failures of other processes in different orders and, in this way, obtain a different perspective of the system's evolution.

- One of the roles of a *group membership* (GM) abstraction is to provide consistent information about which processes have crashed and which processes have not.
- Another role of a membership abstraction is to coordinate the joining of new processes, i.e., those that wish to be included in the system and participate in the computation, or the exclusion of old processes that would voluntarily want to leave this set. As with failure information, it might be desirable that the result of leave and join operations are provided to the processes in a consistent way.

Module 6.5 Interface and properties of group membership

Module:

    Name: GroupMembership (gm).

Events:

    Indication: $\langle$ *gmView* $\mid V$ $\rangle$: Used to deliver update membership information in the form of a *view*. A view V is a tuple (i, M), where $i = V.id$ is a unique view identifier and $M = V.memb$ is the set of processes that belong to the view.

Properties:

    Memb1: *Monotonicity:* If a process p installs view $V^j = (j, M_j)$ after installing $V^i = (i, M_i)$, then $j > i$ and $M_j \subset M_i$.

    Memb2: *Uniform Agreement:* If two processes install views $V^i = (i, M_i)$ and $V'^i = (i, M_i')$, then $M_i = M_i'$.

    Memb3: *Completeness:* If a process p crashes, then eventually every correct process installs $V^i = (i, M_i)$ with $p \notin M_i$.

    Memb4: *Accuracy:* If some process installs a view $V^i = (i, M_i)$ and $q \notin M_i$, then q has crashed.

To simplify the presentation of the group membership concept, we will focus here on the case of process crashes, i.e., the first role above. That is, the initial membership of the group is the complete set of processes, and subsequent membership changes are solely caused by crashes. We do not consider explicit join and leave operations. These can be built as extensions of our basic abstraction. Reference pointers to these operations are given in the historical notes of this chapter.

6.4.2 Specification

The set of processes that participate in the computation is sometimes called a *group*. At any point in time, the current membership of a group is called the *group view*, or simply the *view*. Each view $V^i = (i, M_i)$ is a tuple that contains a unique view identifier i and a set of member processes M. For presentation simplicity, we consider here that the group is initially the entire system. That is, initially, every process installs view $V^0 = (0, \Pi)$, i.e., the initial view of all processes V^0 includes the complete set of processes Π in the system. We consider a *linear group membership* abstraction, where all correct processes are supposed to deliver the same sequence of views: $V^0 = (0, M_0), V^1 = (1, M_1), \ldots$. A process that delivers a view V^i is said to *install* view V^i.

    The group membership abstraction is characterized by the properties listed in Module 6.5. The *uniform agreement* and *local monotonicity* capture the fact that the processes install the same sequence of shrinking views, i.e., the linearity flavor mentioned above. The *completeness* and *accuracy* properties are similar to those of the perfect failure detector abstraction and dictate the conditions under which a process can be excluded from a group.

6.4.3 Algorithm: Consensus-Based Group Membership

Algorithm 6.4 implements the group membership abstraction assuming a uniform consensus and a perfect failure detector abstraction. At initialization, each process installs a view including all the processes in the system. From that point on, the algorithm remains idle until a process is detected to have crashed. Since different processes may detect crashes in different orders, a new view is not generated immediately, i.e., a process does not install a new view in a unilateral way as soon as it detects a failure. Instead, a consensus instance is executed to decide which processes are to be included in the next view. The *wait* flag is used to prevent a process from triggering a new consensus instance before the previous consensus instance has terminated. When the consensus decides, a new view is delivered. Note that, to preserve *agreement*, a process p_i may install a view containing a process that p_i already knows to has crashed, i.e., the perfect failure detector module at p_i have already output that process. In this case, after installing that view, p_i will initiate a new consensus instance to trigger the installation of another view that would exclude the crashed process.

An execution of the membership algorithm is illustrated in Figure 6.3. In the execution, both p_1 and p_2 crash. Process p_3 detects the crash of p_2 and initiates a consensus instance to define a new view. Process p_4 detects the crash of p_1 and proposes a different view to that consensus instance. As a result of the first consensus instance, p_1 is excluded from the view. Since p_3 has already detected the crash of p_2, p_3 triggers a new consensus instance to exclude p_2. Eventually, p_4 also detects the crash of p_2 and also participates in the second consensus instance to install the third view. This view includes only the correct processes.

Correctness. The *Monotonicity* property follows directly from the algorithm. The *agreement* property follows from consensus. The *completeness* and *accuracy* properties follow from those of the perfect failure detector abstraction.

Performance. The algorithm requires at most one consensus execution for each process that crashes.

Variant. We focus here only on the uniform variant of the group membership abstraction: a regular group membership abstraction is specified by replacing the *uniform agreement* property with a regular *agreement* one and a corresponding algorithm might use regular consensus instead of uniform consensus.

Algorithm 6.4 Consensus-Based Group Membership

Implements:
    GroupMembership (gm).

Uses:
    UniformConsensus (uc);
    PerfectFailureDetector ($\mathcal{P}$).

upon event ⟨ *Init* ⟩ **do**
    view := $(0, \Pi)$;
    correct := Π;
    wait := false;
    trigger ⟨ *gmView* | view ⟩;

upon event ⟨ *crash* | p_i ⟩ **do**
    correct := correct $\setminus \{p_i\}$;

upon (correct $\subset$ view.memb) $\wedge$ (wait = false) **do**
    wait := true;
    trigger ⟨ *ucPropose* | view.id+1, correct ⟩;

upon event ⟨ *ucDecided* | id, memb ⟩ **do**
    view := (id, memb);
    wait := false;
    trigger ⟨ *gmView* | view ⟩;

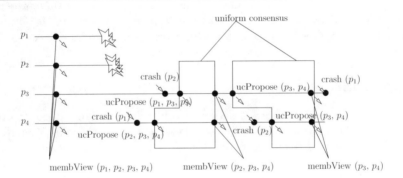

Fig. 6.3: Sample execution of the membership algorithm

6.5 View Synchronous Communication

6.5.1 Overview

The *view synchronous communication* abstraction (we also say view synchrony) is motivated by the combination of two abstractions: reliable broadcast and membership. In the following, we discuss the subtle issue that arises in this combination and motivates the introduction of a first class abstraction.

Consider the following scenario of a group of processes exchanging messages where one of these processes, say, q, crashes. Assume that this failure is detected and that the membership abstraction is used by the processes to install a new view $V = (i, M_i)$ such that $q \notin M_i$. Further assume that, after V has been installed, some process p_i delivers a message m originally broadcast by q. Note that such a scenario is possible, as nothing prevents, in the specification of a reliable broadcast, a message broadcast by a process that has failed from being later delivered. In fact, in order to ensure the *agreement* of the delivery, messages originally broadcast by q are typically relayed by other processes, especially for the case where q has failed. Clearly, it is counterintuitive for the application programmer to handle a message from a process q after q have been declared to be failed and been expelled from the group view. It would thus be desirable for p_i to simply discard m. Unfortunately, it may also happen that some other process p_j has already delivered m *before* delivering view V. So, in this scenario, one may be faced with two conflicting goals: ensuring the reliability of the broadcast, which means that m has indeed to be delivered by p_i, but, at the same time, ensuring the consistency of the view information, which means that m has to be discarded at p_i.

In fact, what is needed is to ensure that the installation of views is ordered with respect to the message flow. If a message m is delivered by a (correct) process before the installation of V, then m should, before the view change, be delivered to all processes that install V. The abstraction that preserves this ordering constraint is called *view synchronous broadcast*, as it gives the illusion that failures are synchronous (or atomic), i.e., that they occur at the same point in time with regard to the message flow.

6.5.2 Specification

View synchronous broadcast is an extension of both reliable broadcast and group membership: as a consequence, the properties we give in Module 6.6 encompass those of reliable broadcast and group membership. Given that we could consider here the properties of regular or uniform reliable broadcast and, optionally, the properties of causal order, we could end up with different possible flavors of view synchronous communication.

In Module 6.6, we illustrate the view synchrony concept by focusing on the combination of group membership (which we have already considered in its uniform form) with regular reliable broadcast. Other combinations are possible. We will come back to the view synchronous broadcast variant obtained by combining the group membership properties with those of uniform reliable broadcast, which will be called uniform view synchronous broadcast.

In addition to the properties of reliable broadcast and group membership, the *view inclusion* property of Module 6.6 orchestrates the way messages should be delivered with respect to view changes, i.e., new view installations. In that property, we state that a process *delivers (or broadcasts) a message*

m *in view* V^i if the process delivers (or broadcasts) the message m after installing view V^i and before installing view V^{i+1}. This property addresses the issue of messages coming from processes already declared to have crashed. Messages are delivered in the same view by different processes, and this view is the view where the messages were broadcast.

Since messages have to be delivered in the view in which they are broadcast, if new messages are continuously broadcast, then the installation of a new view may be indefinitely postponed. In other words, the view synchronous abstraction would be impossible to implement without any control on the broadcast pattern. Therefore, the interface of this abstraction includes two specific events that handle the interaction between the view synchronous abstraction and the application layer (i.e., the upper layer): *block* and *block-ok*. The *block* event is used by the view synchronous abstraction to request the application layer to stop broadcasting messages in the current view. The *block-ok* event is used by that application layer to acknowledge the *block* request.

We assume that the application layer is well behaved in that it indeed stops broadcasting messages (after triggering the *block-ok* event) when it is asked to do so (through the *block* event): new messages can be broadcast after the view is installed. On the other hand, we require from the view synchronous broadcast abstraction that it require the stopping of messages from the application layer only if a new view needs to be installed, i.e., only if a process that is member of the current view has failed. (We do not explicitly state these properties in Module 6.6 as we consider them to be of a different nature than the *view inclusion* property.)

6.5.3 Algorithm: TRB-Based View Synchronous Broadcast

We give a TRB-based algorithm (Algorithm 6.5–6.6) that implements the view synchronous communication abstraction as defined by the properties of Module 6.6. For simplicity, we give the algorithm for a single group, and omit the group identifier from the service interface. The key element of the algorithm is a collective *flush* procedure executed by the processes before installing each new view. This is performed by having the processes trbBroadcast (according to the terminating reliable broadcast semantics) all messages they have been vsDelivered during the current view.

New views (gmViews), that are installed by the underlying group membership abstraction before the flush is complete, are kept in a list of *pending-views* before being actually installed by the view synchronous communication abstraction (vsView). The collective flush is first initiated at each process by requesting the application to stop vsBroadcasting messages in the current view, i.e., before the new view is installed. When this authorization is granted at a given process, the process also stops vsDelivering new messages from the underlying reliable broadcast module. If vsDelivered by any process

---

Module 6.6 Interface and properties of view synchronous communication

Module:

    Name: ViewSynchrony (vs).

Events:

    Request: $\langle$ *vsBroadcast* $\mid g, m$ $\rangle$: Used to broadcast message m to a group of processes g.

    Indication: $\langle$ *vsDeliver* $\mid g, src, m$ $\rangle$: Used to deliver message m broadcast by process src in group g.

    Indication: $\langle$ *vsView* $\mid g, V^i$ $\rangle$: Used to deliver update membership information in the form of a *view*. A view V is a tuple (i, M), where $i = V.id$ is a unique view identifier and $M = V.memb$ is the set of processes that belong to the view.

    Indication: $\langle$ *vsBlock* $\mid g$ $\rangle$: Used to inform the application that a new view needs to be installed and the broadcasting of new messages need to be blocked until that installation.

    Request: $\langle$ *vsBlockOk* $\mid g$ $\rangle$: Used by the application to confirm that the broadcasting of new messages will be temporarily blocked.

Properties:

    VS: *View Inclusion:* If a process p delivers a message m from process q in view V, then m was broadcast by q in view V.

    RB1–RB4: from reliable broadcast.

    Memb1–Memb4: from group membership.

---

in the current view, these messages will be vsDelivered through the TRB abstraction. Using this abstraction, every process, before installing a new view, transmits to all processes the set of messages that it has vsDelivered up to that point. Eventually, when all TRBs are terminated, each process has the set of messages vsDelivered by every other process (that did not fail). A union of all these sets is taken as the set of messages to be vsDelivered before a new view is installed.

An example of the execution of the algorithm is presented in Figure 6.4. Process p_1 vsBroadcasts messages m_1 and m_2 before crashing. Message m_1 is vsDelivered by p_3 and p_4 but not by p_2. On the other hand, m_2 is vsDelivered by p_2 but not by p_3 and p_4. There is also a third message that is vsDelivered by all correct processes before the flush procedure is initiated. When the underlying membership module installs a new view, excluding p_1 from the group, a TRB is initiated for each process in the previous view. Each TRB includes the set of messages that have been vsDelivered. For instance, the TRB from p_2 includes m_1 and m_3 since m_2 has not yet been vsDelivered. The union of these sets, $\{m_1, m_2, m_3\}$, is the set of messages that have to be vsDelivered before installing the new view. Note that m_1 is eventually

---

Algorithm 6.5 TRB-Based View Synchronous Broadcast (data transmission)

Implements:
    ViewSynchrony (vs).

Uses:
    TerminatingReliableBroadcast (trb);
    GroupMembership (gm);
    BestEffortBroadcast (beb).

upon event ⟨ *Init* ⟩ **do**
    pending-views := delivered := trb-done := $\emptyset$;
    next-view := curr-view := $\bot$;
    flushing := false;
    blocked := true;

upon event ⟨ *vsBroadcast* | m ⟩ ∧ (blocked = false) **do**
    delivered := delivered ∪ {(self, m)};
    trigger ⟨ *vsDeliver* | self, m ⟩;
    trigger ⟨ *bebBroadcast* | [DATA, curr-view.id, m] ⟩;

upon event ⟨ *bebDeliver* | src_m,[DATA, vid, m] ⟩ **do**
    if (curr-view.id = vid) ∧ ((src_m, m) ∉ delivered) ∧ (blocked = false) **then**
        delivered := delivered ∪ {(src_m, m)};
        trigger ⟨ *vsDeliver* | src_m, m ⟩;

upon event ⟨ *gmView* | $V = (i, M)$ ⟩ ∧ $(i = 0)$ **do** // initial-view
    curr-view := $(0, M)$
    blocked := false;

upon event ⟨ *gmView* | $V = (i, M)$ ⟩ ∧ $(i > 0)$ **do**
    addToTail (pending-views, V);

---

vsDelivered to p_2 by the underlying reliable broadcast module, but will be discarded; the same will happen to m_2 with regard to p_3 and p_4.

Correctness. Consider first the *view inclusion* property. Let m be any message vsDelivered by some process p in a given view V. If p is the sender of the message, then p directly vsDelivers the message upon vsBroadcasting it, in the same view, V. Consider now the case where the sender q is a different process. There are two possibilities. Either p vsDelivers m after bebDelivering it, or after trbDelivering it. In the first case, the algorithm checks if the view within which the message was vsBroadcast is the current one: if not, the message is discarded. In the second case, the messages proposed to consensus are those vsBroadcast in the current view.

The *no creation* broadcast property directly follows from the properties of the underlying broadcast abstractions. The *no duplication* broadcast property follows from the use of the variable *delivered* and the check that only messages vsBroadcast in a view are vsDelivered in that view. Consider the *agreement*

Algorithm 6.6 TRB-Based View Synchronous Broadcast (view change)

---

upon (pending-views $\neq \emptyset$) $\wedge$ (flushing = false) **do**
    next-view := removeFromHead (pending-views);
    flushing := true;
    trigger $\langle$ *vsBlock* $\rangle$;

upon event $\langle$ *vsBlockOk* $\rangle$ **do**
    blocked := true;
    for j = 1 **to** N **do**
        if j = self **then**
            trigger $\langle$ *trbBroadcast* $|$ p_j, [curr-view.id, delivered] $\rangle$;
        else
            trigger $\langle$ *trbBroadcast* $|$ p_j, $\perp$ $\rangle$;

upon event $\langle$ *trbDeliver* $|$ p_i, m=[vid, del] $\rangle$ $\wedge$ (m=F_{p_i} $\vee$ vid=curr-view.id) **do**
    trb-done := trb-done $\cup$ $\{p_i\}$;
    if m $\neq$ F_{p_i} **then**
        forall (src$_m$, m) $\in$ del: (src$_m$, m) $\notin$ delivered **do**
            delivered := delivered $\cup$ { (src$_m$, m) };
            trigger $\langle$ *vsDeliver* $|$ src$_m$, m $\rangle$;

upon (trb-done = curr-view.memb) $\wedge$ (blocked) **do**
    curr-view := next-view;
    flushing := blocked := false;
    delivered := $\emptyset$;
    trb-done := $\emptyset$;
    trigger $\langle$ *vsView* $|$ curr-view $\rangle$;

---

broadcast property. Assume that some correct process p_i vsDelivers some message m. Every correct process vsDelivers m after bebDelivering it, or upon trbDelivering it if a new view needs to be installed (at least p will trbBroadcast a batch containning that message m).

Consider the *validity* property of the broadcast, and let p be some correct process that vsBroadcasts a message m. Process p directly vsDelivers m and, due to the *agreement* property above, every correct process vsDelivers m. The *monotonicity, group agreement* and *accuracy* properties directly follow from those of the underlying group membership abstraction. The *completeness* property follows from that of the underlying group membership abstraction, the *termination* property of terminating reliable broadcast, and the assumption that the application is well behaved (i.e. it stops vsBroadcasting messages when it is asked to do so).

Performance. During periods where the view does not need to change, the cost of vsDelivering a message is the same as the cost of bebDelivering it. For a view change, however, the algorithm requires the execution of a group membership instance, plus the (parallel) execution of one TRB for each process in the current view, in order to install the new view. Considering the consensus-based algorithms used to implement those abstractions (TRB and

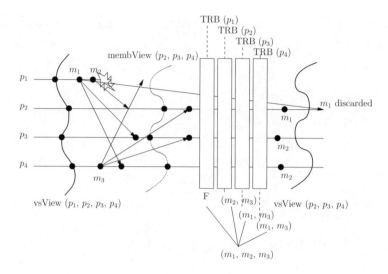

Fig. 6.4: Sample execution of the TRB-based view synchronous algorithm

GM), installing a new view requires one consensus instance for the underlying view membership installation and a parallel execution of several underlying consensus instances, one for each TRB and thus for each process in the view. Through an exercise, we discuss how to optimize Algorithm 6.5–6.6 by running a single instance of consensus to agree both on the new view and on the set of messages to be vsDelivered before the new view is installed.

6.5.4 Algorithm: Consensus-Based Uniform View Synchronous Broadcast

The view-synchronous broadcast algorithm we have just presented (Algorithm 6.5–6.6) is uniform in the sense that no two processes (be they correct or not) install different views. The algorithm is not uniform in the message delivery sense. That is, a process might vsDeliver a message and crash, while no other process vsDelivers that message.

We give here an algorithm (Algorithm 6.7–6.8) that ensures uniformity in both senses: (1) in the sense of group membership and (2) in the sense of view installation. In other words, Algorithm 6.7–6.8 implements a uniform view synchronous broadcast abstraction. To understand this algorithm, it is first important to observe that Algorithm 6.5–6.6 cannot be directly transformed to ensure the uniformity of message delivery simply by replacing the underlying best-effort broadcast abstraction with a uniform reliable broadcast one. The following scenario illustrates that. Consider a process p_i that vsBroadcasts a message m, urbBroadcasts m, and then vsDelivers m after urbDelivering it. The only guarantee here is that all correct processes will

---

Algorithm 6.7 Consensus-Based Uniform View Synchrony (data transmission)

Implements:
    UniformViewSynchrony (uvs).

Uses:
    UniformConsensus (uc);
    BestEffortBroadcast (beb);
    PerfectFailureDetector ($\mathcal{P}$).

upon event $\langle$ *Init* $\rangle$ **do**
    current-view := $(0, \Pi)$; correct := Π;
    flushing := blocked := := wait false;
    delivered := received := $\emptyset$;
    forall m **do** $\text{ack}_m := \emptyset$;
    forall i **do** dset[i] := $\emptyset$;

upon event $\langle$ *uvsBroadcast* $\mid m$ $\rangle$ $\wedge$ (blocked = false) **do**
    received := received $\cup$ {(self, m)};
    trigger $\langle$ *bebBroadcast* $\mid$ [DATA, current-view.id, m] $\rangle$;

upon event $\langle$ *bebDeliver* $\mid p_i,$[DATA, vid, m] $\rangle$ $\wedge$
    (current-view.id = vid) $\wedge$ (blocked = false) **do**
        $\text{ack}_m := \text{ack}_m \cup \{p_i\}$
        if $(m \notin \text{received})$ **then**
            received := received $\cup$ {(p_i, m)};
            trigger $\langle$ *bebBroadcast* $\mid$ [DATA, current-view.id, m] $\rangle$;

upon exists $(src, m) \in$ received **such that**
                (current-view.memb $\subseteq \text{ack}_m$) $\wedge$ ($m \notin$ delivered) **do**
    delivered := delivered $\cup$ {(src, m)};
    trigger $\langle$ *uvsDeliver* $\mid src, m$ $\rangle$;

---

eventually urbDeliver m; they might do so, however, after a new view has been installed, which means that m would not be vsDelivered.

The algorithm (Algorithm 6.7–6.8) uses a best-effort broadcast, a consensus, and a perfect failure detector abstraction. It works as follows. When a process vsBroadcasts a message m, it simply bebBroadcasts m and adds m to the set of messages it has bebBroadcast. When a process p bebDelivers a message m, and m was bebBroadcast by a process q in the same view, p adds m to the set "received" (if it was not there before), and adds q to the set of processes that have acknowledged m, denoted by ack_m. Then p bebBroadcasts m (i.e., acknowledges m) if it did not do so already. When all processes in the current view are in ack_m at a given process q, the message m is vsDelivered by q.

If any process detects the crash of at least one member of the current view, the process initiates a collective flush procedure as in the view synchrony algorithms given in the chapter. The process broadcasts here the set of received messages. It is important to note here that some of these message

---

Algorithm 6.8 Consensus-Based Uniform View Synchrony (view change)

---

upon event $\langle$ *crash* $\mid p_i$ $\rangle$ **do**
    correct := correct $\setminus \{p_i\}$;

upon (correct $\subset$ current-view.memb) $\wedge$ (flushing = false) **do**
    flushing := true;
    trigger $\langle$ *uvsBlock* $\rangle$;

upon event $\langle$ *uvsBlockOk* $\rangle$ **do**
    blocked := true;
    trigger $\langle$ *bebBroadcast* $\mid$ [DSET, current-view.id, received] $\rangle$;

upon event $\langle$ *bebDeliver* $\mid$ src,[DSET, vid, mset] $\rangle$ **do**
    dset[vid] := dset[vid] $\cup$ {(src, mset)};

upon $\forall p \in$ correct $\exists\{(p, \text{mset})\} \in$ dset[current-view.id] $\wedge$ (wait = false) **do**
    trigger $\langle$ *ucPropose* $\mid$ current-view.id+1, [correct, dset[current-view.id]] $\rangle$;
    wait := true;

upon event $\langle$ *ucDecided* $\mid$ id, [memb, vs-dset] $\rangle$ **do**
    forall (p, mset) $\in$ vs-dset: $p \in$ memb **do**
        forall (src$_m$, m) $\in$ mset: (src$_m$, m) $\notin$ delivered **do**
            delivered := delivered $\cup$ { (src$_m$, m) };
            trigger $\langle$ *uvsDeliver* $\mid$ src$_m$, m $\rangle$;
    flushing := blocked := wait := false;
    received := delivered := $\emptyset$;
    current-view := (id, memb);
    trigger $\langle$ *uvsView* $\mid$ current-view $\rangle$;

---

might not have been vsDelivered. As soon as a process p has collected the received set from every other process that p did not detect to have crashed, p proposes a new view through a consensus instance. Besides that view, process p also proposes to consensus the received sets of all processes in the proposed views. Before installing the new view, each process parses all received sets in the consensus decision and vsDelivers those messages it has not vsDelivered yet. Finally the new view is installed and normal operation resumed.

Correctness. The correctness arguments are similar to those of Algorithm 6.5–6.6. The group membership properties follow from the properties of consensus and the perfect failure detector properties. It is also easy to see that no message is vsDelivered twice and it can only be vsDelivered if it was indeed vsBroadcast. Hence the *no creation* and *no duplication* properties. Consider a process that vsDelivers a message. If it does so through consensus before a view change, then all correct processes install that new view and vsDeliver the message. Otherwise, all correct processes must have stored the message in the variable *received*. Hence, every correct process eventually vsDelivers that message. Hence the *agreement* property. A similar argument applies to the *validity* property. The *view inclusion* property directly follows from the algorithm.

Performance. During periods where the view does not need to change, the cost of vsDelivering a message is the same as the cost of a best-effort broadcast primitive by the sender. To install a new view, the algorithm requires the parallel execution of best-effort broadcasts for all processes in the view, followed by a consensus execution to agree on the next view.

6.6 Hands-On

6.6.1 Uniform Total Order Broadcast

The communication stack used to implement the protocol is the following:

Application
Uniform Total Order **(implemented by Consensus-Based UTO)**
Delay
Uniform Consensus (implemented by Flooding UC)
Uniform Reliable Broadcast (implemented by All-Ack URB)
Perfect Failure Detector (implemented by TcpBasedPFD)
Best-Effort Broadcast (implemented by Basic Broadcast)
Perfect Point-to-Point Links (implemented by TcpBasedPerfectP2P)

The protocol implementation is depicted in Listing 6.1.

Listing 6.1. Uniform Total Order Broadcast implementation

```
package appia.protocols.tutorialDA.consensusTO;

public class ConsensusTOSession extends Session{

    InetWithPort iwp;
    Channel channel;
    /*global sequence number of the message ssent by this process*/
    int seqNumber;
    /*Sequence number of the set of messages to deliver in the same round!*/
    int sn;
    /*Sets the beginning and the end of the rounds*/
    boolean wait;
    /* Set of delivered messages. */
    LinkedList delivered;
    /* Set of unordered messages. */
    LinkedList unordered;

    public ConsensusTOSession(Layer l) {
```

```
        super(l);
}

public void handle(Event e) {
    if (e instanceof ChannelInit)
        handleChannelInit((ChannelInit)e);
    else if(e instanceof ProcessInitEvent)
        handleProcessInitEvent((ProcessInitEvent)e);
    else if (e instanceof SendableEvent){
        if (e.getDir()==Direction.DOWN)
            handleSendableEventDOWN((SendableEvent)e);
        else
            handleSendableEventUP((SendableEvent)e);
    } else if (e instanceof ConsensusDecide)
        handleConsensusDecide((ConsensusDecide)e);
    else{
        e.go();
    }
}

public void handleChannelInit (ChannelInit e){
    e.go();

    this.channel = e.getChannel();

    delivered=new LinkedList();
    unordered=new LinkedList();

    sn=1;
    wait=false;
}

public void handleProcessInitEvent (ProcessInitEvent e){
    iwp=e.getProcessSet().getSelfProcess().getInetWithPort();
    e.go();
}

public void handleSendableEventDOWN (SendableEvent e){
    ExtendedMessage om=(ExtendedMessage)e.getMessage();
    //inserting the global seq number of this msg
    om.pushInt(seqNumber);
    e.go();

    //increments the global seq number
    seqNumber++;
}

public void handleSendableEventUP (SendableEvent e){
    ExtendedMessage om=(ExtendedMessage)e.getMessage();
    int seq=om.popInt();

    //checks if the msg has already been delivered.
    ListElement le;
    if (!isDelivered((InetWithPort)e.source,seq)){
        le=new ListElement(e,seq);
        unordered.add(le);
    }

    //let's see if we can start a new round!
    if(unordered.size()!=0 && !wait){
        wait=true;
        //sends our proposal to consensus protocol!
        ConsensusPropose cp;
        byte[] bytes=null;
        cp = new ConsensusPropose(channel, Direction.DOWN, this);
        bytes=serialize(unordered);
```

```
            OrderProposal op=new OrderProposal(bytes);
            cp.value=op;

            cp.go();
        }
}

public void handleConsensusDecide (ConsensusDecide e){
    LinkedList decided=deserialize(((OrderProposal)e.decision).bytes);

    //The delivered list must be complemented with the msg in the decided list!
    for(int i=0;i<decided.size();i++){
        if (!isDelivered ( (InetWithPort)((ListElement)decided.get(i)).se.source,
                    ((ListElement)decided.get(i)).seq )){
            //if a msg that is in decided doesn't yet belong to delivered, add it!
            delivered.add(decided.get(i));
        }
    }

    //update unordered list by removing the messages that are in the delivered list
    for(int j=0;j<unordered.size();j++){
        if(isDelivered ( (InetWithPort)((ListElement)unordered.get(j)).se.source,
                    ((ListElement)unordered.get(j)).seq )){
            unordered.remove(j);
            j--;
        }
    }

    decided=sort(decided);

    //deliver the messages in the decided list, which is already ordered!
    for(int k=0;k<decided.size();k++){
        ((ListElement)decided.get(k)).se.go();
    }
    sn++;
    wait=false;
}

boolean isDelivered(InetWithPort source,int seq){
    for(int k=0;k<delivered.size();k++){
        if ( ((ListElement)delivered.get(k)).getSE().source.equals(source) &&
            ((ListElement)delivered.get(k)).getSeq()==seq)
            return true;
    }

    return false;
}

LinkedList sort(LinkedList list){
    return list;
}

byte[] intToByteArray(int i) {
    byte[] ret = new byte[4];

    ret[0] = (byte) ((i & 0xff000000) >> 24);
    ret[1] = (byte) ((i & 0x00ff0000) >> 16);
    ret[2] = (byte) ((i & 0x0000ff00) >> 8);
    ret[3] = (byte) (i & 0x000000ff);

    return ret;
}

int byteArrayToInt(byte[] b, int off) {
    int ret = 0;
```

```
        ret |= b[off] << 24;
        ret |= (b[off+1] << 24) >>> 8; // must be done this way because of
        ret |= (b[off+2] << 24) >>> 16; // java's sign extension of <<
        ret |= (b[off+3] << 24) >>> 24;

        return ret;
}

private byte[] serialize (LinkedList list ) {
        ByteArrayOutputStream data=new ByteArrayOutputStream();
        byte[] bytes=null;

        //number of elements of the list:int
        data.write(intToByteArray(list. size ()));

        //now, serialize each element
        for(int  i=0;i<list. size (); i++){
                //getting the  list  element
                ListElement le=(ListElement)list.get( i );
                //sequence number:int
                data.write(intToByteArray(le.seq));
                //class name
                bytes=le.se .getClass (). getName().getBytes();
                data.write(intToByteArray(bytes.length));
                data.write(bytes,0, bytes.length );
                //source port:int
                data.write(intToByteArray(((InetWithPort)le.se.source).port));
                //source host:string
                String host=((InetWithPort)le.se.source).host. getHostName();
                bytes=host.getBytes();
                data.write(intToByteArray(bytes.length));
                data.write(bytes,0, bytes. length );
                // message
                bytes=le.se .getMessage().toByteArray();
                data.write(intToByteArray(bytes.length));
                data.write(bytes,0, bytes. length );
        }

        //creating the byte []
        bytes=data.toByteArray();
        return bytes;
}

private LinkedList deserialize (byte[] data) {
        LinkedList ret=new LinkedList();
        int curPos=0;

        //getting the size  of  the  list
        int  listSize =byteArrayToInt(data, curPos);
        curPos+=4;

        //getting the elements of the  list
        for(int  i=0;i<listSize ; i++){
                //seq number
                int seq=byteArrayToInt(data, curPos);
                curPos+=4;
                //class name
                int aux_size=byteArrayToInt(data, curPos);
                String className=new String(data,curPos+4,aux_size);
                curPos+=aux_size+4;
                //creating the event
                SendableEvent se=null;

                se = (SendableEvent) Class.forName(className).newInstance();
                // format known event attributes
```

```
                se.setDir(Direction.UP);
                se.setSource(this);
                se.setChannel(channel);

                //source:porto
                int port=byteArrayToInt(data, curPos);
                curPos+=4;
                //source:host
                aux_size=byteArrayToInt(data, curPos);
                String host=new String(data,curPos+4,aux_size);
                curPos+=aux_size+4;
                se.source=new InetWithPort(InetAddress.getByName(host),port);
                // finally , the message
                aux_size=byteArrayToInt(data, curPos);
                curPos+=4;

                se.getMessage().setByteArray(data,curPos,aux_size);
                curPos+=aux_size;
                se. init ();
                //creating the element that is the unit of the  list
                ListElement le=new ListElement(se,seq);
                //adding this element to the list to return
                ret .add(le);
            }
            return ret;
        }
    }

class ListElement{
    SendableEvent se;
    int seq; /*sequence number*/

    public ListElement(SendableEvent se, int seq){
        this.se=se;
        this.seq=seq;
    }

    SendableEvent getSE(){
        return se;
    }

    int getSeq(){
        return seq;
    }
}
```

Try It

1. Uncomment the eighth line of the *getUnTOChannel* method in file Sam-pleAppl.java, in package demo.tutorialDA. This will insert a test layer that allows the injection of delays in messages sent between process 0 and process 2. After modifying the file, it is necessary to compile it.
2. Open three shells/command prompts.
3. In each shell, go to the directory where you have placed the supplied code.
4. In each shell, launch the test application, SampleAppl, giving a different n value (0, 1, or 2) and specifying the *qos* as **uto**.
   - In shell 0, execute:

     ```
     java demo/tutorialDA/SampleAppl \
     ```

```
-f demo/tutorialDA/procs \
-n 0 \
-qos uto
```

- In shell 1, execute:
  ```
  java demo/tutorialDA/SampleAppl \
      -f demo/tutorialDA/procs \
      -n 1 \
      -qos uto
  ```

- In shell 2, execute:
  ```
  java demo/tutorialDA/SampleAppl \
      -f demo/tutorialDA/procs \
      -n 2 \
      -qos uto
  ```

Note: If the error NoClassDefError has appeared, confirm that you are at the root of the supplied code.

Now that processes are launched and running, you may try the following execution:

1. In shell 0, send a message **M1** (**bcast M1** and press Enter).
   - Note that no process received the message **M1**.
2. In shell 1, send a message **M2**.
   - Note that all processes received message **M1**. The consensus decided to deliver **M1**.
3. In shell 1, send a message **M3**.
   - Note that all processes received message **M2** and **M3**. Now, the consensus decided to deliver these both messages.
4. Confirm that all processes received **M1**, **M2**, and **M3** in the same order.
5. You can keep repeating these steps, in order to introduce some delays, and checking that all processes receive all messages in the same order.

6.6.2 Consensus-Based Non-blocking Atomic Commit

The communication stack used to implement the protocol is the following:

Application
NBAC   **(implemented by Consensus-Based NBAC)**
Uniform Consensus   (implemented by Flooding UC)
Perfect Failure Detector   (implemented by TcpBasedPFD)
Best-Effort Broadcast   (implemented by Basic Broadcast)
Perfect Point-to-Point Links   (implemented by TcpBasedPerfectP2P)

The protocol implementation is depicted in Listing 6.2.

Listing 6.2. Consensus-based Non-Blocking Atomic Commit implementation

```
package appia.protocols.tutorialDA.consensusNBAC;

public class ConsensusNBACSession extends Session {
    public ConsensusNBACSession(Layer layer) {
        super(layer);
    }

    public void handle(Event event) {
        if (event instanceof ProcessInitEvent)
            handleProcessInit((ProcessInitEvent)event);
        else if (event instanceof Crash)
            handleCrash((Crash)event);
        else if (event instanceof NBACPropose)
            handleNBACPropose((NBACPropose)event);
        else if (event instanceof ConsensusDecide)
            handleConsensusDecide((ConsensusDecide)event);
        else {
            event.go();
        }
    }

    private HashSet delivered=null;
    private ProcessSet correct=null;
    private int proposal;

    private void init() {
        delivered=new HashSet();
        proposal=1;
    }

    private void handleProcessInit(ProcessInitEvent event) {
        correct=event.getProcessSet();
        init ();
        event.go();
    }

    private void handleCrash(Crash crash) {
        correct .setCorrect(crash.getCrashedProcess(),false);
        crash.go();

        all_delivered (crash.getChannel());
    }

    private void handleNBACPropose(NBACPropose event) {
        if (event.getDir() == Direction.DOWN) {
            event.getExtendedMessage().pushInt(event.value);
```

```
            event.go ();
        } else {
            SampleProcess p_i=correct.getProcess((InetWithPort)event.source);
            int v=event.getExtendedMessage().popInt();

            delivered.add(p_i);
            proposal*=v;

            all_delivered (event.getChannel());
        }
    }

    private void all_delivered(Channel channel) {
        boolean all_correct=true;
        int i;
        for (i=0 ; i < correct.getSize () ; i++) {
            SampleProcess p=correct.getProcess(i);
            if (p != null)  {
                if (p.isCorrect ()) {
                    if (! delivered.contains(p))
                        return;
                } else {
                    all_correct =false;
                }
            }
        }

        if (! all_correct )
            proposal=0;

        ConsensusPropose ev=new ConsensusPropose(channel, Direction.DOWN, this);
        ev.value=new IntProposal(proposal);
        ev.go ();

        init ();
    }

    private void handleConsensusDecide(ConsensusDecide event) {
        NBACDecide ev=new NBACDecide(event.getChannel(), Direction.UP, this);
        ev.decision=((IntProposal)event.decision).i ;
        ev.go ();
    }
}
```

Try It

1. Setup
   a) Open three shells/command prompts.
   b) In each shell, go to the directory where you have placed the supplied code.
   c) In each shell, launch the test application, *SampleAppl*, giving a different *n* value (0, 1, or 2) and specifying the *qos* as **nbac**.
      - In shell 0, execute

```
java demo/tutorialDA/SampleAppl \
        -f demo/tutorialDA/procs \
        -n 0 \
        -qos nbac
```

- In shell 1, execute

      java demo/tutorialDA/SampleAppl \
          -f demo/tutorialDA/procs \
          -n 1 \
          -qos nbac

- In shell 2, execute

      java demo/tutorialDA/SampleAppl \
          -f demo/tutorialDA/procs \
          -n 2 \
          -qos nbac

d) If the error NoClassDefError has appeared, confirm that you are at the root of the supplied code.

e) Start the *prefect failure detector* by typing **startpfd** in each shell.

2. Run: Now that processes are launched and running, let us try the following execution:

   a) In shell 0, propose **1** (type **atomic 1** and press enter). Any value different from 0 is considered 1, and 0 is 0.

   b) In shell 1, propose **1**. (type **atomic 1** and press Enter).

   c) In shell 2, propose **1**. (type **atomic 1** and press Enter).

   d) Note that all processes *commit* the value **1**.

   e) In shell 0, propose **1**.

   f) In shell 1, propose **1**.

   g) In shell 2, propose **0**. (type **atomic 0** and press Enter).

   h) Note that all processes *commit* the value **0**.

   i) In shell 1, propose **1**.

   j) In shell 2, propose **1**.

   k) In shell 0, kill the test application process.

   l) Note that all processes *commit* the value **0**.

6.6.3 Consensus-Based Group Membership

The communication stack used to implement the protocol is the following:

Application
Group Membership **(Consensus-based GM)**
Uniform Consensus (implemented by Flooding UC)
Perfect Failure Detector (implemented by TcpBasedPFD)
Best-Effort Broadcast (implemented by Basic Broadcast)
Perfect Point-to-Point Links (implemented by TcpBasedPerfectP2P)

The protocol implementation is depicted in Listing 6.3. It follows Algorithm 6.4 very closely. The *view* is represented by an object of class View from package appia.protocols.tutorialDA.membershipUtils. It contains two attributes, the members that compose it, and its *id*. The *id* is an integer. The View class extends Proposal, permitting the comparison between views and allowing its use as a proposal value for consensus. When comparing views, the lowest is the one with the highest id.

Listing 6.3. Consensus-Based Group Membership

```
package appia.protocols.tutorialDA.consensusMembership;

public class ConsensusMembershipSession extends Session {
    public ConsensusMembershipSession(Layer layer) {
        super(layer);
    }

    public void handle(Event event) {
        if (event instanceof ProcessInitEvent) {
            handleProcessInit((ProcessInitEvent)event);
            return;
        }
        if (event instanceof Crash) {
            handleCrash((Crash)event);
            return;
        }
        if (event instanceof ConsensusDecide) {
            handleConsensusDecide((ConsensusDecide)event);
            return;
        }

        event.go();
    }

    private View view=null;
    private ProcessSet correct=null;
    private boolean wait;

    private void handleProcessInit(ProcessInitEvent event) {
        event.go();

        view=new View();
        view.id=0;
        view.memb=event.getProcessSet();
        correct=event.getProcessSet();
        wait=false;
```

```
            ViewEvent ev=new ViewEvent(event.getChannel(), Direction.UP, this);
            ev.view=view;
            ev.go();
        }

        private void handleCrash(Crash crash) {
            correct.setCorrect(crash.getCrashedProcess(),false);
            crash.go();

            newMembership(crash.getChannel());
        }

        private void newMembership(Channel channel) {
            if (wait)
                return;

            boolean crashed=false;
            int i;
            for (i=0 ; i < correct.getSize () ; i++) {
                SampleProcess p=correct.getProcess(i);
                SampleProcess m=view.memb.getProcess(p.getInetWithPort());
                if (!p.isCorrect() && (m != null)) {
                    crashed=true;
                }
            }
            if (!crashed)
                return;

            wait=true;

            int j;
            ProcessSet trimmed_memb=new ProcessSet();
            for (i=0,j=0 ; i < correct.getSize () ; i++) {
                SampleProcess p=correct.getProcess(i);
                if (p.isCorrect())
                    trimmed_memb.addProcess(p,j++);
            }

            View v=new View();
            v.id=view.id+1;
            v.memb=trimmed_memb;

            ConsensusPropose ev=new ConsensusPropose(channel,Direction.DOWN,this);
            ev.value=v;
            ev.go();
        }

        private void handleConsensusDecide(ConsensusDecide event) {
            view=(View)event.decision;

            wait=false;

            ViewEvent ev=new ViewEvent(event.getChannel(),Direction.UP,this);
            ev.view=view;
            ev.go();
        }
}
```

Try It

1. Setup
   a) Open three shells/command prompts.

b) In each shell, go to the directory where you have placed the supplied code.

c) In each shell launch the test application, *SampleAppl*, giving a different n value (0, 1, or 2) and specifying the *qos* as **cmem**.

- In shell 0, execute

```
java demo/tutorialDA/SampleAppl \
        -f demo/tutorialDA/procs \
        -n 0 \
        -qos cmem
```

- In shell 1, execute

```
java demo/tutorialDA/SampleAppl \
        -f demo/tutorialDA/procs \
        -n 1 \
        -qos cmem
```

- In shell 2, execute

```
java demo/tutorialDA/SampleAppl \
        -f demo/tutorialDA/procs \
        -n 2 \
        -qos cmem
```

d) If the error NoClassDefError has appeared, confirm that you are at the root of the supplied code.

e) Start the *prefect failure detector* by typing **startpfd** in each shell.

2. Run: Now that processes are launched and running, let us try the following execution:

a) Observe that an initial view with all members is shown.

b) In shell 0, kill the test application process.

c) Observe that a new view without the failed process is shown.

d) Now, in shell 1, kill the test application process.

e) Observe that in the remaining process a new view, with only one member, is delivered.

6.6.4 TRB-Based View Synchrony

The communication stack used to implement the protocol is the following:

Application
View Synchrony   **(implemented by TRB-based VS)**
Membership   (implemented by Consensus-based Membership)
Reliable Causal Order   (implemented by Garbage Collection Of Past)
Reliable Broadcast   (implemented by Lazy RB)
TRB   **(implemented by Consensus-based TRB)**
Uniform Consensus   (implemented by Flooding UC)
Perfect Failure Detector   (implemented by TcpBasedPFD)
Best-Effort Broadcast   (implemented by Basic Broadcast)
Perfect Point-to-Point Links   (implemented by TcpBasedPerfectP2P)

The role of the significant layers is explained below.

ConsensusTRB. This layer implements the consensus-based terminating reliable broadcast algorithm. It follows Algorithm 6.2 very closely. It functions by assuming that all processes propose the same message for delivery. The result is the message proposed or a failure notification. The layer receives the message proposal within an event of class TRBEvent. It then asks for a consensus decision, either proposing the message or a failure notification. The consensus decision is then notified upward in another TRBEvent.

TRBViewSync. This layer implements the TRB-based View Synchrony algorithm. It follows Algorithm 6.5–6.6 closely. Whenever a new view is given by the underlying membership layer it flushes each member by requesting it to stop sending messages. This is done with a BlockEvent. When the application acknowledges, by sending a BlockOkEvent, it starts to disseminate the messages delivered. This is done in rounds, in which the process with rank equal to the round number disseminates the messages it has delivered, using the *Terminating Reliable Broadcast* primitive. To do this, the layer sends a TRBEvent either with the set, of delivered messages if the round number is equal to its rank, or with *null*. It then waits for the return TRBEvent, delivers any message not yet delivered contained in the received set and advances to the next round. When all rounds are terminated the new view is sent upward. To identify the messages, so as to be able to determine if the message was already delivered or not, each message sent by a process is given a unique identifier, implemented as a simple sequence number. Therefore, the pair $(sender\_process, id)$ globally identifies each message.

The Consensus-Based Terminating Reliable Broadcast implementation is depicted in Listing 6.4 and the TRB-Based View Synchrony implementation is depicted in Listing 6.5.

Listing 6.4. Consensus-Based Terminating Reliable Broadcast implementation

```
package appia.protocols.tutorialDA.consensusTRB;

public class ConsensusTRBSession extends Session {
    public ConsensusTRBSession(Layer layer) {
        super(layer);
    }

    public void handle(Event event) {
        if (event instanceof ProcessInitEvent)
            handleProcessInit((ProcessInitEvent) event);
        else if (event instanceof Crash)
            handleCrash((Crash) event);
        else if (event instanceof ConsensusDecide)
            handleConsensusDecide((ConsensusDecide) event);
        else if (event instanceof TRBSendableEvent)
            handleTRBSendableEvent((TRBSendableEvent) event);
        else if (event instanceof TRBEvent)
            handleTRBEvent((TRBEvent) event);
        else {
            event.go();
        }
    }

    private TRBProposal proposal;
    private ProcessSet correct = null;
    private SampleProcess src;

    private void handleProcessInit(ProcessInitEvent event) {
        event.go();

        correct = event.getProcessSet();
        init();
    }

    private void init() {
        proposal = null;
        src = null;
        // correct filled at handleProcessInit
    }

    private void handleCrash(Crash crash) {
        correct.setCorrect(crash.getCrashedProcess(), false);
        crash.go();

        failed(crash.getChannel());
    }

    private void handleTRBEvent(TRBEvent event) {
        src = correct.getProcess(event.p);

        if (src.isSelf()) {
            TRBSendableEvent ev =
                new TRBSendableEvent(event.getChannel(), Direction.DOWN, this);
            ev.getExtendedMessage().pushObject(event.m);
            ev.go();
        }
```

```
        failed (event.getChannel());
    }

    private void handleTRBSendableEvent(TRBSendableEvent event) {
        if (proposal != null)
            return;

        proposal = new TRBProposal(event.getExtendedMessage().popObject());

        ConsensusPropose ev =
            new ConsensusPropose(event.getChannel(), Direction.DOWN, this);
        ev.value = proposal;
        ev.go();
    }

    private void failed(Channel channel) {
        if (proposal != null)
            return;
        if ((src == null) || src.isCorrect())
            return;

        proposal = new TRBProposal(true);

        ConsensusPropose ev = new ConsensusPropose(channel, Direction.DOWN, this);
        ev.value = proposal;
        ev.go();
    }

    private void handleConsensusDecide(ConsensusDecide event) {
        if (event.decision instanceof TRBProposal) {
            TRBEvent ev = new TRBEvent(event.getChannel(), Direction.UP, this);
            ev.p = src.getInetWithPort();
            if (((TRBProposal) event.decision).failed)
                ev.m = null;
            else
                ev.m = ((TRBProposal) event.decision).m;
            ev.go();

            init ();
        } else {
            event.go();
        }
    }
  }
}
```

Listing 6.5. TRB-Based View Synchrony implementation

```
package appia.protocols.tutorialDA.trbViewSync;

public class TRBViewSyncSession extends Session {
    public TRBViewSyncSession(Layer layer) {
        super(layer);
    }

    public void handle(Event event) {
        if (event instanceof ViewEvent)
            handleView((ViewEvent)event);
        else if (event instanceof BlockOkEvent)
            handleBlockOkEvent((BlockOkEvent)event);
        else if (event instanceof TRBEvent)
            handleTRBEvent((TRBEvent)event);
        else if (event instanceof SendableEvent) {
            if (event.getDir() == Direction.DOWN)
```

```
                handleCSVSBroadcast((SendableEvent)event);
            else
                handleRCODeliver((SendableEvent)event);
        } else {
        event.go();
        }
}

private LinkedList pending_views=new LinkedList();
private HashSet delivered=new HashSet();
private View current_view=null;
private View next_view=null;
private boolean flushing=false;
private boolean blocked=true;
/**
 * trb_done counts the number of processes for wich TRB was used.
 * This is possible because the TRB is used one at a time.
 */
private int trb_done;

private int msg_id=0;

private void handleView(ViewEvent event) {
    if (event.view.id == 0) {
        current_view=event.view;
        blocked=false;

        event.go();

        ReleaseEvent ev=new ReleaseEvent(event.getChannel(), Direction.UP, this);
        ev.go();
    } else {
        pending_views.addLast(event.view);
    }

    moreViews(event.getChannel());
}

private void handleCSVSBroadcast(SendableEvent event) {
    if (blocked)
        return;
    // Assert we have a view
    if (current_view == null)
        return;

    // Chooses a unique identifier for the message
    ++msg_id;

    Msg m = new Msg(current_view.memb.getSelfProcess(),
                    msg_id,
                    event.getClass().getName(),
                    event.getMessage().toByteArray());
    delivered.add(m);

    SendableEvent ev=(SendableEvent)event.cloneEvent();
    ev.source=current_view.memb.getSelfProcess().getInetWithPort();
    ev.setDir(Direction.UP);
    ev.setSource(this);
    ev.init();
    ev.go();

    ((ExtendedMessage)event.getMessage()).pushInt(msg_id);
    ((ExtendedMessage)event.getMessage()).pushInt(current_view.id);
    event.go();
}
```

```java
private void handleRCODeliver(SendableEvent event) {
    SampleProcess src=current_view.memb.getProcess((InetWithPort)event.source);
    ExtendedMessage m=(ExtendedMessage)event.getMessage();
    int vid=m.popInt();
    // Message identifier
    int mid=m.popInt();

    if (current_view.id != vid)
        return;

    Msg msg = new Msg(src, mid, event.getClass().getName(), m.toByteArray());
    if (delivered.contains(msg))
        return;
    delivered.add(msg);

    event.go();
}

private void moreViews(Channel channel) {
    if (flushing)
        return;
    if (pending_views.size() == 0)
        return;

    next_view=(View)pending_views.removeFirst();
    flushing=true;

    BlockEvent ev=new BlockEvent(channel, Direction.UP, this);
    ev.go();
}

private void handleBlockOkEvent(BlockOkEvent event) {
    blocked=true;
    trb_done=0;

    SampleProcess p_i = current_view.memb.getProcess(trb_done);
    TRBEvent ev = new TRBEvent(event.getChannel(), Direction.DOWN, this);
    ev.p = p_i.getInetWithPort();
    if (p_i.isSelf()) {
        ev.m=delivered;
    } else {
        // pushes an empty set
        ev.m=new HashSet();
    }
    ev.go();
}

private void handleTRBEvent(TRBEvent event) {
    HashSet del=(HashSet)event.m;
    trb_done++;

    if (del != null) {
        Iterator iter = del.iterator();
        while (iter.hasNext()) {
            Msg m = (Msg) iter.next();

            if (!delivered.contains(m)) {
                delivered.add(m);

                SendableEvent ev = (SendableEvent) Class.forName(m.eventName).newInstan
                ev.getMessage().setByteArray(m.data, 0, m.data.length);
                ev.setChannel(event.getChannel());
                ev.setDir(Direction.UP);
                ev.setSource(this);
                ev.init();
                ev.go();
```

```
            }
        }
    }

    if (trb_done < current_view.memb.getSize()) {
        SampleProcess p_i = current_view.memb.getProcess(trb_done);
        TRBEvent ev = new TRBEvent(event.getChannel(), Direction.DOWN, this);
        ev.p = p_i.getInetWithPort();
        ev.m = new ExtendedMessage();
        if (p_i.isSelf()) {
            ev.m=delivered;
        } else {
            // proposes an empty set
            ev.m=new HashSet();
        }
        ev.go();
    } else {
        ready(event.getChannel());
    }
}

private void ready(Channel channel) {
    if (!blocked)
        return;
    // because TRB was used one at a time,
    // and this function is only invoqued when all are
    // done, its not required to check the "trb_done" variable.

    current_view=next_view;
    flushing=false;
    blocked=false;

    ViewEvent ev1=new ViewEvent(channel, Direction.UP, this);
    ev1.view=current_view;
    ev1.go();

    ReleaseEvent ev2=new ReleaseEvent(channel, Direction.UP, this);
    ev2.go();

    moreViews(channel);
}
}
```

6.7 Exercices

Exercise 6.1 *Would it make sense to combine the properties of best-effort broadcast with the total-order property?*

Exercise 6.2 *What happens in our "Consensus-Based Total Order" algorithm if the set of messages decided on is not sorted deterministically after the decision but prior to the proposal? What happens in that algorithm if the set of messages decided on is not sorted deterministically at all?*

Exercise 6.3 *Discuss the specifications and algorithms of total order broadcast abstractions in fail-silent and fail-recovery models.*

Exercise 6.4 *Give a specification of a state machine replication abstraction and an underlying algorithm to implement it using a total order broadcast abstraction.*

Exercise 6.5 *Can we implement TRB with the eventually perfect failure detector $\Diamond P$ if we assume that at least one process can crash? What if we assume that any number of processes can crash and every process can trbBroadcast messages?*

Exercise 6.6 *Can we implement TRB with the perfect failure detector P if we assume that any number of processes can crash and every process can trbBroadcast messages?*

Exercise 6.7 *Devise two algorithms that, without consensus, implement weaker specifications of NBAC where we replace the* termination *property with the following ones:*

- (1) weak termination: *let p_i be some process; if p_i does not crash then all correct processes eventually decide;*
- (2) very weak termination: *if no process crashes, then all processes decide.*

Exercise 6.8 *Can we implement NBAC with the eventually perfect failure detector $\Diamond P$ if we assume that at least one process can crash? What if we consider a weaker specification of NBAC where the* agreement *was not required?*

Exercise 6.9 *Do we need the perfect failure detector P to implement NBAC if we consider a system where at least two processes can crash but a majority is correct? What if we assume that at most one process can crash?*

Exercise 6.10 *Give an algorithm that implements a view synchronous abstraction such that a single consensus instance is used for every view change (unlike Algorithm 6.5–6.6), and every process directly vsDelivers every message it vsBroadcasts (unlike Algorithm 6.7–6.8).*

6.8 Solutions

Solution 6.1 The resulting abstraction would not make much sense in a failure-prone environment as it would not preclude the following scenario. Assume that a process p_1 broadcasts a bunch of messages and then crashes. Some correct processes might end up delivering all those messages (in the same order) whereas other correct processes might end up not delivering any message. $\square$

Solution 6.2 If the deterministic sorting is done prior to the proposal, and not a posteriori upon a decision, the processes would not agree on a set but on a sequence, i.e., an ordered set. If they were to toDeliver the messages in this order, we would still have to ensure the total order property.

If the messages that we agree on through consensus are not sorted deterministically within every batch (neither a priori nor a posteriori), then the total order property is not ensured. Even if the processes decide on the same batch of messages, they might toDeliver the messages within this batch in a different order. In fact, the total order property would be ensured with respect only to the *batches* of messages, and not to the messages themselves. We thus get a coarser granularity in the total order.

We could avoid using the deterministic sort function at the cost of proposing a single message at a time in the consensus abstraction. This means that we would need exactly as many consensus instances as there are messages exchanged between the processes. If messages are generated very slowly by processes, the algorithm ends up using one consensus instance per message anyway. If the messages are generated rapidly, then it is beneficial to use several messages per instance: within one instance of consensus, several messages would be gathered, i.e., every message of the consensus algorithm would concern several messages to toDeliver. Agreeing on several messages at the same time reduces the number of times we use the consensus protocol. □

Solution 6.3 Our total order specification and total order broadcast algorithm in the fail-stop model directly apply to the fail-silent model. In this case, we consider underlying uniform reliable broadcast and consensus algorithms in the fail-silent model and assume a correct majority. We discuss below a specification and an algorithm in the fail-recovery model.

We apply the same sort of approach we have used to derive a reliable broadcast or a consensus abstraction for the fail-recovery model. We depart from an abstraction designed from the fail-stop model and adapt the following aspects: interface with adjacent modules, logging of relevant states, and definition of recovery procedures. For the algorithm, we make use of the abstractions implemented in the fail-recovery model, e.g., logged consensus and reliable broadcast.

We illustrate here just the uniform definition, which is presented in Module 6.7. Note that the module exports to the upper layers the sequence of delivered (and ordered) messages.

To implement the abstraction, we give an algorithm (Algorithm 6.9) that closely follows the algorithm for the fail-stop model presented in Section 6.1. The algorithm works as follows. Messages sent by the upper layer are disseminated using the reliable broadcast algorithm for the fail-recovery model. The total order algorithm keeps two sets of messages: the set of *unordered* messages (these are the messages received from the underlying reliable broadcast module) and the set of *ordered* messages (obtained by concatenating the

---

Module 6.7 Interface and properties of logged total order broadcast

Module:

    Name: LoggedUniformTotalOrder (luto).

Events:

    Request: $\langle$ *lutoBroadcast* | m $\rangle$: Used to broadcast message m.

    Indication: $\langle$ *lutoDeliver* | *delivered* $\rangle$: Used to deliver the log of all ordered messages up to the moment the indication is generated.

Properties:

    LUTO1: *Total order:* Let $delivered_i$ be the sequence of messages delivered to process p_i. For any pair (i, j), either $delivered_i$ is a prefix of $delivered_j$ or $delivered_j$ is a prefix of $delivered_i$.

    LRB1 to LRB3: from reliable broadcast in the fail-recovery model.

    LUTO4: *Uniform Agreement:* If there exists p_i such that $m \in delivered_i$ then eventually $m \in delivered_j$ at every process p_j that eventually remains permanently up.

---

results of several consensus instances). A new consensus instance is started when one notices that there are unordered messages that have not yet been ordered by previous consensus instances. The *wait* flag is also used to ensure that consensus instances are invoked in serial order. Upon a crash and recovery, the total order module may reinvoke the same consensus instance more than once. Before invoking the ith instance of consensus, the total order algorithm stores the values to be proposed in stable storage. This ensures that a given instance of consensus is always invoked with exactly the same parameters. This may not be strictly needed (depending on the implementation of consensus) but is consistent with the intuitive notion that each process proposes a value by storing it in stable storage.

The algorithm has the interesting feature of never storing the unordered and delivered sets of messages. These sets are simply reconstructed upon recovery from the stable storage kept internally by the reliable broadcast and consensus implementations. Since the initial values proposed for each consensus instance are logged, the process may reinvoke all past instances of consensus to obtain all messages ordered in previous rounds.

The algorithm requires at least one communication step to execute the reliable broadcast and at least two communication steps to execute the consensus instance. Therefore, even if no failures occur, at least three communication steps are required. No stable storage access is needed besides those needed by the underlying consensus module. $\square$

Solution 6.4 A state machine consists of variables and commands that transform its state and may produce some output. Commands consist of deterministic programs such that the outputs of the state machine are solely de-

---

Algorithm 6.9 Logged Total Order Broadcast

Implements:
 LoggedUniformTotalOrder (luto).

Uses:
 LoggedReliableBroadcast (lrb);
 LoggedUniformConsensus (luc).

upon event ⟨ *Init* ⟩ **do**
    unordered := ∅; delivered := ∅;
    sn := 0; wait := false;
    forall k **do** propose[k] := ⊥;

upon event ⟨ *Recovery* ⟩ **do**
    sn := 0; wait := false;
    retrive (propose);
    while propose[sn] ≠ ⊥ **do**
        trigger ⟨ *lucPropose* | sn, propose[sn] ⟩;
        wait ⟨ *lucDecided* | sn, decided ⟩;
        decided := sort (decided); // some deterministic order;
        delivered := delivered ⊕ decided;
        sn := sn +1;
    trigger ⟨ *lutoDeliver* | delivered ⟩;

upon event ⟨ *lutoBroadcast* | m ⟩ **do**
    trigger ⟨ *lrbBroadcast* | m ⟩;

upon event ⟨ *lrbDeliver* | msgs ⟩ **do**
    unordered := unordered ∪ msgs;

upon (unordered\decided ≠ ∅) ∧ (wait = false) **do**
    wait := true;
    propose[sn] := unordered\delivered; *store* (propose[sn]);
    trigger ⟨ *lucPropose* | sn, propose[sn] ⟩;

upon event ⟨ *lucDecided* | sn, decided ⟩ **do**
    decided := sort (decided); // some deterministic order;
    delivered := delivered ⊕ decided;
    trigger ⟨ *lutoDeliver* | delivered ⟩;
    sn := sn +1; wait := false;

---

termined by the initial state and the sequence of commands it has executed. A state machine can be made fault-tolerant by replicating it on different processes.

A replicated state machine abstraction can be characterized by the properties listed in Module 6.8. Basically, its interface has simply two primitives: i) an *rsmExecute* primitive used by a client to invoke a command of the state machine and ii) an *rsmOutput* used by the state machine to produce an output in response to the execution of a command. For the sake of brevity, we

---

Module 6.8 Interfaces and properties of a Replicated State Machine

Module:

   Name: ReplicatedStateMachine (rsm).

Events:

   Request: ⟨ *rsmExecute* | command ⟩: Used to execute a command.

   Indication: ⟨ *rsmOutput* | output ⟩: Used to indicate the output of a command.

Properties:

   RSM1: Agreement All correct processes observe the exact same sequence of outputs.
   RSM2: Termination Every command eventually produces an output.

Algorithm 6.10 Replicated State Machine

Implements:
   ReplicatedStateMachine (rsm).

Uses:
   UniformTotalOrder (uto);

upon event ⟨ *Init* ⟩ **do**
   state := initial-state ();

upon event ⟨ *rsmExecute* | command ⟩ **do**
   trigger ⟨ *utoBroadcast* | command ⟩;

upon event ⟨ *utoDeliver* | p_i, command ⟩ **do**
   (output, newstate) := execute (command, state);
   state := newstate;
   if output $\neq \perp$ **then**
      trigger ⟨ *rsmOutput* | output ⟩;

---

assume that the *command* parameter of the *rsmExecute* primitive includes both the name of the command to be executed and any relevant parameter for the execution of such a command.

As an example, an atomic register could be implemented as a state machine. In this case, the state of the machine would hold the up-to-date value of the register and the relevant commands would be i) a *write(v)* command that would have the value v to be written as an input parameter and ii) a *read* command that would cause the state machine to output the value of the register. Of course, more sophisticated objects can be replicated the same way.

Algorithm 6.10 implements a replicated state machine simply by enforcing all commands to be disseminated and ordered using a uniform total order broadcast primitive. □

Solution 6.5 No. Consider TRB_i, i.e., the sender is process p_i. We discuss below why it is impossible to implement TRB_i with $\diamond \mathcal{P}$ if one process can crash. Consider an execution E_1 where process p_i crashes initially and consider some correct process p_j. Due to the *termination* property of TRB_i, there must be a time T at which p_j trbDelivers F_i. Consider an execution E_2 that is similar to E_1 up to time T, except that p_i is correct: p_i's messages are delayed until after time T and the failure detector behaves as in E_1 until after time T. This is possible because the failure detector is only eventually perfect. Up to time T, p_j cannot distinguish E_1 from E_2 and trbDelivers F_i. Due to the *agreement* property of TRB_i, p_i must trbDeliver F_i as well. Due to the *termination* property, p_i cannot trbDeliver two messages and will contradict the *validity* property of TRB_i. □

Solution 6.6 We explain below that if we have TRB_i abstractions, for every process p_i, and if we consider a model where failures cannot be predicted, then we can *emulate* a perfect failure detector. This means that the perfect failure detector is not only sufficient to solve TRB, but also necessary. The *emulation* idea is simple. Every process trbBroadcasts a series of messages to all processes. Every process p_j that trbDelivers F_i, suspects process p_i. The *strong completeness* property would trivially be satisfied. Consider the *strong accuracy* property (i.e., no process is suspected before it crashes). If p_j trbDelivers F_i, then p_i is faulty. Given that we consider a model where failures cannot be predicted, p_i must have crashed. □

Solution 6.7 The idea of the first algorithm is the following. It uses a perfect failure detector. All processes bebBroadcast their proposal to process p_i. This process would collect the proposals from all processes that it does not suspect and compute the decision: 1 if all processes propose 1, and 0 otherwise, i.e., if some process proposes 0 or is suspected to have crashed. Then p_i bebBroadcasts the decision to all other processes and decides. Any process that bebDelivers the message decides accordingly. If p_i crashes, then all processes are blocked. Of course, the processes can figure out the decision by themselves if p_i crashes after some correct process has decided, or if some correct process decides 0. However, if all correct processes propose 1 and p_i crashes before any correct process, then no correct process can decide. This algorithm is also called the *Two-Phase Commit (2PC)* algorithm. It implements a variant of atomic commitment that is *blocking*.

The second algorithm is simpler. All processes bebBroadcast their proposals to all processes. Every process waits from proposals from all other processes. If a process bebDelivers 1 from all processes it decides 1; otherwise, it decides 0. Note that this algorithm does not make use of any failure detector. □

Solution 6.8 The answer is no, and, to explain why, we consider an execution E_1 where all processes are correct and propose 1, except some process p_i which proposes 0 and crashes initially. Due to the *abort-validity* property, all correct processes decide 0. Let T be the time at which one of these processes, say, p_j, decides 0. Consider an execution E_2 that is similar to E_1 except that p_i proposes 1. Process p_j cannot distinguish the two executions (because p_i did not send any message) and decides 0 at time T. Consider now an execution E_3 that is similar to E_2, except that p_i is correct but its messages are all delayed until after time T. The failure detector behaves in E_3 as in E_2: this is possible because it is only eventually perfect. In E_3, p_j decides 0 and violates *commit-validity*: all processes are correct and propose 1.

In this argument, the *agreement* property of NBAC was not explicitly needed. This shows that even a specification of NBAC where *agreement* was not needed could not be implemented with an eventually perfect failure detector if some process crashes. □

Solution 6.9 Consider first a system where at least two processes can crash but a majority is correct. We argue below that in this case the perfect failure detector is not needed. To show that, we exhibit a failure detector that, in a precise sense, is strictly weaker than the perfect failure detector and that helps in solving NBAC.

The failure detector in question is denoted by $?P$, and called the *anonymously perfect* perfect failure detector. This failure detector ensures the *strong completess* and *eventual strong accuracy* of an eventually perfect failure detector, plus the following *anonymous detection* property: every correct process outputs a specific value F iff some process has crashed. Given that we assume a majority of the correct processes, failure detector $?P$ implements uniform consensus and we can build a consensus module. Now we give the idea of an algorithm that uses $?P$ and a consensus module to implement NBAC.

The idea of the algorithm is the following. All processes bebBroadcast their proposal to all processes. Every process p_i waits either (1) to bebDeliver 1 from all processes, (2) to bebDeliver 0 from some process, or (3) to output F. In case (1), p_i invokes consensus with 1 as a proposed value. In cases (2) and (3), p_i invokes consensus with 0. Then p_i decides the value output by the consensus module.

Now we discuss in which sense $?P$ is strictly weaker than P. Assume a system where at least two processes can crash. Consider an execution E_1 where two processes p_i and p_j crash initially and E_2 is an execution where only p_i initially crashes. Let p_k be any correct process. Using $?P$, at any time T, process p_k can confuse executions E_1 and E_2 if the messages of p_j are delayed. Indeed, p_k will output F and know that some process has indeed crashed but will not know which one.

Hence, in a system where two processes can crash but a majority is correct, P is not needed to solve NBAC. There is a failure detector that is strictly weaker and this failure detector solves NBAC.

Consider now the second part of the exercise and assume that at most one process can crash. We argue below that in a system where at most one process can crash, we can emulate a perfect failure detector if we can solve NBAC. Indeed, the processes go through sequential rounds. In each round, the processes bebBrodcast a message *I-Am-Alive* to all processes and trigger an instance of NBAC (two instances are distinguished by the round number at which they were triggered). In a given round r, every process waits to decide the outcome of NBAC: if this outcome is 1, then p_i moves to the next round. If the outcome is 0, then p_i waits to bebDeliver $N - 1$ messages and suspects the missing message. Clearly, this algorithm emulates the behavior of a perfect failure detector P in a system where at most one process crashes. □

Solution 6.10 The algorithm we give here (Algorithm 6.11–6.12) uses a reliable broadcast, a consensus, and a perfect failure detector abstraction. It works as follows. When a process detects the crash of at least one member of the current view, the process initiates a collective flush procedure as in the previous algorithm. The purpose of the flush is again to collect all messages that have been vsDelivered by at least one process (not detected to have crashed), and that, as such, must be vsDelivered by all processes that might install the new view. To execute the flush, each process first blocks the normal data flow (by issuing a *block* request and waiting for the corresponding *blockOk*). When the traffic is blocked, the process stops broadcasting and delivering application messages. The process then broadcasts to every other correct process its set of vsDelivered messages.

As soon as a process has collected the vsDelivered set from every other process p that it did not detect to have crashed, p proposes a new view through a consensus instance. More precisely, process p proposes to consensus the new set of view members as well as their corresponding vsDelivered sets. Because the flush procedure might be initiated by processes which have detected different failures (i.e., detected the failures in different order), and some processes might, furthermore, fail during the flush procedure, different processes might propose different values to consensus: what is important to note is that each of these different values contains a valid candidate for the next view and a valid set of vsDelivered messages (the only risk here is to end up vsDelivering messages of processes which have crashed). Consensus guarantees that the same view is selected by all correct processes. Before installing the new view, each process parses the vsDelivered sets of all other correct processes and vsDelivers those messages that it has not vsDelivered yet. Finally the new view is installed and normal operation resumed, i.e., the traffic is unblocked.

Algorithm 6.11 Consensus-Based View Synchrony (data transmission)

Implements:
    ViewSynchrony (vs).

Uses:
    UniformConsensus (uc);
    BestEffortBroadcast (beb);
    PerfectFailureDetector ($\mathcal{P}$).

upon event $\langle$ *Init* $\rangle$ **do**
    current-view := $(0, \Pi)$;
    correct := Π;
    flushing := blocked := wait := false;
    delivered := $\emptyset$;
    forall i **do** dset[i] := $\emptyset$;

upon event $\langle$ *vsBroadcast* $\mid m$ $\rangle$ $\wedge$ (blocked = false) **do**
    delivered := delivered $\cup$ {(self, m)};
    trigger $\langle$ *vsDeliver* $\mid$ self, m $\rangle$;
    trigger $\langle$ *bebBroadcast* $\mid$ [DATA, current-view.id, m] $\rangle$;

upon event $\langle$ *bebDeliver* $\mid$ src$_m$,[DATA, vid, m] $\rangle$ $\wedge$
    current-view.id = vid) $\wedge$ (blocked = false)**do**
        if ((src$_m$, m) $\notin$ delivered) **do**
            delivered := delivered $\cup$ {(src$_m$, m)};
            trigger $\langle$ *vsDeliver* $\mid$ src$_m$, m $\rangle$;

Any message is vsDelivered to its sender as soon as it vsBroadcast. The message is also added to the vsDelivered set of the sender (variable *delivered*). If the sender remains correct, it will be included in the next view (remember that we assume a perfect failure detector). Furthermore, its vsDelivered set will be made available to all non-crashed processes as an output of the consensus that decides the next view. Since all correct processes parse the vsDelivered set for missing messages before they install the next view, the messages are vsDelivered in the same view at all correct processes.

During periods where the view does not need to change, the cost of vsDelivering a message is the same as the cost of rbDelivering it. To install a new view, the algorithm requires the parallel execution of a reliable broadcast for each non-crashed process, followed by a consensus execution to agree on the next view. $\square$

Algorithm 6.12 Consensus-Based View Synchrony (group change)

---

upon event $\langle$ *crash* $|$ p_i $\rangle$ **do**
    correct := correct $\setminus \{p_i\}$;

upon (correct $\subset$ current-view.memb) $\wedge$ (flushing = false) **do**
    flushing := true;
    trigger $\langle$ *vsBlock* $\rangle$;

upon event $\langle$ *vsBlockOk* $\rangle$ **do**
    blocked := true;
    trigger $\langle$ *bebBroadcast* $|$ [DSET, current-view.id, delivered] $\rangle$;

upon event $\langle$ *bebDeliver* $|$ src,[DSET, vid, mset] $\rangle$ $\wedge$ (blocked) **do**
    dset[vid] := dset[vid] $\cup$ {(src, mset)};

upon $\forall p \in$ correct $\exists \{(p, \text{mset})\} \in$ dset[current-view.id] $\wedge$ (wait = false) **do**
    trigger $\langle$ *ucPropose* $|$ current-view.id+1, correct, dset[current-view.id] $\rangle$;
    wait := true;

upon event $\langle$ *ucDecided* $|$ id, memb, vs-dset $\rangle$ **do**
    forall $\{(p, \text{mset})\} \in$ vs-dset: $p \in$ memb **do**
        forall $(\text{src}_m, m) \in$ mset: $(\text{src}_m, m) \notin$ delivered **do**
            delivered := delivered $\cup$ { (src_m, m) };
            trigger $\langle$ *vsDeliver* $|$ src_m, m $\rangle$;
    flushing := blocked := wait := false;
    delivered := $\emptyset$;
    current-view := (id, memb);
    trigger $\langle$ *vsView* $|$ current-view $\rangle$;

6.9 Historical Notes

- The total order broadcast abstraction was specified by Schneider (Schneider 1990), following the work on state machine replication by Lamport (Lamport 1978).
- Our total order broadcast specifications and algorithms in the fail-stop model are inspired by the work of Chandra, Hadzilacos, and Toueg (Chandra and Toueg 1996; Hadzilacos and Toueg 1994).
- Our total order broadcast specification and algorithms in the crash-recovery model were defined more recently (Boichat, Dutta, Frolund, and Guerraoui 2003a; Boichat and Guerraoui 2005; Rodrigues and Raynal 2003).
- We considered that messages that need to be totally ordered were broadcast to all processes in the system, and hence it was reasonable to have all processes participate in the ordering activity. It is also possible to consider a total order multicast abstraction where the sender can select the subset of processes to which the message needs to be sent, and require that no other process besides the sender and the multicast set participates in the

ordering (Rodrigues, Guerraoui, and Schiper 1998; Guerraoui and Schiper 2001).

- It is possible to design total order algorithms that exploit particular features of concrete networks. Such algorithms can be seen as sophisticated variants of the basic strategy presented here (Chang and Maxemchuck 1984; Veríssimo, Rodrigues, and Baptista 1989; Kaashoek and Tanenbaum 1991; Moser, Melliar-Smith, Agarwal, Budhia, Lingley-Ppadopoulos, and Archambault 1995; Rodrigues, Fonseca, and Veríssimo 1996; Rufino, Veríssimo, Arroz, Almeida, and Rodrigues 1998; Amir, Danilov, and Stanton 2000).

- The atomic commit problem was introduced by Gray (Gray 1978), together with the two-phase commit algorithm, which we studied in the exercice section. The atomic commit (sometimes called *atomic commitment*) problem corresponds to our NBAC specification without the *termination* property.

- The non-blocking atomic commit (NBAC) problem was introduced by Skeen (Skeen 1981) and was then refined (Guerraoui 2002; Delporte-Gallet, Fauconnier, Guerraoui, Hadzilacos, Kouznetsov, and Toueg 2004). The NBAC algorithm presented in this chapter is a modular variant of Skeen's decentralized three-phase protocol. It is more modular in the sense that we encapsulate many tricky issues of NBAC within consensus.

- The terminating reliable broadcast problem was studied by Hadzilacos and Toueg (Hadzilacos and Toueg 1994) in the context of crash failures. This abstraction is a variant of the Byzantine Generals problem (Lamport, Shostak, and Pease 1982). While the original Byzantine Generals problem considers processes that might behave in an arbitrary manner and, in particular, be malicious, the terminating reliable broadcast abstraction assumes that processes may only fail by crashing.

- The group membership problem was initially discussed by Birman and Joseph (Birman and Joseph 1987a). They also introduced the view synchronous abstraction. The specification we consider for that abstraction was introduced later (Friedman and van Renesse 1995). This is a strong specification as it ensures that messages are always delivered in the view in which they were broadcast. Weaker specifications were also considered (Babaoglu, Bartoli, and Dini 1997; Chockler, Keidar, and Vitenberg 2001; Fekete, Lynch, and Shvartsman 2001; Fekete and Lesley 2003; Pereira, Rodrigues, and Oliveira 2003).

7. Concluding Remarks

*The world must be coming to an end. Children no longer obey their parents
and every man wants to write a book.*
(Writing on a tablet, unearthed not far from Babylon and dated back to
2800 B.C.)

In many areas of computing, theory and practice were able to sediment a
number of basic abstractions that are now taught to students and provided
to programmers in the forms of libraries, or even programming language
constructs.

The basic abstractions of sequential computing include data structures
like *set*, *record*, and *array*, as well as control structures like *if-then-else*, and
loops. In concurrent computing, fundamental abstractions include *thread*, *mu-
tex*, *transaction*, and *semaphore*, whereas the underlying abstractions of operating systems include *address space* and *file*.

This book studies abstractions for distributed programming: *broadcast*,
shared memory, *consensus*, and its variants. Some of these might become, if
they are not already, the basic building blocks for building reliable distributed
applications.

We mention in the following practical systems that support (some) of
these abstractions as well as alternative books that describe their underlying
algorithms and implementations.

7.1 Further Implementations

The abstractions we studied have all been developed within the *Appia* library. This library was written in Java with the goal of supporting flexible
protocol compositions. Originally built for pedagogical purposes, *Appia* has
subsequently been used in many different research projects (Miranda, Pinto,
and Rodrigues 2001).

In the following, we enumerate other programming libraries that implement some of the abstractions we considered in this book. We then also give pointers for more details on theoretical studies around the algorithmic aspects of these abstractions.

V. The V distributed System was developed at Stanford University as part of a research project to explore communication issues in distributed systems. The process group abstraction was introduced there to encapsulate distribution (Cherriton and Zwaenepoel 1985).

Amoeba. The Amoeba microkernel-based system was developed at the Vrije University of Amsterdam to devise applications on a collection of workstations or single board computers (Kaashoek, Tanenbaum, Hummel, and Bal 1989).

Delta-4. An European project that defined an architecture to build dependable system based on reliable (group) communication abstractions. Many of the ideas underlying Delta-4 were later incorporated in the FT-CORBA standard (Powell, Barret, Bonn, Chereque, Seaton, and Verissimo 1994; Rodrigues and Veríssimo 1992).

Replicated RPC. One of the first systems to use the group communication abstraction to access replicated servers (Cooper 1984).

Isis/Horus/Ensemble/Spinglass. These were developed at Cornell University to experiment with the group membership and view synchrony abstractions (Birman and Joseph 1987a; van Renesse, Birman, and Maffeis 1996). Isis, the first in the suite, was a commercial product and, for many years, was a reference system in the area (Birman and van Renesse 1993). Horus was a modular implementation of Isis, and Ensemble an implementation of it in the ML programming language with several optimizations of the communication stack (Hayden 1998). Spinglass, the youngest in the family, was based on gossip-based algorithms and designed for highly scalable systems (Birman, van Renesse, and Vogels 2001).

Transis. A group communication system with algorithms defined for both local-area and wide-are networks. The work on this system highlighted the importance of uniform primitives (Amir, Dolev, Kramer, and Malki 1992).

Psync/Consul/Cactus/Coyote. A suite of group communication systems inspired by the x-kernel protocol composition framework. Consul was one of the first systems to relax total order based on application semantics for improved performance (Peterson, Bucholz, and Schlichting 1989; Mishra, Peterson, and Schlichting 1993). Cactus was a follow-up on Consul based on a microprotocol decomposition of group services. Many useful protocol composition lessons were extracted from this work (Bhatti, Hiltunen, Schlichting, and Chiu 1998).

GARF/OGS/BAST. A suite of distributed programming libraries developed at EPFL. The consensus abstraction was promoted as a first class citizen of the libraries. A fine-grained composition methodology was proposed to guide the programmer (Felber and Guerraoui 2000; Guerraoui, Eugster, Felber, Garbinato, and Mazouni 2000).

Arjuna. An object-oriented distributed system integrating group communication and transaction abstractions (Parrington, Shrivastava, Wheater, and Little 1995).

Totem. A group communication protocol suite well-known for a very efficient implementation of total order on local-area network. It was used to build FT-CORBA compliant systems (Moser, Melliar-Smith, Agarwal, Budhia, Lingley-Ppadopoulos, and Archambault 1995).

Spread. A group communication suite with support for wide-area communication (Amir, Danilov, and Stanton 2000).

JGroups. A group communication protocol suite (written in Java) widely used at the time of writing of this book (Ban 1998).

7.2 Further Readings

We enumerate, in the following, several books that also present distributed programming abstractions. Some of the abstractions are different than those we studied in this book. Some are similar but presented in a different manner.

- **Tel(1994), Lynch(1996), Attiya and Welch(1998).** These books survey the theory of distributed computing and address aspects like complexity, which we did not cover here. Algorithms are written in a very abstract way, making it easier to prove their correctness in a modular and precise manner (Lynch 1996). Different computing models are considered, with special emphasis on their similarities and the discrepancies between them (Attiya and Welch 1998).

- **Birman (1996), Veríssimo and Rodrigues(2001), Birman(2005).** These books take the perspective of the designer of a distributed system and discuss crucial architectural decisions for achieving dependability.

- **Colouris, Dollimore, and Kindberg(1994), Tanenbaum(2002).** These books present the operating system perspective of a distributed system, including aspects like transactions, security, and naming.

- **Raynal(1986).** This book focuses on the allocation of resources to distributed processes and presents different solutions in an intuitive and coherent framework.

References

Abraham, I., G. V. Chockler, I. Keidar, and D. Malkhi (2004). Byzantine disk paxos: optimal resilience with byzantine shared memory. In *Proceedings of the ACM Symposium on Principles of Distributed Computing (PODC)*, pp. 226–235.

Aguilera, M., W. Chen, and S. Toueg (2000, May). Failure detection and consensus in the crash recovery model. *Distributed Computing 2*(13).

Alpern, B. and F. Schneider (1985). Defining lineness. Technical Report TR85-650, Cornell University.

Amir, Y., C. Danilov, and J. Stanton (2000, June). A low latency, loss tolerant architecture and protocol for wide area group communication. In *International Conference on Dependable Systems and Networks (FTCS-30, DCCA-8)*, New York, USA.

Amir, Y., D. Dolev, S. Kramer, and D. Malki (1992, July). Transis: A communication sub-system for high availability. In *22nd Annual International Symposium on Fault-Tolerant Computing (FTCS), Digest of Papers*, pp. 76–84. IEEE.

Attiya, H., A. Bar-Noy, and D. Dolev (1995, June). Sharing memory robustly in message passing systems. *Journal of the ACM 1*(42).

Attiya, H. and J. Welch (1998). *Distributed Computing*. Mc Graw Hill.

Avoine, G., F. Gärtner, R. Guerraoui, and M. Vukolic (2005). Gracefully degrading fair exchange with security modules. In *Proceedings of the European Dependable Computing Conference (EDCC)*, pp. 55–71.

Babaoglu, Ö., A. Bartoli, and G. Dini (1997). Enriched view synchrony: A programming paradigm for partitionable asynchronous distributed systems. *IEEE Trans. Computers 46*(6), 642–658.

Baldoni, R., J.-M. Hélary, M. Raynal, and L. Tangui (2003). Consensus in byzantine asynchronous systems. *J. Discrete Algorithms 1*(2), 185–210.

Ban, B. (1998). Jgroups: A toolkit for building fault-tolerant distributed applications in large scale.

Ben-Or, M. (1983). Another advantage of free choice: Completely asynchonous agreement protocols. In *Proceedings of 2nd ACM Symposium on Principles of Distributed Computing (PODC'83)*, Montreal, Canada, pp. 27–30.

Bhatti, N., M. Hiltunen, R. Schlichting, and W. Chiu (1998, November). Coyote: A system for constructing fine-grain configurable communication services. *ACM Trans. on Computer Systems 16*(4), 321–366.

Birman, K. (1996). *Building Secure and Reliable Network Applications*. Prentice Hall.

Birman, K. (2005). *Reliable Distributed Systems: Technologies, Web Services and Applications*. Springer.

Birman, K., M. Hayden, O. Ozkasap, Z. Xiao, M. Budiu, and Y. Minsky (1999, May). Bimodal multicast. *ACM Transactions on Computer Systems 17*(2).

Birman, K. and T. Joseph (1987a, February). Reliable communication in the presence of failures. *ACM Transactions on Computer Systems 1*(5).

Birman, K. and T. Joseph (1987b, February). Reliable Communication in the Presence of Failures. *ACM, Transactions on Computer Systems 5*(1).

Birman, K. and R. van Renesse (1993). *Reliable Distributed Programming with the Isis Toolkit.* IEEE Computer Society Press.

Birman, K., R. van Renesse, and W. Vogels (2001, June). Spinglass: Secure and scalable communications tools for mission-critical computing. In *International Survivability Conference and Exposition*, Anaheim, California, USA.

Boichat, R., P. Dutta, S. Frolund, and R. Guerraoui (2001, January). Deconstructing paxos. Technical Report 49, EPFL, CH 1015, Lausanne.

Boichat, R., P. Dutta, S. Frolund, and R. Guerraoui (2003a, March). Deconstructing paxos. In *ACM SIGACT News Distributed Computing Colomn*, Number 34 (1).

Boichat, R., P. Dutta, S. Frolund, and R. Guerraoui (2003b, June). Reconstructing paxos. In *ACM SIGACT News Distributed Computing Colomn*, Number 34 (2).

Boichat, R. and R. Guerraoui (2005). Reliable and total order broadcast in a crash-recovery model. *Journal of Parallel and Distributed Computing.*

Chandra, T., V. Hadzilacos, and S. Toueg (1996). The weakest failure detector for consensus. *Journal of the ACM.*

Chandra, T. and S. Toueg (1996). Unreliable failure detectors for reliable distributed systems. *Journal of the ACM 43*(2), 225–267.

Chang, J. and N. Maxemchuck (1984, August). Reliable broadcast protocols. *ACM, Transactions on Computer Systems 2*(3).

Cherriton, D. and W. Zwaenepoel (1985, May). Distributed process groups in the v kernel. *ACM Transactions on Computer Systems 3*(2).

Chockler, G., I. Keidar, and R. Vitenberg (2001). Group communication specifications: A comprehensive study. *ACM Computing Surveys 33*(4), 1–43.

Colouris, G., J. Dollimore, and T. Kindberg (1994). *Distributed Systems, Concepts and Designs.* Addison Wesley Publishing Company.

Cooper, E. (1984, August). Replicated procedure call. In *Proceedings of the 3rd ACM symposyum on Principles of Distributed Computing*, Berkeley, USA. ACM.

Delporte-Gallet, C., H. Fauconnier, and R. Guerraoui (2002, October). Failure detection lower bounds on consensus and registers. In *Proceedings of the International Conference on Distributed Computing Systems (DISC'02).*

Delporte-Gallet, C., H. Fauconnier, and R. Guerraoui (2005). The weakest failure detectors to implement atomic objects in message passing systems. Technical report, Ecole Polytechnique Fédérale de Lausanne (EPFL), School of Computer and Communication Systems.

Delporte-Gallet, C., H. Fauconnier, R. Guerraoui, V. Hadzilacos, P. Kouznetsov, and S. Toueg (2004, July). The weakest failure detectors to solve certain fundamental problems in distributed computing. In *In Proceedings of the 23rd ACM Symposium on Principles of Distributed Computing (PODC 04)*, St.John's.

Doudou, A., B. Garbinato, and R. Guerraoui (2005). Tolerating arbitrary failures with state machine replication. In *Dependable Computing Systems Paradigms, Performance Issues, and Applications. Wiley.*

Dutta, D. and R. Guerraoui (2002, July). The inherent price of indulgence. In *Proceedings of the ACM Symposium on Principles of Distributed Computing (PODC'02).*

Dwork, C., N. Lynch, and L. Stockmeyer (1988, April). Consensus in the presence of partial synchrony. *Journal of the ACM 35*(2), 288–323.

Eugster, P., R. Guerraoui, S. Handurukande, P. Kouznetsov, and A.-M. Kermarrec (2003). Lightweight probabilistic broadcast. *ACM Trans. Comput. Syst. 21*(4), 341–374.

Eugster, P., R. Guerraoui, and P. Kouznetsov (2004, March). Delta reliable broadcast: A probabilistic measure of broadcast reliability. In *Proceedings of the IEEE International Conference on Distributed Computing Systems (ICDCS 2004)*, Tokyo, Japan.

Ezhilchelvan, P., A. Mostefaoui, and M. Raynal (2001, May). Randomized multivalued consensus. In *Proceedings of the Fourth International Symposium on Object-Oriented Real-Time Distributed Computing*, Magdeburg, Germany.

Fekete, A. and N. Lesley (2003). Providing view synchrony for group communication services. *Acta Informatica 40*(3), 159–210.

Fekete, A., N. Lynch, and A. Shvartsman (2001). Specifying and using a partitionable group communication service. *ACM Transactions on Computer Systems 19*(2), 171–216.

Felber, P. and R. Guerraoui (2000). Programming with object groups in corba. *IEEE Concurrency 8*(1), 48–58.

Fidge, C. (1988). Timestamps in Message-Passing Systems that Preserve the Partial Ordering. In *Proceedings of the 11th Australian Computer Science Conference*.

Fischer, M., N. Lynch, and M. Paterson (1985, April). Impossibility of distributed consensus with one faulty process. *Journal of the Association for Computing Machinery 32*(2), 374–382.

Friedman, R. and R. van Renesse (1995, March). Strong and weak virtual synchrony in horus. Technical Report 95-1537, Department of Computer Science, Cornell University.

Garbinato, B., F. Pedone, and R. Schmidt (2004). An adaptive algorithm for efficient message diffusion in unreliable environments. In *Proceedings of the IEEE International Conference on Dependable Systems and Networks (DSN)*, pp. 507–516.

Golding, R. and D. Long (1992, October). Design choices for weak-consistency group communication. Technical Report UCSC–CRL–92–45, University of California Santa Cruz.

Gray, C. and D. Cheriton (1989, December). Leases: An efficient fault-tolerant mechanism for distributed file cache consistency. In *Proceedings of the Twelfth ACM Symposium on Operating Systems Principles*, Litchfield Park, Arizona, pp. 202–210.

Gray, J. (1978). Notes on database operating systems. *Lecture Notes in Computer Science*.

Guerraoui, R. (2000, July). Indulgent algorithms. In *Proceedings of the ACM Symposium on Principles of Distributed Computing (PODC'00)*.

Guerraoui, R. (2002). Non-blocking atomic commit in asynchronous distributed systems with failure detectors. *Distributed Computing 15*(1), 17–25.

Guerraoui, R., P. Eugster, P. Felber, B. Garbinato, and K. Mazouni (2000). Experiences with object group systems. *Softw., Pract. Exper. 30*(12), 1375–1404.

Guerraoui, R. and R. Levy (2004, March). Robust emulations of a shared memory in a crash-recovery model. In *Proceedings of the IEEE International Conference on Distributed Computing Systems (ICDCS 2004)*, Tokyo, Japan.

Guerraoui, R., R. Oliveria, and A. Schiper (1997). Stubborn communication channels. Technical Report TR97, EPFL.

Guerraoui, R. and M. Raynal (2004). The information structure of indulgent consensus. *IEEE Trans. Computers 53*(4), 453–466.

Guerraoui, R. and A. Schiper (2001). Genuine atomic multicast in asynchronous distributed systems. *Theoretical Computer Science 254*, 297–316.

Gupta, I., A.-M. Kermarrec, and A. Ganesh (2002, October). Adaptive and efficient epidemic-style protocols for reliable and scalable multicast. In *Proceedings of Symposium on Reliable and Distributed Systems (SRDS 2002)*, Osaka, Japan.

Hadzilacos, V. (1984). Issues of fault tolerance in concurrent computations. Technical Report 11-84, Harvard University, Ph.D thesis.

Hadzilacos, V. and S. Toueg (1994, May). A modular approach to fault-tolerant broadcast and related problems. Technical Report 94-1425, Cornell University, Dept of Computer Science, Ithaca, NY.

Hayden, M. (1998). *The Ensemble System*. Ph. D. thesis, Cornell University, Computer Science Department.

Herlihy, M. and J. Wing (1990, July). Linearizability: a correctness condition for concurrent objects. *ACM Transactions on Programming Languages and Systems 3*(12).

Israeli, A. and M. Li (1993). Bounded timestamps. *Distributed Computing 4*(6), 205–209.

Jelasity, M., R. Guerraoui, A.-M. Kermarrec, and M. van Steen (2004, October). The peer sampling service: Experimental evaluation of unstructured gossip-based implementations. In H.-A. Jacobsen (Ed.), *Middleware 2004, ACM/I-FIP/USENIX International Middleware Conference*, Lecture Notes in Computer Science 3231, Toronto, Canada, pp. 79–98. Springer.

Kaashoek, F. and A. Tanenbaum (1991, May). Group communication in the Amoeba distributed operating system. In *Proceedings of the 11th International Conference on Distributed Computing Systems*, Arlington, Texas, USA, pp. 222–230. IEEE.

Kaashoek, F., A. Tanenbaum, S. Hummel, and H. Bal (1989, October). An efficient reliable broadcast protocol. *Operating Systems Review 4*(23).

Kermarrec, A.-M., L. Massoulie, and A. Ganesh (2000, October). Reliable probabilistic communication in large-scale information dissemination systems. Technical Report MMSR-TR-2000-105, Microsoft Reserach, Cambridge, UK.

Koldehofe, B. (2003). Buffer management in probabilistic peer-to-peer communication protocols. In *Proceedings IEEE Symposium on Reliable Distributed Systems (SRDS)*.

Kouznetsov, P., R. Guerraoui, S. Handurukande, and A.-M. Kermarrec (2001, October). Reducing noise in gossip-based reliable broadcast. In *Proceedings of the 20th Symposium on Reliable Distributed Systems (SRDS)*, NewOrleans,USA.

Ladin, R., B. Liskov, L. Shrira, and S. Ghemawat (1990). Lazy replication: Exploiting the semantics of distributed services. In *Proceedings of the Ninth Annual ACM Symposium of Principles of Distributed Computing*, pp. 43–57.

Lamport, L. (1977). Concurrent reading and writing. *Communications of the ACM 11*(20), 806–811.

Lamport, L. (1978, July). Time, clocks and the ordering of events in a distributed system. *Communications of the ACM 21*(7), 558–565.

Lamport, L. (1986a). On interprocess communication, part i: Basic formalism. *Distributed Computing 2*(1), 75–85.

Lamport, L. (1986b). On interprocess communication, part ii: Algorithms. *Distributed Computing 2*(1), 86–101.

Lamport, L. (1989, May). The part-time parliament. Technical Report 49, Digital, Systems Research Center, Palo Alto, California.

Lamport, L., R. Shostak, and M. Pease (1982, July). The byzantine generals problem. *ACM Transactions on Prog. Lang. and Systems 4*(3).

Lin, M.-J. and K. Marzullo (1999, September). Directional gossip: Gossip in a wide area network. In *Proceedings of 3rd European Dependable Computing Conference*, pp. 364–379.

Lynch, N. (1996). *Distributed Algorithms*. Morgan Kaufmann.

Lynch, N. and A. Shvartsman (1997). Robust emulation of shared memory using dynamic quorum acknowledged broadcasts. In *Proceedings of the International Symposium on Fault-Tolerant Computing Systems (FTCS'97)*.

Lynch, N. and A. Shvartsman (2002, October). Rambo: A reconfigurable atomic memory service for dynamic networks. In *Proceedings of the International Conference on Distributed Computing Systems (DISC'02)*.

Malkhi, D. and M. K. Reiter (1997). Byzantine quorum systems. In *Proceedings of the ACM Symposium on the Theory of Computing (STOC)*, pp. 569–578.

Martin, J.-P. and L. Alvisi (2004). A framework for dynamic byzantine storage. In *Proceedings of the IEEE International Conference on Dependable Systems and Networks (DSN)*, pp. 325–334.

Miranda, H., A. Pinto, and L. Rodrigues (2001, April). Appia, a flexible protocol kernel supporting multiple coordinated channels. In *Proceedings of the 21st International Conference on Distributed Computing Systems*, Phoenix, Arizona, pp. 707–710. IEEE.

Mishra, S., L. Peterson, and R. Schlichting (1993, October). Experience with modularity in consul. *Software Practice and Experience 23*(10), 1059–1075.

Moser, L., P. Melliar-Smith, A. Agarwal, R. Budhia, C. Lingley-Ppadopoulos, and T. Archambault (1995, June). The totem system. In *Digest of Papers of the 25th International Symposium on Fault-Tolerant Computing Systems*, pp. 61–66. IEEE.

Neiger, G. and S. Toueg (1993, April). Simulating synchronized clocks and common knowledge in distributed systems. *Journal of the ACM 2*(40).

Parrington, G., S. Shrivastava, S. Wheater, and M. Little (1995). The design and implementation of arjuna computing systems. *The Journal of the USENIX Association 8*(3).

Pereira, J., L. Rodrigues, and R. Oliveira (2003, February). Semantically reliable multicast: Definition, implementation and performance evaluation. *IEEE Transactions on Computers, Special Issue on Reliable Distributed Systems 52*(2), 150–165.

Peterson, G. (1983). Concurrent reading while writing. *ACM Transactions on Prog. Lang. and Systems 1*(5), 56–65.

Peterson, L., N. Bucholz, and R. Schlichting (1989). Preserving and using context information in interprocess communication. *ACM Transactions on Computer Systems 7*(3), 217–246.

Postel (1981). Transmission control protocol: Internet rfc 793. Technical report, Information Sciences Institute, University of Southern California.

Powell, D., P. Barret, G. Bonn, M. Chereque, D. Seaton, and P. Verissimo (1994). The delta-4 distributed fault-tolerant architecture. *Readings in Distributed Systems, IEEE, Casavant and Singhal (eds)*.

Raynal, M. (1986). *Algorithms for Mutual Exclusion*. MIT Press.

Raynal, M., A. Schiper, and S. Toueg (1991, September). The causal ordering abstraction and a simple way to implement it. *Information processing letters 39*(6), 343–350.

Rodrigues, L., H. Fonseca, and P. Veríssimo (1996, May). Totally ordered multicast in large-scale systems. In *Proceedings of the 16th International Conference on Distributed Computing Systems*, Hong Kong, pp. 503–510. IEEE.

Rodrigues, L., R. Guerraoui, and A. Schiper (1998). Scalable atomic multicast. In *IEEE Proceedings of IC3N'98*.

Rodrigues, L., S. Handurukande, J. Pereira, R. Guerraoui, and A.-M. Kermarrec (2003, June). Adaptive gossip-based broadcast. In *Proceedings of the IEEE International Symposium on Dependable Systems and Networks*.

Rodrigues, L. and M. Raynal (2003). Atomic broadcast in asynchronous crash-recovery distributed systems and its use in quorum-based replication. *IEEE Transactions on Knowledge and Data Engineering 15*(4).

Rodrigues, L. and P. Veríssimo (1992, October). *x*AMp: a Multi-primitive Group Communications Service. In *Proceedings of the 11th Symposium on Reliable Distributed Systems (SRDS'11)*, Houston, Texas, pp. 112–121. IEEE.

Rufino, J., P. Veríssimo, G. Arroz, C. Almeida, and L. Rodrigues (1998, July). Fault-tolerant broadcasts in CAN. In *Digest of Papers, The 28nd International Symposium on Fault-Tolerant Computing*, Munich, Germany, pp. 69–73. IEEE.

Schneider, F. (1990). Implementing fault-tolerant services with the state machine approach. *ACM Computing Surveys* (22 (4)), 300–319.

Schneider, F., D. Gries, and R. Schlichting (1984). Fault-tolerant broadcasts. *Science of Computer Programming* (4), 1–15.

Schwarz, R. and F. Mattern (1992, February). Detecting causal relationships in distributed computations: In search of the holy grail. Technical report, Univ. Kaiserslautern, Kaiserslautern, Germany.

Shao, C., E. Pierce, and J. Welch (2003, October). Multi-writer consistency conditions for shared memory objects. In *Proceedings of the 17th Symposium on Distributed Computing (DISC 2003)*, Sorrento,Italy.

Skeen, D. (1981, July). A decentralized termination protocol. In *Proceedings of the 1st Symposium on Reliability in Distributed Software and Database Systems*, Pittsburgh, USA. IEEE.

Tanenbaum, A. and M. van Steen (2002). *Distributed Systems: Principles and Paradigms*. Prentice Hall.

Tel, G. (1994). *Introduction to Distributed Algorithms*. Cambridge University Press.

van Renesse, R., K. Birman, and S. Maffeis (1996, April). Horus: A flexible group communication system. *Communications of the ACM 4*(39).

Veríssimo, P. and L. Rodrigues (2001). *Distributed Systems for System Architects*. Kluwer Academic Publishers.

Veríssimo, P., L. Rodrigues, and M. Baptista (1989, September). AMp: A highly parallel atomic multicast protocol. In *Proceedings of the SIGCOM'89 Symposium*, Austin, USA, pp. 83–93. ACM.

Vidyasankar, K. (1988, August). Converting lamport's regular register to atomic register. *Information Processing Letters* (28).

Vidyasankar, K. (1990, June). Concurrent reading while writing revisited. *Distributed Computing 2*(4).

Vitanyi, P. and B. Awerbuch (1986). Atomic shared register by asynchronous hardware. In *Proceedings of the IEEE Symposium on Foundations of Computer Science (FOCS'86)*, pp. 233–243.

Voulgaris, S., M. Jelasity, and M. van Steen (2003, July). A robust and scalable peer-to-peer gossiping protocol. In G. Moro, C. Sartori, and M. Singh (Eds.), *Agents and Peer-to-Peer Computing, Second International Workshop*, Lecture Notes in Computer Science 2872, Melbourne, Australia. Springer.

Wensley, J. e. a. (1978, October). The design and analysis of a fault-tolerant computer for air craft control. *IEEE 10*(66).

Xiao, Z., K. Birman, and R. van Renesse (2002, June). Optimizing buffer management for reliable multicast. In *Proceedings of The International Conference on Dependable Systems and Networks (DSN 2002)*, Washington, USA.

Yin, J., J.-P. Martin, A. Venkataramani, L. Alvisi, and M. Dahlin (2003). Separating agreement from execution for byzantine fault tolerant services. In *Proceedings of the ACM Symposium on Operating System Principles of Operating Systems (SOSP)*.

Index

springer.com

Denis Caromel, Ludovic Henrio

A Theory of Distributed Objects

346 p., Hardcover
Springer-Verlag, ISBN 3-540-20866-6

Preface by Luca Cardelli

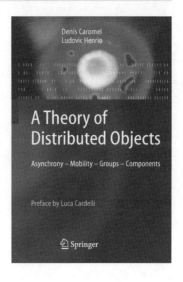

Distributed and communicating objects are becoming ubiquitous. In global, Grid and Peer-to-Peer computing environments, extensive use is made of objects interacting through method calls. So far, no general formalism has been proposed for the foundation of such systems.

Caromel and Henrio are the first to define a calculus for distributed objects interacting using asynchronous method calls with generalized futures, i.e., wait-by-necessity – a must in large-scale systems, providing both high structuring and low coupling, and thus scalability. The authors provide very generic results on expressiveness and determinism, and the potential of their approach is further demonstrated by its capacity to cope with advanced issues such as mobility, groups, and components.

Researchers and graduate students will find here an extensive review of concurrent languages and calculi, with comprehensive figures and summaries.
Developers of distributed systems can adopt the many implementation strategies that are presented and analyzed in detail.

Printing: Krips bv, Meppel
Binding: Stürtz, Würzburg